WARLORD

Yen Hsi-shan

in Shansi Province

1911-1949

WARLORD
Yen Hsi-shan
in Shansi Province
1911-1949

BY DONALD G. GILLIN

PRINCETON, NEW JERSEY
PRINCETON UNIVERSITY PRESS
1967

To my Father and Mother

PREFACE

IN THE PAST, students of the history of the Chinese Republic have been concerned largely with the so-called national or central governments which came to power in Peking and Nanking after the overthrow of the Ch'ing dynasty in 1911. They have devoted considerably less attention to the military regimes set up in various provinces by professional soldiers, commonly known as warlords. Yet these governments were for the most part independent of Peking and Nanking and played an equally important, sometimes paramount role in the history of the Republic. This inquiry into the career and policies of Marshal Yen Hsi-shan, whose armies dominated all or part of the northwestern province of Shansi between 1911 and 1949, has been undertaken in the hope that a study of one of these warlord regimes will result in a broader understanding of warlordism as a political phenomenon, illuminating further the whole subject of regional government in China during the first half of the twentieth century. It describes the efforts of an ill-educated, autocratic, but nonetheless able and often modern-minded Chinese leader to effect political, social, and economic changes which he felt were imperative if China was to survive the impact of Western civilization and meet the challenge of communism and Japanese imperialism. Hampered by his own conservatism and parochial outlook, as well as by that of his subjects, he encountered difficulties and experienced disappointments which plagued other conservative reformers in China. But he helped generate forces destined to alter fundamentally the structure of Chinese society.

In the course of writing this study I have received invaluable assistance from a number of people.

Considerable information was given by the late Yen Hsi-shan, as well as by persons formerly associated with him. These include H. H. K'ung, who assisted Yen in innumerable ways and especially in the economic development of Shansi, Yang Ai-yüan, a general in Yen's army, Keng Shih and Wang Huai-i, secretaries to Yen Hsi-shan, and H. R. Williamson, Percy T. Watson, E. D. Hawkins, and Wynn C. Fairfield, who served as missionaries in Shansi during the decades preceding the Japanese invasion. Mr. Uno Shigeaki of the Japanese

Foreign Office and Professor James T. C. Liu of Princeton told me several interesting things about Yen's relations with the Japanese. I likewise appreciate the financial support I received from the Ford Foundation, the American Inter-University Program for Field Training in Chinese, the Rockefeller Foundation, the Joint Committee on Contemporary China of the Social Science Research Council, the Duke University Research Council, and Stanford University's Committee for Far Eastern Studies. Finally, I wish to express my gratitude for the help given me by Mr. Eugene Wu, Mr. Tamotsu Takase, Mr. David Tseng, and other members of the staff of the East Asian Collection of the Hoover Institution, Stanford University, where much of the research for this book was carried out. All of the views expressed in the following pages, however, are exclusively my own.

CONTENTS

ILLUSTRATIONS, following page 66

1. Yen and Sun Yat-sen, 1912, from a photograph in the possession of the author

2. Yen as Warlord, around 1920, from *Who's Who in China*, 1925

3. Yen in Taiwan, May 1957, from a photograph in the possession of the author

MAPS

ABBREVIATIONS

Archives · Hatano Ken'ichi, *Gendai Shina no kiroku* (*Modern China Archives*). Tokyo, 1924-1932.

CCCK · Chien-cheng chou-k'an min-chung chien-sheng-yün-tung hui (Shansi Association for the Promotion of Popular Supervision of the Government), pub., *Chien-cheng chou-k'an* (*Supervisorial Weekly*), January 1, 1935. Taiyuan.

CEB · The National Government of China, pub., *The Chinese Economic Bulletin*, Peking and Nanking, 1920-1937.

CEJ · *The Chinese Economic Journal*, 1926-1937. Shanghai.

CEM · The National Government of China, pub., *The Chinese Economic Monthly*, Peking, 1925-1926.

CSSH · Chin-Sui she-hui ching-chi tiao-ch'a t'ung-chi hui (Association for the Promotion of Statistical Investigation of the Economies and Societies of Shansi and Suiyuan), pub., *Chin-Sui she-hui ching-chi tiao-ch'a t'ung-chi she nien-kan* (*Annual of the Association for the Promotion of Statistical Investigation of the Economies and Societies of Shansi and Suiyuan*), 1935. Taiyuan.

CT · *China Today*, New York, 1934-1941.

CWR · *The China Weekly Review*, Shanghai, 1920-1950.

CYB · *The China Year Book*, London and Tientsin, 1916-1932, and Shanghai, 1934-1939.

Fairfield · Wynn C. Fairfield, letter to myself, dated July 18, 1958.

Hatano, *History of the C.C.P., 1936* · Hatano Ken'ichi, *Chūgoku kyōsantō shi, ichi ku san roku nen* (*The History of the Chinese Communist Party, 1936*). Tokyo, 1961.

HHFY · Fan Ch'ang-chiang, *et al.*, *Hsi-hsien feng-yün* (*Wind and Clouds on the Western Front*). Shanghai, 1937.

HHHCC · Fan Ch'ang-chiang, *et al.*, *Hsi-hsien hsieh-chan chi* (*An Account of the Bloody Fighting on the Western Front*). No date or place of publication.

Hirano, *Komoto* · Hirano Reiji, *Manshu no imbōsha: Kōmoto Daisaku no ummei teki na ashioto* (*The Manchurian Intriguer: the Fateful Trail of Kōmoto Daisaku*). Tokyo, 1959.

Hirano, *Prisoner* · Hirano Reiji, *Chūkyō ryoshū ki* (*I Was a Prisoner of the Chinese Communists*). Tokyo, 1957.

HNT · Nung-ts'un chiao-yü kai-chin she (Society for the Improvement of Village Education), pub., *Hsin nung-ts'un* (*New Village*), May 15, 1936. Taiyuan.

HPCY · Fan Ch'ang-chiang, *et al.*, *Hsi-pei chan-yün* (*War Clouds Over the Northwest*). Shanghai, 1938.

HPH · Fan Ch'ang-chiang, *Hsi-pei hsien* (*Northwestern Front*). Hankow, 1938.

Hsü Fan-t'ing, *Letter* · Hsü Fan-t'ing, "Chi Shan-hsi t'u huang-ti Yen Hsi-shan te i-feng wu-ch'ien yen-shu" ("A Five Thousand Word Letter to the Local Emperor of Shansi, Yen Hsi-shan"), Ch'en Po-ta, *Yen Hsi-shan p'i-p'an* (*A Criticism of Yen Hsi-shan*). Kalgan, 1945.

HTPL · *Hsien-tai p'ing-lün* (*The Contemporary Review*). Peking, 1925-1926.

Industrial Gazetteer · Shih-yeh pu, Kuo-chi mao-i chü (Industry Section, Board of International Trade), pub., *Chung-kuo shih-yeh chih, Shan-hsi sheng* (*The Chinese Industrial Gazetteer, Shansi Province*). Shanghai, 1937.

Industrial Monthly · Chung-hua shih-yeh hsieh-hu (Chinese Industrial Association), pub., *Chung-hua shih-yeh yüeh-k'an* (*Chinese Industrial Monthly*), September 1, 1935. Taiyuan.

IPC · *International Press Correspondence, Moscow*, 1935-1936.

Japanese Biographical Survey, 1937 · Gaimushō, jōhō bu (Information Section, Japanese Ministry of Foreign Affairs), comp., *Gendai Chūka minkoku manshu teikoku jimmei kan* (*Current Survey of Important Men in the Chinese Republic and the Manchu Empire*). Tokyo, 1937.

Japanese Steel Survey · Naikaku sōri daijin kambō chō-sashitsu (Cabinet Research Office), comp., *Chūkyō tekkō gyō chōsa hōkokusho* (*Survey Report on the Steel Industry of Communist China*). Tokyo, 1956.

Japanese Monograph No. 178 · United States Army, Forces in the Far East, *North China Area Operations Record*, July 1937-May 1941, Japanese Monograph Number 178. Washington, 1955.

Kuomintang Biographies · Chinese Communist Party, comp., *Biographies of Kuomintang Leaders.* Yenan, 1945. English translation published by Harvard University Committee on International and Regional Studies. Cambridge, 1948.

K'ung · Letter to myself from H. H. K'ung, dated December 5, 1957.

KWCP · *Kuo-wen chou-pao* (*The Weekly Gazette*). Tientsin, 1927-1938.

Lectures · Yen Hsi-shan, *Yen Po-ch'uan hsien-sheng yen lün lei-pien* (*The Collected Addresses of Mr. Yen Hsi-shan*), Volumes I-IX, Shanghai, 1938.

Manshū jihen · Taiheiyō sensō gen'in kenkyūbu, Nihon kokusai seiji gakkai (Committee to Study the Origins of the Pacific War of the Japanese Association of International Relations), ed., *Taiheiyō sensō no michi: kaisen gaikō shi* (*The Road to the Pacific War: A Diplomatic History before the War*), II, *Manshū jihen* (*The Manchurian Incident*). Tokyo, 1962-1963.

NCH · *The North China Herald.* Shanghai, 1910-1941.

NYT · *The New York Times.* New York, 1931-1950.

PT · *The People's Tribune.* Shanghai, 1931-1937.

SMR Survey · Shiryō-ka, Sōmu bu, Minami Manshū kabushiki kaisha (Research Section, General Affairs Department, South Manchurian Railroad Company), pub., *Hoku Shi jijo sōran* (*General Survey of Conditions in North China*). Hsin-king, 1935.

Statistical Annual · Shan-hsi sheng cheng-fu (The Provincial Government of Shansi), pub., *Shan-hsi sheng t'ung-chi nien-chien* (*Shansi Statistical Annual*), I and II. Taiyuan, 1934.

TPLC · Kao K'e-fu, ed., *Ti-pa-lu chün tsai Shan-hsi* (*The Eighth Route Army in Shansi*). Shanghai, 1938.

U.S. Foreign Relations Papers, 1936 · United States Department of State, pub., *Papers Relating to the Foreign Relations of the United States, 1936.* Washington, 1954.

Village Rules · Yen Hsi-shan, *Ts'un-cheng fa-kuei ling-wen chi-yao* (*A Compilation of Rules Governing Village Administration*). Taiyuan, 1925.

Williamson · Letter to myself from H. R. Williamson, dated December 11, 1957.

Wu Pao-san, Part I · Wu Pao-san, "Ch'a Sui Chin lü-hsing kuan-kan" ("Impressions from a Trip through Chahar, Suiyuan, and Shansi"). Part I, *Tu-li p'ing-lün* (*Independent Commentary*), November 10, 1935, pp. 14-18.

Wu Pao-san, Part II · The foregoing author, title, and periodical, Part II, November 17, 1935, pp. 14-20.

Yang Ai-yüan · Letter to myself from Yang Ai-yüan, dated April 12, 1958.

WARLORD

Yen Hsi-shan
in Shansi Province
1911-1949

CHAPTER ONE

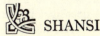 SHANSI

The Geography of Shansi

THE PROVINCE of Shansi is in the northwest of China, approximately 200 miles west of Peking. It is a high plateau, 175 miles wide and 350 miles long, which slopes gradually southward. Bordered on the east by Chahar and Hopei, it faces Honan in the south, Suiyuan in the north, and Shensi in the west. On all sides are imposing mountains and rivers. In the northeast there are the Wu-t'ai Mountains while along the southern and southeastern borders lie the T'ai-hang and Chung-t'iao ranges, rising thousands of feet within a few miles.

Between Shansi and Shensi flows the Yellow River, its bed generally several thousand feet below the elevation of the adjacent highlands. At Fen-ling-tu it turns eastward and for a hundred miles forms the border between Shansi and Honan. The Tatung basin in the northeastern corner of Shansi is more accessible than other parts of the province. Only two sections of the Great Wall separate it from Suiyuan; however, the basin itself is cut off from the rest of Shansi by the formidable Hengshan Range.[1]

These barriers virtually isolate Shansi from its neighbors. The surrounding mountains are pierced by major passes only at three places—Ning-wu in the north and Niang-tzu and Yen-men in the east. Narrow and precipitous, these passes can be defended against an attacking army by a handful of men.[2] In the west and southwest the turbulent Yellow River forms an equally effective obstacle to invasion. This natural isolation explains in part why Yen Hsi-shan was able to rule undisturbed in Shansi during the disorderly decade that followed the overthrow of the Ch'ing Dynasty.

The interior of Shansi is a maze of mountains, precipices, and rocky plateaus, bisected by a longitudinal structural de-

[1] *Chung-kuo fen-sheng t'u* (Atlas of the Provinces of China) (Hong Kong, 1954), Section 19, and Paul O. Elmquist, *The Nature of the Chinese Foothold in Shansi, 1937-1939* (unpublished manuscript), pp. 22-24.

[2] Evans F. Carlson, *Twin Stars of China* (New York, 1940), p. 231.

pression which extends northeastward from Feng-ling-tu to the Heng-shan Mountains. Through this depression flow swift rivers which in the course of centuries have deposited in the surrounding loess-covered valleys a thick layer of alluvium. The most important of these fertile alluvial regions are the valley of the Fen River in the south, the Taiyuan basin in central Shansi, the valley of the Hu-t'o River in the north, and the Tatung basin. Within them are concentrated the agricultural resources of the province,[3] for with the exception of a few smaller valleys and fertile upland areas, the rest of Shansi is barren and ill-suited for agriculture.[4]

The People of Shansi

In 1920 there were in Shansi approximately 11 million people.[5] The bulk of them lived in the four major alluvial basins. Of these the most densely populated was the area around Taiyuan or Yang-ch'ü, the provincial capital. Set on the east bank of the Fen River in the middle of the fertile central plain, Taiyuan was the commercial and industrial as well as the political center of Shansi. South of Taiyuan were the smaller but prosperous cities of Yü-tz'u, Taiku, P'ing-yao, and Fen-yang. Under the Ch'ing the merchants of these towns had controlled Shansi's famed banks. Larger than Taiyuan and of equal commercial and industrial importance was the northern city of Tatung. In the east and southeast the major cities were Chin-ch'eng, the gateway to southern Shansi, Ch'ang-chih, the commercial center of the South, and P'ing-ting, a coal-mining community which faced the Niang-tzu Pass. Hsin-chiang and Lin-fen were the chief settlements in the valley of the Fen River.[6] Most of these towns were enclosed by high walls and fortified with antique cannon. Clustered around them and scattered throughout the province were thousands of villages. In more remote areas these frequently consisted of not more than five houses, and many people lived in caves dug into the sides of cliffs.[7]

[3] Paul O. Elmquist, *op.cit.*, pp. 23-26.

[4] Hsia Ching-feng, "Shan-hsi lü-hsing chi" ("A Trip through Shansi"), *Ti-hsüeh tsa-chih* (*The Geographer's Magazine*), Jan. 1, 1916, p. 2a.

[5] *The China Year Book*, hereafter cited as *CYB*, *1921-1922*, p. 3.

[6] *Chung-kuo fen-sheng t'u*, Section 19.

[7] Hsia Ching-feng, "Shan-hsi lü-hsing chi," *Ti-hsüeh tsa-chih*, Feb. 2, 1916, p. 5b.

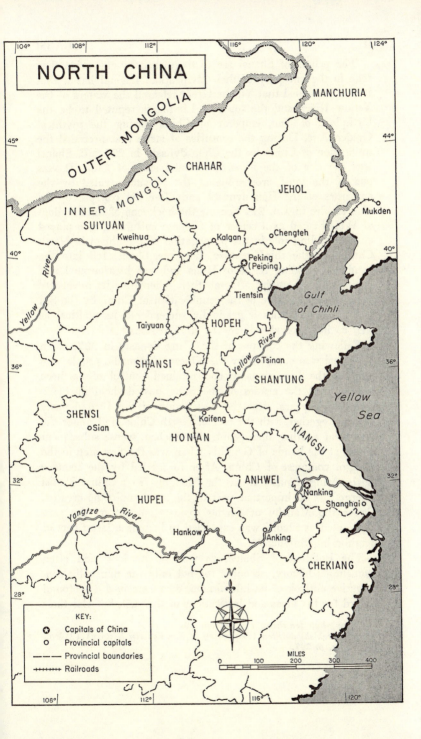

NORTH CHINA

OUTER MONGOLIA

INNER MONGOLIA

MANCHURIA

CHAHAR

JEHOL

SUIYUAN

Kweihua

Kalgan

Chengteh

Mukden

Peking
(Peiping)

Tientsin

Gulf
of Chihli

Taiyuan

HOPEH

Yellow River

SHANSI

Yellow River

Tsinan

SHANTUNG

Yellow Sea

SHENSI

Sian

Kaifeng

HONAN

KIANGSU

HUPEI

ANHWEI

Nanking

Shanghai

Yangtze River

Hankow

Anking

CHEKIANG

N

KEY:
⊛ Capitals of China
○ Provincial capitals
– – – Provincial boundaries
++++++ Railroads

MILES
0   100   200   300   400

The people of Shansi are distinguished by the pride they take in the antiquity of their civilization. Legend has it that it was in Shansi that Yü the Great released the waters of the Yellow River and the town of Lin-fen is reputed to be the birthplace of Yao, emperor of China during the mythical Golden Age. During the centuries of strife that preceded the unification of China by the Ch'in dynasty in 221 B.C. Shansi was the site of the important feudal state of Chin. It was one of the most prosperous of the provinces ruled by the emperors of the Han dynasty and after the collapse of the Han empire in A.D. 221 became the backbone of the kingdom of Wei. Famed as a center of Chinese culture, it also played an outstanding role in the propagation of Buddhism in North China.[8] In the third century, however, Shansi fell into the hands of invading tribes of Huns and was incorporated into one ephemeral empire after another. Thereafter its prosperity declined and in spite of the reunification of China by the Sui and T'ang dynasties it gradually surrendered its political as well as its cultural primacy to other regions.[9]

Following the collapse of the T'ang dynasty in 907, much of Shansi was occupied by the Khitan, a nomadic people who founded the Liao dynasty and retained control of northern Shansi until the armies of the Sung ousted them in 1122. Only seven years after the destruction of the Liao dynasty Shansi, together with the rest of North China, fell under the control of another alien people, the Juchen, whose subsequent defeat at the hands of Genghis Khan was the first step in the Mongol conquest of China. After forces led by the founder of the Ming dynasty drove the Mongols from China, Shansi emerged as an important part of the new empire he created. Under the Manchu or Ch'ing dynasty, moreover, the area designated as Shansi was expanded to include a large part of neighboring Suiyuan.[10]

The isolation of Shansi, as well as its long and often momentous history, accounts for not only the unusually conservative outlook of its inhabitants, who conceived a profound regard for the ideas and institutions of the past, but also their

[8] *Chung-kuo fen-sheng t'u*, Section 19.
[9] *Tōyō rekishi daijiten* (*Dictionary of Far Eastern History*) (Tokyo, 1937), III, p. 397.
[10] *Ibid.*

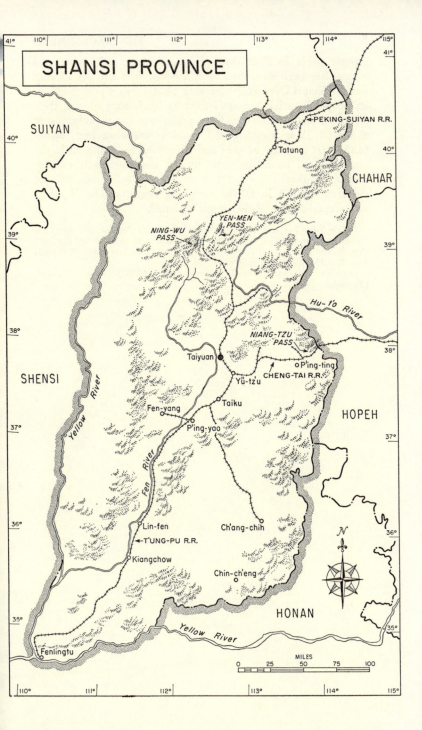

SHANSI PROVINCE

SUIYAN

CHAHAR

PEKING-SUIYAN R.R.

Tatung

NING-WU PASS

YEN-MEN PASS

Hu-t'o River

NIANG-TZU PASS

SHENSI

Taiyuan

Yü-tzu

P'ing-ting

CHENG-TAI R.R.

Fen-yang

Taiku

HOPEH

P'ing-yao

Yellow River

Fen River

Ch'ang-chih

Lin-fen

T'UNG-PU R.R.

Kiangchow

Chin-ch'eng

N

HONAN

Fenlingtu

Yellow River

MILES

0   25   50   75   100

intense pride in their own province. Their attitude toward Shansi has been described as *"Chin-kuo t'ian-hsia mo ch'iang yen"*—"Shansi Over all!"[11] Because Shansi was a poor province its people likewise became famed for their shrewdness, their diligence and persistence, their preference for planning, and, above all, their frugality and acquisitiveness. In fact, owing to the vast quantity of gold and silver said to be buried in the backyards of its inhabitants, during the nineteenth century Shansi acquired the reputation of being a solid mountain of precious metal.[12] In all the foregoing respects, Yen Hsi-shan was representative of the people he ruled.

[11] Jen Y-ing-lun and Kuo Chien-fu, "Chin-shih-nien-lai chih Shan-hsi min-chung yün-tung" ("The Mass Movement in Shansi during the Past Ten Years"), p. 2. *Chien-cheng chou-k'an* (*Supervisorial Weekly*), Jan. 1, 1935, hereafter referred to as *CCCK*.

[12] Hsieh Hui-tzu, *Chin-jih chih hua-pei* (*North China Today*) (Nanking, 1939), p. 25.

CHAPTER TWO

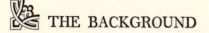 THE BACKGROUND

Yen's Education

YEN HSI-SHAN was born in 1883 in the village of Ho-pien, located not far from Taiyuan in the Wu-t'ai district of north-eastern Shansi, where for generations members of his family had been minor bankers and merchants.[1] As a boy he pursued a classical education in the village school while at the same time serving an apprenticeship in his father's bank. The failure of his father's bank, however, compelled him to enroll in the tuition-free military academy maintained by the Manchu government in Taiyuan for the purpose of training officers for the new army which the Manchus were endeavoring to build in an effort to strengthen China's defenses against foreign aggression. Ambitious and eager to restore the fortunes of his family, Yen undoubtedly realized that the traditional political and social order was doomed and that the future belonged to those trained in the skills and techniques introduced from the West.

At the National Military College (*Kuo-li wu-pei hsüeh-tang*) Yen studied mathematics, physics, geography, and other subjects generally regarded as "modern."[2] In 1904 he accompanied his class to Japan, where he spent the next two years at the *Shimbu Gakkō*, a preparatory school for Chinese who intended to enroll in the Imperial Military Academy (*Nippon shikan gakkō*). After devoting an additional year to field training as a member of the Komae Regiment of the Japanese Army, he entered the Imperial Military Academy from which he graduated in 1909. Among the more than 200 Chinese attending the academy at this time there were many destined to play an important role in the subsequent overthrow of the Ch'ing dynasty.[3]

The five years Yen spent in Japan influenced him pro-

[1] A letter to myself from H. R. Williamson, dated Dec. 11, 1957, and hereafter referred to as *Williamson*, p. 1.

[2] Wynn C. Fairfield, *China's Model Province and its Governor* (an unpublished manuscript), p. 2.

[3] Interview with *Yen Hsi-shan*, Taipei, Taiwan, Dec. 27, 1956.

foundly. Like most Chinese studying in Japan, he was awed and chagrined by the rapidity with which the Japanese were modernizing their country. While a patient in a Japanese hospital, for example, he encountered for the first time drugs, X-ray machines, and the other paraphernalia of modern medicine, although he was almost as impressed by the Japanese government's efforts to stamp out what it regarded as primitive customs such as the practice of blackening one's teeth.[4] Whereas the nations of the West were remote places populated by people whose affairs were too alien and unintelligible to attract the close attention of a conservative and relatively unsophisticated Chinese like Yen, the progress being made by the hitherto despised and backward inhabitants of one of China's nearest neighbors convinced him that his own country was falling dangerously behind the rest of the world. This reaction accounts in part for his efforts to modernize Shansi after he became the ruler of his native province.

Yen concluded that Japan was forging ahead of China largely because of the skill with which the Japanese government mobilized popular support behind its policies. He was impressed especially by the results of the Japanese government's campaign to glorify the armed forces. He observed that in Japan the government strove to convince the people that soldiers and sailors are the cornerstone of society and therefore more worthy of respect than mere civilians. While on maneuvers with the Japanese Army, he noted how soldiers were treated like heroes by the countrypeople who welcomed the servicemen into their homes, fed them, and even washed their clothing.[5] When Japan defeated Russia in 1905, Yen attributed her surprising victory to the enthusiastic support her armed forces received from the Japanese public. He recalled that in the temples and public buildings in Tokyo there were set up exhibits depicting the assault on Port Arthur, the destruction of the Russian fleet, and other Japanese victories, while at the same time the newspapers were used to whip up hatred of the Russians until virtually everyone "thirsted for Russian blood."[6] Confronted with a society dominated by

---

[4] Yen Hsi-shan, *Yen Po-ch'üan hsien-sheng yen-lün lei-pien* (*The Collected Speeches of Mr. Yen Po-ch'üan*) (Shanghai, 1939), hereafter referred to as *Lectures*, III-B, p. 39 (Jan. 1919).

[5] *Lectures*, V, p. 37 (May 1915).

[6] See *ibid.*, p. 32.

the army, Yen remembered with anger the shabby treatment commonly meted out to soldiers in China.

After returning to China, Yen wrote a booklet warning his countrymen that they could overtake Japan only by assigning soldiers a higher social status and otherwise cultivating a Chinese version of bushidō.[7] He had become a Spencerian, arguing that life is a ceaseless struggle in which the strong and the fit destroy the weak and the unfit, proclaiming that warfare is the highest form of this struggle and the state merely a device for mobilizing the people. He contended that therefore the Chinese must reject abstract morality as useless and instead evaluate all ideas and institutions solely in terms of their contribution to the power and military might of the state. "China can save herself only by embracing militarism," he declared in 1915.[8] Although a number of the values he formed while a student in Japan remained with him and continued to color his opinions, renewed contact with Confucianism, as well as the defeat of Germany at the hands of the democracies in the First World War, caused Yen to lose much of his youthful enthusiasm for militarism. His admiration for the Japanese likewise was tempered by the realization that they menaced the independence of China. During a visit to Korea in 1909 he was exposed to the misery and servility of the Koreans and returned to China with the conviction that "nothing is more terrible than the loss of one's country."[9] But most of the young men he sent abroad for further education went to Japan and he repeatedly urged his subjects to emulate the Japanese. As late as 1923 the repertoire of government-supported drama troupes in Shansi included a play entitled *The Patriotism of Marquis Ito.*[10] Furthermore, Yen maintained his friendship with many of the Japanese who had been his classmates at the Imperial Military Academy and who subsequently achieved high rank in the Japanese Army.[11] These friendships, along with a persistent belief in at least some of the principles of Japanese

[7] See *ibid.,* p. 21.   [8] See *ibid.,* p. 3.
[9] *Lectures,* III-A, p. 40 (April 1918).
[10] The *North China Herald,* hereafter referred to as *NCH,* March 24, 1923, 788:2.
[11] *Ching-pao* (*Capital News*), Dec. 29, 1930, as quoted in Hatano Ken'ichi, *Gendai Shina no kiroku* (*Modern China Archives*), hereafter referred to as *Archives,* December, 1930, p. 372.

militarism, explain in part why he and other Chinese military leaders trained in Japan found it so difficult to offer whole-hearted opposition to the Japanese Army when it invaded their country after 1937.

Prelude to the Revolution

When Yen left China in 1904 he was disgusted by the corruption of Ch'ing officials in Shansi. He recalled that they invariably decided law suits brought before them in favor of the litigant who gave them the largest bribe.[12] As a boy, moreover, he had been convinced by books like Hsü Chi-yu's *A Brief Description of the Ocean Circuit* (*Ying-huan chih-lüeh*) that the unprogressiveness and inept foreign policy of the Manchu dynasty largely was responsible for China's helplessness in the face of foreign aggression. Hsü was a native of Yen's own district and at one time had served as viceroy of Fukien and Chekiang. He had been dismissed from his posts and exiled to Shansi, however, because in his book he adopted an objective attitude toward the countries of the West and neglected to employ the sign of the dog when transliterating the word England so as to designate it a barbarian country.[13] Yen was impressed by Hsü's book and conceived the utmost contempt for the government that had persecuted its author.[14] During the Boxer Uprising, when Manchu forces attempted to advance through Ho-pien in order to attack the invading troops of the Allied Powers, Yen helped his fellow villagers drive the Imperial soldiers from the village. Owing perhaps to Hsü's influence, he regarded the Boxers as a stupid response to the challenge of the West.[15]

Upon arriving in Japan, Yen was urged by everyone he encountered to join Sun Yat-sen's antidynastic party, later known as the Revolutionary Brotherhood or *T'ung Meng Hui*. Yet in spite of his hostility toward the Manchu government, Yen hesitated to become part of a revolutionary conspiracy against it and therefore initially inclined toward the Reformers led by K'ang Yu-wei and Liang Ch'i-ch'ao. But

[12] Interview with *Yen Hsi-shan*, Taipei, Taiwan, Jan. 13, 1957.
[13] *Lectures*, III-B, p. 9 (June 1918).
[14] Yen Hsi-shan, pub., *Sung-k'an hsien-sheng ch'üan-chi* (*The Complete Works of Hsü Chi-yu*) (Wu-t'ai, 1915), I, pp. 1a-1b.
[15] Yen Hsi-shan, *Yen yüan-chang cheng-lün chi-yao* (*The Collected Political Addresses of Premier Yen*) (Taipei, 1950), I, p. 1.

Sun's writings, especially a pamphlet entitled *The Soul of China* (*Chung-kuo hun*), soon persuaded him that China's only salvation lay in revolution. After conversing with Sun Yat-sen, he joined the T'ung Meng Hui and thereafter devoted himself to mobilizing support for the revolutionary cause among other Chinese studying in the Imperial Military Academy. His efforts along this line took the form of organizing some twenty-eight of his fellow students into a Blood and Iron Society (*T'ieh-hsieh chang-fu t'uan*), which he apparently hoped would play a role in the Chinese revolution similar to that carried out by Bismarck and the Prussian military class in the creation of a strong and united Germany.[16]

In 1907 Yen returned to Shansi on a mission for the T'ung Meng Hui. In addition to enlisting support for the revolutionaries among students, teachers, merchants, and members of the Buddhist clergy, he also delivered bombs to conspirators plotting to assassinate the provincial governor.[17] This was followed by another sojourn in Japan while he completed his studies at the Imperial Military Academy. Upon graduating from the academy in 1909 Yen returned to Shansi, where he was awarded the second-class degree of *chü-jen* and appointed director of the local military school (*lu-chün hsiao-hsüeh*).[18] A year later he was promoted to the post of commander of the Second Brigade of the New Shansi Army and subsequently became a colonel in charge of two thousand men. The New Army was a recently organized force, made up exclusively of soldiers recruited in Shansi and commanded for the most part by returned students from Japan.[19] The majority of its officers either were members of the T'ung Meng Hui or else so dissatisfied with the conduct of the government that they were prepared to support the revolutionaries. Nothing could better exemplify the dilemma which confronted the Ch'ing

[16] Fang Yen-kuang, *Yen Po-ch'üan hsien-sheng yü Shan-hsi cheng-chih te k'e-kuan chi-shu* (*Objective Accounts of Mr. Yen Hsi-shan and the Government of Shansi*) (Nanking, 1948), p. 2.

[17] Interview with Yen Hsi-shan, Taipei, Taiwan, Jan. 13, 1957.

[18] This was not the orthodox literary degree of *chü-jen* but instead a special degree conferred only upon returned students from abroad. Letter to myself from Yang Ai-yüan, dated April 12, 1958, and hereafter referred to as *Yang Ai-yüan*, p. 13a.

[19] Wen Kung-chih, *Tsui-chin san-shih-nien Chung-kuo chün-shih shih* (*A Military History of China during the Last Thirty Years*) (Shanghai, 1930), I, p. 125.

government. In order to strengthen China's defenses the dynasty needed a modern army commanded by men trained in the technology and military tactics of the West. To its dismay, the students it sent abroad to study these subjects returned determined to overthrow the dynasty. Because it was unable to do without their services, the government sought to win their support by appointing them to positions of authority, with the result that large elements of the Imperial Army passed into the hands of the enemies of the dynasty.

The Revolution

When Yen left Japan in 1909 he was convinced that a revolution in China was imminent. Sun Yat-sen had told him that the T'ung Meng Hui would strike first in the South, where disaffection was most widespread, and then march northward; that Yen was to wait until the insurgents reached Honan, then turn on the Manchus, drive them from Shansi, and lead the advance on Peking.[20] Yen was compelled to act prematurely, however, by the vigorous reaction of the Imperial authorities in Shansi when an insurrection broke out at Hankow on October 10, 1911. Victories won by the insurgents in Hupei and neighboring Shensi frightened the governor of Shansi, Lu Chung-ch'i, into taking immediate steps to suppress the revolutionaries in his own province. Besides garrisoning Taiyuan with Manchu troops, he attempted to divide the forces of the revolutionaries by ordering a large part of the New Army to proceed northward while at the same time despatching the remaining units to the extreme south, supposedly for the purpose of defending against an invasion by revolutionaries from neighboring provinces.[21] Upon perceiving that the governor intended to oppose the revolution, Yen and his followers concluded that the dispersal of the New Army would be followed by a purge of officers having revolutionary sympathies. For this reason, they tried to induce Lu to withdraw his orders by agreeing to do as instructed only if he complied with what they felt were impossible demands which he would be obliged to reject. Instead, he accepted their con-

[20] Sun Yat-sen, *Tsung-li ch'üan-shu yen-chiang* (*The Complete Speeches of Sun Yat-sen*) (Taipei, 1951), I, p. 168.

[21] Yen Hsi-shan, *Shan-hsi kuang-fu chih ching-kuo* (*The Revolution of 1911 in Shansi*) (an unpublished manuscript), p. 4.

ditions but continued to insist that they march their forces away from Taiyuan, with the result that they were compelled to rebel.[22]

Yen was certain of support from his own brigade since many of its officers and noncommissioned officers were members of the T'ung Meng Hui. The rest were followers of Liang Ch'i-ch'ao's Reform Party but were outraged by the government's persecution of the reformers and therefore prepared to follow the revolutionaries. The higher-ranking officers of the Second Brigade, on the other hand, were loyal to the dynasty, although its commander was Yen's friend Huang Kuo-liang, who enjoyed the backing of most of its junior and noncommissioned officers. On October 28 Huang and his supporters arrested the officers opposed to them and distributed to the troops the weapons stored in the arsenal. When a Manchu officer attempted to interfere he was hurled down a well.[23] Then in order to deceive the governor Huang moved his headquarters to the south, taking care to leave the bulk of his brigade near Taiyuan where it might cooperate with Yen's.

Throughout the night of October 28 Yen sat by the telephone in his headquarters listening anxiously as the governor warned the garrison commander of impending danger. The garrison commander declined to mobilize his forces, however, perhaps because he had been taken in by the removal of Huang Kuo-liang's headquarters to the south. Consequently, on the morning of October 29, when Yen's soldiers attacked the Manchu garrison in Taiyuan they enjoyed the advantage of complete surprise. After overwhelming the garrison the rebels shot the governor and his family and commenced shelling the Manchu quarter. It quickly surrendered and was thrown open to looting. Meanwhile in other parts of the province there occurred similar but generally more violent risings which within a few days delivered most of Shansi into the hands of the insurgents.[24] Its independence from the Ch'ing government was

[22] Tsou Lu, ed., *Chung-kuo Kuo-min-tang shih-kao* (*A Draft History of China's Kuomintang*) (Changsha, 1938), I, p. 869.

[23] Yen Hsi-shan, *op.cit.*, p. 9.

[24] See *ibid.*, pp. 10-11. There seems to be a controversy over precisely how much violence occurred in Shansi during the first weeks of the Revolution of 1911. A foreigner who witnessed the uprising in Taiyuan says that no more than thirty Manchus died and that all who wished to were allowed to leave their compound in safety. Letter to myself from Wynn C. Fairfield, dated Sept. 12, 1958. On the other hand, according

proclaimed by the provincial assembly, a hitherto purely deliberative body that had been created by the Manchus as part of an effort to appease the mounting demand for representative government.

The young army officers who led the insurrection against the Ch'ing in Shansi attacked the dynasty for failing to repel foreign aggression and promised political changes so sweeping that Yen likened the revolution to a dawn which would dispel the darkness that had engulfed China since the triumph of Ch'in in 221 B.C. Perhaps the failures and disappointments that followed have obscured the feverish enthusiasm for reform generated in Shansi by the Revolution of 1911; however, Yen subsequently admitted that the vast majority of those who took part in the revolution were bent solely on securing for themselves the power and wealth possessed by the Manchus.[25] It likewise would seem that by persecuting proponents of reform the dynasty alienated moderates who otherwise might have come to its defense. Yet, as in other provinces, the revolution in Shansi resulted largely from the antagonism of a provincially minded population to a government represented for the most part by officials from areas outside the province. This hatred of outsiders was so intense and universal in Shansi that even bankers and merchants contributed to the revolutionary cause, notwithstanding the fact that as creditors of the dynasty they would suffer a financial loss if it were overthrown.[26]

Aftermath of the Revolution

Owing to the authority he exercised over the army, as well as the prestige he enjoyed within the ranks of the local T'ung Meng Hui, Yen Hsi-shan was elevated to the post of "military governor" (*tu-tu*) in the new revolutionary regime. It has been suggested that few of his comrades desired an office likely to invite immediate decapitation if the Ch'ing succeeded in

---

to two other sources, in areas remote from Taiyuan the Manchus frequently were murdered by the revolutionaries and their supporters. See Hsia Ching-feng, *op.cit.*, p. 5a, and *NCH*, Nov. 25, 1911, 520:2. Perhaps Yen's authority spared the Manchus in Taiyuan but was less effective in the countryside.

[25] *Lectures*, VI, p. 78 (July 1921).

[26] Hsia Ching-feng, *op.cit.*, p. 5b.

putting down the revolution.[27] Yen immediately led his army to the Niang-tzu Pass, the gateway to eastern Shansi, for the purpose of repelling the attack he was certain Peking would launch against Shansi. At the Niang-tzu Pass he conferred with Wu Lu-chen, who commanded the Imperial forces in neighboring Hopei.[28] Although under orders to suppress the revolution in Shansi, Wu promised to cooperate with Yen and upon returning to his headquarters despatched a telegram instructing his commanders to attack the Manchus. As a returned student from Japan, Wu instinctively leaned toward the revolutionaries; however, he also was under the influence of a Japanese named Kawashima Naniwa, who wished to prevent Yuan Shih-k'ai from establishing in China a powerful central government capable of resisting Japan's demands and therefore urged Wu to dispute Yuan's control of Peking and the rest of North China.[29] Since Yen seems to have been unacquainted with Kawashima, he probably was not a party to this plot, which was exposed when Wu's telegram fell into the hands of Yuan Shih-k'ai. Yuan reacted with characteristic vigor; his soldiers surrounded and attacked Wu's headquarters, took Wu and his staff prisoner, and executed them on the spot.[30] Then Yuan ordered his troops, under the command of Ts'ao Kun and Wu P'ei-fu, to assault Niang-tzu Pass and suppress the revolution in Shansi.

Late in November, Yen advanced into Hopei with the intention of routing the Imperial troops being concentrated near the rail junction of Ching-hsing. To his dismay his own army was put to flight and saved from destruction only by the virtual impregnability of Niang-tzu Pass, whose defenders withstood repeated assaults on the part of Yuan's victorious soldiers. Yen must have perceived the hopelessness of further resistance because he entered into negotiations with Yuan Shih-k'ai, who used these talks to lull his rival into complacency and then mounted a new attack against the pass. This time, Yen's soldiers threw down their weapons and fled in terror, allowing the Imperial troops to penetrate the pass and

[27] Letter to myself from Wynn C. Fairfield, dated July 18, 1958, and hereafter referred to as *Fairfield*, p. 4.

[28] Yen Hsi-shan, *Yen yüan-chang cheng-lün chi-yao*, I, p. 1.

[29] Yoshino Sakuzō and Katō Shigeru, *Shina kakumei shi* (*A History of the Chinese Revolution*) (Tokyo, 1922), pp. 277-281.

[30] Tsou Lu, *op.cit.*, pp. 7a-7b.

advance into Shansi.[31] Instead of risking what remained of his shattered army by attempting to defend Taiyuan, Yen withdrew into the northwestern corner of Shansi, where he joined forces with insurgents from the neighboring province of Shensi. With their assistance, he succeeded in keeping his army intact until the abdication of the dynasty ended hostilities and allowed him to reassume the post of military governor.[32] By demonstrating the utter futility of opposing Yuan Shih-k'ai's armies in the North, Yen's defeat must have helped shape Sun Yat-sen's determination to relinquish the presidency of the new Republic and come to terms with his enemy. On the other hand, the defection of Shansi made it clear that North China, like the provinces of the South, was prepared to rise against the Manchus and consequently may have convinced Yuan Shih-k'ai that only the abolition of the Ch'ing dynasty would end the civil war.

[31] *NCH*, Dec. 23, 1911, 793:1 and 794:3.
[32] *NCH*, Jan. 12, 1912, 98:2-3, and "Lü," "Shan-hsi shu-cheng t'an" ("On the Government of Shansi"), *Hsien-tai p'ing-lün* (*The Contemporary Review*), hereafter referred to as *HTPL*, Aug. 28, 1926, pp. 10-11.

CHAPTER THREE

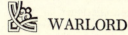 WARLORD

Yen Hsi-shan and Yuan Shih-k'ai

YEN HAS INFERRED that he owed his confirmation as military governor of Shansi to his membership in the T'ung Meng Hui and therefore to his association with Sun Yat-sen.[1] Nevertheless, when Sun visited Shansi in the fall of 1912 he spoke at length about the dangers of sectionalism and urged his fellow revolutionaries to subordinate their own interests to the common good, which suggests that he was uncertain of Yen's loyalty to the principles of the Revolution. Since Sun warned against "crafty men who are trying to divide and conquer us," he also may have feared that Yen would desert the recently organized Kuomintang in the event that it clashed with Yuan Shih-k'ai.[2] His fears were justified because in 1913 Yen remained neutral when Yuan suppressed the Kuomintang and drove its leaders from the country. On the contrary, in 1914 he accepted from Yuan the honorary rank of field marshal and a year later joined him in denouncing Sun Ch'uan-fang and other militarists who were defying his authority.

Convinced by his defeat in 1911 of the futility of waging war against Yuan's powerful army, Yen likewise appears to have admired the realistic and military-minded Yuan more than the dreamy and less effectual Sun Yat-sen. As late as 1957 he referred to Yuan as a highly intelligent man who invariably accomplished whatever he set out to do.[3] It would seem, moreover, that Yuan helped Yen maintain his authority in Shansi. For example, he came to Yen's rescue in 1912 when revolutionaries from southern Shansi declared that region independent of Yen's regime. With the aid of troops sent into Shansi by Yuan Shih-k'ai, Yen suppressed this uprising and sent its leaders in chains to Peking.[4] Yuan also ignored the claims of Yen's chief rival, Hsü Hsi-feng, whose

[1] Interview with Yen Hsi-shan, Taipei, Taiwan, Jan. 13, 1957.
[2] Sun Yat-sen, *op.cit.*, pp. 165-168.
[3] Interview with Yen Hsi-shan, Taipei, Taiwan, Jan. 13, 1957.
[4] Ts'ai Tung-fan, *Min-kuo t'ung-su yen-i* (*The Romance of the Republic*) (Shanghai, 1926), III, p. 34a.

forces had succeeded in driving the Manchus out of northern Shansi at the same time that Yen was suffering defeat in the south. After a brief tenure as police commissioner in Yen's new government, Hsü denounced Yen as a reactionary and tried to use the police to overthrow him, only to be defeated and driven from the province.[5]

In return for these favors, Yen permitted Yuan's henchmen to dominate the provincial government of Shansi. They held all of the key posts, including the office of civil governor, which was conferred on a close friend of Yuan's who brought with him a police force almost as large as Yen's army.[6] Yen was obliged to reduce the size of his own forces and share control of northern Shansi with one of Yuan's commanders. When he asked Peking to underwrite his efforts to establish military colonies in neighboring Suiyuan, Yuan rejected his petition and attempted to thwart his plans by giving someone else jurisdiction over the territory Yen proposed to colonize. Yuan's behavior indicated that he distrusted Yen; however, he probably allowed him to retain the military governorship of Shansi for fear of offending the intense sectionalism of the local population, especially since Yuan's own troops were extremely unpopular in Shansi owing to depredations they had committed in the course of their campaign against Yen's forces in 1911.[7] Yen must have resented bitterly Yuan's attempts to keep him from extending his influence northward because when soldiers from Outer Mongolia crossed the border into Suiyuan he used this incident as a pretext for occupying most of the province. Furthermore, he challenged Yuan's authority within Shansi by publicly urging the civil governor to surrender much of his power to the district magistrates and other local officials who made up the bulk of Yen's supporters. In 1915 Yen charged that under the Republic Chinese were no better off than they had been when ruled by the Manchus,[8] which may explain why a Peking newspaper accused him of

---

[5] Harvard Committee on International and Regional Studies, pub., *Biographies of Kuomintang Leaders*, compiled by the Publication Information Association of the Chinese Communist Party, Yenan, 1945 (Cambridge, 1948), hereafter referred to as *Kuomintang Biographies*, the biography of Chao P'i-lien. Also see *Yang Ai-yüan*, p. 4b.

[6] *Yang Ai-yüan*, pp. 7b-8a, and letter to myself from H. H. K'ung, dated Dec. 5, 1957, and hereafter referred to as *K'ung*.

[7] *NCH*, March 9, 1912, 633:3.

[8] *Lectures*, III-A, pp. 2-5 (Sept. 1915).

"fomenting dangerous rumors."[9] According to Yen, in 1916 he was denounced by Yuan's agents in Shansi and barely escaped being executed for treason. Nevertheless, when Yuan announced that he intended to reestablish the monarchy by ascending the throne as the founder of a new dynasty, Yen pledged his support, accepted a title of nobility, and tried to demonstrate his loyalty by sending his own parents to Peking to serve as hostages.[10] Even after revolts in various provinces exposed the weakness of Yuan's regime, Yen continued to acknowledge the authority of the Peking government, although in reality he remained aloof from the conflict between Yuan and his enemies. Yuan's death in the summer of 1916 ended the civil war but Yen waited almost a year before ousting the dead man's supporters from the government of Shansi.[11]

The history of Yen Hsi-shan's relations with Yuan Shih-k'ai suggests that the political unity of China did not dissolve immediately after the overthrow of the Ch'ing dynasty. Although unable to reestablish completely the authority of the central government in most provinces, Yuan was powerful enough to impose his will on their leaders. The collapse of his power in 1916 left Yen and the other provincial governors in undisputed possession of their domains and ushered in a period of genuine disunity which I shall call the warlord period.

The Warlord Period

The decade that followed the death of Yuan Shih-k'ai witnessed a long and bitter struggle between rival militarists for regional and later national hegemony. The defeat of his forces in neighboring Honan in 1919 seems to have convinced Yen that Shansi was too underdeveloped to support an army powerful enough to compete effectively in this contest. Therefore, he tried to remain aloof from the struggle for power and

[9] *NCH*, Aug. 14, 1915, 418:1.
[10] Hsi Jung, *Yen Hsi-shan te tsui-chuang* (*The Crimes of Yen Hsi-shan*) (Yenan, 1945), p. 2, Wen Kung-chih, *op.cit.*, p. 126, interview with *Lo Chia-lun*, chairman of the Historical Committee of the Kuomintang, Taipei, Taiwan, May 17, 1957, *NCH*, June 10, 1916, 571:2, and Hsü Fan-t'ing, "Chi Shan-hsi t'u huang-ti Yen Hsi-shan te i-feng wu-ch'ien yen shu" ("A Five Thousand Word Letter to the Small-time Emperor of Shansi, Yen Hsi-shan"), p. 3, hereafter referred to as Hsü Fan-t'ing, *Letter*, Ch'en Po-ta, *Yen Hsi-shan p'i-p'an* (*A Criticism of Yen Hsi-shan*) (Kalgan, 1945).
[11] Wen Kung-chih, *op.cit.*, p. 127, and Fairfield, *op.cit.*, p. 1.

concerned himself almost exclusively with the problem of modernizing Shansi and developing its resources. His enthusiasm for modernization was inspired for the most part by his experiences in Japan but also may have resulted from an epidemic which ravaged much of Shansi in 1918. Yen was impressed profoundly by the zeal, talents, and modern outlook of the doctors and other personnel sent into Shansi by foreign relief agencies for the purpose of helping him combat the plague. He subsequently compared these foreigners favorably to his own generally benighted and apathetic officials.[12] Conversations with other proponents of Westernization such as John Dewey, Hu Shih, and Yen's close friend H. H. K'ung, principal of the Oberlin-supported schools in Taiku, likewise must have reinforced his determination to modernize Shansi. At any rate, the reforms he carried out there won for him widespread acclaim and for Shansi the reputation of being the "Model Province."

Meanwhile, in order to preserve his control of Shansi, Yen shifted from one warring clique to another, invariably emerging on the winning side. Initially he was a protégé of perhaps the most powerful of the northern warlords, Tuan Ch'i-jui, who succeeded to Yuan Shih-k'ai's rule in Peking. In 1916 Tuan had interceded on Yen's behalf when Yuan contemplated having him executed for treason.[13] Yen returned the favor a year later by helping Tuan thwart Chang Hsün's attempt to restore the Ch'ing dynasty to power. Tuan allowed Yen to oust Yuan's appointees from Shansi, bestowed on him the title of Model Governor of Shansi, and used the Shansi Army against Honanese militarists who had defied his Peking regime, with the result that Yen came to be regarded as an important member of Tuan's so-called Anfu clique.[14] Yen reciprocated by annually paying Tuan a large sum of money; however, the defeat of his army in Honan caused him to hesitate when Tuan ordered him to suppress another uprising, this time in neighboring Shensi. Although he ordered one of his divisions to advance into Shensi, he secretly assured the in-

[12] *Lectures*, III-A, p. 143 (Dec. 1918).

[13] Interview with Yen Hsi-shan, Taipei, Taiwan, Jan. 13, 1957.

[14] "Lü," *op.cit.*, p. 7, *Yang Ai-yüan*, and Teng and Ingalls, trans., Li Chien-nung, *The Political History of China 1840-1928* (Princeton, 1956), p. 503.

surgents there that his troops would not interfere with their activities.[15] Tuan, on the other hand, pressed Yen to transfer civil authority over Shansi to men hand-picked by the Peking government. Thus the relationship between Yen and Tuan Ch'i-jui remained as unstable as most warlord alliances.

In 1920 Yen foresaw the downfall of the Anfu clique and purchased the good will of the victorious Chihli faction, while at the same time continuing to send money to the defeated Anfu generals in the hope that they would remain friendly to him and permit him to retain control of Shansi if they succeeded in regaining their power.[16] Two years later he backed the Chihli leaders, Wu P'ei-fu and Ts'ao Kun, during their successful struggle with the forces of the Manchurian overlord Chang Tso-lin, chiefly in order to mollify their powerful subordinate, Feng Yü-hsiang, whose armies controlled neighboring Chahar. He received as a reward the rank of marshal but struggled incessantly against efforts on the part of the Peking government to undermine his authority in Shansi. In 1924, when the Chihli clique became involved in another war with Chang Tso-lin, Feng Yü-hsiang betrayed Wu and Ts'ao, seized Peking, and formed an alliance with Chang Tso-lin and Tuan Ch'i-jui. Yen tried to ingratiate himself with the victors by sending troops to occupy the Honanese rail junction of Shih-chia-chuang so as to prevent Wu P'ei-fu from reinforcing his armies to the north; however, in the hope of retaining Wu's good will he subsequently dismissed the commander of these troops on the ground that this officer exceeded his orders when he turned back Wu's reinforcements.[17] It would appear that Feng Yü-hsiang was not taken in by Yen's deviousness because after appointing himself "Defense Commissioner for the Northwest" he claimed jurisdiction over parts of northern Shansi. Yen benefited, on the other hand, from the support of Tuan Ch'i-jui, who was considerably weaker than either Feng or Chang and therefore eager to regain Yen's backing.[18] Ultimately, Yen and Tuan emerged as members of a coalition

[15] "Lü," op.cit., p. 10.
[16] Wang Chen-i, "Mo-fan tu-chün chih hsia Shan-hsi-chih kai-kuan" ("A Picture of Shansi under the Rule of the Model Governor"), Hsin min-kuo (New Republic), June 1924, p. 3.
[17] Wen Kung-chih, op.cit., p. 127 and NCH, Nov. 29, 1924, 356:5.
[18] "Lü," "Shan-hsi shu-cheng t'an," HTPL, Aug. 21, 1926, p. 7.

formed by Wu P'ei-fu and Chang Tso-lin for the purpose of destroying Feng's power.

Yen's policies with respect to other warlords were an outgrowth of his own vulnerability. Although weaker than most of his rivals, he often held the balance of power between them, and consequently even those he betrayed hesitated to attack him lest they need his support in the future. His behavior exemplifies the hypocrisy and unabashed opportunism of Chinese politics during the warlord period, but nonetheless the inhabitants of the Model Province were able to enjoy peace during perhaps the most disorderly years in the history of modern China.

The Shansi Army

Yen returned from Japan in 1909 with the conviction that in order to survive in the modern world China must embrace militarism. "The three great duties of the people," he remarked in a booklet issued early in 1919, "are to serve in the army, to pay taxes, and to receive education. The vital spirit of the people is the attaching of importance to things military. To protect the nation, the army is needed; to prepare to fight, wealth is needed."[19] He also extolled Germany as the most powerful nation in Europe, and in other works he called for universal conscription along German and Japanese lines, while urging parents to give their children toy knives and spears "in order to nourish in them an admiration for military prowess."[20] However, defeats suffered by the Shansi Army in neighboring Honan, together with the collapse of Germany after the First World War, caused Yen to reassess the value of militarism as a way of life. During the years that followed he delivered comparatively few speeches dealing with the army and in these exhorted his soldiers to fulfill their responsibilities to the civilian population. In an effort to save money he systematically reduced the size of his army until by 1923 there were fewer troops in Shansi than in most of the other provinces of China.[21] In fact, when Tuan Ch'i-jui asked him to recruit

[19] Harrison K. Wright, "What the People Ought to Know," *The Chinese Recorder*, Nov. 1919, p. 746.

[20] *Lectures*, v, p. 23 (May 1915) and F. C. H. Dreyer, "Yen Shi-shan: A Progressive Governor," *The Chinese Recorder*, July 1920, p. 479.

[21] *CYB, 1923*, p. 583.

more troops in order to strengthen the forces of the Anfu clique, Yen complied by simply promoting all of the officers in one of his regiments to brigade rank without increasing even slightly the number of men under their command.[22]

All of this ended in 1923 after rumors circulated that neighboring warlords were planning to invade Shansi. Yen began conscripting the youth of Shansi into his army and created a large civilian reserve consisting of conscripts who, after being discharged into civilian life, periodically came together for additional military training. The existence of this rural militia (*hsiang-chün*) freed Yen from the expense of maintaining a large standing army but assured him of the services of 100,000 trained men.[23] Although inspired for the most part by what Yen had seen in Japan, the rural militia also seems to have been patterned after the American National Guard. Conscription and the creation of a civilian reserve aroused considerable opposition among the peasants, who not only resented the absence of their sons but likewise complained that after enjoying the comparative ease and comfort of life in the army, farmboys generally were unwilling to return to the fields. In a desperate effort to keep his son from being drafted, one peasant even mutilated the boy by cutting off his index finger. But because Yen conscripted his troops from the local population and maintained a large civilian reserve, the Shansi Army was for the most part a citizens' army and perhaps the only army in China composed exclusively of soldiers from the province in which it was stationed.[24] For this reason, and because the Model Governor insisted that his soldiers repair roads and help the peasants in the fields as well as pay for whatever they took from civilians, during the 1920's Yen's troops seem to have enjoyed substantially more popularity than the hordes of rapacious mercenaries employed by many warlords.[25] In this respect his policies foreshadowed Chinese Communist attempts to mobilize popular support for their army by inducing the masses to regard Communist soldiers as merely fellow citizens responsible for safeguarding the interests of the common people.

[22] "Lü," *op.cit.*, p. 7.
[23] Wen Kung-chih, *op.cit.*, pp. 124-125, and Wang Chen-i, *op.cit.*, p. 3.
[24] Wen Kung-chih, *op.cit.*, pp. 124-125.
[25] *NCH*, Feb. 2, 1924, 165:5, and Jan. 17, 1925, 92:4.

Leadership and Training in the Shansi Army

Since Yen Hsi-shan was preoccupied with politics and civil administration, he left to his subordinates most of the decisions concerning the training and actual operations of the Shansi Army. Initially, his troops were commanded by his old comrade Huang Kuo-liang; however, in 1917, perhaps as part of an effort to make himself undisputed master of Shansi, Yen dismissed Huang and replaced him with Shang Chen, who remained his chief of staff until 1930. Inasmuch as Shang Chen came from outside Shansi and therefore did not enjoy a personal following within the Shansi Army,[26] Yen probably feared him less than the more popular Huang Kuo-liang. Together with the comparative smallness of the Shansi Army, Yen's distrust of able commanders may explain why young men eager for a military career normally left Shansi and joined the army of Wu P'ei-fu in neighboring Honan.[27] Among Yen's generals only Fu Tso-yi seems to have been an adroit tactician and an inspiring field commander. Others, like Sun Ch'u and Yang Ai-yüan, owed their exalted rank to their loyalty and trustworthiness rather than their military abilities.

Candidates for commissions in the Shansi Army were chosen from the ranks of elementary school graduates and given two years of middle school education before entering the army as junior officers. In order to qualify for higher rank they were obliged to attend the Paoting Military Academy in Hopei or enlist in Yen's own Military Instruction Corps (*lu-chün chiao-tao t'uan*). Since all of this training was provided at the expense of the provincial government, a career as an officer in Yen's army probably attracted persons unable to secure an education by other means. According to Yen, the officers and men of his army were subjected to the kind of punishing training common in the Japanese Army. He recommended starving the recruits, beating them, exposing them to the elements, and working them to the point of exhaustion to "toughen" them up. "Because they are ill-treated and made

[26] Gaimushō jōhō bu (Information Bureau, Japanese Foreign Ministry), comp., *Gendai Chūka minkoku manshu teikoku jimmei kan* (*A Current Survey of Famous Persons in the Chinese Republic and the Manchurian Empire*) (Tokyo, 1937), hereafter referred to as *Japanese Biographical Survey, 1937*, p. 242.

[27] *NCH*, March 19, 1921, 727:3.

to suffer during their training, Japanese soldiers do not flee from the battlefield or turn against their officers," he once remarked.[28] To improve further the discipline of his troops he organized them into a Soldier's Heart-Washing Society (*chün-jen hsi-hsin she*) and tried in other ways to inculcate in them a spirit of enthusiasm, loyalty, obedience, and self-sacrifice. For example, officers were expected to familiarize themselves with the background, outlook, and personality of every soldier under their command, with a view to adopting the most appropriate and effective methods of indoctrinating them with the tenets of Yen's peculiar ideology.[29]

In spite of such measures, Yen's soldiers failed to live up to his expectations. It would appear that in reality their training program consisted of nothing more severe than daily exercises under the supervision of drill instructors from Taiyuan. Furthermore, their morale and discipline were so poor that in skirmishes with bandits they occasionally ignored their officers and after firing their rifles into the air scurried for shelter, moving Yen to observe that "soldiers who do not take aim are immoral."[30] Yen implied that cowardice and disobedience were responsible for the defeat of his army in Honan in 1919. He placed much of the blame on his officers, who either misconstrued his instructions or else were out of sympathy with his objectives. Many habitually disregarded the orders of their own superiors and when called upon to lecture their soldiers on the virtues of loyalty and obedience, simply delivered senseless harangues made up of unrelated passages from their instruction manuals.[31] Yen's own comments suggest that the majority of his officers neither understood nor sympathized with his objectives but instead had entered his service solely in the hope of acquiring prestige and a higher standard of living.[32]

The Taiyuan Arsenal

Although its training left something to be desired, the Shansi Army probably was as well-equipped as any army in China. In 1923 rumors to the effect that neighboring war-

[28] *Lectures*, v, p. 30 (May 1915).
[29] See *ibid.*, p. 45 (July 1918).
[30] *Lectures*, III-C, p. 17 (Nov. 1918).
[31] *Lectures*, v, p. 44 (July 1918).
[32] See *ibid.*, pp. 53-54 (July 1919).

lords were preparing to invade Shansi confronted Yen with the necessity of rearming his troops, whose weapons antedated the First World War and were hopelessly obsolete, in addition to being imported from so many different foreign countries that frequently ammunition issued to the soldiers did not fit their rifles.[33] Rather than incur the expense of importing new weapons from abroad, Yen expanded his gun repair shop into a large, modern arsenal. Machinery for the Taiyuan Arsenal was purchased mostly in Germany and operated under the supervision of a staff of Chinese technicians headed by several Swedish and German engineers. Most of the Chinese technicians had been educated in the United States, but some may have been graduates of Yen's own Shansi Military Technical School (*Shan-hsi wu-yeh chuan-men hsüeh-hsiao*), where soldiers who demonstrated an aptitude for science and technology were given training in chemistry, physics, and engineering.[34] During the first year of its existence, the director of the arsenal was Yen's former chief of staff, Huang Kuo-liang.

By 1926 the Taiyuan Arsenal employed 8,000 workers and was among the largest and most productive arsenals in China.[35] Besides turning out daily 4,500 grenades, 120,000 cartridges, and 3,200 mortar and artillery shells, it also produced each month 1,500 rifles, 500 pistols, and 300 mortars, as well as 30 machine guns and a smaller number of field guns and howitzers, ranging in size from 75 millimeter to 105 millimeter.[36] This was sufficient to supply the needs of Yen's entire army.[37] Moreover, Yen set up a research department in the Military Technical School and, at the suggestion of a German technician, created an Arms Committee (*ping-ch'i wei-yuan-hui*), which offered liberal rewards to anyone who invented a new weapon or succeeded in improving an existing one. This committee was responsible for the development of more rapid firing automatic weapons, a new 88 millimeter howitzer, and a device that enabled Yen's riflemen to fire grenades a distance

[33] *Lectures*, VIII, p. 15 (Jan. 1919).

[34] Bureau of Economic Information of the Chinese Government, comp., *The Chinese Economic Bulletin*, hereafter referred to as *CEB*, July 25, 1925, p. 55.

[35] "Lü," *op.cit.*, p. 9.   [36] *CYB, 1931*, p. 441.

[37] The Tientsin *I Shih-pao* (*Wide World Daily*), May 29, 1926, as quoted in *Archives*, May 1926, p. 396.

of several hundred yards. Soon the grenade became perhaps the most effective weapon used by the Shansi Army, although, according to a foreign reporter, the large number of casualties among troops equipped with the new grenade launcher indicated that this device was by no means perfected.[38] This may explain why Yen's soldiers often regarded their new weapons with suspicion, for he complained that many of them preferred the spears and swords traditionally carried by Chinese fighting men.[39] In his eagerness to modernize his army, Yen even purchased two aircraft, built a repair shop for them, hired several Japanese flying instructors, and set about creating his own flying corps, notwithstanding the fact that during its first flight over Taiyuan one of his new planes crashed and was destroyed.[40]

The history of the Taiyuan Arsenal demonstrates that as early as the 1920's Yen Hsi-shan was keenly aware of the need for military modernization and determined to manufacture his own armaments. Yet in spite of its excellent weapons, the Shansi Army generally was considered no match for the better-trained and numerically superior forces commanded by other warlords.[41] Consequently, if Yen was able to rule almost undisturbed in Shansi for two decades, he owed his success chiefly to his own wiliness and the natural impregnability of Shansi.

[38] *CEB*, April 4, 1925, p. 196 and *CYB*, 1928, p. 1281.
[39] *Lectures*, v, p. 58 (Aug. 1921).
[40] *CEB*, Dec. 5, 1925, p. 329.
[41] *Fairfield*, p. 1, and "Chao," "Shan-hsi wen-t'i" ("The Shansi Question"), *HTPL*, Sept. 19, 1925, p. 4.

CHAPTER FOUR

GOVERNMENT AND POLITICS

Social Control

SHANSI'S comparative immunity from foreign invasion left Yen Hsi-shan free to use his army to suppress banditry within the Model Province and otherwise uphold his authority over his domain. During the early years of his rule, he battled incessantly against hordes of brigands who each winter ravaged the countryside, robbing and murdering whoever they encountered. Although the local population sought refuge in walled towns and villages, frequently even these citadels were stormed and looted by armies of brigands who fled into the mountains before Yen's troops arrived on the scene.[1] For this reason, Yen tried to supplement the work of his army by organizing able-bodied villagers into militia (*pao-wei t'uan*). Whenever their labor was not needed in the fields, militiamen trained under the command of members of the local gentry who had served for three months in the Shansi Army. Furthermore, each year they spent one month taking part in maneuvers and undergoing examinations at a nearby army camp. Proficiency was rewarded with the Order of the Vigilant Lion and a gift of money to the recipient's native village. Militiamen who killed or captured bandits also were given money, along with persons who revealed to the authorities information that resulted in the death or apprehension of brigands.[2]

Because militiamen received only nominal wages and were virtually self-supporting, the militia cost Yen very little to maintain. Even its weapons consisted for the most part of inexpensive items like staves, spears, and old-fashioned muskets. But these were relatively ineffective against well-armed bandits, especially since in many instances militiamen went into battle equipped with nothing more lethal than knives and sharpened stones. Then too, many of the peasants were indifferent fighters who loafed when they should have been training

[1] *NCH*, Dec. 22, 1917, 716:3, and Aug. 11, 1917, 316:1-2.
[2] Yen Hsi-shan, *Ts'un-cheng fa-kuei ling-wen chi-yao* (*A Compilation of Rules Concerning Village Administration*) (Taiyuan, 1925), hereafter referred to as *Village Rules*, pp. 25b-26b.

and promptly went into hiding whenever bandits appeared. As for their officers, frequently they were so incompetent that they were easily outwitted by able and more experienced bandit chieftains.[3] Moreover, not only the common people but a large percentage of Yen's officials lived in such dread of the brigands that they were reluctant to report their whereabouts to the army. When Yen installed a system of military telephones in an effort to facilitate the suppression of banditry, some local officials actually refused to use the phones for fear that they would not be compensated for the cost of the call.[4] Nevertheless, with the forces at his disposal Yen succeeded in virtually eradicating banditry in Shansi.[5] "We travelled day or night throughout the area without any reason for concern," remarked a former resident.[6] Yen probably owed much of his success to his own ruthlessness. In 1911 he executed outright more than two hundred persons caught looting in Taiyuan after his forces overthrew Manchu rule in that city.[7] Yet he also tried to eliminate a major cause of lawlessness by obliging his soldiers to learn a trade so that upon being released from the army they would not be compelled to turn to banditry for a livelihood.[8]

Besides relying on his army and the members of the militia, Yen employed thousands of policemen to keep everyone in the province under continual surveillance and to report to Taiyuan any violations of provincial laws. Although attached to the subdistricts (*ch'ü*) and paid out of local revenues, these policemen received their training in Taiyuan and were responsible to the provincial government, in the form of the district magistrate. Since the salaries of the police were meager, however, Yen found it difficult to recruit able and honest men into his police force, so that often village headmen

---

[3] See *ibid.*, p. 27a, and *NCH*, Dec. 16, 1922, 727:2.

[4] *Lectures*, III-B, p. 46 (Jan. 1919).

[5] Wang Ch'ien, *Erh-shih-ch'i nien Shan-hsi cheng-chih kai-k'uang* (*Twenty-Seven Years of Government in Shansi*) (an unpublished manuscript written in 1938), p. 16b, *NCH*, July 15, 1922, 158:1-2, and Han Lu, "Ai Shan-hsi" ("Alas for Shansi"), *HTPL*, July 3, 1926, p. 6.

[6] Letter to myself from F. S. Hutchins, formerly a missionary in Shansi, dated Sept. 12, 1957.

[7] Letter to myself from Wynn C. Fairfield, dated Sept. 12, 1958.

[8] *CEB*, Nov. 7, 1925, p. 271, and Mansfield Freeman, "Has China Found a New Moses?" *Asia*, April 1924, pp. 323-324.

and their assistants had to serve as local constables in addition
to performing their other duties. Yen likewise complained repeatedly about incompetence, corruption, and downright crim-
inal behavior on the part of the police.[9] This is why he urged
students attending the law school of Shansi University to
emulate lawyers in the West by becoming policemen after
they graduated.[10]

In spite of these obstacles Yen succeeded in reducing appreciably the number of crimes committed in Shansi. According to one of his followers, in 1924 there occurred only seven-
teen robberies in the entire province.[11] But in their eagerness
to please Yen and reassure him of their zeal and diligence,
local officials frequently reported slight infractions of even the
most insignificant regulations, causing the provincial ministry
of justice to become so involved in the investigation of mis-
demeanors that often it lacked the time to deal with more important matters. In order to extend still further the authority
of his government Yen introduced an annual census and retained the system of collective responsibility that had existed
under the Ch'ing dynasty. Local officials were punished for the
misbehavior of anyone living under their jurisdiction, heads
of families suffered for the misdeeds of their relatives, and
businessmen and landlords were penalized for the crimes of
their associates or tenants. "No individual must be allowed to
slip through the net" warned Yen.[12] In his eagerness to control their behavior, he openly encouraged his subjects to spy
on one another, urging them to report "bad persons" to the
police and "idle women" to their husbands.[13] Nor did his professed respect for filial piety deter him from exhorting children
to report to the authorities the misconduct of their parents.[14]
In fact, he explicitly called on his subjects to tender to the
state the loyalty they traditionally had reserved exclusively
for their own families, on the grounds that China's weakness
in the face of foreign aggression was a result of the extreme
clannishness of her population, which fostered disunity and

9 *Lectures*, III-B, pp. 11 and 155 (June 1918 and Aug. 1924).
10 *Lectures*, VI, p. 13 (Sept. 1918).
11 Wang Ch'ien, *op.cit.*, p. 16b.
12 *Lectures*, III-A, pp. 59-60 (May 1918).
13 Leon Wieger, *Chine Moderne*, IV, (Hien-hien, 1924), p. 355.
14 *Lectures*, III-C, p. 126 (Aug. 1923), and *Village Rules*, p. 9a.

selfish indifference to the fate of the nation.[15] In a widely distributed booklet entitled *What Families Must Know* (*Chia-t'ing hsü chih*) he laid down rules governing virtually every aspect of family life. At least one of these was aimed at undermining the solidarity of the extended family, for it urged fathers to encourage independence on the part of their married sons by allowing them to establish separate households.[16] "Exclusive preoccupation with the interests of one's own family has made Chinese society stink like a bedbug," Yen maintained.[17]

Moral Regeneration

The ubiquity of Yen's government is exemplified by the extent to which he interfered in the private lives of his subjects. For example, he insisted that everyone remove the long plaits of hair mandatory under the Ch'ing and ordered the police to clip off the queues of conservatives who disobeyed. At his behest, the authorities even lured people into theaters with the promise of a free theatrical performance and then proceeded to cut the hair of the hapless audience. The police coveted the money to be made from the sale of human hair and often used the campaign against queues as a pretext for extortion;[18] however, Yen's own motives were quite different. Like many returned students, he was keenly aware that most foreigners regarded the Chinese as backward and uncivilized. "They think that Chinese are little more than animals," he complained.[19] He even accused the American government of periodically recalling its nationals from China for fear that if they remained in that country too long they would become contaminated.[20] Consequently, he was eager to stamp out in Shansi every practice likely to invite the contempt of foreigners and especially anachronisms like the wearing of queues. "How can we match the achievements of the foreigners if we can't even look like them?" asked Yen.[21]

[15] Mansfield Freeman, *op.cit.*, 297:1-2.
[16] F. C. H. Dreyer, *op.cit.*, pp. 478, 479.
[17] *Lectures*, v, p. 46 (July 1918).
[18] *NCH*, May 11, 1918, 335:3, and Wang Chen-i, *op.cit.*, p. 2.
[19] *Lectures*, III-C, p. 14 (Nov. 1918).
[20] *Lectures*, v, p. 47 (July 1918).
[21] *Lectures*, III-A, pp. 88-89 (Aug. 1918).

Another convention that aroused Yen's wrath was the custom of binding the feet of young girls. In Shansi the wrappings came up to the knee so that the lower parts of the legs became mere crippled sticks. Women nonetheless refused to remove the bindings out of fear that this would destroy their marriage prospects. In an effort to rid the province of foot binding, Yen established in each district a branch of his Society for the Liberation of Feet (*T'ien-tsu hui*) and encouraged students to wear badges proclaiming that they would not marry girls having bound feet. He threatened to punish young men who wed such girls and frequently sentenced mothers who continued to bind the feet of their daughters to hard labor in state-owned factories.[22] As a result, the number of women having bound feet in Shansi declined appreciably, although Yen admitted that the campaign against foot binding was extremely unpopular, owing to the fact that the local officials again took the chance to extort money from the public.[23]

Yen's antagonism toward foot binding also may have been inspired by a feeling that this practice prevented women from playing a more active role in the economic life of Shansi. In much of Shansi women seldom took up any occupation aside from their purely domestic duties, and as these idle women comprised nearly 25 percent of the potential labor force, Yen was determined to put them to work.[24] He erected in each district at least one vocational training school where peasant girls were given the rudiments of literacy and taught skills like spinning, weaving, and sericulture.[25] Perhaps the largest of these institutions was the Shansi Women's Vocational Factory (*Shan-hsi nü-tzu chih-yeh kung-ch'ang*) in Taiyuan.[26] Yen argued that largely because women were uneducated they suffered mistreatment at the hands of their parents, husbands, and in-laws. But he refused to let girls pursue their studies beyond the primary grades, on the grounds that they did not need higher education in order to run their households proper-

[22] Wang Chen-i, *op.cit.*, p. 9a, and *Lectures*, III-C, p. 33 (Nov. 1918).
[23] *Lectures*, III-B, p. 225 (Jan. 1934).
[24] *CEB*, Nov. 14, 1925, p. 276.
[25] *Ibid.*, and Mansfield Freeman, *op.cit.*, 296:2-297:1.
[26] Shih-yeh pu, Kuo-chi mao-i chü (Industry Section, Board of International Trade), pub., *Chung-kuo shih-yeh chih, Shan-hsi sheng* (*The Chinese Industrial Gazetteer, Shansi Province*) (Shanghai, 1937), hereafter referred to as *Industrial Gazetteer*, p. 20-szu.

ly.[27] As with men, he was less interested in educating women than in indoctrinating them, for in addition to limiting the amount of education they could acquire, he also had girls attending his schools taught how to read his own works and encouraged them to communicate his doctrines to their children. All of this changed after 1925, however, when victories won by the Kuomintang armies in the South generated in Shansi so much enthusiasm for the principles of the Kuomintang, including women's rights, that Yen was compelled to let girls enroll in the middle schools and colleges of Taiyuan, where to his dismay they promptly formed a women's association (*fu-nü lien-ho hui*).[28]

Queue wearing, foot binding, and female illiteracy were only a few of the "social evils" which Yen attempted to stamp out in Shansi. Eager to put an end to homosexuality and prostitution, he convened a conference to determine the best way of "ensuring constancy and regularity of sexual intercourse between husbands and wives."[29] Moreover, every morning members of the Early Rising Society (*Ts'ao-ch'i hui*) knocked on the doors of houses in Taiyuan and reported persons still in bed after six o'clock. Also outlawed were idleness, gambling, sloppiness, brawling, excessive merrymaking, and the use of the old lunar calendar. Members of the Boy Scouts and other organizations shared with local officials the responsibility of making certain that everybody observed these prohibitions. Often school children were encouraged to gather outside the homes of malefactors and curse the occupants until they came out and promised to mend their ways.[30] Other miscreants were surrounded by crowds which lamented their behavior in language commonly reserved for funerals or were pursued through the streets by bands of small girls chanting, "Bad man, won't you be good!"[31] Yen likewise anticipated the techniques of the Chinese Communists by imprisoning habitual

[27] *Lectures*, VI, pp. 17, 84 (Dec. 1918 and July 1922).

[28] *Huang-pao* (*The Yellow Paper*), July 8, 1927, as quoted in *Archives*, July 1927, pp. 112-113, *NCH*, Nov. 14, 1925, 289:3, and Jen Ying-lun and Kuo Chien-fu, *op.cit.*, p. 3.

[29] Yen Hsi-shan, pub., *Chin Shan hui-i lu* (*The Records of the Conference for the Promotion of Progress in Shansi*) (Taipei, 1957), pp. 15-16.

[30] *Lectures*, III-C, p. 126 (Sept. 1922).

[31] *NCH*, Oct. 14, 1922, 77:3, and Leon Wieger, *op.cit.*, p. 342.

lawbreakers in state-owned factories, where attempts were made to "redeem them through labor."[32]

Public Health

Yen's enthusiasm for public health and sanitation was a product of his experiences in Japan; however, it was made more intense by outbreaks of diphtheria, influenza, and bubonic plague which occurred in Shansi during the early years of his rule. Yen's efforts to quarantine the sick to prevent these diseases from reaching epidemic proportions were frustrated by the indifference of local officials and the opposition of the masses. Few people were willing to be so unfilial as to turn their backs on a sick or dying relative, especially since, in the absence of trained doctors and adequately equipped hospitals, those who fell ill were doomed unless cared for by their families.[33] As a result, the sick infected the healthy until in some areas so many had perished that carpenters could not keep up with the demand for coffins. Several districts reported as many as 8,000 deaths within the course of a single year.[34]

Many who survived these years of pestilence owed their lives to the knowledge and skill of foreign medical missionaries, who comprised much of the staff of the organization Yen created for the purpose of fighting disease in Shansi.[35] Yen was so impressed by these foreign doctors that he erected in Taiyuan a modern hospital and medical school, which he proposed to staff with graduates of the Peking Union Medical College. Although neither of these institutions ever amounted to much,[36] foreign drugs as well as Western medical and surgical techniques became increasingly popular in Taiyuan.[37] But in the countryside the vast majority of the population continued to patronize herbalists and others dealing in the traditional medical lore of China. Besides prescribing weird and often ridiculous remedies, such as a diet of human flesh, these self-styled doctors frequently resorted to acupuncture and cauterization, but were so ignorant of elementary hygiene that they neglected to sterilize their instruments, with what

[32] Wang Ch'ien, op.cit., p. 14a.
[33] Lectures, III-C, p. 1 (April 1918).
[34] NCH, Dec. 21, 1918, 725:3.
[35] Lectures, III-A, p. 143 (Dec. 1918) and Fairfield, pp. 2-3.
[36] K'ung, p. 29, and Lectures, VIII, p. 20 (April 1919).
[37] CEB, Aug. 1, 1925, p. 59.

generally must have been catastrophic results.[38] In an effort to correct this situation, Yen established schools where such people were taught the basic principles of modern medicine. Nevertheless, because he was unwilling to expend the enormous sum necessary in order to achieve a genuine breakthrough in the field of public health and sanitation, epidemics continued to decimate the population of Shansi.[39]

Christian missionaries also helped Yen combat the famines that devastated much of Shansi during the early 1920's. By the end of 1922 three successive years of drought had created desperate conditions in much of Shansi. A third of the population was starving, many already had died, and thousands were turning to banditry.[40] Yen's own attempts to alleviate suffering failed because local officials remained indifferent to his pleas, while the rich ignored his prohibitions against hoarding grain and violated the ceiling he placed on the price of foodstuffs.[41] But he received invaluable assistance from the American Red Cross and missionary organizations like the American Mission Board and the China International Famine Relief Commission. The Famine Relief Commission spent in Shansi more than half a million dollars not only in the form of direct relief but also for motor roads constructed in order to facilitate the movement of relief supplies and agricultural experiments aimed at increasing farm output.[42] Yen worked closely with the members of the commission, who included both his trusted advisor H. H. K'ung and his commissioner of police, Nan P'ei-lan.[43] According to a foreign member of the Famine Relief Commission, its efforts, together with the resumption of rainfall in 1923, averted what otherwise would have been an "appalling calamity."[44] In the hope of preventing

[38] *Lectures*, III-C, p. 73 (April 1921), and VIII, pp. 20-21 (April 1918).

[39] Letter to myself from Dr. Percy Watson, formerly a medical missionary in Shansi, dated Oct. 5, 1957, and *NCH*, Feb. 24, 1923, 505:3, Dec. 8, 1923, 662:1-2, and Jan. 26, 1924, 123:5.

[40] Interview with *Yen Hsi-shan*, Taipei, Taiwan, Nov. 6, 1957.

[41] *NCH*, Nov. 25, 1922, 503:3, and Feb. 24, 1923, 506:3, and *Lectures*, VI, p. 77 (April 1921), and VIII, p. 38 (Aug. 1920).

[42] This estimate is based on a survey of reports issued annually throughout the 1920's by the China International Famine Relief Commission.

[43] China International Famine Relief Commission, pub., *Annual Report, 1923*, p. 50, and *Annual Report, 1925*, p. 86.

[44] *NCH*, May 5, 1923, 300:2, and *Fairfield*, p. 14.

the recurrence of such a catastrophe Yen ordered village
headmen to exact annually from each family under their jurisdiction a certain amount of grain, which was stored in the local
temple under the custody of the village elders. He was confident that this scheme would result in the accumulation by
each village of enough surplus food to feed the local population if for some reason the land failed to yield an adequate
harvest. The local gentry, however, frequently embezzled the
grain entrusted to them so that it was not available for distribution to the needy.[45]

Yen likewise endeavored to protect his subjects against
the evils of drug addiction. In 1916 at least 10 percent of
Shansi's 11 million people were habitual consumers of opium.[46]
The drug especially was popular in Taiku, Yü-tz'u, and other
urban areas where the decline of Shansi's commercial prosperity
had caused widespread unemployment and poverty. In addition to being alarmed by the physical and moral deterioration
that inevitably result from addiction to opium, Yen also was
concerned about the economic implications of the drug traffic.
He complained that every year more than CH$10 million
left Shansi in payment for opium imported from neighboring provinces.[47] The responsibility of preventing the sale and
consumption of narcotics in Shansi was given to the Society for
the Suppression of Opium Smoking (Chieh-yen hui). Yen
hoped that with the cooperation of local officials the association
would succeed in slowing down the traffic in drugs to the
point where the price of narcotics rose beyond the reach of
most addicts. Every year the authorities seized tons of opium
and imprisoned or shot hundreds of people caught dispensing
narcotics.[48] Even persons merely suspected of trafficking in
drugs were thrown into prison unless guaranteed by members
of their families or business associates. "Those who sell
narcotics are abominable!" thundered Yen. "Kill them! Kill
them!"[49]

[45] *Village Rules*, p. 31a, *Williamson*, p. 15, and *Fairfield*, p. 14.
[46] *Lectures*, III-A, p. 69 (May 1918), and Hsia Ching-feng, "Shan-hsi
lü-hsing chi," *Ti-hsüeh tsa-chih*, Feb. 2, 1916, p. 6b.
[47] *Lectures*, III-B, p. 68 (Aug. 1919). With respect to the exchange
rate between Chinese and American dollars, according to Sidney
Gamble, *North China Villages* (Berkeley, 1963), p. x, in 1933 Chinese
dollars were exchanged into American dollars at the rate of 3.84 to 1.
[48] *NCH*, Nov. 4, 1922, 290:1-2.
[49] Wang Ch'ien, *op.cit.*, p. 15b.

Yen initially treated addicts with equal severity. Besides having to pay substantial fines, they generally were subjected to the humiliation of public exposure, along with their friends and relatives. Those unable to secure guarantees had to labor in government-operated factories or on the roads, and habitual offenders were thrown into prison, where most of them died from ailments brought on by the sudden withdrawal of narcotics.[50] Yen subsequently admitted that he did not have enough cells to accommodate all of the addicts imprisoned in Shansi during the early years of his rule.[51] Largely because of the hardship inflicted on the families of those arrested, however, the harsh treatment meted out to addicts aroused considerable opposition on the part of the public. People became unwilling to report cases of addiction to the authorities, and so few volunteered to guarantee former addicts that Yen was reduced to having them vouch for each other.[52] Consequently, in 1922 he abandoned his policy of punishing addicts in favor of attempting to rehabilitate them. In addition to bringing enormous pressure to bear on them through their families, he erected for their benefit sanitariums which dispensed medicinal compounds designed to assuage and gradually destroy their craving for narcotics. "How pitiful are drug addicts!" chanted the students of Taiyuan as they marched through the streets. "Save them! Save them! Save them!"[53]

At first glance it would appear that Yen's campaign against drug addiction in Shansi was extraordinarily successful. He boasted that after 1922 the number of persons addicted to opium declined by as much as 80 percent,[54] and his claim is substantiated in the writings of independent observers.[55] But in the absence of similar efforts by neighboring warlords, Yen's attempts to prevent the manufacture or sale of opium in Shansi simply caused the price of narcotics there to rise so steeply that vast quantities of drugs were attracted into his domain from other provinces.[56] Many who found opium too

[50] See *ibid.*, p. 10a, and *NCH*, Feb. 14, 1925, 261:5.
[51] *Lectures*, III-C, p. 208 (March 1932).
[52] See *ibid.*, p. 130 (Sept. 1922).   [53] Wang Ch'ien, *op.cit.*, p. 15b.
[54] *Lectures*, III-C, p. 129 (Oct. 1922).
[55] *CYB, 1926*, p. 639, and "Lü," "Shan-hsi shu-cheng t'an," *HTPL*, Sept. 25, 1926, p. 12.
[56] Wang Meng-chou and Chang Lan-t'ing, "I-nien-lai Shan-hsi chih chin-tu" ("The Fight Against Narcotics in Shansi during the Past Year"), p. 3, *CCCK*.

expensive changed over to tiny compounds of morphine and heroin known as pills of immortality (*chin-tan*), which were more easily secreted and considerably less difficult to administer than opium. Whereas an opium smoker needed a conspicuous and often expensive pipe, the *chin-tan* addict could "fly in the airplane" merely by consuming the drug off a piece of tin foil.[57] Although Yen returned to a policy of imprisoning addicts and beheaded anyone caught selling *chin-tan*, drugs of all kinds continued to enter the Model Province. Smugglers were frequently escorted by soldiers from neighboring provinces, whom Yen dared not attack for fear of provoking a war. Persons guilty of selling or consuming narcotics, moreover, often possessed considerable wealth and influence, which saved them from punishment.[58] "The gentry are some of the worst offenders," complained Yen.[59] This is why local officials, who came for the most part from the privileged class, seldom enforced Yen's decrees outlawing the use of narcotics. In fact, so many of Yen's own officials were involved in the drug traffic[60] that ultimately he abandoned his efforts to suppress it and instead attempted to establish a government monopoly over the production and sale of opium in Shansi.[61] All of this suggests that without the cooperation of the gentry warlords like Yen Hsi-shan were unable to carry out even the most urgent and reasonable reforms.

The Structure of Government in Shansi

When Yen returned from Japan in 1909, he believed that China's salvation lay in military autocracy along German and Japanese lines. He attributed Germany's remarkable strength to its system of government which he felt instilled in the German people a willingness to sacrifice their own interests to those of the state.[62] The defeat of the Germans in the First

[57] Chao Shu-li, *Li-chia-chuang te pien-ch'ien* (*Li Village Turns Over*) (Shanghai, 1947), p. 33.

[58] Wang Chen-i, *op.cit.*, p. 2, Chao Shu-li, *op.cit.*, pp. 6-7, and *NCH*, Feb. 23, 1924, 279:3-4, and Aug. 23, 1924, 289:2.

[59] *Lectures*, III-C, p. 51 (March 1921).

[60] Wang Chen-i, *op.cit.*, p. 2, Chao Shu-li, *op.cit.*, p. 13, and *NCH*, Nov. 10, 1917, 279:3-4, and Aug. 23, 1924, 565:3.

[61] *Lectures*, III-B, p. 187 (Sept. 1921), Haldore E. Hanson, "Leaks in the Opium Barrel," *The China Weekly Review*, hereafter referred to as *CWR*, March 7, 1936, p. 20, and *NCH*, May 15, 1926, 292:2-3.

[62] *Lectures*, V, p. 34 (May 1915).

World War, however, momentarily shook Yen's faith in the superiority of authoritarianism. In 1918 he called the Germans "enemies of mankind" and imposed a boycott against their goods, while at the same time hailing the allied powers as "champions of morality."[63] He was impressed profoundly by the unanimity and enthusiasm with which the peoples of the democracies supported their governments during the war and endeavored to secure comparable popular support for his own policies by draping his fundamentally despotic regime in the trappings of Western democracy. The result was what he called "government that makes use of the people" (*yung-min cheng-chih*).[64] In addition to demanding that headmen be elected by villagers, he set up in each village a deliberative assembly composed of representatives of every family living in the community. While Yen hailed these innovations as first steps in the creation of political democracy, real power in Shansi remained in the hands of Yen's own clique, which compelled the village assemblies to sanction whatever policies it chose to follow. This was equally true with respect to the provincial assembly, whose members were hand picked by Yen and apparently rarely stood for reelection.[65] According to one of his own followers, most of the assemblymen were "useless pigs," who did nothing but play mah-jongg and smoke opium.[66] Since in 1919 they devoted themselves exclusively to authorizing expenditures already made by the provincial government two years before, their irresponsibility was at least in part a result of Yen's unwillingness to give them any genuine authority. As for the much publicized election of village headmen, Yen instructed district magistrates to make certain that headmen chosen by the villagers were "good men" and even suggested that the magistrates visit the villages and designate those who should be elected.[67] His conception of representative government is illustrated by his claim that he was putting into effect a form of self-government which had flourished in China under the ancient Chou dynasty. "He believes in making

---

[63] *Lectures*, III-A, p. 106 (Aug. 1918).

[64] Wang Chen-i, *op.cit.*, p. 3b.

[65] Wang Chen-i, *op.cit.*, p. 3a, and *Archives*, June 1927, p. 127.

[66] Hsüeh Ch'in, "Tang-shih hui-i" ("Reflections about the Party"), p. 5, *CCCK*.

[67] *Williamson*, p. 3, and *Lectures*, III-A, p. 224 (March 1922), and III-C, p. 135 (Oct. 1922).

progress by going backward," commented one of his advisers.[68]

Yen contended that he dared not confer on the people of Shansi the power to play a more active role in determining the policies of the state until they had acquired sufficient experience and sophistication to fulfill the obligations which he was convinced must accompany this power. After he and his officials concluded that the masses were ready for self-government, they would voluntarily share their power with the people in the same manner that a father gradually relinquished his authority over his children as they attain maturity.[69] To Yen representative government did not mean the achievement of popular sovereignty, which they equated with anarchy; it was instead simply a device for arousing public enthusiasm for the policies of their governments. Yen frequently pointed to the prevalence of disorder and misery in the world as proof of the evils of democratic government and contrasted these conditions with the peace and prosperity enjoyed by the Chinese under the rule of capable and benevolent emperors.[70] In 1921 he charged that the existence of political parties in the United States had undermined the American government and thwarted the will of the American people.[71] Nevertheless, he maintained that China must adopt representative institutions because they were effective instruments for mobilizing popular resistance to foreign aggression. He even found a Chinese precedent for his policy of *yung-min cheng-chih* in the views of the eleventh century thinker and statesman Wang An-shih, who, according to Yen, tried to strengthen the ruling dynasty by persuading its subjects to lend it active support instead of merely serving it.[72]

Inasmuch as Yen was raised in an authoritarian society and educated in autocratic Japan, it is not surprising that he almost instinctively feared and disliked democracy. This predilection for paternal but despotic government seems to have been reinforced by a conviction that he was a latter-day sage whose mission it was to regenerate mankind. For this reason

[68] Mansfield Freeman, *op.cit.*, 298:1.
[69] *Lectures*, III-B, pp. 102-103 (July 1922).
[70] *Lectures*, VII, p. 42 (1919).
[71] *Lectures*, VI, p. 75 (March 1921).
[72] *Lectures*, III-B, p. 9 (June 1918).

he insisted that his portrait, together with excerpts from his speeches and writings, be displayed prominently in every village.[73] Besides building for himself a residence like the palace of an emperor, he also emulated the monarchy by traveling in great pomp and couching his orders and proclamations in terms reminiscent of imperial edicts.[74] In fact, a person who knew him well says that he regarded Shansi as his little kingdom.[75]

Yen's exalted opinion of himself caused him to dislike forthrightness in his subordinates. In 1913 his most capable general, Huang Kuo-liang, was expelled from Shansi for having questioned the wisdom of aligning with Yuan Shih-k'ai against Sun Yat-sen and the Kuomintang.[76] Subsequent differences over administrative matters cost Yen the services of his best civil official, Ma Tao-yin, who resigned in disgust, presumably because of the Model Governor's intransigence.[77] In keeping with his hostility toward political parties, Yen outlawed them in Shansi, along with secret societies, which he described as organizations of "low-class people" created for the purpose of promoting "Boxerism."[78] In 1927 he dealt ruthlessly with members of two pseudoreligious sects that had gained a foothold in southern Shansi. When they boasted of their immunity to bullets, he had some of them shot in order to convince the rest that they were mistaken.[79]

Southern Shansi in general was a center of disaffection, for in 1913 and again in 1917 it was the scene of major rebellions against Yen's rule. The popularity of the rebels and the nature of their demands suggest that these uprisings were provoked by a widespread feeling in the south that Yen was exploiting that region for the benefit of his native district and other areas to the north. When peasants rioted in support of the second of those rebellions, Yen punished the men responsible by

[73] Leon Wieger, *op.cit.*, pp. 344, 350.

[74] *Ibid.*, and *NCH*, Aug. 12, 1922, 452:3.

[75] Interview with Wang Huai-i, formerly English-language secretary to Yen Hsi-shan, Taipei, Taiwan, Jan. 13, 1957.

[76] *K'ung*, p. 3, "Lü," "Shan-hsi shu-cheng-t'an," *HTPL*, Aug. 28, 1926, p. 7, and letter to myself from Professor Lao Kan, formerly a student in Shansi, dated May 1, 1958.

[77] *NCH*, Oct. 7, 1922, 13:2.

[78] *Lectures*, III-B, p. 51 (Jan. 1919).

[79] *Ch'en-pao* (*The Morning News*), March 10, 1927, as quoted in *Archives*, March 1927, pp. 138-140.

chaining them together through holes punched in their collarbones.[80]

He was equally merciless toward Hsü Hsi-feng and other liberals, whom he executed or drove from the province because they criticized his regime.[81] Small wonder that during the early years of his rule he seldom left his residence for fear of being assassinated and then ventured out only after traffic had been stopped and guards posted in the streets.[82] There even circulated rumors to the effect that when he was being shaved a soldier stood by and held a pistol to the temple of the barber.[83] In 1923 fear that other warlords intended to attack him caused Yen to place his entire domain under martial law, with the result that freedom of speech and assembly virtually ceased to exist in Shansi. In addition to controlling the press, Yen's regime also censored the mails and banned organizations of private individuals, lest they become focal points of opposition to the provincial government.[84] Antagonism toward Yen persisted among important elements in Shansi, however; and in 1924 he was obliged to behead a number of army officers for collaborating with his enemies.

Yen not only used force to maintain his authority over Shansi, but likewise enlisted the support of important groups or cliques within the population by appointing their leaders to high office in his government. The most significant of these men was Chao Tai-wen, a person considerably older than Yen, who had been his teacher and for whom he had the utmost respect. Chao had studied in Japan, where he was active in Sun Yat-sen's movement, and upon returning to Shansi became a leader of the revolutionaries in that province. After the Revolution of 1911, he served as Yen's chief of staff and later was appointed vice-governor of Shansi. His influence on Yen's policies was profound and his family was second in importance only to Yen's own clan.[85] Together with Nan P'ei-lan, another returned student from Japan who held the post of police commissioner in Shansi for more than two decades, Chao represented the conservative, Japanese-oriented element in Yen's

[80] *NCH*, Sept. 1, 1917, 493:1.
[81] Hsu Fan-t'ing, *Letter*, p. 5.
[82] *NCH*, July 21, 1917, 428:2.
[83] John Gunther, *Inside Asia* (London, 1939), p. 312.
[84] Wang Chen-i, *op.cit.*, p. 3.
[85] *Japanese Biographical Survey*, 1937, p. 355.

regime. Several of Yen's lieutenants were graduates of English universities and one, H. H. K'ung, had obtained degrees from Oberlin and Yale before becoming the principal of the Christian schools maintained in Taiku by Oberlin College. K'ung mobilized volunteer forces in support of Yen during the Revolution of 1911 and subsequently became Yen's chief adviser on education and economic affairs.[86] Even radicalism found its way into Yen's regime, in the form of Chao P'i-lien, a member of the Chao clan who nevertheless had been sympathetic to Hsü Hsi-feng.

A foreigner who knew Yen says that he was less able than many of his subordinates but that their hostility toward one another prevented them from challenging his leadership.[87] Yen deliberately encouraged this factionalism within his regime by filling it with men belonging to mutually antagonistic cliques, perhaps in an effort to obtain the services of capable people without endangering his own authority. In that event, a common loyalty to Yen must have been the only force that held most of his followers together, and inasmuch as he also reserved for himself all real powers of decision, this may explain why by 1930 he was so indispensable that in his absence the structure of government in Shansi threatened to collapse.[88]

Yen likewise owed his power to the fact that he possessed a considerable amount of political charisma. Foreigners invariably came away impressed by his graciousness and charm;[89] however, the popularity he enjoyed in Shansi also was the result of other traits in his personality. Not only his

[86] See *ibid.*, p. 159, and Emily Hahn, *The Soong Sisters* (New York, 1943), pp. 90, 102.

[87] *Fairfield*, p. 4.

[88] *Ching-pao*, Nov. 27, 1930, and *Ta Kung Pao* (*Impartiality*), Nov. 22, 1930, as quoted in *Archives*, Nov. 1930, pp. 358, 327, respectively. This interpretation was suggested to me by the methods which Chiang Kai-shek employed in order to maintain his supremacy within the Kuomintang, as described in Ch'ien Tuan-sheng, *The Government and Politics of China* (Cambridge, 1950), pp. 128-132, 136-167, 225-226. Ch'ien's observations concerning the impact of these tactics on Chiang Kai-shek's regime are provocative and merit the attention of all scholars interested in events in China under the warlords.

[89] For example, see Edna Lee Booker, *News is My Job* (New York, 1940), pp. 107-110, R. W. Swallow, "Taiyuanfu Revisited," *NCH*, Nov. 22, 1932, 196:3, and A. Doak Barnett, *China on the Eve of Communist Takeover* (New York, 1963), p. 180. My own relations with Yen during the period 1956-1957 were extraordinarily pleasant.

cunning, which later caused an American to call him Foxy Grandpa,[90] but even his acquisitiveness must have appealed to the people of Shansi, whose own shrewdness and avarice were proverbial in China, especially since Yen tempered his greed by periodically making substantial gifts of money to be used for the public welfare.[91] Yen's unusual accessibility was also responsible for his popularity. He readily accommodated anyone who came to him seeking a small loan in order to buy land, build a house, or finance a marriage.[92] Under the Ch'ing, Shansi had been ruled by haughty mandarins who held themselves aloof from the population, but after the early years of his rule Yen deliberately mingled with his subjects in an effort to find out how they felt about his policies and in the hope that personal contact with him would cause them to support his program. He traveled continually and in the course of these excursions talked in a frank and informal manner with people from all walks of life, including a large number of ordinary farmers and shopkeepers, for he was keenly aware of their problems and their grievances against the government.[93] In fact, during these trips he behaved much like a person seeking election to public office. When he initiated a scheme aimed at radically changing the structure of village government, for example, he visited a multitude of villages, where he shook the hands of the local gentry, dined with them, and distributed pastries among the villagers. Even a writer who detested Yen infers that this kind of behavior won for

[90] Charles J. V. Murphy, "China Reborn," *Life*, Nov. 12, 1945, p. 13.
[91] *NCH*, Sept. 4, 1935, 382:4. With regard to Yen's cunning and its impact on his popularity in Shansi, if, as Graham Peck suggests on pages 491-492 of *Two Kinds of Time* (Boston, 1950), the Chinese admire in their leaders the qualities exemplified by the heroes of the famous novel *San-kuo yen-i* (*The Romance of the Three Kingdoms*), it would appear that in China honesty and consistency in political life have commanded less popular respect than wiliness and downright deviousness and opportunism. This raises the question of whether the Chinese define "political integrity" in a sense that differs radically from the connotation normally given to this phrase in the West. Obviously, this whole problem has broad implications with respect to the history of China under the warlords.
[92] Hsü Ying, "Chui-hua Shan-hsi" ("Reflections about Shansi"), *Kuo-wen chou-pao* (*The Weekly Gazette*), hereafter referred to as *KWCP*, Nov. 22, 1937, p. 51.
[93] For example, see *Lectures*, III-A, pp. 299-300 (June 1932), and III-C, pp. 211, 257 (March 1932 and Aug. 1938), as well as *NCH*, May 15, 1926, 292:3.

him appreciable popular support.[94] All of this suggests that because of their different background—their humble origin and lack of education, for instance—warlords like Yen Hsi-shan did not share fully the aristocratic outlook of the manda-rins who preceded them and therefore were less inclined to set themselves apart from the people they governed. They possessed what might be called "the common touch," and in this respect their conduct foreshadowed the Communist Party's efforts to persuade the masses that the party's leaders were fellow members of the working class.

Yen Hsi-shan also perceived the advantages of persuading his subjects to identify their interests with his government and actively support it instead of merely compelling them to accept his rule. The attempts he made to mobilize popular support for his government did not result in the creation of anything approaching political democracy; however, by giv-ing his subjects at least a nominal voice in affairs of state he may have discredited the authoritarianism of the past in the eyes of many and caused them to yearn for a government more responsive to the popular will. Yen also served the forces of change in China by attacking the age-old particularism of his countrymen. The magistrates who ruled Shansi's 105 districts, as well as their assistants, received their training in Taiyuan at institutions like the Training Academy (*yu-ts'ai kuan*) and the Institute of Political Administration (*hsing-cheng yen-chiu so*), which Yen created expressly for this purpose. After being indoctrinated with loyalty to Yen and his ideas, they were given unprecedented authority over the villages under their jurisdiction.[95] Besides presiding over the election of village headmen and their assistants, the district magistrate enjoyed the right to remove from office any village official who displeased him. Yen expected his magistrates to spend much of their time visiting towns and villages in their districts to make certain that their instructions were carried out. Village officials had to submit annual reports and attend weekly lectures dealing with their responsibilities to the provincial government. In order to bring them even more closely under his scrutiny, Yen created the Bureau of Villages (*ts'un-cheng chu*), which employed a large force of special investigators and

[94] Wang Chen-i, *op.cit.*, p. 2.
[95] *Hsin Chung-kuo* (*New China*), Nov. 15, 1919, p. 6.

divided every district into from three to six subdistricts (*ch'ü*), each headed by a deputy magistrate (*ch'ü-chang*) trained and appointed by the provincial government.[96] As most of the police received their training in Taiyuan, Yen succeeded in reducing the autonomy customarily enjoyed by village officials in Shansi. Perhaps the warfare between rival militarists after 1911 obscured the achievement by at least some of them of an unprecedented degree of cohesiveness at the provincial level which helped to lay the groundwork for the reunification of the country under the Kuomintang and the Chinese Communists.

In addition to demanding absolute loyalty from his officials, Yen urged them to befriend those under their jurisdiction and seek to win the affection and cooperation of the people by eating coarse food, wearing plain clothing, and otherwise trying to identify themselves with the masses.[97] He found that widespread hostility toward his officials was frustrating his attempts to mobilize popular support for his regime. "The people must stop regarding the magistrate's yamen as a breeding place of devils," he warned, "and come to look upon it as a temple of Bodhisattvas."[98]

Nonetheless, the ignorance of Yen's officials and their indifference to his objectives continued to interfere seriously with the implementation of his program. Because there existed a shortage of educated personnel he frequently was compelled to employ as officials semiliterate men whose inability to understand orders prevented them from communicating these instructions to others.[99] Since many of his officials were too incompetent or lazy to perform their duties effectively, their authority fell into the hands of more able but ill-educated and unscrupulous subordinates who used it to extort money from the public. Corruption was so common within the bureaucracy that Yen likened it to an overflowing privy and hesitated to adopt a merit system for fear that this would result in the dismissal of the great majority of his officials.[100] His speeches leave the impression that much of the bureaucracy lived extravagantly and met their expenses by levying excessive

[96] *Williamson*, p. 3, and *Lectures*, III-C, p. 79 (April 1922).
[97] *Lectures*, VI, p. 113 (Aug. 1925), and III-B, p. 112 (May 1923).
[98] *Lectures*, III-A, p. 237 (Oct. 1922).
[99] *Lectures*, III-A, pp. 57-58, 114 (May 1918 and Sept. 1918).
[100] *Lectures*, III-A, pp. 44-45, 107 (April, Aug. 1918).

fines, soliciting bribes, and embezzling public funds. For example, magistrates about to leave for a new post often sold the furnishings in their official residence and sometimes auctioned off the building itself.[101] Yen likewise accused his officials of employing or favoring their own friends and relatives whenever possible. But he was responsible himself for much of the corruption and nepotism that he professed to deplore in his bureaucrats. He paid most of them so little that inevitably they were tempted to supplement their income through corruption and exploitation.[102] Furthermore, his own behavior was out of keeping with the austerity and impartiality which he demanded on the part of his officials. He lived in the utmost luxury;[103] by 1930 there circulated rumors that he had accumulated a personal fortune of CH$70 million, and his opulence became almost proverbial among his subjects.[104] A Japanese writer refers to all of Shansi as Yen's "family property" (chia-ch'u).[105] Besides enriching himself, Yen also let his chief followers amass great wealth. A foreigner who was entertained in Yen's palatial home in the 1920's recalls that the wives of his chief ministers wore expensive silks and costly jewels.[106] According to another writer, the house belonging to Yen's police commissioner, Nan P'ei-lan, occupied a space the size of several city blocks. He says that in

[101] See *ibid.*, p. 50 (April 1918).

[102] *K'ung*, p. 18, and "Lü," "Shan-hsi shu-cheng t'an," *HTPL*, Sept. 11, 1926, p. 9.

[103] For example, see Edna Lee Booker's description of a visit to Yen's home in Hopients'un during the 1920's in Booker, *op.cit.*, pp. 107-110.

[104] *The New York Times*, hereafter referred to as *NYT*, Aug. 15, 1931, 6:3, Percy H. Kent, *The Twentieth Century in the Far East* (London, 1937), p. 130, and Kao K'e-fu, ed., *Ti-pa-lu chün tsai Shan-hsi* (*The Eighth Route Army in Shansi*) (Shanghai, 1938), hereafter referred to as *TPLC*, p. 181.

[105] Hatano Ken'ichi, *Chūgoku kyōsantō shi, ichi ku san roku nen* (*A History of the Chinese Communist Party, 1936*) (Tokyo, 1961), hereafter referred to as Hatano, *History of the C.C.P., 1936*, p. 6. A writer sympathetic to the Communists says that he was told by Yen's nephew that Yen secreted his wealth, in the form of opium and bullion, in the walls of his house and on the grounds of his estate, set up machine gun emplacements to guard it, and then executed the laborers who performed this work for fear that they might reveal the hiding place of his treasure. See *San Man Po* (*The New Evening News*), Nov. 14, 1958, p. 2. In my opinion, however, the authenticity of this story is doubtful since the "nephew" gave the writer the mistaken impression that Yen's ancestral home was in Taiku rather than Hopients'un.

[106] Edna Lee Booker, *op.cit.*, p. 108.

Shansi it was not uncommon for high-ranking officials to gamble away vast sums in the course of a single night and mentions one who provided his daughter with a dowry so large that it filled hundreds of palanquins in her wedding procession.[107] Yen also protected his friends and relatives when they broke the law; for example, his son was not punished in spite of being involved in numerous traffic accidents while driving his automobile through the streets of Taiyuan.[108] The provincial government likewise ignored the behavior of Chao Tai-wen's clan, whose members abused and exploited the other families living in their native village.[109] All of this helps to explain why the rank and file of Yen's officials disregarded his pleas for honesty and failed to heed his denunciations of favoritism.

Yen's attempt to create a modern and more effective bureaucracy in Shansi was frustrated as well by the lethargy and conservatism of his officials. He upbraided many of them for neglecting their duties and charged that they spent too much time writing poetry, practicing calligraphy, and otherwise pursuing the traditional pastimes of the scholar-official. According to a foreigner who lived in Shansi during the 1920's, local officials seldom acted and then only when coerced.[110] Even district magistrates were reluctant to leave their yamens in order to ascertain whether or not their orders actually were being carried out.[111] The many special investigators employed by the Bureau of Villages seem to have been completely ineffectual, for in addition to accepting bribes from local officials they failed to interest themselves in the mundane realities of village life and alienated much of the rural population by their arrogance and meddlesome behavior. "The inspectors frequently do more harm than good," admitted Yen.[112] An obstacle of still greater magnitude was the ill-concealed opposition offered by officials who regarded Yen's schemes as too radical or looked upon them as threats to their own power and prerogatives. Yen repeatedly charged that his reforms were being sabotaged at the local level by headmen and other officials

107 Hsü Fan-t'ing, *Letter*, pp. 9-11.   108 See *ibid.*, p. 10.
109 Fukada Yuzō, *Shina kyōsangun no gensei* (*The Current Condition of the Chinese Communist Army*) (Tokyo, 1939), p. 359.
110 *Fairfield*, p. 6.
111 *Lectures*, VIII, p. 13 (Jan. 1919).
112 *Lectures*, III-B, p. 153 (Aug. 1924).

who either encouraged the people to disregard his instructions or else merely promulgated his orders without taking steps to see that they were implemented.[113] His experience underscores the difficulty of effecting reforms without first making certain that those charged with the task of putting them into effect are in favor of the proposed changes or at least not antagonistic to them. Yen tried to overcome this difficulty by replacing uncooperative officials with men more devoted to his aims, but he dared not pursue this policy too far lest it arouse the anger of the landed gentry, from whose ranks came most of the local officials.

The Role of the Gentry

Yen shared the values of the gentry, and the innovations he advocated were designed to preserve the existing order and in this way sustain the primacy of the landholding class in Shansi. The gentry often withheld their cooperation, however, and frequently used their wealth and influence to discredit or subvert his campaign to centralize the administration of government, promote mass literacy, and stamp out drug addiction and corruption. Yen also accused the rich of hampering his efforts to alleviate suffering in famine-stricken parts of Shansi by frustrating his attempt to stabilize the value of the currency and hold down the price of foodstuffs.[114] Wealthy landowners disregarded the moderate ceiling Yen imposed on the price of cereals and disposed of their hoards of grain for from three to four times the normal price; they embezzled the contents of the public granaries and turned over to their own relatives or sold on the black market provisions given to them by the government for distribution to the starving.[115] Yen's complaints about tenantry and usury suggest that the gentry also were exploiting the poor by charging exorbitant rents and interest rates. In fact, the rapacity of the small number of persons who possessed a degree of wealth and education and their indifference to the misery of those around them appear to have been salient characteristics of the society Yen came to dominate. Brought on by ceaseless and intense competition for the limited resources of a stagnant economy, their

[113] *Lectures*, III-A, pp. 52, 205 (April 1918 and April 1920).
[114] *Lectures*, VIII, p. 38 (Aug. 1920).
[115] *NCH*, Nov. 25, 1922, 503:3.

ruthless behavior engendered a profound hostility to the gentry on the part of other elements of the population.

Yen professed to fear that, unless checked, the irresponsible conduct of the privileged class would undermine the stability of his regime by provoking widespread unrest,[116] especially since the gentry often used his own program as a pretext for plundering the rest of the population.[117] He publicly accused the rich of "victimizing" the peasants[118] and declared that his own government represented the antithesis of gentry rule.[119] He reminded the gentry that under the Ch'ing the literati had been extremely unpopular because they assumed that their exalted position gave them the right to cheat and bully their less fortunate neighbors. "When a man was awarded the first degree he became a threat to his village," he recalled, "and a *chü-jen* was regarded as a menace to the entire district."[120] Besides erecting in various places stone tablets bearing inscriptions denouncing avaricious and uncooperative members of the gentry, [121] Yen set out to reduce the authority which the gentry traditionally enjoyed in the countryside. District magistrates not only were given unprecedented authority over the villages under their jurisdiction,[122] but also were rotated less frequently in order to make them less dependent on the gentry for advice and information about local conditions.[123] Then too, many offices that formerly had been reserved for the local gentry were filled with outsiders trained in Taiyuan.[124] In his anger, Yen behaved much like certain English and French kings who sought the assistance of the common people against their disobedient nobility, for innovations such as the village assemblies and the election of headmen represented an attempt to impose a popular check on the power of the gentry.[125] Significantly, both of these reforms were

[116] *Lectures*, VII, p. 64 (March 1921).
[117] Wang Chen-i, *op.cit.*, pp. 1-2.
[118] *Lectures*, III-A, p. 216 (March 1921).
[119] *Lectures*, III-C, p. 121 (Sept. 1922).
[120] *Lectures*, III-A, p. 141 (Dec. 1918).
[121] *NCH*, Nov. 5, 1921, 365:3.
[122] *Hsin Chung-kuo*, Nov. 15, 1919, p. 6, and Haldore E. Hanson, "Chinese War Lord Dreams of Russia," *CWR*, Feb. 8, 1936, p. 356.
[123] *Lectures*, III-B, p. 157 (Aug. 1924), and Ch'en Po-ta, "Yen Hsi-shan p'i-p'an," p. 51 in the anthology of the same name.
[124] Wang Ch'ien, *op.cit.*, pp. 4b-5a.
[125] *Lectures*, III-B, p. 109 (Nov. 1921), and III-A, pp. 185-188 (Dec. 1919).

introduced as part of a campaign to reorganize the villages of Shansi in such a way as to bring their officials more closely under the control of the provincial government. Beginning in 1922 Yen held village headmen personally responsible for the implementation of his program, but at the same time divided the villagers into groups of twenty-five households called areas (*lü*), whose chiefs constituted a village council and presumably shared the authority of the headman and his assistants. In an effort to enlist the backing of the gentry for this scheme, Yen compelled many of them to come to Taiyuan and attend schools which he set up for the purpose of indoctrinating them with loyalty to his own principles.[126] Meanwhile, model village committeemen (*ts'un-fan wei-yuan*) descended on the villages, where they lectured to village officials about the necessity of placing the interests of Yen's government ahead of every other consideration. One writer accuses Yen of trying to enslave the gentry and says that his policies had the effect of making Shansi a one-man dictatorship.[127] Thus it seems that owing to his lust for power and his determination to mobilize at least a moderate amount of popular support for his regime, Yen's interests sometimes ran counter to those of the gentry.

Nothing illustrates this phenomenon more vividly than Yen's struggle to overhaul the administration of justice in Shansi. He proposed to govern his domain through the medium of the law[128] and for this reason broke with tradition by endeavoring to make the law known to everyone so that all would be aware of their legal rights and obligations.[129] He even allowed villagers to enact their own laws, inasmuch as he conferred on their elected assemblies the right to draft local ordinances, provided that these outlawed gambling, drug addiction, prostitution, brawling, loafing, foot binding, and other commonly accepted practices which he regarded as undesirable. Furthermore, whereas in the past lawsuits were referred to local officials, who generally decided them in favor of litigants having wealth and influence, Yen tried to correct such abuses by creating a system of courts patterned after those existing in the countries of the West. He reminded his followers that in Shansi popular dissatisfaction with the

---

[126] Wang Chen-i, *op.cit.*, p. 1.   [127] *Ibid.*

[128] *Lectures*, v, p. 48 (July 1918).

[129] F. C. H. Dreyer, *op.cit.*, p. 477, and Harrison K. Wright, *op.cit.*, p. 744.

judgments handed down by Ch'ing magistrates was a major cause of the Revolution of 1911.[130] Because these reforms menaced their interests and prerogatives, however, not only the gentry but many of Yen's own bureaucrats opposed them and in most instances succeeded in making them ineffectual. Yen denounced local officials for encouraging the rest of the population to ignore the law and accused them of neglecting to remit lawsuits to his new courts. But too often judges were less intent on dispensing justice than on demonstrating their erudition or their proficiency in the realm of abstract reasoning, with the result that the courts did not inspire much confidence on the part of the public.[131]

Yen attacked these problems by attempting to get rid of lawsuits altogether. In each village he set up a six-man Council for the Prevention of Litigation (*Hsi-sung hui*). Those elected to membership in this organization arbitrated disputes between the rest of the villagers, who were compelled to submit their grievances to the council before appealing to the courts or the nearest magistrate. Yen's avowed purpose was to discourage litigation by providing his subjects with faster and less expensive justice at the hands of the people least likely to be taken in by false accusations and specious evidence, namely their fellow villagers.[132] "There is no place for lawsuits in an ideal community," he maintained.[133] He professed to be acting on behalf of the poor,[134] and his claim is supported by the testimony of several persons having an intimate knowledge of conditions in Shansi during the 1920's. According to them, the gentry habitually initiated lawsuits, with the aim of defrauding their poorer neighbors who were unable to offer comparable bribes to dishonest magistrates or bear the cost of prolonged litigation.[135] Although hostile to Yen Hsi-shan, one of these writers implies that frequently members of the Council for the Prevention of Litigation did not come from the gentry and therefore were inclined to oppose the rich when they tried to exploit other villagers.[136]

[130] *Lectures*, III-A, p. 205 (April 1920).
[131] See *ibid.*, p. 51 (April 1918).
[132] See *ibid.*, p. 205 (April 1920).
[133] *Village Rules*, p. 22b.　　　[134] *Lectures*, III-B, p. 84 (1922).
[135] *Williamson*, p. 4, *NCH*, Jan. 27, 1923, 222:3, and Chao Shu-li, *op.cit.*, pp. 6-7.
[136] Chao Shu-li, *op.cit.*, pp. 3, 10-11. Chao refers to the person I have in mind as a *t'iao-chieh yüan* or "arbiter"; however, the functions he

Among the reasons Yen was antagonistic to the gentry was their opposition to his demands for a larger share of the agricultural surplus. In an effort to secure money for the reconstruction of Shansi's depressed economy, Yen sponsored a thrift movement (*chieh-chien yün-tung*) and encouraged his subjects to make their savings available to his regime by depositing them in government-operated banks. Persons wealthy enough to have savings did not trust his banks, however, and were able to earn considerably more interest by lending their money to speculators and poor farmers.[137] Yen threatened to seize the funds he needed,[138] and according to a well-informed writer much of the capital used to finance economic modernization in Shansi during the 1920's was taken from the rich in the form of forced loans.[139] Beginning in 1926 Yen used rising military expenditures as an excuse for exacting additional large sums from the gentry and other members of the privileged class, who resisted his demands and had to be coerced into meeting them.[140] Taxes in Shansi more than doubled between 1915 and 1920, only to soar even higher after 1923 as Yen became increasingly preoccupied with building a powerful army and furthering his ambitions in North China.[141] In 1926, for example, he not only raised the land tax but started gathering it a year in advance. Since throughout the 1920's millions of peasants in Shansi were too poor to pay additional taxes,[142] much of the extra revenue which Yen collected during these years must have been squeezed out of the rich. This is suggested by the fact that the gentry repeatedly conspired with local officials to evade taxes and otherwise defraud the government.[143] One writer maintains that all of the reforms which Yen introduced after 1920 as part of his campaign to

---

ascribes to him are identical in most respects with those performed by members of the Council for the Prevention of Litigation.

[137] Leon Wieger, *op.cit.*, p. 347, *NCH*, July 9, 1921, 95:3, and *Lectures*, IV, p. 13 (Dec. 1919).

[138] *Lectures*, III-B, p. 196 (Aug. 1929).

[139] Anonymous, "Model Governor's Example for China," *The Trans-Pacific*, March 29, 1924, p. 5.

[140] *Ch'en-pao*, March 5, 1927, as quoted in *Archives*, March 1927, pp. 78-79, and Chao Shu-li, *op.cit.*, p. 48.

[141] Wang Chen-i, *op.cit.*, pp. 3, 6-7, and F. C. H. Dreyer, *op.cit.*, p. 476.

[142] *NCH*, July 12, 1924, 48:5.

[143] *Lectures*, III-A, pp. 52, 115 (April and Sept. 1918), III-C, p. 133 (Oct. 1922), and *NCH*, Sept. 23, 1922, 868:1.

reorganize the villages of Shansi were simply devices for taxing their inhabitants more effectively.[144] In addition to demanding from each village a yearly account of its receipts and expenditures,[145] he also held headmen and village elders personally responsible for the payment of taxes levied by the provincial authorities.[146] He farmed out to merchants a large number of taxes normally collected by village officials and boasted that thereafter these assessments yielded considerably more revenue. Perhaps he wanted the support of the merchants against the gentry, because he spoke about the enormous influence they enjoyed among the masses, expressed the hope that they would use this influence on behalf of his policies, and rebuked his officials for spending too much of their time with the gentry and not enough with the merchants.[147] Significantly, in Chao Shu-li's fictional account of village life in Shansi during the 1920's the government-appointed "arbiter" in Li Village is a merchant, whose sympathies are with the poor rather than the rich.[148]

In his eagerness to secure undisputed control of agriculture, Yen even urged that all land be turned over to the government, which would proceed to distribute it more equally among the persons cultivating it. He predicted that as soon as land and other kinds of property had been redistributed according to need, social distinctions would vanish and there would grow up in Shansi a classless, and presumably more stable and productive, society.[149] Besides accusing the gentry of enlarging their estates at the expense of their poorer neighbors, he denounced them as well for lending out money at exorbitant interest and spoke of combatting such usury by extending cheap credit to poor farmers, who, according to Yen, also were given low-priced fertilizer and encouraged to form cooperatives.[150] "We must protect the poor from exploitation

---

[144] Anonymous, "Plight of the Shansi Peasantry," *The People's Tribune*, hereafter referred to as *PT*, Jan. 16, 1932, p. 132.

[145] *CEB*, Oct. 25, 1924, p. 12.

[146] *CEB*, April 18, 1925, p. 233, *Village Rules*, p. 5a, and Chen Han-seng, "The Good Earth of China's Model Province," *Pacific Affairs*, Sept. 1936, p. 378.

[147] *Lectures*, III-B, p. 101 (July 1922).

[148] Chao Shu-li, *op.cit.*, p. 3.

[149] Leon Wieger, *op.cit.*, pp. 335-336.

[150] Yen Hsi-shan, *Chin Shan hui-i lu*, p. 21, *Lectures*, IV, p. 11 (Dec. 1919), and *Williamson*, p. 17.

at the hands of parasitical landlords and capitalists," he declared.[151] There is no evidence, however, indicating that before 1935 he actually tried to alter drastically the situation existing in the countryside.

Owing to the poor quality of much of the land in Shansi, tenantry was unfeasible in most areas; however, in those having comparatively fertile soil the rich ignored Yen's protests and continued to add to their landholdings. An investigation conducted in 1930 revealed that in two districts in eastern Shansi more than 60 percent of the arable land belonged to a mere 14 percent of the rural population.[152] Tenantry must have been equally widespread in the region around Taiyuan, where Yen and his followers invested so much of their wealth in real estate that the price of land more than doubled within the course of a single decade.[153] During the famine that ravaged Shansi in the early 1920's, moreover, Yen encouraged hungry farmers to mortgage their land and set up semiofficial agencies to facilitate such transactions. Although his preoccupation with enriching himself and his supporters evidently outweighed his enthusiasm for land reform, he likewise was too dependent on the cooperation of the gentry to translate into effective action his conviction that the popular unrest which menaced his regime could be ended only by rectifying the gross maldistribution of wealth in the countryside. The gentry enjoyed so much power and influence in the villages that their antagonism was enough to discredit any of Yen's policies. Popular opposition to the confiscation of land for the construction of new irrigation ditches only ceased after the government solicited the support of the local gentry.[154] Furthermore, Yen found that since officials had to be drawn from the ranks of the gentry, whose members alone possessed the requisite amount of leisure and education, posts like that of village headman remained virtually the property of wealthy clans. In most villages the popularly elected assembly and the Council for the Prevention of Litigation also fell under the domination of the gentry, who used them to exploit the rest

[151] Yen Hsi-shan, *Chin Shan hui-i lu*, p. 10.
[152] Chen Han-seng, *op.cit.*, pp. 370-371.
[153] *CEB*, Feb. 14, 1925, p. 89, and Anonymous, *op.cit.*, p. 133.
[154] *Lectures*, III-B, p. 5 (June 1918).

of the population.[155] Yen complained that not only village officials but even district magistrates habitually favored the rich,[156] but he admitted that he could not govern without the cooperation of the gentry and therefore urged his officials to treat them with the utmost courtesy and respect.[157] For these reasons the gentry continued to enjoy almost undisputed authority over the villages of Shansi,[158] although Yen's expressions of animosity toward them may have damaged their prestige and intensified their unpopularity.

[155] See *ibid.*, p. 169 (Aug. 1927) and *Williamson*, p. 3.
[156] *Lectures*, III-B, p. 169 (Aug. 1927).
[157] See *ibid.*, p. 163 (Oct. 1926), and III-C, p. 67 (April 1921).
[158] *Williamson*, p. 3, *Fairfield*, p. 5, and Chao Shu-li, *op.cit.*, pp. 1-11.

CHAPTER FIVE

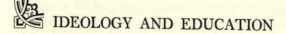 IDEOLOGY AND EDUCATION

The Confucian Revival

YEN HSI-SHAN devoted much of his life to the task of formulating and propagating what he hoped would be an appealing and effective ideology. As a young man he embraced militarism and the tenets of Social Darwinism, only to renounce them after the First World War. "The Great War was the worst tragedy in history," he declared, "and would not have occurred if the West had heeded the teachings of China's sages."[1] Thereafter he shared with most Chinese conservatives a conviction that reform is an ethical question and professed to believe that the problems confronting China could be solved only through the moral rehabilitation of its people. He contended that not until his subjects experienced a change of spirit and became better men and women would they be able to bring about the material changes which would procure for them the blessings of modernization. Consequently he tried to resuscitate Confucianism in Shansi and make it once again a universally accepted ideology. He was emotionally committed to Confucianism by virtue of his upbringing, but also because it seemed to offer an acceptable alternative to the disorder and instability of the times. Many of his speeches intimate that he lived in fear of a popular uprising that would overthrow the existing order and destroy his power. This may explain why he conceived such an extravagant admiration for the principles of harmony and moderation exemplified by the Confucian Doctrine of the Mean. In short, he looked upon Confucianism as an historically effective means of inculcating respect for authority and disseminated it in the hope that it would strengthen his hold on the people of Shansi.[2] Even the reforms he introduced were offered in a spirit of *noblesse oblige* and with the intention of demonstrating to all that the Model Governor was a superior man (*chün-tzu*) and thus the epitome of virtue from the Confucian point of view.

[1] *Lectures*, VII, p. 8 (April 1918).
[2] *Lectures*, VI, p. 96 (Nov. 1918), and VIII, p. 5 (Sept. 1918).

The tenets of Yen's Confucianism were borrowed for the most part from the Neo-Confucianism popular under the Ching dynasty. He told his subjects that each of them possessed an innate capacity for goodness, but that in order to fulfill this capacity they must subordinate their emotions and desires (*kan-chih*) to the dictates of conscience (*liang-chih*). He especially admired Lu Chiu-yüan and Wang Yang-ming, the Ming philosophers whose teachings disparaged mere knowledge, and urged men to act on the basis of an intuitive understanding.[3] In keeping with their doctrines, he held that human beings could suppress evil desires and attain perfection only by means of intense self-criticism and self-cultivation. He established in every town a Heart-Washing Society (*Hsi-hsin she*), made up of officials, members of the local gentry, and older students who each Sunday gathered in a temple-like structure to meditate and listen to uplifting sermons based on themes drawn from the Confucian classics. Everyone attending these meetings was supposed to rise and confess aloud his misdeeds of the past week, inviting the criticism of the rest of the congregation.[4] Such "confessions" played an equally important role in the colorful rallies which the authorities staged weekly for the benefit of younger students and the general public. Meanwhile, Yen initiated in each village a Good People's Movement (*hao-jen yün tung*) to inculcate in his subjects qualities subsequently extolled by Chiang Kai-shek's regime as part of its so-called New Life Movement. These included honesty, friendliness, dignity, diligence, modesty, thrift, personal neatness, and obedience, for no matter what the nominal subject of his sermon might be, whenever a speaker addressed a meeting of the Heart-Washing Society he

[3] *Lectures*, VII, pp. 12-29 (Sept. 1918 to July 1919). For a perceptive discussion of the role played by theories of "knowledge" and "action" in the development of Chinese thought during the past three centuries see David S. Nivison, "The Problem of 'Knowledge' and 'Action' in Chinese Thought since Wang Yang-ming," Arthur F. Wright, ed., *Studies in Chinese Thought* (Chicago, 1953), pp. 112-145.

[4] *Lectures*, III-A, pp. 197-198 (April 1920). Since in the past the Chinese have looked upon the heart rather than the brain as the seat of the human intellect, the phrase *hsi-hsin* might more properly be translated into English as "brainwashing," with all that that implies for those who contend that this concept was introduced into China by the Chinese Communists.

repeatedly exhorted his listeners to respect the authority of Yen Hsi-shan and obey his orders without question.[5]

Although Yen professed to be reviving Confucianism, and his ideology reflects profoundly the influence of Chao Tai-wen, whose education in the classics was superior to Yen's, in reality he borrowed ideas from almost every conceivable system of thought. These ranged from Buddhism and Legalism to Western ideologies like militarism, liberalism, and Christianity. Yen attributed to Christianity much of the strength enjoyed by the peoples of the West and felt that only by fashioning out of their own tradition a religion equally inspiring could the Chinese acquire enough vitality to overtake the foreigners.[6] He especially admired the work being carried out in Shansi under the direction of American missionaries from Oberlin College, who maintained at Taiku a complex of modern schools. On more than one occasion Yen spoke to the graduating classes of these schools, although foreigners charge that his officials frequently discouraged students from enrolling in them for fear that what they learned there would undermine their faith in traditional Chinese values and institutions.[7] According to the person in charge of Oberlin's effort in Shansi, Yen contributed to the support of an indigenous Christian church in Taiyuan and contemplated using Christian chaplains in his army.[8] He also let Christian preachers address meetings of the Heart-Washing Society and deliberately patterned that organization after the Christian church, even to the point of having its services conclude with the singing of hymns in praise of Confucius. Many of the doctrines that he espoused through the medium of the Heart-Washing Society were also inspired by Christianity.[9] For example, he broke with tradition by urging his subjects to place their faith in a supreme being which he called *shang-ti* and for whom he professed to find a sanction in the Confucian classics; however, he described this deity in terms reminiscent

[5] F. C. H. Dreyer, *op.cit.*, pp. 478-479, and *NCH*, May 25, 1918, 457:3.

[6] *Lectures*, VI, p. 8 (June 1918).

[7] *NCH*, March 18, 1922, 736:3.

[8] Kenneth Scott Latourette, *A History of Christian Missions in China* (New York, 1929), pp. 678, 775-776.

[9] *Lectures*, III-A, p. 74 (May 1918), and *NCH*, Oct. 11, 1918: 86:1.

of the Christian concept of God. He hoped that if the people of Shansi came to believe in divine retribution they would be less likely to break the law and otherwise misbehave. "The sinner, were there no law, and no heaven, and no fear of the scorn of men would be a degenerate in this life and an evil spirit in the life to come," he explained. "I, the Military Governor, warn you that every man ought to fear God, the law, and public opinion."[10] He probably owed to Christianity another notion which permeated his ideology, the belief that acceptance of its tenets was tantamount to being regenerated or reborn. Nevertheless, Christians were not allowed to refer directly to their faith while speaking to members of the Heart-Washing Society, and Yen failed to come to their defense after 1925 when a nationwide feeling of revulsion against foreigners provoked anti-Christian demonstrations in Taiyuan.[11] It would seem that he was not inclined toward Christianity, but simply used certain of its doctrines to achieve his own purposes.

Yen's policy with respect to Buddhism was equally calculating and equivocal. Owing in large part to the materialistic outlook which he acquired while in Japan, upon returning to Shansi he condemned Buddhism on the grounds that it fostered complacency and superstition.[12] Initially he had many temples torn down or else emptied of their idols and converted into meeting places for the Heart-Washing Society;[13] however, this aroused such unrest that eventually he was obliged to abandon his campaign against Buddhism and restore most of its temples. Thereafter, instead of persecuting Buddhists, he merely tried to bring them more closely under the control of the state by setting up in each district a Buddhist Association (*fo-chiao hui*), headed by a priest who presumably was responsible to the provincial authorities. His intervention undoubtedly explains why one of his closest friends became abbot of the famous Ch'ung-shan temple in Taiyuan and a leading figure in the Buddhist hierarchy in Shansi.[14] Although Yen's

[10] Harrison K. Wright, *op.cit.*, pp. 744-745.

[11] *NCH*, Jan. 9, 1926, 53:2, and Feb. 6, 1926, 228:4-5, *K'ung*, p. 25, and *Fairfield*, p. 12.

[12] *Lectures*, v, p. 37 (May 1915).

[13] *NCH*, Feb. 21, 1925, 298:5, and F. C. H. Dreyer, *op.cit.*, p. 481.

[14] Hirano Reiji, *Manshu no imbōsha: Kōmoto Daisaku no ummeiteki na ashiato* (*The Manchurian Intriguer: the Fateful Trail of Komoto*

more tolerant attitude toward Buddhism reflected the influence of Chao Tai-wen, who was a devout Buddhist, as well as
his own disillusionment with materialism as a result of the
First World War, he likewise must have perceived the usefulness of Buddhism since he deliberately incorporated many
of its elements into the ritual and doctrines of the Heart-
Washing Society.[15] Nor was he above making use of Taoist
cults, such as Court of the Way (*Tao-yuan*), whose adherents
believed that the truth would be revealed to them through the
spirits of the dead and therefore held seances in the course
of which they communed with the spirits of not only Confucius
and Lao-tzu but also persons like Abraham Lincoln and the
Virgin Mary.[16] In fact, Yen once boasted that he had formulated an ideology embodying the best features of "militarism,
nationalism, anarchism, democracy, capitalism, communism,
individualism, imperialism, universalism, paternalism, and uto-
pianism (*ta-t'ung chu-i*)."[17] No combination of ideas appears to
have been too incongruous for him if he felt that it might win
for him additional supporters or enable him to promote his interests in other ways.

Yen looked upon Chinese nationalism as merely another idea
which could be used to advance his own objectives. He achieved
power as an apostle of nationalism, repeatedly denounced imperialism, and tried to make himself still more powerful under
the guise of strengthening China's defenses against foreign
aggression. Students attending middle schools in Shansi were
reminded continually of the concessions extorted from China
by the foreigners, while the rest of the population was urged
to hold itself in a perpetual state of military preparedness. In
addition, Yen organized the Boy Scouts along paramilitary
lines,[18] built shrines to honor national heroes such as the
Han warrior Kuan Yü and the Sung general Yüeh Fei,[19] and
declared that the chief aim of the Heart-Washing Society was

Daisaku) (Tokyo, 1959), hereafter referred to as Hirano, *Komoto*, p.
198.

[15] *Williamson*, p. 11, and *Lectures*, VII, pp. 15, 53-54 (Jan. 1918
and June, 1920).

[16] Leon Wieger, *op.cit.*, pp. 67-68, 344.

[17] *Lectures*, III-A, pp. 241-242 (March 1925).

[18] Leon Wieger, *op.cit.*, p. 358, *Williamson*, p. 12, and *Fairfield*,
p. 12.

[19] *Lectures*, VII, p. 19 (1919), and *NCH*, March 18, 1922, 736:3.

to inculcate patriotism by reviving the Confucian church.[20] This is why a foreigner accused him of attempting to create in Shansi a Confucian version of Shinto.[21] Nevertheless, Yen regarded Sun Yat-sen's doctrines as a threat to his authority and therefore discouraged their propagation in Shansi. To counteract Sun's influence he even brought out his own version of the Three Principles of the People, omitting the principles of nationalism and democracy and recommending instead virtue and knowledge.[22] In 1919, after students inspired by the May Fourth Movement in Peking staged antiforeign demonstrations in the streets of Taiyuan, Yen condemned their behavior as "disorderly" and warned them that patriotism, like rainfall, is beneficial only when moderate.[23] But less then ten years later, when the triumph of the resurgent Kuomintang appeared to be inevitable, he ordered his subjects to embrace Sun's ideology and reemerged as the champion of Chinese nationalism, only to go down to defeat within three years at the head of a coalition formed to prevent the realization of national unity under the leadership of Chiang Kai-shek. He seems to have been sincerely alarmed by the disunity of China and its consequent helplessness in the face of foreign aggression, but nonetheless he resisted the efforts of the Kuomintang to unify the country because he feared that unification would mean the destruction of his own power in Shansi.

Yen's Efforts to Disseminate His Ideology and Its Impact on the Public

In order to disseminate his ideas, Yen issued millions of handbooks in which he spelled out his opinions on virtually every aspect of life. The authorities distributed these booklets free of charge to students, teachers, and officials, who were expected to read them aloud to their illiterate neighbors. Titles ranged from *What the People Must Know* (*Jen-min hsü chih*) to *What Families Must Know* (*Chia-t'ing hsü chih*), *What Village Headmen Must Know* (*Ts'un-chang hsü chih*), and *General Information for Merchants* (*Shang-jen t'ung-shih*).[24]

---

[20] Harrison K. Wright, *op.cit.*, p. 747.

[21] *Ibid.*

[22] *Lectures*, III-A, pp. 12-24 (April 1918).

[23] *Lectures*, VIII, p. 29 (May 1919).

[24] *Lectures*, III-A, p. 18 (April 1918), and Millard's Review, pub., *Who's Who in China, 1920*, p. 263.

Yen and Sun Yat-sen, 1912

Yen as Warlord, around 1920

Yen in Taiwan, May 1957

In addition, Yen published a multitude of newspapers, including a village daily entitled *Village Talk* (*Ts'un-hua*), and likewise made use of posters, lectures, slogans, and plays. The
latter were performed by traveling companies, made up largely
of students and officials. Yen himself periodically visited important towns and villages with the aim of enlisting public
support for his regime. "People! People!" he usually began.
"Come quickly and listen! Look at me and know my heart!
My only desire is to love the people!"[25] He frequently delivered
such speeches at massive rallies which were attended by the
entire population of a town or region. For example, in 1922
several hundred thousand people gathered in Taiyuan to hear
one speaker after another extol Yen's efforts to "turn Shansi into
a paradise," while in the background bands played the "Hymn
of the Federation of Municipalities and Villages." This was
followed by a torchlight procession of students and soldiers,
who marched through the streets waving placards and shout-
ing slogans.[26] Less spectacular but equally effective must have
been the Young People's Groups, whose members studied Yen's
writings and practiced something referred to only as "reciprocal
surveillance."[27]

Nevertheless, Yen did not succeed in making his peculiar
form of Confucianism a widely accepted ideology in Shansi.
Most of his subjects refused to believe that his objectives
differed substantially from those of past regimes. They distrusted his innovations, mocked at his propaganda, fled from his
censors, and ridiculed or slandered his officials. He charged that
the public misunderstood the reasons for his policies because
officials, gentry, and other educated persons neglected to explain his ideas to the common people. "They feel that the
masses are too contemptible to waste their time on," he complained.[28] In many instances local officials misappropriated
money given to them for the purpose of financing propaganda
activities. Others tried to reach the masses but wrote in language too sophisticated for the public to understand or spoke
about subjects so esoteric and irrelevant that their listeners
became confused and irritated. Besides remaining indifferent

[25] *Lectures*, III-B, p. 82 (July 1922).
[26] Leon Wieger, *op.cit.*, p. 342.
[27] See *ibid.*, p. 339.
[28] *Lectures*, III-B, p. 129 (Aug. 1923).

to Yen's ideology, most of his officials behaved in a manner which discredited it in the eyes of the ordinary villager. Instead of attempting to generate popular enthusiasm for Yen's regime by disseminating his propaganda, they coerced the common people into obeying their orders and ruled through fear rather than persuasion.[29] Yen castigated them for meting out unnecessarily harsh punishment and accused local policemen of indulging in needless brutality. "Two thirds of the village headmen have arrogated to themselves the pomp and power of little princes," remarked a foreign observer.[30]

Certain aspects of Yen's ideology also explain why it failed to win many converts among the masses. Especially repugnant to most of his poverty stricken subjects must have been his bland assurance that all of their problems would vanish as soon as they learned how to repress their desires. As for the Heart-Washing Society, after 1925, when Yen became too preoccupied with politics to compel their attendance, officials and the gentry remained away from its meetings in such large numbers that the society closed most of its temples. Even the students and other young people, who had been singled out for special attention by Yen's propagandists, remained indifferent to his ideas. For example, Yen attacked members of the Boy Scouts for being less interested in spiritual mobilization than in wearing colorful uniforms and playing soldier.[31] Confucianism and the other dogmas of the past were too stale and discredited to command widespread respect any longer, and by indiscriminately grafting on to them components of more recent systems of thought Yen only confused the ignorant and invited the contempt of the educated. Subsequent events demonstrated that an ideology consisting of little more than an invitation to trust and obey the Model Governor could not compete with the more universal and explicit doctrines expounded by Sun Yat-sen and the Kuomintang.

Educational Policies: Primary Schooling

Because Yen used newspapers and other written material to communicate much of his propaganda he was disturbed by the prevalence of illiteracy in Shansi. In 1911, when he became

[29] See *ibid.*, pp. 125-126 (Aug. 1923).
[30] *NCH*, Feb. 3, 1923, 305:2.
[31] *Lectures*, III-B, p. 69 (Aug. 1919).

their ruler, more than 99 percent of Shansi's 11 million inhabitants could neither read nor write.[32] Said a foreign observer:

> The Grammar Schools (of which there were 170) are said to have enrolled 8,500 pupils in the autumn of 1914. We have received quite a number of students from government grammar schools into our academy [the Oberlin-in-Shansi Memorial Academy at Taiku]. In almost every case their preparation has been found to be incomplete. . . . Going on down into the Primary Schools, of which there were said to be 1,484 for boys, with 135,000 pupils, and 216 for girls, with 3,240 pupils, we find conditions still worse. In many cases the only "modern" thing about the primary school is the sign-board over the front gate, while within the school an old-time unscientific pedagogue is teaching the old-time classics in the old-time unscientific way. In other schools, half-baked boys from nearby Grammar Schools have essayed the role of village pedagogue, to the disgust of the patrons, who have been seeking to restore the old system, under which a gentleman with whom everyone in the village was acquainted, and who was universally respected, dealt out the time-honored platitudes, and at least did no harm even if he didn't do much good. In a word, the whole educational situation in Shansi, from top to bottom, is extremely unsatisfactory, not to speak in harsher terms.[33]

Beginning in 1918, as part of his campaign to eradicate such conditions, Yen insisted that most of the children in his domain attend school for at least four years,[34] with the result that by 1923 there were in Shansi about 800,000 children receiving some kind of elementary education, a considerably larger number than those reported attending primary schools in any other province.[35] To house all of these school children, Yen built

---

[32] *Lectures*, III-C, p. 26 (Nov. 1918).

[33] From an anonymous report quoted in a letter to myself from Wynn C. Fairfield, dated Sept. 25, 1958.

[34] Ma Shao-po and Ts'ao Tzu-chung, "I-nien-lai Shan-hsi chih chiao-yü" ("Education in Shansi during the Past Year"), p. 3, *CCCK*.

[35] *CYB, 1925-1926*, p. 257, and *NCH*, May 15, 1926, 292:2. Even a writer hostile to Yen admits that between 1917 and 1919 the number of children attending school in Shansi rose from 342,693 to 1,035,356, which represents an increase of almost 300 percent. See Wang Chen-i, *op.cit.*, p. 8.

68   IDEOLOGY AND EDUCATION

more than 26,000 people's schools (*kuo-min hsüeh-hsiao*). In
an effort to make these structures symbols of modernization,
he outfitted them with such things as window frames, paneled
doors, and Norman arches, creating what one foreigner called
"hideous caricatures of European dwellings rendered more
incongruous by poor workmanship and florid coloring."[36] In
the countryside, children attended the people's schools during
slack periods when their labor was not needed in the fields, and
to this extent Yen's new schools foreshadowed the so-called
winter schools which the Chinese Communists subsequently
established in the areas they occupied in northwestern China.
Although operated and subsidized by the provincial authorities, the people's schools were maintained largely out of the
proceeds of an income tax paid by the residents of each district.
In this way, Yen compelled the rich to provide for the education of children from poorer families, who also were given
money and textbooks by the provincial ministry of education.[37]
Between 1917 and 1919 the amount of money which the provincial government invested in education more than doubled
and four years later constituted the largest single item of
expenditure in its budget.[38]

In selecting a curriculum for the people's schools, Yen seems
to have been influenced profoundly by the American educator
and pragmatic philosopher John Dewey, who in 1919 delivered several lectures in Shansi. This explains in part why
Yen condemned the Chinese classics as too impractical for
school children and ordered the people's schools to teach instead subjects more closely geared to the everyday needs of
their pupils.[39] In addition to learning how to read newspapers
and government circulars, the students were taught how to
write funeral notices, marriage contracts, and simple letters.[40]
To help them master these skills Yen had all newspapers and

[36] *NCH*, Nov. 27, 1920, 594:3.
[37] Leon Wieger, *op.cit.*, p. 353.
[38] Wang Chen-i, *op.cit.*, p. 8, and *CEB*, Nov. 7, 1925, p. 274. Wang
Chen-i points out, however, that the increase in spending for educational
purposes failed to keep pace with the threefold expansion in total enrollment and accuses Yen of spending ten times as much on his army,
whose expenses were not included in the provincial government's annual budget. Nevertheless, it would appear that Yen invested heavily in
education.
[39] *Fairfield*, p. 8, and Mansfield Freeman, *op.cit.*, 296:1.
[40] Yen Hsi-shan, *Yen yüan-chang cheng-lün chi-yao*, p. 8b.

other reading matter issued by the provincial government written in the vernacular. Frequently, such publications employed a system of phonetic spelling—the *chu-yin tzu-mu*—which Yen hoped would facilitate the recognition of characters and encourage uniformity of pronunciation. Books explaining this system were distributed free of charge, and the government expected at least one member of every family to have mastered it. Yen likewise opened night schools and public reading rooms for illiterate adults, and to make certain that everyone learned their lessons he instructed merchants not to sell to any customer unable to identify characters written on signs placed in their shops.[41] He felt that the welfare of the state depended on how quickly every man under forty and every woman under thirty learned how to read.[42] "The three great duties of the people are to serve in the army, to pay taxes, and to receive an education," he remarked.[43]

Yen's desire to make education in Shansi as practical as possible accounts for the important role assigned vocational training and athletics in the curriculum of the people's schools. Besides offering courses on sericulture, animal husbandry, and other agricultural subjects, these schools maintained shops where the pupils manufactured things like clothing, furniture, and pottery. Yen was intent on modernizing Shansi's domestic handicraft industries and therefore needed a class of literate, well-trained manual workers.[44] As for athletics, he attached so much importance to a healthy body that he dismissed officials unable to pass periodic physical fitness examinations; students were encouraged to join the Provincial Athletic Association (*Shan-hsi t'i-yü hui*).

Notwithstanding the educational value of such innovations, the principal function of the people's schools appears to have been ideological rather than pedagogical. When admonished by conservatives who feared that the population would become rebellious if educated, Yen replied that unless the people were educated they would be unable to distinguish right from wrong and would become dangerous to those in authority. "Mass education consists of instilling within the mass of the people the

[41] *Lectures*, III-C, p. 26 (Nov. 1918).
[42] F. C. H. Dreyer, *op.cit.*, p. 478.
[43] Harrison K. Wright, *op.cit.*, p. 747.
[44] *CEB*, May 16, 1925, p. 285.

proper attitudes and virtues," he declared.[45] Thus he was more interested in inculcating a pattern of behavior than in provoking thought, and this may explain why he was attracted to the theories of John Dewey, who contended that knowledge divorced from action is incomplete. Such an argument appeared to conform with the teachings of the Neo-Confucian philosophers Lu Chiu-yüan and Wang Yang-ming, whose activism Yen hailed as "the shortest road to perfection."[46] Because Yen looked on education as a potent means of indoctrinating the masses with loyalty to his own regime he insisted that the people's schools use as textbooks his own writings, such as *What the People Must Know* and *On National Militarism*. Many of the teachers employed in the people's schools came from poorer families and were trained at the expense and under the supervision of the provincial government at the People's Normal School (*Kuo-min shih-fan hsüeh-hsiao*) in Taiyuan,[47] where they were encouraged to serve as the spearhead of Yen's campaign to enlarge his own power at the expense of local autonomy.[48] After graduating they were made responsible directly to the provincial ministry of education, which kept them under the closest surveillance. Such tactics proved effective, and Yen came to regard the primary school students as his most zealous supporters and frequently used them to spy on local officials.[49] All of this suggests that in an effort to reduce the power traditionally enjoyed in the countryside by the landed gentry, Yen tried to create a completely new elite which because of its humble origin would be dependent on him and therefore willing to champion his interests against those of the gentry.

Children who attended the people's schools received an education of questionable value. One writer accused Yen of teaching his subjects only enough characters to read his propaganda.[50] Furthermore, many of the instructors employed in the people's schools were too ill-educated to understand the contents of Yen's textbooks, which they compelled their pupils to

[45] *Lectures*, v, p. 19 (May 1915).

[46] *Lectures*, vII, pp. 52-56 (June 1920).

[47] Nym Wales, *Red Dust* (Stanford, 1952), pp. 143-144.

[48] *NCH*, May 10, 1919, 367:1, and *Lectures*, III-B, pp. 113-114 (1923).

[49] *Lectures*, III-B, p. 101 (July 1922).

[50] Wang Chen-i, *op.cit.*, p. 8.

commit to memory, just as the students of former days had memorized the Chinese classics. Others found the utilitarian character of Yen's modern curriculum repugnant and continued to teach only the outmoded classics. In the hope of improving the quality of primary school instruction Yen sent out teams of model instructors (*mo-fan chiao-shou*) to advise local teachers and supervise their conduct. The wages paid teachers remained so meager, however, that able men sought more lucrative posts in the bureaucracy, with the result that even the model instructors generally were too young and ill-educated to command the respect or cooperation of local officials and gentry. For reasons already suggested, many of the landholding class considered Yen's program of mass education such a threat to their interests that they used their influence to discredit it and impede the construction of schools.[51] Finally, because local officials neglected to record births, large numbers of peasants were able to evade Yen's regulations and keep their children out of school. Such parents complained that after attending school peasant youngsters no longer were willing to work on the land but instead wished to become officials or take up another occupation more befitting an educated person. These obstacles prevented Yen from realizing his dream of universal primary school education in Shansi,[52] but he probably succeeded in increasing appreciably the number of persons able to read and write. In 1922 he boasted to an American newswoman that in Shansi 80 percent of the children of school age were attending school.[53]

Educational Policies: Secondary Schooling

Yet it would seem that Yen was less interested in educating the youth of Shansi than in indoctrinating them in his people's schools. What he wanted from his school system was an army of trained farmers and workers able to read his propaganda, yet not educated enough to question it. This accounts for his indifference to secondary education. For graduates of the people's schools who desired more education there was in each district an upper primary school (*kao hsiao-hsueh*), but since

[51] *NCH*, Sept. 17, 1921, 852:3, and *Lectures*, III-C, pp. 39-41 (Dec. 1918).
[52] *Fairfield*, p. 9.
[53] Edna Lee Booker, *op.cit.*, p. 108.

the annual tuition was CH$20, these schools attracted less than 2 percent of the primary school population. Although between 1914 and 1922 middle school enrollment increased at the rate of 100 percent a year, in 1922 there were only 12,000 middle school pupils in Shansi.[54] All of them came from families wealthy enough to pay a tuition of CH$400, a sum far beyond the reach of the overwhelming majority of the population. Even rich peasants hesitated to send their children to middle school for fear that, after graduating, their sons and daughters would be unable to secure jobs lucrative enough to compensate their families for the cost of their education. In fact, professional opportunities were so scarce in underdeveloped Shansi that frequently middle school graduates were less qualified to make a living than youths who had foregone schooling in order to acquire more practical skills.[55]

Although students in government-supported middle schools received instruction in mathematics, natural science, foreign languages, and other "modern" subjects, they also were subjected to ideological indoctrination comparable to that carried on in the primary schools. They wore uniforms, underwent continual military training, and were required to demonstrate the unquestioning loyalty and obedience normally expected only of soldiers. According to one writer, middle school students were taught that loyalty to Yen Hsi-shan was the highest virtue and reminded that in the future they would be sustained by their virtue.[56] Teachers lashed pupils who defied them, and the government expelled from school youngsters daring enough

54 An anonymous report, quoted in a letter to myself from Wynn C. Fairfield, dated Sept. 25, 1958, says that in 1914 there were in Shansi only fifteen middle schools, having a total enrollment of 1,500 students. The figure of about 12,000 students by 1922 is taken from an estimate made by the provincial government and reprinted in the *CYB, 1925-1926*, p. 245. On page 257 of the same volume, however, the editor asserts that there were only 863 students attending middle school in Shansi. On the other hand, not only Yen but also one of his most outspoken critics maintain that by 1925 there were between 20,000 and 30,000 pupils in Shansi's middle schools. See *Lectures*, III-B, p. 37 (Jan. 1919), and "Lü," "Shan-hsi shu-cheng t'an," *HTPL*, Sept. 25, 1926, p. 10. The problem of reconciling contradictory statistics has confronted me throughout the preparation of this study. The figure I have selected in this instance lends support to H. H. K'ung's contention that Yen neglected middle school education in the 1920's. See *K'ung*, p. 19.

55 *Lectures*, VI, p. 67 (Dec. 1919).

56 Wang Chen-i, *op.cit.*, p. 8.

to challenge Yen's doctrines and opinions.[57] Chao Tai-wen, who for many years served as the principal of the People's Normal School, had one of his sons thrown into prison, where he died, because the boy attacked Yen's regime and he threatened to have a second son arrested if he returned from Peking, where he was active in the student movement.[58] Chao's antagonism toward returned students from Peking was shared by Yen Hsi-shan, who refused to employ graduates of Peking University on the grounds that all of them were Bolsheviks.[59]

Nevertheless, Yen failed to prevent the youth from Shansi from becoming caught up in the wave of nationalism generated in China by the May Fourth Movement of 1919. Students attending middle schools in the provincial capital defied the government by trooping into the streets where they shouted their opposition to the concessions given Japan in the Treaty of Versailles. Yen must have been overawed by these demonstrations because in 1922 he allowed graduates of Peking University to establish their own middle school in Taiyuan. Then, in 1925, after British police touched off a nationwide anti-foreign movement by firing on Chinese demonstrators in Shanghai, a mob of angry students descended on Yen's home and, after compelling him to dismiss officials they considered pro-foreign, forced him to authorize a boycott against British and Japanese goods. This boycott was enforced by members of the Student Association, which set up branches in every middle school and college in the province. The associations sent bands of students to break up the shops of merchants guilty of violating the boycott and even attacked the provincial government when Yen continued to sell cotton to Japan.[60] In the months that followed, the Student Association fell under the domination of radicals, who used their enormous power to intimidate Yen and his government.[61] After Yen imposed new taxes, the association ordered middle school students to remain away from classes, and when Chao Tai-wen tried to prevent students attending the People's Normal School from taking part in the strike, they chased their teachers from the school and demolished the homes of several high-ranking of-

[57] Nym Wales, *op.cit.*, p. 143.   [58] *Ibid.*
[59] Wang Chen-i, *op.cit.*, p. 9.
[60] *NCH*, July 18, 1925, 20:3, July 21, 1925, 169:1, and July 29, 1925, 244:4.
[61] *NCH*, Nov. 14, 1925, 244:4.

ficials. Yen was so terrified by this rebellion on the part of those he had hoped would be the bulwark of his regime that he lowered taxes, replaced Chao Tai-wen with a more liberal principal, and virtually handed over control of the normal school to the Student Association.[62] Since he had created the normal school for the purpose of training teachers who would disseminate his ideology among the pupils in his new elementary schools, his experience illustrates how innovations introduced by conservative leaders in the hope of bolstering their authority frequently contributed to the destruction of the existing order.

As the students became more powerful, the quality of the education offered in Shansi's middle schools declined. Instructors who gave difficult examinations or otherwise aroused the wrath of their pupils were accused of being pro-foreign and either boycotted or coerced into resigning. One middle school principal was ousted because he refused to let the students look over the questions before their examination.[63] The result was that teachers lost control of their pupils, who not only habitually cheated on examinations but also brawled in the classroom and destroyed the books and other equipment given them.[64] Instead of trying to maintain discipline, the average instructor disclosed examination questions beforehand and otherwise sought to win the friendship of his students in the hope that they would come to his support if his job was threatened. Teachers were so demoralized that many embezzled school funds or extorted money from the parents of their pupils, while all remained away from class for prolonged periods. Furthermore, the students frequently staged demonstrations and strikes solely out of a desire to avoid assignments and examinations.[65] In one district they boycotted their classes for weeks simply because a policeman had pushed back a student trying to force his way to the front of a crowd watching a fire. And when Yen's ministry of education set aside only forty days for a winter vacation, students everywhere expressed their dissatisfaction by staying away for more than two months.[66] According to Yen, in 1921 middle school students in the provincial capital attended classes for only half a year and spent

62 "Lü," "Shan-hsi shu-cheng t'an," *HTPL*, Sept. 11, 1926, p. 9.
63 *NCH*, May 15, 1926, 292:2.
64 *Lectures*, III-C, p. 25 (Nov. 1918), and VI, p. 83 (July 1922).
65 *Fairfield*, p. 9.   66 *NCH*, March 8, 1924, 358:3-4.

most of their time carousing in brothels and opium dens.[67] In the words of Nathaniel Peffer: "When patriotism became a vocation, intellectual growth was stunted."[68]

Educational Policies: Higher Education

Since Yen was eager to industrialize his domain he was compelled to interest himself in higher education. Engineers graduated from existing colleges and universities proved to be too incompetent to build anything more complicated than an old-fashioned wooden bridge. Yen complained that their knowledge hardly exceeded that of an elementary school graduate in the West.[69] Accordingly, he set out to improve the quality of technical training available in Shansi. In addition to building an industrial technical college (*kung-chüan hsüeh-hsiao*), which he outfitted with the most modern laboratory equipment,[70] he also revamped completely the operations of Shansi University. This institution had been established in the nineteenth century and was famed as a center of traditional learning. Yen abolished the privileged position of Chinese studies, increased substantially the size of the university's budget, conferred the presidency of the university on a returned student from England who had majored in engineering, and tried to modernize its curriculum by constructing a machine shop and introducing courses in mining, metallurgy, electricity, and other branches of science and technology.[71] At the suggestion of a missionary, he likewise set up a language school where students were taught how to read technical works written in Western languages.[72]

The faculty of Shansi University consisted of missionaries and of Chinese who had been educated abroad at the expense of the provincial government.[73] After enjoying the comparative luxury of life in foreign lands, however, these returned students rebelled against the meager salaries and other hardships endured by teachers in Shansi. Perhaps their experiences

---

[67] *Lectures*, VI, pp. 82, 98 (July 1921 and Aug. 1922).
[68] Nathaniel Peffer, *The Far East* (Ann Arbor, 1958), p. 333.
[69] *Lectures*, VIII, p. 3 (Aug. 1918).
[70] *CEB*, July 25, 1925, p. 54.
[71] Lady Hosie, "Shansi After Twenty-Five Years," *NCH*, Dec. 16, 1936, p. 470, and Wang Chu-hsien, *Shan-hsi ta-hsüeh chiao-shih* (*A Sketch of Shansi University*) (an unpublished manuscript), p. 3.
[72] "Lü," "Shan-hsi shu-cheng t'an," *HTPL*, Sept. 25, 1926, p. 11.
[73] *NCH*, Aug. 30, 1919, 535:1.

abroad likewise made them skeptical about the wisdom of Yen's policies and less inclined to obey his orders. At any rate, eventually Yen stopped sending people overseas and instead used his money to build a new technical school in Shansi. He may have also wished to end the chaos created by continual quarreling between professors educated in Western countries, generally England,[74] and those trained in Japan.[75]

In the opinion of a writer who professed to have an intimate knowledge of conditions in Shansi during the 1920's, no matter where they secured their schooling, Yen's teachers and technicians were extraordinarily ill-trained. He says that the blindness of geologists on the staff of Shansi University, who were unable to distinguish quartz from other kinds of white rock, was matched by the incompetence of their colleagues in civil engineering, who knew so little about mathematics that they spent an entire semester trying to determine the dimensions of a lake small enough for a well-trained person to survey in a day.[76] According to this writer, another of Yen's engineers, charged with separating silver from lead in newly mined ore, ruined a costly furnace because he used a catalyst containing sulphur, with the result that gases accumulated and fused ore, catalyst, and furnace into a single indistinguishable mass.[77] He claims that owing to the scarcity of qualified linguists the language school came to be staffed by carpenters, iron mongers, cobblers, and other semiliterate workmen whose familiarity with Western languages must have been confined to a smattering picked up while in the employ of foreigners.[78] As for the missionaries employed on the faculty, according to this writer, the one who taught mechanical engineering was unfamiliar with the simplest mathematical equations and turned out to be helpless when the university's power plant stopped functioning.[79] He maintains that another who headed the foreign language school, was demented but nevertheless stayed on as director of the school until he affronted Yen by refusing to remove his wet weather clothing during a banquet held in his honor. If these charges are true, it would seem that among the problems which confronted Chinese leaders eager to

[74] R. N. Swallow, *op.cit.*, 196:2.   [75] *Williamson*, p. 10.
[76] "Lü," *op.cit.*, p. 11.
[77] "Lü," "Shan-hsi shu-cheng t'an," *HTPL*, Oct. 9, 1926, p. 12.
[78] "Lü," "Shan-hsi shu-cheng t'an," *HTPL*, Sept. 25, 1926, p. 11.
[79] *Ibid.*

modernize their country none were more perplexing than those created by the scarcity of personnel trained in the technology and languages of the West.

The ignorance of Yen's professors accounts to a large extent for the apathy displayed by their pupils. Moreover, most of the students attending colleges in Shansi hoped to become officials in the government and for this reason were less interested in technical training than in acquiring a knowledge of the law. In order to combat this, Yen provided scholarships for poorer students who because of their peasant origin would be more likely to choose careers in industry; however, he complained that too often district magistrates bestowed these funds on undeserving but influential members of the local gentry.[80] On the other hand, Yen allocated to colleges and universities less than a seventh of the money he spent each year on education.[81] Perhaps the turbulent nationalism of the middle school students caused him to fear that too much education would undermine his hold on the youth of the province. After 1927, when he became involved in a series of costly and ultimately catastrophic campaigns against other warlords, Yen seems to have abandoned higher education altogether. By 1930 Shansi University was little more than a vast resort, presided over by professors who supplemented their inadequate wages by gambling with their pupils, and attended by students so indifferent to learning that the library closed its doors for want of patronage.[82]

Conclusions

By attempting to provide tuition-free elementary schooling for everyone, Yen Hsi-shan departed radically from the traditional practices of Chinese governments and succeeded in expanding significantly the number of school children in Shansi. Between 1920 and 1925 the number of printing establishments in Taiyuan increased by 50 percent, largely because of the growing demand for books generated by Yen's program of mass education.[83] The new subjects he introduced into the curriculum of Shansi's schools represent an equally important

[80] *Lectures*, III-A, pp. 51-52 (April 1918).
[81] *CYB, 1925-1926*, p. 245, and *K'ung*, p. 22.
[82] Yen Ching-yüeh, "Militarizing the Model Province," *CWR*, May 31, 1930, p. 539.
[83] *CEB*, April 11, 1925, p. 226.

step in the direction of modernization. But Yen violated the spirit of his own reforms when, like former Chinese rulers, he insisted on subordinating learning to ideological indoctrination. This caused him to neglect secondary and higher education, which also suffered from the chaos created in the schools by the student movement. The impact of all this on the young people attending Yen's schools must have been profound but can be determined only by additional research. Most likely, these students came away without sufficient knowledge to evaluate in a sophisticated manner the ideologies competing for their support. If such conditions existed in schools elsewhere in China, they may explain to some extent the capriciousness and extremism of Chinese political life during the decades to come.

CHAPTER SIX

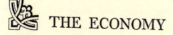 THE ECONOMY

General Conditions

BECAUSE of its extensive commercial and banking interests Shansi enjoyed considerable prosperity during the eighteenth and nineteenth centuries. Many of the banks in the Chinese Empire belonged to natives of Shansi, while at the same time merchants from that province carried on most of China's trade with Russia and Mongolia.[1] Each year these merchants and bankers remitted to Shansi more than CH$40 million, with the result that their families became some of the wealthiest in China. In fact, until 1900 bullion was so plentiful that instead of developing the resources of their own province the inhabitants of Shansi imported much of their food and most of the manufactured goods they required.[2] Beginning in the last decades of the nineteenth century, however, this prosperity vanished so completely that by 1920 Shansi was one of the poorest provinces in China. In addition to being weakened by losses resulting from the disorders that accompanied the Taiping Rebellion and the Boxer Uprising, most of Shansi's bankers operated on too small a scale and were too ignorant of modern banking to compete with more liberally capitalized banks organized along Western lines.[3] Their ruin was completed by the Revolution of 1911, which destroyed the wealth and power of the ruling bureaucrats, to whom they had loaned great sums.[4] Whereas in 1911 there still were twenty-six old style banks (p'iao-hao) in Shansi, by 1930 all but three had gone out of business. Meanwhile in Russia and in much of Mongolia foreign competition and economic nationalism, in

[1] Ch'ü Chih-sheng, "Shan-hsi te ching-chi hsien-chuang yü ching-chi t'ung-chih" ("Economic Controls and Present Economic Conditions in Shansi"), *KWCP*, March 12, 1934, p. 2.

[2] Ch'üan-kuo ching-chi wei-yüan-hui (National Economic Committee), pub., *Shan-hsi k'ao-ch'a pao-kao shu* (*Report of an Investigation of Shansi*) (Shanghai, 1936), hereafter referred to as *Shansi Report*, p. 3.

[3] Ch'en Ch'i-t'ien, *Shan-hsi p'iao-chuang k'ao-lüeh* (*An Examination of the Shansi Banks*) (Shanghai, 1936), pp. 36-41.

[4] *NCH*, Feb. 27, 1915.

the form of extortionate taxes and official restrictions, gradually reduced the volume of trade handled by merchants from
Shansi until most of them went bankrupt and were compelled
to return home. Since they had accumulated large holdings
of Russian currency, they also suffered catastrophic losses when
the First World War and the Bolshevik Revolution in Russia
destroyed the value of the ruble.[5] As a result of all this, by
1921 in one formerly prosperous district of Shansi there were
between 4,000 and 5,000 unemployed merchants,[6] while in
the once flourishing towns of Taiku and Yü-tz'u businessmen
were reduced to selling their wives and children in an effort
to satisfy their creditors.[7] Their misery was shared by much
of the farming population, whose income had declined substantially, owing largely to the deterioration of Shansi's handicraft industries under the impact of foreign competition but
likewise because other provinces in North China stopped buying grain from Shansi as soon as the construction of the
Peking-Suiyuan Railroad made it possible to procure less expensive foodstuffs from Suiyuan.[8]

Inasmuch as the population of Shansi was increasing rapidly,
these conditions produced growing unemployment and distress.
In 1918 Yen complained about the presence in Shansi of more
than a million jobless persons, whom he euphemistically referred to as "vagrants."[9] "It is not poverty to be without
money, but it is true poverty to be without a trade," he told
his people.[10] An economist writing in the *Chinese Economic
Journal* says that during the 1920's one sixth of the labor
force in Shansi was unemployed.[11] The collapse of Shansi's
banking and mercantile empire, moreover, caused remittances
from outside Shansi to fall off so drastically that Yen's subjects were compelled to liquidate their reserves of bullion in

---

5 *Chung-wai ching-chi chou-k'an* (*Sino-foreign Economic Weekly*),
No. 124, as quoted in *Archives*, Aug. 1925, pp. 106-110.
6 See *ibid.*, p. 108.   7 *Lectures*, III-C, pp. 91-96 (July 1922).
8 *Lectures*, III-A, p. 369 (July 1934).
9 Yen Hsi-shan, *Yen tu-chün cheng-shu* (*The Political Handbook of
Military Governor Yen*) (Shanghai, 1930), p. 1b. According to a foreign writer, "vagrants" was the term commonly used by the provincial
authorities to designate the unemployed. See *NCH*, July 14, 1923,
89:1.
10 F. C. H. Dreyer, *op.cit.*, p. 480.
11 C. F. Ma, "Notes on Chinese Labor Population," *The Chinese
Economic Journal*, hereafter referred to as *CEJ*, Nov. 1930, p. 1285.

order to pay for the goods they imported from other provinces. Although after 1920 Yen succeeded in cutting down appreciably Shansi's annual trade deficit of more than CH$75 million,[12] in 1922 specie still was leaving the province at the rate of well over CH$20 million a year.[13] The deflation that resulted from this continual loss of specie had a profoundly depressive impact on Shansi's economy. According to Yen, by 1935 nine out of every ten families in Shansi were poverty-stricken.[14] He perceived that unless he could modernize the economy of his underdeveloped domain and increase its productivity, popular unrest would grow and he might be unable to avert a popular uprising against his regime, much less mobilize enough strength to prevent Shansi from being overrun by the powerful armies of neighboring warlords. Consequently, he adopted the slogan, "strengthen the nation by enriching the country" (*fu-kuo ch'iang-kuo*) and endeavored to reorganize Shansi's economy along more productive lines.[15]

Commerce and Industry

Yen aimed to export as much as possible while reducing substantially the volume of goods being brought into Shansi, which explains his close supervision of the activities of merchants and other businessmen. Although he tried to enlist their support for his regime, and perhaps against the gentry, he frequently denounced them for being old-fashioned and unimaginative. Because they went into business only with members of their own clan and insisted that investors assume unlimited liability for debts, the businessmen of Shansi were unable to amass enough capital to compete with enterprises organized along Western lines.[16] Furthermore, they rejected the impersonal relationships characteristic of economic activity in the West and continued to subordinate everything to the interests of their own families, with the result that in most business concerns nepotism flourished and with it corruption and mismanagement. Dishonesty and obsolete methods, for example, were responsible for the failure of the privately operated

[12] Wang Chen-i, *op.cit.*, p. 7.   [13] *Lectures*, IV, p. 23 (1922).
[14] *Lectures*, III-A, p. 370 (July 1935).
[15] *Lectures*, III-B, p. 67 (1922).
[16] *Lectures*, III-C, p. 27 (Nov. 1918), and IV, pp. 12, 15, 24 (Dec. 1919, Jan. 1920, and 1922), and Hsia Ching-feng, "Shan-hsi lü-hsing chi." *Ti-hsüeh tsa-chih*, Jan. 1, 1916, p. 6a.

Taiyuan Electric Light Company in 1923, as well as the
decline of Shansi's once thriving salt and brewing industries.[17]
Perhaps the extraordinary preeminence and prosperity formerly
enjoyed by the merchants and bankers of Shansi left them
convinced of the correctness of their own methods and made
them even less inclined than businessmen elsewhere in China
to embrace practices introduced from the West. At any rate,
their lack of organization, haphazard methods, and ignorance
of business conditions outside Shansi placed them at an enormous disadvantage with respect to more alert and modern-
minded competitors from other provinces.[18]

In an effort to remedy this situation, Yen set up in each
district a chamber of commerce, introduced a uniform system
of weights and measures, and published a weekly newspaper
containing information of value to merchants and businessmen, only to find that in Shansi the business community was
less interested in productive investments than in reaping exorbitant profits from speculation and short-term loans to individuals. "The most prosperous businessmen in the province
. . . are speculators and usurers," he charged.[19] The rapid
rise in the price of land in Shansi during the 1920's indicates
that many merchants and bankers also were using their profits to buy their way into the ranks of the landed gentry. Their
behavior raises the question of whether much of China not
only was bypassed by the Industrial Revolution but likewise
failed to experience the "commercial revolution" that preceded
and made possible the growth of industry in the West. In many
instances, moreover, merchants responsible for collecting taxes
on behalf of the provincial government induced momentary
fluctuations in the value of the currency which enabled them to
exact from the peasants sums considerably larger than those demanded by the provincial authorities. "They rob the public
and blame the government," complained Yen.[20]

Yen's disdain for local merchants and businessmen explains
in part why, after events in the Soviet Union seemed to demonstrate the feasibility of socialism, he denounced capitalism

17 *CEB*, Jan. 24, 1925, p. 52, Feb. 21, 1925, p. 99, and March 28,
1925, p. 173.
18 *NCH*, Feb. 2, 1924, 165:5.
19 Yen Hsi-shan, *Chin Shan hui-i lu*, p. 28.
20 *Lectures*, III-A, pp. 182-183 (Nov. 1919).

as usury and called its proponents simply parasites living off the labor of others.[21] He professed to be horrified by the power exercised by financiers and manufacturers in the countries of the West and probably feared that the growth of large private-ly owned enterprises in Shansi would be followed by the rise of a class of wealthy and independent entrepreneurs which ultimately would contest his authority. In spite of his antipathy to the gentry and his efforts to win support among business-men, his antagonism toward private enterprise also may have sprung from a perhaps unconscious desire to disassociate him-self from the commercial background of his own family by embracing the prejudices of the landed gentry, membership in which was the traditional objective of parvenus like the Model Governor. Throughout the 1920's Yen's attitude with respect to the gentry was ambivalent, and his opinions frequently re-flected the agrarian viewpoint of the landowning class, which conceded the necessity of setting up industries and improving communications in order to strengthen China's defenses but at the same time wished to keep the commercial classes power-less lest they challenge its own privileged position. Then too, socialism appeared not in the least radical to one accustomed to the official monopolies of the Ch'ing dynasty. For these rea-sons, and because he perceived the enormous profits to be har-vested, Yen declared himself in favor of "state capitalism" (*kung-tzu chu-i*) and tried to establish a government monopoly over manufacturing.[22]

In 1920 fear of an invasion by the better equipped forces of the neighboring warlord Han Fu-chü caused Yen to adopt a policy of what he called "salvation through productivity" (*tsao-ch'an chiu-kuo*).[23] In addition to building the Taiyuan Arsenal, whose operations already have been described, he constructed a sulphates factory, a small but modern iron works, a CH$600,-000 machine tool factory, and refineries that conducted experi-ments looking toward the extraction of petroleum from coal and shale rock. Attached to the machine tool plant was a steel works having a meager capacity but nevertheless enough to

[21] Yen Hsi-shan, *op.cit.*, pp. 10-13. [22] See *ibid.*, p. 34.
[23] Naikaku sōri daijin kambō chosashitsu (Cabinet Research Office), comp., *Chūkyō tekkōgyō chōsa hōkokusho* (*Survey Report on the Steel Industry of Communist China*) (Tokyo, 1956), hereafter referred to as *Japanese Steel Survey*, pp. 405-408.

produce steel in greater quantities than most of the other mills in China and likewise at much lower cost, owing to Shansi's abundant supply of cheap coal.[24] Yen used these enterprises for the purpose of training an industrial working force and talked about expanding them into a complex of heavy industries capable of manufacturing not only a wide range of weapons but also the machinery he needed in order to modernize Shansi's economy.[25] His preoccupation with other matters prevented him from carrying out his plans, however, and as late as 1930 Shansi still had, in the words of one writer, "no heavy industry worthy of the name."[26]

Yen's efforts to compensate for the decline of Shansi's handicraft industries by promoting the growth of light industry were equally ineffectual. Besides subsidizing various kinds of cottage industries, he built two flour mills, a cigarette factory, a paper mill, and a large and comparatively modern cotton textile mill, which, together with a number of smaller, privately operated mills, turned out each year more than CH$3.5 million worth of cloth and yarn.[27] His aim was to revive the manufacture of consumer goods in Shansi by introducing methods of production borrowed from the West. As part of this campaign he erected more than a score of small factories and workshops where soldiers and the unemployed were taught how to make candles, soap, clothing, and a host of other commodities.[28] Nevertheless, only the textile mills flourished; Shansi's other industries were undercapitalized, badly managed, and so primitive and unproductive that well-informed observers dismissed them as "not worth mentioning."[29] Consequently, Yen's subjects remained dependent on foreign countries and other prov-

[24] *Shansi Report*, pp. 12, 61-84, 169, *CEB*, Aug. 23, 1924, p. 10, Feb. 7, 1925, p. 79, Feb. 21, 1925, p. 107, July 11, 1925, p. 25, and Anonymous, "Hsi-pei yü-ts'ai lien-kang chi-ch'i ch'ang" ("The Northwestern Yü Ts'ai Steel and Machine Plant"), *Chung-hua shih-yeh yüeh-k'an* (*The Chinese Industrial Monthly*), hereafter referred to as *Industrial Monthly*, Sept. 1, 1935, p. 119.

[25] *CEB*, April 11, 1925, pp. 203-204.

[26] *Shansi Report*, p. 144.

[27] See *ibid.*, pp. 7-8, 118-121, 126-127, and *Industrial Gazetteer*, pp. 7-szu, 104-106-chi.

[28] *Industrial Gazetteer*, pp. 695-699-chi, and *CEB*, Sept. 1, 1924, p. 9, Dec. 27, 1924, p. 13, May 16, 1925, p. 285, May 30, 1925, p. 317.

[29] *Shansi Report*, p. 131, and Ch'ü Chih-sheng, *op.cit.*, p. 1. The opinion of these writers is shared by Wang Chen-i, *op.cit.*, p. 5.

inces for manufactured goods and continued to export great quantities of specie in order to pay for these commodities.[30]

Yen failed to achieve a significant degree of industrialization in Shansi in part because the atmosphere of the province discouraged enterprise and impeded specialization. The abundance and cheapness of labor dissuaded entrepreneurs from introducing technological innovations that might have increased output. The low status of women, who were constrained to stay in the household and make it as self-sufficient as possible, likewise hindered economic development by removing the incentive for specialization. Many of the values held by the people of Shansi, moreover, were incompatible with industrial growth. Because they had grown up in an isolated and stagnant society, most of them were unfamiliar with the Western concept of an expanding economy and rejected the concomitant belief that men can augment their wealth most rapidly by investing in productive enterprises. Instead, they chose to spend their savings on elaborate weddings and other forms of conspicuous consumption or sought to enlarge their share of already existing wealth by purchasing land. Thrift and initiative were stifled too by the extended family system, which imposed on enterprising and successful individuals the responsibility of providing for their indigent and often less venturesome relatives.

These obstacles to economic growth might have been overcome by an ambitious but realistic program of industrial development sustained by bold and imaginative leadership; Yen's projects on the contrary were mismanaged and suffered from a lack of planning and coordination, as he subsequently acknowledged.[31] Furthermore, he readily sacrificed his economic objectives whenever they threatened to interfere with his military and political ambitions. He repeatedly complained about a shortage of investment capital, for example, but spent on the army at least half of his government's annual income.[32] By his own admission, extortionate taxes frustrated efforts to promote economic growth in Shansi;[33] however, he must bear much of the responsibility for this situation because he levied

---

[30] Ch'ü Chih-sheng, *op.cit.*, p. 1.
[31] *Lectures*, III-A, p. 314 (Dec. 1932).
[32] *Lectures*, V, p. 51 (July 1918).
[33] *Lectures*, III-A, p. 314 (Dec. 1932).

many of these taxes himself.[34] Then too, although he appreciated the military and economic value of modern industry, he
was uneasy about its social and political implications. Many
of the speeches he delivered in the 1920's betray a distaste for
individualism, urbanization, large-scale enterprise, and other
phenomena associated with economic growth in the countries
of the West.[35] Perhaps he feared that by subverting traditional
values and disrupting the existing order modernization would
produce social instability and bring about the collapse of his
authority. He virtually outlawed labor unions[36] and in 1926
used troops against the striking workers of a cotton mill in
which he had invested.[37] Like the mandarins of the Ch'ing
dynasty, he considered farming to be by far the most productive and socially desirable occupation. This is why he replied
in response to a query about the apparent prosperity of Japan
and other industrial countries that in all these nations the development of industry had resulted in a critical shortage of
food.[38]

Yen's preoccupation with agriculture led him to conclude
that reforestation would yield greater profits than coal mining,[39] in spite of the fact that buried in the earth beneath
Shansi is more than half of the coal in China.[40] In addition to
being unusually accessible, these beds contain most of China's
high-grade anthracite.[41] For this reason, in 1907 a British
syndicate purchased from the Imperial government in Peking
the right to mine Shansi's coal, only to encounter a storm of
opposition on the part of antiforeign elements among the gentry
in Shansi, who formed their own syndicate, the Pao Chin
Mining Company, which persuaded the British to relinquish
their newly acquired concessions in exchange for a cash pay-

[34] *CEB*, Feb. 21, 1925, pp. 97-98, March 14, 1925, pp. 148-149, May
30, 1925, p. 318, June 13, 1925, p. 346, Nov. 21, 1925, p. 300,
Dec. 26, 1925, p. 361.
[35] For example, see pp. 91-100 in *Lectures*, III-C (July 1922).
[36] Anonymous, "Labor Conditions in Shansi," *The Chinese Economic
Monthly*, hereafter referred to as *CEM*, June 1925, pp. 23-24.
[37] *NCH*, Oct. 23, 1926, 156:2.
[38] Yen Hsi-shan, *op.cit.*, p. 27.
[39] Wang Ch'ien, *op.cit.*, p. 10b, and *Lectures*, III-C, p. 62 (May
1921).
[40] Kojima Seiichi, *Hoku Shi keizai tokuhon* (*An Economic Primer of
North China*) (Tokyo, 1937), I, p. 40.
[41] Takagi Rikurō, *Hoku Shi keizai annai* (*An Economic Guide to
North China*) (Tokyo, 1937), p. 164.

ment of 20 million taels. This enormous ransom consumed so much of the Pao Chin Company's assets, however, that it lacked enough capital to buy modern machinery and operate on a large scale.[42] Most of its collieries were merely shallow pits, having a circumference of less than 14 feet and worked by a handful of ill-trained coolies who used shovels to hack coal from the walls of these holes, hauled it to the surface chunk by chunk with the aid of a windlass and an iron hook, and then trundled it away on their backs or in tiny pushcarts. The largest of these so-called mines yielded no more than 400 tons of coal a day and the smallest only 3 tons. In many instances their production costs were so high, owing to inefficient and dishonest management as well as low output, that keeping them in operation cost more than they brought in, and they continued to function solely at the behest of the provincial government.[43]

Notwithstanding his keener interest in reforestation, Yen professed to attach great importance to Shansi's immense deposits of coal. "Our future prosperity lies beneath our feet!" he exclaimed.[44] Upon becoming civil governor of Shansi in 1917, he declared that all of the province's mineral wealth was the property of the state, and in order to encourage and supervise its exploitation he created the Shansi Bureau of Public Mines (*Chin min-kung k'uang chü*). Although he left to private entrepreneurs the task of actually carrying out mining operations, he supplied much of the CH$1.5 million invested in the Share-the-Wealth (*T'ung-pao*) Mining Company, which undertook to exploit large deposits of coal lying in and around the city of Tatung to the north, and he probably was a major stockholder in other privately run concerns organized for the purpose of working the even richer coal fields at Yangch'üan near P'ingting in eastern Shansi.[45] Some of these companies procured foreign machinery and tried to employ more up-to-date methods of mining, with the result that between 1920 and 1926 coal production nearly doubled, only to drop off rapidly after 1926 because of dislocations created by Yen's involvement in a series of wars with other militarists.[46] Even during

---

[42] Letter to myself from Wynn C. Fairfield, dated Sept. 23, 1958.
[43] Hsia Ching-feng, *op.cit.*, pp. 4a-4b, and "Lü," "Shan-hsi shu-cheng t'an," *HTPL*, Oct. 9, 1926, p. 11.
[44] *Lectures*, III-B, p. 61 (March 1919).
[45] "Lü," *op.cit.*, p. 12, and *Fairfield*, p. 18.
[46] *Industrial Gazetteer*, p. 17-wu, and *CYB*, *1929-1930*, p. 51.

their most productive years, however, Shansi's collieries failed to keep pace with mines in Hopei and Shantung,[47] both provinces having considerably less coal than Shansi but where mining operations were largely in the hands of foreign concerns. Consequently, coal continued to make up less than a third of Shansi's exports, and in much of the province remained so scarce and expensive that millions of Yen's subjects were compelled to shiver through the winters without sufficient fuel to keep warm.[48]

In the absence of a substantial investment of additional capital, mining remained largely a primitive, costly, and unproductive enterprise. Working conditions in most of Shansi's mines were so intolerable, for example, that there existed a chronic shortage of miners, inasmuch as only criminals hiding from the police and other desperate persons were ready to risk their lives in the ill-ventilated and perennially flooded pits.[49] In the case of Yen's T'ung Pao Mining Company, much of the firm's capital, which otherwise might have been used to modernize its operations, was frittered away in the form of exorbitant salaries and bonuses to Yen's own friends and relatives, who served as the concern's "directors" and "assistant managers."[50] Then too, the rich declined to invest their money in mining unless first guaranteed extravagant profits. In an effort to raise extra capital, Yen proposed to lease certain coal and iron-rich lands in southern Shansi to a wealthy Anglo-Chinese syndicate from outside the province, but was compelled to abandon his plan when students boycotted their classes and staged massive demonstrations aimed at convincing the public that he was preparing to sell Shansi's interests out to the foreigners. "Under no circumstances will foreigners be allowed to mine coal in Shansi," promised Yen.[51] Although this pledge did not deter him from subsequently granting concessions to an English mining company, he demanded in return virtually full control over any operations that resulted, as well as most of the profits, which may explain why nothing

47 *CYB*, *1929-1930*, pp. 50-51.
48 Wang Chen-i, *op.cit.*, p. 5, and *NCH*, Dec. 22, 1923, 816:2, and May 31, 1924, 331:3.
49 *CEB*, Feb. 2, 1924, p. 10, and "Lü," *op.cit.*, p. 11.
50 "Lü," *op.cit.*, p. 12.
51 *Lectures*, III-C, pp. 65-66 (April 1921).

seems to have come of this venture.[52] The most productive mines in Shansi, conversely, were operated at Tatung by the T'ung Chi Mining Company, a privately owned firm having its headquarters in Tientsin and having a large number of Japanese stockholders. Nevertheless, because of the intense xenophobia of his subjects Yen was unable to explore seriously the possibility of using foreign capital to finance the exploitation of Shansi's mineral resources.

Lack of an adequate rail system prevented Yen from developing a substantial market for coal mined in Shansi and is another important reason why his efforts to promote mining were not successful.[53] Tatung, in the north, enjoyed access to the Peking-Suiyuan Railroad which belonged to the central government in Peking; but there were no railroads in the western and southern parts of Shansi, and in the east only a strip of narrow gauge track winding through the mountains that separate Taiyuan from the border of Hopei. This so-called Cheng Tai Railroad was under the management of a French syndicate which had built the line before the Revolution of 1911 and thereafter reaped an annual return on its investment of almost 25 percent by charging the highest freight rates in China.[54] These rates were so high, in fact, that in spite of its comparatively low price at the pithead, by the time coal mined in Shansi and transported over the Cheng Tai line reached industrial centers elsewhere in China it was too expensive to compete with coal from mines serviced by other railroads.[55]

Nevertheless, Yen was unwilling to shoulder the cost of laying down additional track and expected the central government in Peking to build for him the railroads he needed in order to utilize the mineral resources of his domain. Peking agreed but insisted on using track of standard width instead of the narrow gauge variety Yen had specified, with the result that he withdrew his request and abandoned his plans to open new

[52] Hsin-wen pao (The News), Oct. 1926, as quoted in Archives, Oct. 1926, pp. 372-375.

[53] "Lü," op.cit., p. 12, and interview with Ch'üan Han-sheng, Professor of the Economic History of Modern China in the National Taiwan University, Taipei, Taiwan, Oct. 3, 1956.

[54] Shansi Report, pp. 246-247.

[55] Anonymous, "Coal Mining in Shansi," CEM, Nov. 1925, p. 28, NCH, Jan. 10, 1934, 44:1, and Chung-wai ching-chi chou-k'an, No. 120, as quoted in Archives, Aug. 1925, p. 212.

mines, fearing that the central government would employ the new railroads to extend its authority into Shansi, and he preferred to have no railroads rather than ones that could be used by the rolling stock of an invading army.[56] Furthermore, in his eagerness to secure money in order to meet military expenses, Yen levied heavy taxes against coal and other commodities hauled by the Cheng Tai Railroad.[57] Together with overregulation and other forms of government harassment, such taxes were enough to discourage the exploitation of Shansi's unusually rich deposits of sulphur.[58] Nothing could underline more forcefully the extent to which political disunity and militarism impeded the economic modernization of China during the 1920's.

Yen's policy with respect to road building illustrates vividly how his desire for military power and political control interfered with his efforts to promote economic growth in Shansi. Under the Ch'ing, most of the roads in Shansi were narrow ruts worn so deeply into the soft loess that traffic passing over them could not be seen from the surrounding fields. Such thoroughfares filled with water and were unusable whenever it rained. In much of the province there were no roads but simply trails suitable for use by mules, camels, and human beings. Freight was often hauled to the top of a mountain by mules and then slid down the other side in carts outfitted with skids. Small wonder that by the time goods reached their destination they were too expensive for all but the very rich to buy. Nor was economic specialization feasible in a land where the virtual absence of railroads and the inadequacy of other forms of transportation isolated one region from another and made local self-sufficiency essential.

Considerations other than a wish to encourage trade, however, caused Yen to become aware that Shansi needed more and better roads. During the drought that afflicted Shansi for three years beginning in 1919, he was obliged to transport from the comparatively unaffected north enough grain to feed

---

[56] Interview with *Ch'üan Han-sheng*, "Lü," *op.cit.*, p. 12, *Fairfield*, p. 19, and *K'ung*, p. 34.

[57] "Coal Mining in Shansi," pp. 28, 30, and *Chung-wai ching-chi chou-k'an*, No. 124, as quoted in *Archives*, Aug. 1925, p. 243.

[58] *Chung-wai ching-chi chou-k'an*, No. 104, as quoted in *Archives*, June 1926, pp. 15-19.

the starving inhabitants of the famine-stricken south, but found that owing to the poor quality and small number of roads in his domain this task would require the use of 30,000 mules and even then could not be accomplished in less than six months. He complained that he might just as easily use a glass of water to extinguish a fire in a wood pile as try to prevent famine without an adequate system of roads.[59] Consequently, Yen put his soldiers to work building roads and with the assistance of the American Red Cross and the China International Famine Relief Commission succeeded in laying down well over a thousand miles of roadway.[60] By 1929 motor roads linked Taiyuan with almost every district in the province, while at the same time a newly erected network of telephone and telegraph lines enabled Yen to communicate instantaneously with all of the district capitals and military headquarters in his domain.[61] Whereas in the past it had taken five or six days to travel the distance between Taiyuan and Tatung, now the trip could be made by motor car in only twelve hours. According to one writer, during the famine that ravaged northwestern China in 1929 the people of Shansi suffered much less than the population of neighboring provinces because Yen's motor roads gave relief authorities in the Model Province easy and inexpensive access to most of the stricken areas.[62] Yen's road-building program altered to some extent the notoriously parochial outlook of most of his subjects,[63] for in many instances the new roads extended into areas so remote and isolated that their inhabitants had never seen a cart, much less a bicycle or bus.[64]

Notwithstanding their value as instruments of political control and social change, as well as their usefulness in time of famine, the roads that Yen built during the 1920's did not contribute significantly to the economic development of Shansi. Because he tried to save money by leaving many of them un-

[59] *Lectures*, VIII, p. 37 (Aug. 1920).

[60] *CEJ*, May 1930, p. 547, and *Shansi Report*, pp. 276-277.

[61] Anonymous, "Plight of the Shansi Peasantry," *PT*, Jan. 16, 1932, p. 132, and *Industrial Gazetteer*, pp. 63-75-jen.

[62] John Philip Emerson, *Yen Hsi-shan, A Warlord and his Province 1911-1948* (An unpublished manuscript), p. 32.

[63] Even Yen's most uncompromising critics acknowledged the success of his road-building program. For example, see Chen Han-seng, *op.cit.*, p. 378.

[64] *NCH*, Aug. 20, 1921, 537:1.

surfaced they often were eaten away by washouts or blocked by landslides, since his engineers economized by removing as little earth as possible whenever it was necessary to cut through a hill or mountain.[65] Instead of allocating money for the up-keep of the roads, Yen ordered local officials to maintain them out of their own revenues. Large stretches of roadway were al-lowed to become overgrown with weeds and bushes, while bridges frequently deteriorated to the point of being useless;[66] and travel by motor vehicle became so hazardous that generally merchants preferred to employ traditional forms of transporta-tion like camels and rickshaws.[67] Then too, in return for the enormous payments which he demanded from companies oper-ating trucks or buses on the public highways, Yen permitted these carriers to charge for their services at exorbitant rates that discouraged his subjects from using the roads for commercial purposes.[68] His indifference to economic considerations caused many of the roads he built to come to an end at the pro-vincial border and not to juncture with roads outside Shansi.[69] A well-informed writer says that not only Yen's motor roads but also his new system of telecommunications were used exclusively for military and administrative purposes and made almost no impact on Shansi's economy.[70]

Agriculture

Yen Hsi-shan was emotionally disposed to favor agriculture and perceived that the bulk of his revenue must come from the agricultural sector of the economy; unless he succeeded in in-creasing appreciably the output of Shansi's farms he would be unable to redress his province's adverse balance of trade.[71] His efforts to step up agricultural productivity took the form of trying to bring more land under cultivation through an ambitious program of water control and afforestation. Although Shansi normally enjoys an annual rainfall of more than sixteen inches, this precipitation is extremely uneven and occurs for the

[65] Lady Hosie, *op.cit.*, p. 470, and *NCH*, Sept. 23, 1922, 868:1 and Aug. 4, 1923, 309:1.
[66] *NCH*, Sept. 26, 1925, 428:1, and Dec. 14, 1932, 412:3.
[67] *NCH*, Dec. 1, 1923, 397:2-3, and Lady Hosie, *op.cit.*, p. 470.
[68] *NCH*, Dec. 9, 1922, 648:3, and *Shansi Report*, pp. 279-280.
[69] *Shansi Report*, p. 276.
[70] Wang Chen-i, *op.cit.*, p. 6. In the case of the telephone and tele-graph system, this observation is confirmed by *K'ung*, p. 35.
[71] *Lectures*, IV, pp. 2-3 (Oct. 1916).

most part during the summer. Peasants living outside the river valleys were obliged to store up enough water during the wet months to irrigate their crops after the rains ceased. Since most of them did not have sufficient capital or skill to do this effectively, Yen employed for their benefit a large staff of technical advisors and created the Bureau of Water Control (*shui-li chü*), which built new irrigation canals and offered to rent peasants the latest kind of machinery for use in sinking wells and constructing reservoirs. He also undertook to plant trees on the barren slopes of Shansi's hills and mountains in the hope that the presence of vegetation would reduce the number of flash floods and slow the process of soil erosion. Whereas in the remote past Shansi had been heavily forested, by 1920 indiscriminate cutting had resulted in the destruction of all but an infinitesimal number of trees. Yen's aim was to reforest more than 27 million acres or approximately one quarter of the province.[72] Working through local branches of the semiofficial Society for the Promotion of Forestation (*Lin-yeh ts'u-chin hui*), he distributed millions of seedlings to his subjects and exhorted each of them to plant and care for at least one tree a year. His enthusiasm for reforestation even caused him to judge the vitality of a community by the number of trees he found in it. "The United States has many trees because the Americans are a vigorous people," he remarked.[73]

Yen was equally determined to coerce and cajole the farmers of Shansi into practicing a more diversified kind of agriculture. Much of the irrigation work undertaken by the Bureau of Water Control, for example, was aimed at encouraging peasants in northern Shansi to grow cotton instead of cereals. Cotton fetched a higher price and Yen predicted that it would flourish in the north if enough water was available. Besides rewarding farmers who planted cotton, he maintained at least five cotton experimentation stations (*mien-yeh shih-yen ch'ang*) where specialists showed peasants how to cultivate cotton and carried out experiments looking toward the development of improved strains.[74] Similarly, in an effort to promote animal husbandry in Shansi, he imported from Australia a thousand head of Merino sheep, which he intended to mate with the

---

[72] *CEB*, June 13, 1925, p. 387.
[73] *Lectures*, III-C, p. 73 (April 1921).
[74] *Industrial Gazetteer*, pp. 89-90-ting.

hardier but less attractive indigenous breeds to produce a breed hardy enough to withstand the rigors of Shansi's climate but having wool comparable to the Merino.[75] The manufacture of silk was another occupation that Yen encouraged his subjects to take up, not only through the distribution of mulberry seedlings and silkworm eggs but also by setting up a modern silk-weaving factory as well as a number of schools for the purpose of teaching the peasants the fundamentals of sericulture.[76] The creation of these schools was only a part of a broad program designed to circulate knowledge of the latest agricultural techniques. In each district there was an agricultural experimentation station, run by graduates of the Provincial College of Agriculture (*Shan-hsi nung-chuan hsüeh-hsiao*) who conducted experiments, maintained an information service for the benefit of local farmers, and otherwise promoted the modernization of agriculture.[77] In addition to supporting the Provincial College of Agriculture, Yen likewise operated a middle school that prepared students for a career in agriculture, and every year he had a hundred especially able peasants, including many women, brought to Taiyuan for a prolonged period of study under the guidance of agricultural specialists. It was expected that after returning home these peasants would communicate their new knowledge and skills to their fellow villagers. All of these attempts to improve agriculture in Shansi benefited additionally from the advice and research of European agronomists in the employ of the provincial government and American missionaries belonging to the faculty of the Department of Agriculture in the Oberlin-in-Shansi Memorial School at Taiku.

Although Yen's efforts resulted in a threefold increase in the amount of land planted with cotton in Shansi,[78] the rest of his agricultural program was a failure. A foreigner having wide experience in the field of water control found Yen's accomplishments in this area unimpressive and blamed the drought that ravaged Shansi in 1928 and again in 1929 and 1930 on

[75] *CEB*, June 9, 1924, p. 4, and Oct. 17, 1925, pp. 221-222.
[76] Wang Ch'ien, *op.cit.*, p. 7b, and Anonymous, "Sericulture in Shansi," *CEM*, Dec. 1925, pp. 8-16.
[77] *CEB*, May 2, 1925, pp. 253-254.
[78] *Industrial Gazetteer*, pp. 90-91-ting.

inadequate irrigation.[79] Less than a fifth of the trees Yen planted survived, and this was not enough to yield the returns he had anticipated.[80] As for the Merino sheep, all but a handful of them died,[81] while his attempts to develop a viable silk industry met with such little success that his silk-weaving factory went bankrupt.[82] Overall agricultural productivity remained so low that in 1927 Shansi still was exporting CH$7 million worth of specie a year, in part to pay for food imported from other areas.[83] Yen's lack of success explains why the peasants, who comprised the overwhelming majority of the population of Shansi, continued to live in the utmost poverty. One writer charges that in 1930 a farmer in Shansi usually received an annual income considerably smaller than that enjoyed by most of the peasants in impoverished lands like India and the Philippine Islands.[84] According to articles in the *Chinese Economic Bulletin*, in 1925 80 percent of the peasants in Shansi were living from hand to mouth and subsisting for the most part on a diet of potatoes and cereals.[85] Since to survive the average poor peasant found it necessary to spend considerably more than he earned,[86] much of the rural population was hopelessly in debt. Although conditions were better in the cities and towns of Shansi,[87] the countryside remained impoverished and observers generally agree that Yen

[79] Oliver J. Todd, *Two Decades in China* (Peiping, 1938), pp. 84-85, 156-159, 539-550. Todd's adverse opinion with respect to the effectiveness of Yen's water control program was shared by other well-informed observers, such as Wang Chen-i, *op.cit.*, p. 2, and *Williamson*, p. 16.

[80] Leon Wieger, *op.cit.*, p. 356, *CEB*, Jan. 3, 1925, p. 10, and *Lectures*, IV, p. 38 (Dec. 1921).

[81] *Lectures*, III-A, p. 473 (Aug. 1936).

[82] Wang Chen-i, *op.cit.*, p. 2, and *CEB*, March 28, 1925, p. 183.

[83] Ch'ü Chih-sheng, *op.cit.*, p. 1. An article in the *CEB*, Sept. 26, 1925, p. 183, more or less confirms Ch'ü's observation.

[84] Chen Han-seng, *op.cit.*, p. 379. Another writer says that as late as the summer of 1924 millions of peasants in Shansi were living on the margin of starvation. See *NCH*, July 12, 1924, 48:5.

[85] *CEB*, July 11, 1925, p. 23, and Nov. 14, 1925, p. 277.

[86] According to the *CEB*, Sept. 6, 1924, pp. 5-7, and July 11, 1925, p. 23, the average yearly income of a poor peasant living in Shansi was CH$34 and his annual expenses almost CH$50.

[87] *NCH*, Feb. 23, 1924, 279:3, June 28, 1924, 487:5, and July 12, 1924, 46:5, and *CEB*, March 14, 1925, p. 5, July 25, 1925, p. 54, and Oct. 10, 1925, p. 212.

failed to develop the resources of his domain enough to raise appreciably the living standards of most of his subjects.[88]

Yen must bear much of the blame for the failure of his own policies with respect to agriculture. Too often his projects existed largely on paper or were formulated without taking into consideration the planning and technique necessary to implement them. For example, most farmers could not afford to rent well-digging machinery from the Bureau of Water Control and were compelled to employ methods so primitive that they rarely found water and if successful had no way of bringing it to the surface or of keeping it from becoming contaminated with mud from the sides of the well; small wonder that many of them gave up in disgust after digging a few shallow holes.[89] Yen's efforts to use Shansi's rivers for irrigation were equally haphazard and nearly as fruitless. Instead of attempting to control the turbulent waters of the Fen River by constructing masonry dams equipped with check gates, he relied on a system of old-fashioned earthen dams which because they lacked check gates had to be destroyed each year and then rebuilt for use the following year.[90] Inasmuch as his dikes too were made largely of earth, they gave way quickly under the pressure of the water, leaving the river to wander at will across the floor of its valley, frequently taking hundreds of lives and causing considerable property damage.[91] Yen demonstrated so little interest in dam building that none of his new motor roads came within forty miles of the best location for a dam on the river Fen. A foreign authority on water control who visited Shansi after 1930 found that the situation with respect to rivers in other parts of the province was still worse and criticized the provincial government for neglecting even to gather the hydraulic data necessary to initiate a serious program of water conservation.[92]

According to another foreigner, Yen was unable to secure the services of experienced personnel from outside Shansi

[88] *Williamson*, p. 21, and "Lü," "Shan-hsi shu-cheng t'an," *HTPL*, Sept. 11, 1926, p. 10.
[89] *CEB*, April 4, 1925, p. 194, and *Lectures*, IV, p. 39 (Dec. 1921).
[90] Oliver J. Todd, *op.cit.*, pp. 539-550.
[91] See *ibid.*, p. 158, and *NCH*, Aug. 18, 1923, 448:2-3, and Sept. 22, 822:3.
[92] Oliver J. Todd, *op.cit.*, pp. 159, 533, 549-551.

and did not make use of the trained men available.[93] Perhaps this is why he insisted on raising sheep and planting trees in regions where these activities were bound to result in failure, owing to lack of pasturage and poor soil.[94] Many of the sheep that died, moreover, were victims of rinderpest and other diseases which might have been overcome if Yen had not ignored the need for properly trained veterinarians.[95] He likewise spent much money trying to promote sericulture, an industry ill-suited to the cold and dry climate of Shansi,[96] but which he may have introduced simply because in the Confucian classics it is hailed repeatedly as an effective means of enriching the country. Finally, he seems to have been less interested in taking realistic steps to rehabilitate the economy of Shansi than in planting trees along the sides of the highways and carrying out other pretentious but comparatively valueless projects designed to attract the attention of visitors and leave them with the impression that he was a progressive ruler.

Yen's program also miscarried because local officials who were responsible for implementing it had not enough interest and insufficient training to undertake anything as demanding and technically complicated as economic modernization. Many of them placed saplings they received from the government in dry and rocky ground where the young trees quickly died; others aroused the wrath of the peasants by coercing them into irrigating newly planted trees with water they needed for their crops or ordered them to plant trees in soil normally used to grow foodstuffs.[97] Furthermore, inspection tours undertaken with the professed aim of examining dikes and irrigation projects generally were used as opportunities for enjoying a holiday in the countryside.[98] In addition to blaming local officials for the failure of his efforts to promote sericulture in Shansi,[99] Yen accused them of retaining for use as scrap paper the information bulletins periodically given to them by the agricultural experimentation stations for distribution to the peasants.[100]

[93] *Fairfield*, p. 13.
[94] *CEB*, May 2, 1925, p. 253, and Oct. 17, 1925, p. 222.
[95] *NCH*, March 29, 1924, 480:5.
[96] *Fairfield*, p. 16.   [97] Wang Ch'ien, *op.cit.*, p. 7a.
[98] *NCH*, July 21, 1917, 140:2.
[99] *Lectures*, III-B, p. 3 (June 1918), and III-A, pp. 42, 80 (April, May 1918).
[100] *Lectures*, III-B, p. 3 (June 1918).

Since the bulk of these officials came from the landholding class it is possible that many of them deliberately sabotaged Yen's program, lest its unsettling effect on the peasantry upset the status quo in the countryside. Yen was forced to admit also that peasants brought to Taiyuan to learn more advanced methods of farming "become so sophisticated and fond of luxury that they are unwilling to return to their villages."[101]

In the final analysis, however, Yen was unable to vitalize agriculture in Shansi because he neglected to effect changes in the system of land ownership and other reforms that would encourage peasants to employ the new methods of farming he urged upon them. Most farmers were unwilling to adopt innovations as long as landlords and moneylenders would continue to appropriate the greater part of any increase in productivity that resulted. Together with the ignorance of the peasants, their conservative outlook, and their deep-seated hostility toward government, this explains why the bulk of the farming population resisted tenaciously Yen's efforts to implement his program. For example, the peasants refused to feed or otherwise care for the Merino sheep Yen forced upon them, not only because they regarded these animals as government property but also for fear that if they acquired more livestock their taxes would be raised.[102] Besides neglecting to water or actually destroying most of the trees they planted at Yen's behest,[103] they normally were unwilling to surrender land which the Bureau of Water Control needed in order to construct wells and irrigation ditches, generally on the grounds that they would not benefit from these innovations but sometimes because the bodies of their ancestors were buried in the land demanded from them.[104] Needless to say, the extra taxes that Yen imposed for the purpose of financing the work of the Bureau of Water Control, as well as other aspects of his program, aroused considerable opposition,[105] causing him to complain that his subjects were misconstruing the slogan "Strengthen the Nation by Enriching the Country" (*fu-kuo ch'iang-kuo*) to mean simply higher taxes and larger conscription quotas.[106] Similar-

[101] *Lectures*, VII, p. 75 (1922).
[102] *Lectures*, III-A, p. 473 (Aug. 1936), and III-B, p. 70 (Dec. 1919).
[103] Leon Wieger, *op.cit.*, p. 356.
[104] *Lectures*, III-B, p. 5 (June 1918).
[105] *Lectures*, III-A, p. 240 (Aug. 1924).
[106] *Lectures*, III-B, p. 67 (Aug. 1919).

ly, although the price of cotton rose steadily throughout the 1920's and Yen offered substantial rewards to persons who cultivated it, most of the peasants stubbornly continued to grow cereals until Yen began punishing severely farmers who ignored his orders.[107]

Even the schools that he founded with the aim of teaching children from peasant families how to practice modern farming failed to generate much enthusiasm among the peasants, who generally were not anxious to have their children become farmers, but instead wanted them to take up studies that would prepare them for a career in the bureaucracy.[108] Yen could have reassured the peasants and won their support for his program only by enacting land reforms and reducing their dependence on moneylenders through the extension of cheap credit, low-priced fertilizer, and crop insurance; however, before 1931 he was too conservative and too overawed by the gentry and the banking interests in Shansi to do more than talk vaguely about the desirability of land reform and the greater productivity that would result from it.[109]

Money and Banking

Because Yen did not succeed in increasing appreciably the output of Shansi's economy, specie continued to leave the province, causing the value of money in Shansi to fluctuate wildly. Yen professed to be alarmed by the popular unrest this aroused,[110] and in 1919 he created his own bank of issue, the Provincial Bank of Shansi (*Shan-hsi sheng-li yin-hang*), which quickly acquired a dominant position with respect to other banks in Shansi and attempted to prevent prices from rising any higher by seeking to withdraw from circulation all notes except its own.[111] Although nominally a privately operated enterprise, in reality the new bank was controlled by Yen, who contributed much of its capital, dictated its policies, and appointed its directors and managers, generally from among

[107] The Bureau of Village Administration of the Shansi Provincial Government, comp., *Shan-hsi liu-cheng san-shih hui-pien* (*A Compilation of Documents Relating to the Six Policies and Three Matters in Shansi*) (Taiyuan, 1929), II, p. 1b.

[108] *Fairfield*, p. 16.   [109] Yen Hsi-shan, *op.cit.*, p. 21.

[110] *Lectures*, III-C, pp. 30-31 (Nov. 1918).

[111] *Industrial Gazetteer*, p. 118-i, and *Ching-chi* (*Economics*), Oct. 16, 1924, as quoted in *Archives*, Oct. 1924, p. 203.

his own friends and relatives.[112] It appears to have been a highly profitable venture for everyone concerned, and its currency remained comparatively stable throughout most of the 1920's,[113] perhaps because it deliberately located its branch offices in obscure and inaccessible places with a view to discouraging most of the population from exchanging their banknotes for specie.[114]

The activities of Yen's new bank did not solve the monetary problems afflicting Shansi, however. Money changers and privately owned banks still issued copper certificates and usually in amounts far in excess of their capital,[115] while at the same time a large quantity of debased and counterfeit coins entered Yen's domain from neighboring provinces, so that between 1913 and 1923 the value of copper coins and certificates in Shansi depreciated by 50 percent.[116] In 1923 this situation provoked a financial panic that brought ruin to hundreds of banks and money-changing shops. Yen responded by curtailing substantially the right of such establishments to issue copper certificates and outlawed speculation, which was another major cause of Shansi's chronic monetary instability. In the absence of a significant increase in agricultural or industrial productivity, however, currency and copper coins being used in the Model Province continued to decline in value. By the end of 1924, for example, they were worth 80 percent less than at the beginning of the year,[117] much to the discomfiture of the laboring class; the growing shortage of specie brought on soaring interest rates as well.[118] In the past interest rates rarely exceeded 10 percent in Shansi, but by 1925 they averaged 24 percent and rates of up to 100 percent were by no means uncommon.[119] Yen attempted to remedy this situation by establishing at least five farmer-worker banks (*nung-kung yin-hang*) for the purpose of extending

[112] Wang Chen-i, *op.cit.*, p. 5, and *Hua-pei jih-pao* (*North China Daily*), Dec. 15, 1930, as quoted in *Archives*, Dec. 1930, p. 199.

[113] Ch'ü Chih-sheng, *op.cit.*, p. 2, and E. Kann, "Copper Banknotes in China," *CEJ*, July 1929, p. 571.

[114] *NCH*, Oct. 30, 1926, 206:2.

[115] E. Kann, *op.cit.*, p. 571, and *NCH*, Nov. 10, 1923, 373:1, and Feb. 2, 1924, 165:5.

[116] *CEB*, April 25, 1925, p. 239.

[117] *Ibid.*   [118] *CEB*, Nov. 14, 1925, p. 277.

[119] *CEB*, Oct. 25, 1924, p. 11, Jan. 31, 1925, p. 69, April 4, 1925, p. 199.

low-interest loans to farmers and laborers. These banks failed to win the confidence of the public, however, owing to irresponsible management, and there is evidence that interest rates continued to rise.[120] Yen denounced his own officials for encouraging the inflationary spiral by printing money for their personal use and accused them of conspiring with speculators bent on profiting from fluctuations in the value of the currency.[121] Yet he too was responsible for the monetary troubles that plagued his regime, since in his eagerness to raise more revenue he provoked additional inflation by minting his own copper coins and allowing them to circulate in competition with coins from other provinces.[122] No wonder he attacked the use of money and called for its replacement with some form of barter.

Summary and Conclusions

For a variety of reasons, during the latter half of the nineteenth century and the first decades of the twentieth Shansi's economy deteriorated rapidly. The result was a perennial trade deficit which by draining specie out of the province caused deflation and chronic monetary instability. Yen tried to remedy this situation by promoting the manufacture in Shansi of goods normally imported from foreign countries or other provinces; but his efforts in this direction were half-hearted and the industries he erected, too small, and inadequately capitalized to compete with factories outside Shansi. Lack of rail transportation in much of Shansi also militated against industrialization and prevented Yen from exploiting a potentially valuable source of foreign exchange in the form of Shansi's enormous reserves of coal. Farm output remained low, moreover, owing in part to the absence of vital modern water control projects but chiefly because in Shansi farms were minuscule in size and worked in a primitive fashion by ignorant and impoverished peasants whose exploitation at the hands of the rich discouraged them from adopting innovations which might have resulted in larger yields. All of this suggests that in Shansi economic growth depended on economic and social

[120] *Industrial Gazetteer*, p. 130-hsin, *CEB*, Oct. 24, 1925, p. 238, and Chao Shu-li, *op.cit.*, pp. 19-20.
[121] *CEB*, April 25, 1925, p. 239, and *Shansi Report*, pp. 308-309.
[122] Yen Hsi-shan, *op.cit.*, pp. 26-29.

changes so thoroughgoing that they could not come about as long as the men who ruled the province were committed to tradition and had a large stake in the existing order. Yen Hsi-shan's interest in economic modernization was genuine, but until the 1930's it was not profound enough to overcome the conservatism that kept him from initiating the sweeping changes necessary to pursue it effectively.

CHAPTER SEVEN

THE STRUGGLE FOR POWER

A Period of Revolution

FENG YÜ-HSIANG's seizure of Peking in 1923 must have alarmed Yen Hsi-shan profoundly, for among the men close to Feng was Yen's old rival, Hsü Hsi-feng, who urged Feng to oust Yen from Shansi before making war upon the Manchurian warlord Chang Tso-lin.[1] Perhaps at Hsü's behest, but also because Yen had been intriguing against Feng in neighboring Honan, in 1925 the armies of Fan Chung-hsiu, a Honanese militarist allied with Feng, invaded Shansi. Initially, Yen's forces were so badly beaten that they retired into the cities and allowed the invaders to ravage the countryside; however, owing largely to his new motor roads, Yen was able to throw the bulk of his army into the conflict and after a series of hard-fought battles succeeded in driving Fan's soldiers back across the border into Honan.[2]

The following year, Feng's Peoples' Army (*Kuominchün*) retreated into northwest China after suffering repeated defeats at the hands of Chang Tso-lin, Wu P'ei-fu, and other militarists who had formed a coalition with the aim of destroying Feng's army and ending forever his power in North China. Although Yen tried to remain aloof from this struggle, lest the warring armies invade and devastate Shansi, fear of antagonizing Chang and Wu compelled him to resist the Kuominchün when it attempted to withdraw along the Peking-Suiyuan Railroad through Tatung into the comparative safety of Inner Mongolia.[3] Feng's troops retaliated by seizing much of northern Shansi, but halted their advance toward Taiyuan after the fighting elsewhere ended in victory for the armies of the coalition and Feng conceded defeat by departing for Russia.[4] Yen

---

[1] Hsü Fan't'ing, *op.cit.*, p. 6.

[2] "Lü," "Shan-hsi shu-cheng t'an," *HTPL*, Aug. 28, 1926, p. 9, and *NCH*, Jan. 9, 1936, 53:1-2, and May 15, 1926, 292:4.

[3] "Lü," Aug. 28, 1926, p. 10, *Fairfield*, p. 1, and *NCH*, Oct. 23, 1926, 156:1.

[4] Jermyn Chi-Hung Lynn, *Political Parties in China* (Tientsin, 1930), pp. 151-152, and *Huang Pao*, June 19, 1926, as quoted in *Archives*, June 1926, p. 251.

accepted their surrender and permitted them to remain in Shansi as his "guests," not only because his army still was no match for them but also in the hope that their presence would discourage Chang and Wu from attempting to extend their influence into Shansi. Besides declining Chang's offer to send Manchurian troops into Shansi to help him disarm the Kuominchün, he recruited tens of thousands of new soldiers for his own army and occupied all of Suiyuan in order to keep that province out of Chang's hands.[5] "Thus this worthy man defended himself equally well against both his friends and his enemies," comments one writer.[6]

Meanwhile, to the south the armies of the resurgent Kuomintang inflicted defeat after defeat on Wu P'ei-fu as they moved northward in their campaign to seize Peking and reunify China under the rule of the newly organized National Government at Canton, which soon moved its capital to the city of Hankow. The Kuomintang had reestablished itself in Shansi as early as 1921, when returned students from Peking, led by Miao P'ei-ch'eng and Han K'e-wen, began agitating on its behalf among the students attending Yen's schools. Owing in large part to nationalist feeling generated by the May Fourth Movement of 1919, they won considerable support and in 1924 set up a "provisional party headquarters" (lin-shih tang-pu).[7] During the summer of 1925 the popularity of the Kuomintang increased rapidly as students in Shansi became caught up in the May Thirtieth Movement, a nationwide expression of anti-foreign sentiment that resulted from a clash between Chinese students and British police in the International Settlement at Shanghai. Under the leadership of the Kuomintang, students in Taiyuan not only demonstrated against imperialism but likewise attacked Yen Hsi-shan, who quickly granted their demands for lower taxes and more freedom because he feared that otherwise they would go over to Feng Yü-hsiang.[8] This so encouraged the Kuomintang that it stepped up its organizing activities and in December 1926 convened a provincial party congress (ch'uan-sheng tai-piao ta-hui), made up of rep-

[5] Grover Clark, In Perspective (China 1927) (Peking, 1927), pp. 35-41, and Wen Kung-chih, op.cit., p. 131.
[6] Leon Wieger, Chine Moderne, VIII, p. 35.
[7] Hsueh Ch'in, "Tang-shih hui-i" ("Reflections about the Party"), p. 4, CCCK.
[8] Nym Wales, op.cit., p. 144.

resentatives from all parts of Shansi, which in turn created a permanent party headquarters; nevertheless, the authorities continued to regard party members as subversives and generally they were obliged to meet and act clandestinely in order to escape arrest.[9]

This situation changed radically in the spring of 1927 after additional Kuomintang victories virtually destroyed the power of Wu P'ei-fu and gave the National Government at Hankow at least nominal control over much of China. In an effort to secure Yen's assistance against this new enemy, Chang Tso-lin offered him a high command in his Peace Preservation Army (*Ankuochün*), while at the same time emissaries from the Kuomintang also came to Taiyuan to solicit Yen's support for their own cause. Inasmuch as both sides appeared to be equally powerful, Yen was unwilling to antagonize either one and for this reason feigned illness in order to avoid meeting their representatives.[10] He was impressed by the strength of the Kuomintang armies, however, and was under considerable pressure to join forces with them, primarily because Feng Yü-hsiang had reassumed command of the Kuominchün and declared in favor of the Kuomintang but also on account of the large number of young people in Shansi, including many of his own subordinates, who sympathized with the anti-imperialist objectives of the Kuomintang.[11] On the other hand, he was frightened profoundly by the radicalism of the Hankow government, which was attempting to extend its authority into Shansi, where it enjoyed much support among left-wing students opposed to Yen's regime.[12] The most important of these students were Wang Ying, P'eng Chen, and Po I-po, two of whom were destined to figure prominently in the Communist movement in China. Under their leadership, students reputed to be sympathetic to the aims of the Chinese Communist Party

[9] Anonymous, *Shan-hsi ch'ing-tang ch'ien-hou chi-lüeh* (*A Brief Description of Events Leading up to and Following the 'Party Purification Movement' in Shansi*) (date and place of publication unknown), pp. 1-3. I am grateful to Professor John Israel of Clermont College for calling my attention to this manuscript.

[10] *I-shih pao*, March 31, 1927, as quoted in *Archives*, March 1927, p. 414.

[11] Anatol Kotenev, *New Lamps for Old* (Shanghai, 1931), pp. 277, 317, and *NCH*, Oct. 8, 1927, 48:2.

[12] *Huang-pao*, June 10, 1927, *Ch'en-pao*, June 16, 20, 1927, as quoted in *Archives*, pp. 122, 198, and 255-256, respectively.

came to dominate the Taiyuan Municipal Labor Union (*T'ai-yüan shih kung-hui*) and engaged in a fierce struggle with anti-Communists for control of the local Kuomintang. On at least one occasion this conflict provoked a wild riot that lasted for three days and ended only after the police intervened on behalf of the anti-Communists.[13] Since radicals within the Kuomintang frequently attacked provincial officials as well,[14] their behavior must have terrified Yen Hsi-shan, who lived in fear of a popular uprising against his regime. This is why he was overjoyed when Chiang Kai-shek withdrew from the Hankow Government on the grounds that it was being taken over by the Communists and established a new anti-Communist National Government at Nanking. Perhaps at Yen's behest, Feng Yü-hsiang joined him in supporting the Nanking Government, with the result that the Hankow regime was obliged to surrender to Chiang Kai-shek and purge itself of Communists. Meanwhile, in Shansi, Communist-inclined students were expelled from the local Kuomintang and either arrested by Yen's police or else compelled to leave the province.[15] These events must have dissipated much of Yen's animosity toward the Kuomintang because in June he raised its flag and accepted from the National Government an appointment as Commander in Chief of the Northern Route Revolutionary Army (*ke-ming chün pei-lu tsung-szu-ling*).[16]

By going over to the Kuomintang Yen endeared himself to students and other young people in Shansi;[17] however, his decision aroused much less enthusiasm among his older followers. Many were urging him to side with Chang Tso-lin,[18] and there circulated rumors to the effect that one of the most influential men in his regime, Nan P'ei-lan, was preparing to resign in protest against the alliance with the Kuomintang.[19] Perhaps opposition from conservatives explains why he was obliged to coerce shopkeepers and others into displaying

[13] Anonymous, *op.cit.*, pp. 1-4.

[14] Jen Ying-lun and Kuo Chien-fu, *op.cit.*, p. 3, *CCCK*.

[15] "Party Purification in Shansi," p. 3, and *I-shih pao*, Sept. 20, 1927, as quoted in *Archives*, Sept. 1927, p. 254.

[16] *Ch'en-pao*, June 8, 1927, as quoted in *Archives*, June 1927, p. 86.

[17] *Ch'en-pao*, June 10, 1927, as quoted in *Archives*, June 1927, pp. 124-127.

[18] *I-shih pao*, Oct. 2, 1927, as quoted in *Archives*, Oct. 1927, p. 24.

[19] *I-shih pao*, Sept. 23, 1927, as quoted in *Archives*, Sept. 1927, pp. 295-296.

Kuomintang flags and portraits of Sun Yat-sen.[20] Since he also permitted students belonging to the Kuomintang to oust and mistreat the members of the provincial assembly,[21] whose chairman was the leading spokesman of the gentry,[22] it would seem that his new enthusiasm for the Kuomintang caused him to break with some of the more conservative elements in his regime. He continued, however, to employ as his principal subordinates men who had been his trusted lieutenants for many years, and the changes he introduced as a result of the alliance with the Kuomintang amounted to little more than *i-chih kai-ming*—"raising the flag and altering the names"—i.e. he simply abolished the titles and other appellations formerly used in his army and the provincial government and replaced them with a nomenclature more in keeping with the revolutionary pretensions of the Kuomintang.[23] Nor did he alter immediately his policy with respect to Chang Tso-lin. Instead of attacking the Manchurian forces stationed in neighboring Hopei and Chahar, he tried to effect a reconciliation between Chang and Chiang Kai-shek, chiefly in order to forestall an invasion of Shansi by Chang's powerful armies, but also because the complete defeat of either side would leave Shansi at the mercy of the victor.[24] Chang Tso-lin rejected Chiang Kai-shek's terms, however, and mounted a counteroffensive in the hope of overwhelming the momentarily inactive Kuomintang armies before Chiang succeeded in reuniting them under his own command and was able to initiate a new drive toward Peking. As part of this strategy he sent troops southward along the Peking-Hankow Railroad with the intention of attacking Kuomintang forces in Honan and Hopei, only to have their advance stalled by units of the Shansi Army, which had occupied the important rail junction Shihchiachung. When Yen's soldiers also crossed the border into Chahar in order to prevent the Manchurian armies from using the Peking-Suiyuan Railroad, Chang ar-

[20] *Ch'en-pao*, June 10, 1927, as quoted in *Archives*, June 1927, p. 128.

[21] See *ibid.*, p. 127, and Hsüeh Ch'in, *op.cit.*, p. 5.

[22] *Fairfield*, p. 4.

[23] *Ch'en-pao*, June 14, 1927, as quoted in *Archives*, June 1927, pp. 165, 170-171.

[24] *CWR*, June 18, 1927, pp. 70-71, *Chiao-t'ung jih-pao* (*Communications Daily*), July 2, 1927, as quoted in *Archives*, July 1927, pp. 21-22, and *I-shih pao*, Sept. 16, 1927, as quoted in *Archives*, Sept. 1927, p. 201.

rested the representatives Yen had sent to Peking and vowed that he would invade Shansi and drive Yen from power. In the fighting that followed the ill-trained and outnumbered Shansi Army suffered one defeat after another and probably was saved from destruction only by timely action on the part of the Kuominchün, which advanced into Hopei and frightened Chang Tso-lin into abandoning his plans for an invasion of Shansi.[25]

In spite of their poor showing against the Manchurians during the fall of 1926, Yen's soldiers played an important role in the campaign that followed the reunification of the Kuomintang under Chiang Kai-shek and which finally delivered Peking into the hands of the Kuomintang in the summer of 1928. While Chiang invaded Shantung and the Kwangsi Army, commanded by Li Tsung-jen, marched north along another route, Yen and Feng Yü-hsiang advanced toward Peking from the west across Chahar and Hopei, with the result that when the Japanese turned back Chiang Kai-shek's army at Tsinan in Shantung the race to take Peking turned into a contest between Yen's forces and the Kuominchün. At the urging of the Japanese, as well as many of his own supporters, Chang Tso-lin decided to withdraw from North China, but it would appear that because he feared and distrusted Yen less than Feng he ordered his commanders to resist stubbornly the advance of the Kuominchün while at the same time giving way before Yen's troops.[26] On June 3 he departed for Manchuria, only to die from the effects of an explosion that wrecked his train as it was entering the city of Mukden early in the morning of June 4. His son, Chang Hsüeh-liang, inherited his authority over Manchuria but recalled all of the Manchurian troops remaining in North China and subsequently raised the Kuomintang flag and accepted from Chiang Kai-shek an appointment as governor-general of Manchuria. According to a Japanese writer, while the Manchurian forces were in the process of evacuating Peking the general commanding the Japanese forces stationed at Tientsin

[25] J. C. H. Lynn, *op.cit.*, p. 215 and *NCH*, Dec. 3, 1927, 397:1.
[26] Anatol Kotenev, *op.cit.*, p. 333, and Williamson, *Letter*, p. 2. On June 11, 1957, Yen Hsi-shan told me that early in 1928 he was approached by a man purporting to be a Manchurian agent, who told him that if the Shansi Army advanced toward Peking, Chang Tso-lin's soldiers would fall back after offering merely token resistance.

warned Feng Yü-hsiang against trying to occupy the old capital and invited Yen to take possession of Peking.[27] Whereas Feng was an outspoken enemy of the Japanese and therefore an obvious threat to their interests in Manchuria and North China, during the summer of 1927 Yen had suppressed anti-Japanese demonstrations in Shansi,[28] although he joined with the demonstrators in denouncing Japan for sending additional troops into Shantung.[29] At any rate, Yen's army was the first to enter Peking and if this happened because the Japanese intervened on his behalf, they must have acted with the approval of Chiang Kai-shek, who already had appointed Yen commander of the Nationalist garrisons in Peking and Tientsin, apparently in order to prevent control of those cities from falling into the hands of Feng Yü-hsiang.[30] Yen's subsequent election to membership in the People's Political Council and the Central Executive Committee of the Kuomintang and his elevation to the posts of Minister of the Interior and vice-chairman of the all-important Military Affairs Commission in the National Government were a tacit admission on the part of Chiang Kai-shek that Yen now shared with Feng Yü-hsiang the mastery of North China.

Yen's success, however, must be measured against the disasters that overtook his subjects as a result of these campaigns. Much of Shansi was devastated by invading armies, while throughout the province banditry flourished, owing to the presence of so many disbanded and ill-disciplined soldiers.[31] In an effort to increase the size of his army as quickly as possible, Yen recruited into its ranks well over one hundred thousand additional men, many of them bandits from neighboring provinces, whom his officers found it impossible to indoctrinate or control.[32] For example, soldiers quartered on the premises of the new petroleum refinery damaged its

[27] Maruyama Shizuo, *Ushinawaretaru kiroku* (*The Story of Defeat*) (Tokyo, 1950), p. 171.
[28] *Huang-pao*, July 25, 1927, as quoted in *Archives*, July 1927, pp. 330-331.
[29] *Ch'en-pao*, June 20, 1927, as quoted in *Archives*, June 1927, p. 272.
[30] *Williamson*, p. 1, and Harley F. MacNair, *China in Revolution* (Chicago, 1931), p. 135.
[31] *Lectures*, III-B, pp. 182, 185 (Sept. 1928), and *NCH*, Dec. 3, 1927, 397:1-2, and Nov. 24, 1928, 297:3.
[32] *NCH*, May 15, 1926, 292:5, and March 17, 1928, 423:4.

machinery so badly that the refinery was obliged to shut down.[33] Perhaps for the same reason, the output of iron in Shansi after 1928 declined by more than 25 percent.[34]

By then, however, Yen was preoccupied completely with his army and the struggle for power in North China, which meant that matters affecting the economy or involving the civilian population were left to local officials, who generally did not share his enthusiasm for reform and modernization.[35] Their indifference explains why the "peoples' schools" began closing their doors for lack of funds, although Yen must share the blame for the deterioration of his school system, inasmuch as he diverted to the army much of the money earmarked for the schools and encouraged his officials to embezzle the rest by reducing their already inadequate salaries. He was compelled to do this because the cost of equipping and otherwise maintaining not only his own vastly enlarged army but also much of the Kuominchün threatened to bankrupt his regime. In 1928 the expenses of the provincial government were 350 percent greater than in 1925, with the result that between those years its annual deficit soared from CH$685,571 to CH$13,647,000, notwithstanding the fact that after 1925 Yen imposed a multitude of new taxes which caused the income of his government to more than double by 1928.[36] Since he attempted to overcome this deficit by printing unbacked paper currency,[37] his subjects suffered from the effects of rampant inflation, as well as the exorbitant taxes, and this may account for the reoccurrence of famine in Shansi beginning in 1929.[38]

A Period of Rebellion

The uneasy alliance between Feng Yü-hsiang and Chiang Kai-shek broke down in the summer of 1929. When the Japanese finally retired from Shantung, Feng prepared to occupy the northern half of that province, only to be stymied by Chiang, who moved his own troops in first. Feng retaliated

---

[33] *Shansi Report*, p. 169.   [34] See *ibid.*, p. 53.

[35] Wang Ch'ien, *op.cit.*, p. 17a, and Arthur Holcombe, *The Chinese Revolution* (Harvard, 1930), p. 25.

[36] Ch'i T'ien-yü, "I-nien-lai Shan-hsi chih ts'ai-cheng," ("Fiscal Administration in Shansi during the Past Year"), pp. 2, 8, *CCCK*.

[37] *NCH*, March 20, 1926, 519:5, and Oct. 30, 1926, 206:3.

[38] Tuan Liang-ch'en, "I-nien-lai chih Shan-hsi ching-chi," ("The Economy of Shansi during the Past Year"), p. 7, *CCCK*.

by mobilizing his forces and had them take up positions along the border between Shantung and Hopei, while at the same time he denounced Chiang for filling the National Government with his own supporters and accused him of aspiring to be a dictator.[39] Chiang, in turn, bribed two of Feng's commanders into defecting from the Kuominchün, and Feng conceded defeat by giving up his command with the avowed intention of going abroad; however, this merely encouraged Chiang to mount an offensive against the Kuominchün, which he undoubtedly hoped would destroy once and for all Feng's power in North China. At this point Yen intervened on Feng's behalf by publicly announcing that if Feng left China he would insist on accompanying him. "Together we will see the world, hand in hand," he told Feng.[40] His purpose was to warn Chiang Kai-shek that in order to destroy the Kuominchün he must defeat Yen's forces as well. Upon learning that Yen had declared his solidarity with Feng, Chiang hurried to Peking, now renamed Peiping, and after conversing with Yen not only called off his offensive against the Kuominchün but likewise allowed Feng to reassume command of his army and even gave him money to pay his troops. During the months that followed, both sides prepared for war, although in a vain effort to break up the alliance against him Chiang appointed Yen deputy commander in chief of the Kuomintang armies. Yen accepted the post but nevertheless in the winter of 1930 demanded that Chiang resign from the government and when this demand was ignored ordered his forces to attack Chiang's troops in Shantung and Honan. On April 1 he expelled Chiang's representatives from Peiping, reiterated Feng's charges against Chiang, and proclaimed himself commander in chief of the armies opposing the Nanking regime, with Feng and Li Tsung-jen as his principal subordinates.[41]

Yen came to the aid of the Kuominchün chiefly because he perceived that if he allowed Chiang Kai-shek to destroy Feng

[39] *NCH*, May 25, 1929, 294:2.
[40] *CWR*, June 8, 1929, p. 52.
[41] Nihon Kokusai Seiji Gakkai Taiheiyō Sensō Gen'in Kenkyūbu (The Japan Association of International Relations, the Committee to Study the Origins of the Pacific War), ed., *Taiheiyō sensō no michi: kaisen gaikō-shi* (*The Road to the Pacific War: A Diplomatic History before the War*) (Tokyo, 1962-1963), Vol. II, *Manshū jihen* (*The Manchurian Incident*), hereafter referred to as *Manshū jihen*, p. 243.

Yü-hsiang's army he would be isolated and helpless to resist subsequent demands that he share with Nanking his authority in Shansi and other parts of North China.[42] Statements made by a writer loyal to Yen suggest that under the guise of expelling Communists, Kuomintang leaders in Shansi also ousted from their party members whose sympathies lay with Yen Hsi-shan in his fight to prevent the Nanking government from extending its authority into Shansi.[43] This may be the reason that after breaking with the Nanking regime in 1930 Yen suppressed the Kuomintang in Shansi,[44] even while professing to champion the rights of Kuomintang members everywhere against Chiang Kai-shek, whom he accused of betraying Sun Yat-sen's principles.[45] Then too, he probably feared losing control of the Peiping-Tientsin area, since he urgently needed additional territory in order to acquire more revenue for the support of his armies, as well as commands for his generals and lucrative jobs for the unemployed graduates of his new schools.[46] His efforts to integrate closely the economies of Shansi and Hopei[47] indicate that he regarded his new possessions as a part of his personal empire and intended to retain them indefinitely. Certainly his commanders must have looked forward to enjoying a long sojourn in Peiping because one of them built there a fine residence he initially had contemplated erecting in Taiyuan.[48] Perhaps, as several writers imply, Yen's appetite for national power was whetted by Feng Yü-hsiang,[49] whom he later denounced for having "tricked" him into opposing the National Government.[50] According to a foreigner who lived in Peiping during its occupation by the Shansi Army, Yen also feared that unless he wrested from Nanking

---

[42] Ch'ien Tuan-sheng, *op.cit.*, p. 102, and *Fairfield*, p. 2.

[43] Jen Ying-lun and Kuo Chien-fu, *op.cit.*, p. 3.

[44] Anonymous, *Shan-hsi ch'ing-tang ch'ien-hou chi-lüeh*, p. 5.

[45] *Manshū jihen*, p. 244.

[46] *NCH*, May 15, 1926, 292:4-5, and Oct. 23, 1926, 156:5.

[47] Shiyro-ka, Somu-bu, Minami Manshū Kabushiki Kai Sha (Research Section, General Affairs Department, South Manchurian Railroad Company), comp. *Hoku shi jijō sōran* (*A General Survey of Conditions in North China*) (Hsinking, 1935), hereafter referred to as *SMR Survey*, p. 236.

[48] Chao Shu-li, *op.cit.*, p. 22.

[49] Leon Wieger, *Chine Moderne*, Vol. IX, p. 17, and Hatano Ken'ichi, *Gendai Shina no seiji to jimbutsu* (*Politics and Outstanding Men in Contemporary China*) (Tokyo, 1937), p. 117.

[50] Interview with *Yen Hsi-shan*, Taipei, Taiwan, on June 11, 1957.

the leadership of the nation and prevented Chiang from setting himself up as the sole spokesman of Chinese nationalism the youth of Shansi would desert to the Kuomintang.[51] This may be why he attacked the Nanking government for failing to get rid of the unequal treaties,[52] although his own relationship with the Japanese inspired rumors that Japan was supplying him with arms and money.[53] On the other hand, Yen and his allies benefited enormously from popular discontent aroused by the behavior of the southern carpetbaggers whom Chiang invariably sent to represent his regime in the North. This caused Japanese writers to describe the fighting that followed as "the great war between North and South."[54]

While the armies of Feng and Chiang Kai-shek fought a savage war of attrition in Honan, Yen's soldiers advanced virtually unopposed into Shantung, where they occupied the provincial capital and threatened to outflank Chiang's entire force. These early victories encouraged Yen to go ahead with his plans for the creation of a new national government. Among those invited to take part in this government were Wang Ching-wei, the leader of the dissatisfied left wing of the Kuomintang, several members of the equally dissatisfied right wing of Chiang Kai-shek's party, and disgruntled militarists like Li Tsung-jen and Tuan Ch'i-jui. Inspired by a common fear of Chiang Kai-shek, these men put aside their differences and came together in the Enlarged Party Conference (*hung-ta tang hui-i*) to draft a constitution for the new regime. Their deliberations were interrupted, however, by the news that Chiang Kai-shek had attacked and virtually annihilated Yen's

[51] Interview with *Henri Vetch*, a former resident of Peiping, in Hong Kong on March 31, 1958.

[52] *Manshū jihen*, p. 243.

[53] Hallet Abend, *My Life in China: 1926-1941* (New York, 1943), p. 95, and Israel Epstein, *The Unfinished Revolution in China* (Boston, 1947), pp. 67, 72. These rumors were widely believed to be true; however, an exhaustive investigation has failed to reveal any evidence which substantiates them. On the contrary, as late as May 24, 1930, the Japanese Consul-General in China had no knowledge of any Japanese assistance to Yen and very much doubted if such aid really was being extended. See Nishida's letter to Shidehara in the Gaimushō or "Foreign Office" file entitled *Honpō no chihō-seifu oyobi kojin ni taisuru shakkan kankei zakken: Sensei oyobi Kyosei sho no bu, ji Shōwa go-nen gogatsu shido roku-nen gogatsu* (*Miscellaneous Matters Relating to Our Country's Loans to Local Governments and Individuals: Section on Shansi and Shensi Provinces, May, 1930 to May, 1931*) (Tokyo, 1931).

[54] *Manshū jihen*, p. 245.

forces in Shantung. In addition to being so large that he was unable to keep it adequately supplied, by this time Yen's army consisted for the most part of hastily trained militiamen and ex-bandits whose knowledge of modern warfare must have been extremely limited since many were unfamiliar with shrapnel and upon encountering it concluded that their enemies had developed a completely new weapon.[55] A foreigner who saw Yen's soldiers in action called them a horde of "ill-fed, unpaid, and half-equipped bumpkins who haven't the slightest idea of warfare and don't want to learn."[56] Small wonder that when attacked by Chiang Kai-shek's troops most of them dropped their weapons and fled in terror.[57] After routing them, Chiang attacked the Kuominchün along its left flank, as well as from the front, and drove it northward in the direction of Shansi.

Yen and his allies endeavored to save themselves by securing assistance from the Manchurians and for this reason invited the "Young Marshal" of Manchuria, Chang Hsüeh-liang, to become a member of their new government. This government came into existence early in September, only to be dissolved a month later after Chang sided with Chiang Kai-shek and threatened to send troops into Hopei if Yen and Feng continued to resist the Nanking government. Besides needing Chiang Kai-shek's support against Russian intrigue and Japanese imperialism in Manchuria, Chang Hsüeh-liang disliked and distrusted his father's old enemy, Feng Yü-hsiang,[58] and was anxious to use intervention on behalf of the Nanking regime as a pretext for reasserting Manchurian control over North China.[59] According to the Japanese, in return for Chang's aid Chiang offered to let the Young Marshal rule everything north of the Yellow River and promised to set aside for his followers at least four cabinet posts in the National Government.[60] Chang's apparent desire for greater influence in the Nanking regime indicates that he was swayed as well by his Australian advisor, William Henry Donald, who regarded Yen as a reactionary and hoped that after helping Chiang Kai-shek defeat him Chang could persuade Chiang to

---

[55] *Ch'en-pao*, Aug. 16, 1927, as quoted in *Archives*, Aug. 1927, pp. 220-222, Chao Shu-li, *op.cit.*, p. 25, and *CWR*, July 5, 1930, p. 129.

[56] *CWR*, July 5, 1930, p. 129. [57] *CYB*, 1931.

[58] Johnson to Stimson, Oct. 13, 1930, *Papers Relating to the Foreign Relations of the United States*, 1930, II (Washington, 1945), p. 39.

[59] *Manshū jihen*, p. 244. [60] See *ibid.*, p. 245.

pursue more liberal policies.[61] Finally, Chiang gave Chang Hsüeh-liang CH$10 million,[62] whereas the notoriously tight-fisted Yen offered him a much smaller sum.[63]

Upon receiving Chang's ultimatum Yen resigned from the new government, withdrew what was left of his army into Shansi, and threw himself on the mercy of Chang Hsüeh-liang by asking the Young Marshal to intercede on his behalf with the Nanking government. This time he did not allow the bulk of Feng Yü-hsiang's troops to take refuge in Shansi, with the result that the Kuominchün suffered one defeat after another and finally surrendered en masse to Chiang Kai-shek. The struggle was over, but not before more than one hundred thousand men had died[64] in what an American reporter has called "one of the bloodiest and most costly civil wars in the history of the Chinese Republic."[65]

Yen was defeated by Chiang Kai-shek not only on account of the inferior training and morale of his troops but also because Shansi and the other parts of North China that had fallen into his hands were too underdeveloped to support a force capable of resisting the well-equipped armies at the disposal of Nanking. This is why he found it difficult to pay the foreign concerns which were supplying him with weapons and other war material.[66] In a desperate effort to raise additional revenue, he levied still heavier taxes and began collecting the land tax three years in advance.[67] Persons who were unwilling or not able to meet these new demands were imprisoned until their relatives paid their taxes for them. The authorities used the same tactics to coerce the rich into purchasing vast quantities of worthless government securities.[68] Nevertheless, the government collected much less than it spent and Yen continued to issue unbacked paper currency in order

[61] Earl Selle, *Donald of China* (New York, 1948), pp. 263-264.

[62] *Manshū jihen*, p. 245.

[63] Interview with Wang Huai-i in Taipei, Taiwan, June 11, 1957. According to Carsun Chang, it was common knowledge that Chang Hsüeh-liang was an inveterate gambler. Chiang Kai-shek gave each of his representatives a checkbook and told them to play mah-jongg with Chang until he came over to Nanking's side. See Carsun Chang, *The Third Force in China* (New York, 1952), p. 92.

[64] *Manshū jihen*, p. 245.   [65] Hallet Abend, *op.cit.*, p. 117.

[66] *CWR*, June 21, 1930, p. 92.

[67] Anonymous, "Plight of the Shansi Peasantry," *PT*, Jan. 16, 1932, p. 135.

[68] Yen Ching-yüeh, *op.cit.*, p. 538.

to balance the provincial budget. By the summer of 1930 his money was worth less than half of its original value,[69] and prices in Shansi were so high that much of the population could not afford to buy food.[70] Food had become increasingly expensive as agricultural output dwindled, owing in part to a prolonged famine but likewise because the countryside swarmed with bandits, who treated the peasants so cruelly that many of them abandoned their farms and took refuge in the cities.[71] One writer says that at least half of Yen's subjects were reduced to eating grass and bark.[72] Meanwhile, bankers, merchants, and craftsmen went out of business, first by the hundreds and then by the thousands, after Yen's defeat at the hands of Chiang Kai-shek caused popular confidence in his currency to evaporate completely.[73] By November teachers, policemen, and other civil servants were clamoring for higher salaries and threatening to strike unless their income kept pace with the soaring cost of living. Some of their anger was directed at the assistant manager and other executives of the semiofficial Provincial Bank of Shansi, who had provoked additional inflation by speculating in scarce commodities.[74] Yen punished these men for their disloyalty to his regime; however, in most instances he allowed his officials to do as they pleased, so long as they succeeded in raising the enormous sums he demanded from them,[75] and in the absence of his continual prodding and supervision civil government in Shansi quickly disintegrated. For example, because of connivance on the part of officials, including those having the highest rank, the drug traffic flourished, with the result that addiction became widespread in the army and so prevalent in the countryside that in at least one village well over a sixth of the inhabitants were habitual users of narcotics.[76] Instead of attempting to correct this situation, Yen imposed heavy

[69] *CWR*, June 21, 1930, p. 92.

[70] Ch'u Chih-sheng, *op.cit.*, p. 2, and Yen Ching-yüeh, *op.cit.*, pp. 538-539.

[71] Wang Ch'ien, *op.cit.*, p. 17a, and Yen Ching-yüeh, *op.cit.*, p. 538.

[72] Tuan Liang-ch'en, *op.cit.*, p. 7.

[73] Yen Ching-yüeh, *op.cit.*, p. 538, and *I-shih pao*, Nov. 5, 1930, as quoted in *Archives*, Nov. 1930, p. 67.

[74] *Hua-pei jih-pao*, Dec. 5, 1930, as quoted in *Archives*, Dec. 1930, p. 200.

[75] Yen Ching-yüeh, *op.cit.*, p. 538.

[76] See *ibid.*, p. 539, "Plight of the Shansi Peasantry," p. 135, and Chao Shu-li, *op.cit.*, pp. 27, 29, 30.

taxes on the consumption of narcotics and began peddling his own drugs under the guise of selling medicine to addicts.[77] "The province is rapidly going back to its conditions of twenty years ago," concluded the writer of an article on drug addiction in Shansi.[78] His comment is an appropriate epitaph for virtually all of the reforms and achievements which had caused many to call Yen's domain the Model Province.

[77] Anonymous, *op.cit.*, p. 135.   [78] *CYB*, *1931*, p. 598.

CHAPTER EIGHT

A PERIOD OF STRIFE

Yen Goes into Exile

YEN UNDOUBTEDLY HOPED that the withdrawal of his army from the Peking-Tientsin area would mollify the Nanking government and dissuade Chiang Kai-shek from invading Shansi. Yet, although the Kuomintang armies remained outside the Model Province, Chiang's bombing planes repeatedly raided Taiyuan and other cities in Shansi, where they did much damage and aroused considerable hysteria among the inhabitants.[1] Consequently, even Yen's closest followers urged him to leave Shansi in the hope that his departure would persuade Chiang to end the air raids and forestall an invasion by the victorious Kuomintang forces.[2] On November 4 Yen complied to the extent of resigning from the provincial government, on the grounds that he was suffering from ulcers; however, he merely retired to his native village and from there continued to govern Shansi while his emissaries conferred with Chang Hsüeh-liang at the latter's headquarters in Manchuria. Chang was unwilling to let Chiang Kai-shek extend his authority into North China by invading and occupying Shansi, and his attitude, together with Japanese intervention

[1] *Ta Kung Pao*, Nov. 22, 1930, as quoted in *Archives*, Nov. 1930, p. 358. These raids against Taiyuan and other cities may be the first instances in which airplanes were used in China to terrify and demoralize the civilian population. For an especially vivid description of the hysteria provoked in Taiyuan by Chiang's bombers see Chao Shu-li, *op.cit.*, pp. 34, 36. The whole subject of the impact of the airplane on the military and political history of modern China merits special attention. Because of his superior financial resources Chiang Kai-shek was able to buy warplanes on a scale beyond the reach of his rivals, with the result that he enjoyed an enormous advantage over them, since in addition to being useful in battle, airplanes also were symbols of power and prestige whose very presence often was enough to overawe an enemy army. According to the daughter of an official close to Yen in 1930, Yen was stunned and dismayed by the discovery that his mountainous and formerly impregnable province was vulnerable to attack by Chiang Kai-shek's aircraft. (Interview with Miss Wang Huai-i, Taipei, Taiwan, Jan. 13, 1957.)

[2] For example, on Oct. 11 representatives of the provincial gentry urged Yen to retire from public life for the sake of the province. See *I-shih pao*, Oct. 13, 1930, as quoted in *Archives*, Oct. 1930, p. 137.

on Yen's behalf, explains in large part why Chiang permitted Yen's subordinates to retain control of Shansi, provided that Yen himself left the province immediately.[3] Besides responding to pressure from Chang and the Japanese, Chiang Kai-shek may have feared that if he demolished the power structure already existing in Shansi, the instability that resulted might create a situation in that province favorable to the growth of radicalism and communism. By 1930 Yen was a person of such importance in Shansi and so indispensable that in the absence of his influence the machinery of government was likely to disintegrate as various army commanders in the province struggled with each other to fill the vacuum left by the collapse of his power.[4]

For these reasons, the Nanking government appointed Shansi's new rulers from among Yen's own adherents. Authority over what remained of his army was given to two of his veteran commanders, Hsü Yung-ch'ang and Fu Tso-i, while Shang Chen succeeded Yen as chairman of the provincial government. Unlike most of Yen's officers, Shang Chen was not a native of Shansi and had entered Yen's service late in life, which may explain why he risked Yen's anger by opposing the war against the Kuomintang.[5] As a general in the Shansi Army but at the same time a Kuomintang sympathizer, Shang Chen must have been the only person acceptable to both Yen and the Nanking government. After becoming chairman of the provincial government he openly sided with Chiang Kai-shek and accepted an appointment to the Central Executive Committee of the Kuomintang; however, Chiang's triumph in Shansi was more apparent than real, since Shang Chen's authority did not extend beyond Taiyuan, where his power depended on his army and the support he received from the leaders of the provincial Kuomintang. The rest of the province

[3] *Manshū jihen*, p. 245. According to Mr. Uno Shigeaki of the Japanese Foreign Office, who has examined the telegraphic correspondence between Chang Hsüeh-liang and the Nanking government, Chang urged the central government to let Yen remain in Shansi; however, Chiang Kai-shek insisted that Yen leave, perhaps because his departure would create the impression that Chiang had won a decisive victory. (Interview with Mr. *Uno Shigeaki*, Stanford, Nov. 27, 1962).

[4] *Ching Pao*, Nov. 27, 1930, and *Ta Kung Pao*, Nov. 22, 1930, as quoted in *Archives*, Nov. 1930, pp. 358, 327, respectively.

[5] *CWR*, Nov. 29, 1930, p. 463, and the biography of Shang Chen in *Kuomintang Biographies*.

was governed by other generals of the Shansi Army,[6] who probably tolerated Shang Chen's control of the capital only because they hoped that he could secure from the central government money for the payment of their troops as well as the reconstruction of Shansi's shattered economy. Perhaps they followed the advice of Yen's close friend H. H. K'ung, who currently was serving as Minister of Industry in the central government. K'ung lent them his support early in February 1931, when they formally asked Nanking for financial assistance. In his reply Chiang Kai-shek expressed concern about the plight of Shansi's economy but refused to extend aid to the stricken province until Yen's generals reduced drastically the amount of money they were spending for the upkeep of their armies.[7] This provoked another appeal on the part of the Shansi generals, who now spoke in the name of the provincial Kuomintang and pointedly referred to Yen as a "rebel."[8] Shortly after, Shang Chen assumed the chairmanship of the provincial government, which immediately received from the central government a loan of CH$24 million to be used for the purpose of stabilizing the value of Shansi's currency.[9]

In spite of this assistance the provincial government was unable to halt the deterioration of Shansi's economy, owing largely to the voracious demands of the various armies in and around the province. Many of these armies had belonged to the Kuominchün or were made up of ex-bandits whom Yen had recruited from neighboring provinces. Now they threatened to raise havoc in Shansi unless supported by the provincial authorities.[10] Consequently, in 1931 Shang Chen's government was obliged to spend CH$24 million on the armed forces, in addition to another CH$17,750,000 for nonmilitary purposes. Inasmuch as its income that year amounted to less than CH$11 million, it incurred a deficit of CH$30 million,[11] which

[6] *Ta Kung Pao*, Nov. 21, 1930, as quoted in *Archives*, Nov. 1930, p. 291, and the biography of Yen Hsi-shan in *Kuomintang Biographies*.
[7] *Hua-pei jih-pao*, Feb. 2, 1931, as quoted in *Archives*, Feb. 1931, pp. 145-146.
[8] *I-shih pao*, Feb. 12, 1931, as quoted in *Archives*, Feb. 1931, pp. 147-148.
[9] In Feb. 1931 the provincial authorities asked the central government for a loan of CH$24 million and in May urged the government to *reissue* this loan, which indicates that such a loan actually was extended. See *CWR*, Feb. 21, 1931, p. 430, and May 30, 1931, p. 476.
[10] Ch'ü Chih-sheng, *op.cit.*, p. 2, and *CWR*, Feb. 28, 1931, p. 444.
[11] *CWR*, May 30, 1931, p. 459, and *CYB, 1934*, p. 512.

it succeeded in overcoming only because in May and again in June it received from the central government loans totaling more than CH$30 million.[12] Nevertheless, it was unable to do more than make a gesture in the direction of retiring the vast quantities of unbacked paper currency issued by Yen before 1931, with the result that the value of this money continued to decline and prices rose still higher.[13]

Yen Regains His Power

While Shang Chen grappled with the problems afflicting Shansi's economy, Yen remained in Manchuria, where he had fled after finally leaving Shansi in December 1930. He apparently feared death at the hands of assassins in the employ of Chiang Kai-shek, since he journeyed to Tientsin incognito, made his home there in the British and Japanese concessions, and before going to Manchuria demanded that Chang Hsüeh-liang guarantee his personal safety.[14] From his retreat in the city of Dairen he took part in at least two conspiracies aimed at overthrowing Chiang Kai-shek. The first of these involved negotiations with Chiang's enemies at Canton[15] and the second, collaboration with Shih Yü-san, a former general in the Kuominchün, who in August 1931 declared western Hopei independent of the central government. Yen was certain Shih would succeed and returned to Shansi, again traveling incognito, with the intention of reestablishing his authority there.[16] Perhaps Chang Hsüeh-liang encouraged him to go back in the hope that his return would halt the growth of Chiang Kai-shek's influence in Shansi. Probably because he was aware of Yen's complicity in Shih's rebellion, Shang Chen attacked Shih's army in the name of the central government and after defeating it occupied western Hopei. This setback discouraged Yen from openly defying Nanking by making himself head of the provincial government; however, instead of leaving Shansi he retired to his native village where he met with Hsü Yung-

[12] CWR, Aug. 8, 1931, p. 375.

[13] NCH, March 31, 1931, 433:2, and Hua-pei jih-pao, April 2, 1931, as quoted in Archives, April 1931, p. 29.

[14] Hua-pei jih-pao, Dec. 4, 5, 1930, as quoted in Archives, Dec. 1930, pp. 49, 67-68.

[15] NYT, June 10, 1931, 10:5, and Japanese Biographical Survey, 1937, p. 16.

[16] Japanese Biographical Survey, 1937, p. 16, and CWR, Aug. 1, 1931, p. 337, and Aug. 15, 1931, p. 416.

ch'ang and other generals of the Shansi Army. They must have given him their support, for Shang Chen immediately resigned from the provincial government, although his forces remained in control of western Hopei.[17] Owing to a rebellion on the part of his rivals at Canton, Chiang Kai-shek was unwilling to take up arms against the Shansi Army and therefore allowed Hsü Yung-ch'ang to assume the chairmanship of the provincial government in return for a promise that Yen would remain in the background and not reenter public life.[18]

Nanking's failure to resist Japan's occupation of Manchuria in September 1931 provided Yen and his followers with an opportunity for overthrowing the leaders of the provincial Kuomintang, who had set up their own yamen, recruited for themselves a small army of police, and otherwise behaved as if they governed Shansi.[19] Yen benefited from the existence of widespread animosity toward the provincial Kuomintang, especially among the students, on account of the arrogance of its leaders, their refusal to tolerate criticism or opposition, and their exploitation of the local population.[20] On December 18 a large number of students gathered near the party's headquarters in Taiyuan to protest the central government's policy of not fighting the Japanese. This demonstration was supported by the provincial authorities, who may have instigated it,[21] but nevertheless became so violent that frightened party police fired into the crowd.[22] Hsü Yung-ch'ang retaliated by arresting and deporting many of the party's leaders.[23] The rest left voluntarily because this "Massacre of December Eighteenth" outraged local opinion to such an extent that they were in danger of being murdered if they attempted to remain in the province.[24] As a result the Kuomintang ceased to exist in Shansi, except in the form of a dummy organization whose

[17] *CWR*, Aug. 15, 1931, pp. 416-417, *NCH*, Aug. 31, 1931, 218:2, and the biography of Shang Chen in *Kuomintang Biographies*.

[18] *CWR*, Aug. 29, 1931, p. 525.

[19] Li Ch'ang-sheng, "Pen-hui kung-tso chih hui-ku yü chan-wang," ("The Work of Our Association in Retrospect and its Outlook for the Future"), p. 2, *CCCK*.

[20] *Ibid.*

[21] Interview with Professor Claude Buss, formerly an American diplomat in China, Stanford University, April 12, 1963. Professor Buss visited Shansi and spoke to Shang Chen shortly before Shang's resignation.

[22] *NCH*, Dec. 14, 1932, 415:3.

[23] Anonymous, *Shan-hsi ch'ing-tang ch'ien-hou chi-lüeh*, p. 5.

[24] *NCH*, Dec. 14, 1932, 415:3.

members were loyal to Yen Hsi-shan rather than the Nanking government.[25]

Meanwhile, Chiang Kai-shek had been compelled to yield at least nominal control over the central government to a coalition of his rivals from Canton. Although Yen's sympathies lay with Chiang's enemies, he negotiated with both sides and it is not certain whether Chiang or the Canton faction subsequently conferred on him the title of Pacification Commissioner of Taiyuan and Suiyuan (*T'aiyüan Sui ching chu-jen*).[26] As Pacification Commissioner he commanded the armies of Shansi and Suiyuan; in reality, he also gave orders to the men who nominally were in charge of civil affairs in these provinces—Hsü Yung-ch'ang in Shansi and Fu Tso-i in Suiyuan.[27] During the years that followed, Yen resisted tenaciously Chiang Kai-shek's efforts to extend his authority into Shansi. When an exiled leader of the provincial Kuomintang returned to Taiyuan from his refuge in Nanking, for example, he was set upon by a mob of students and almost beaten to death.[28] Moreover, laws promulgated by the central government were not heeded in Shansi,[29] while publications issued under the auspices of Yen's regime repeatedly accused the Kuomintang of being corrupt, dictatorial, and indifferent to the needs of the masses.[30] The attitude of most of Yen's subjects toward his struggle with the central government probably was expressed by persons critical of him, who nevertheless when asked if they preferred to be governed by Chiang Kai-shek replied: "God forbid! We want a Shansi man for Shansi."[31]

[25] "Party Purification in Shansi," p. 5, and Hsüeh Ch'in, *op.cit.*, p. 5.

[26] Even usually well-informed Japanese observers were confused by Yen's maneuvers. One Japanese account has him consorting with the Canton faction. See *Japanese Biographical Survey, 1937*, p. 16. Another maintains that he owed his appointment to Chiang Kai-shek. See Hatano Ken'ichi, *op.cit.*, p. 117. A report in *CWR*, Jan. 2, 1932, p. 138, says that he was in league with the Canton faction.

[27] *NCH*, Dec. 14, 1932, 415:3, and Jan. 10, 1934, 44:3. A foreign reporter who visited Shansi in 1932 when Yen still held only the title of Pacification Commissioner found him living in the provincial governor's mansion. See R. N. Swallow, *op.cit.*, 196:3.

[28] *NCH*, Oct. 4, 1933, 11:2.

[29] Ch'ü Chih-sheng, *op.cit.*, p. 1.

[30] For example, see the articles by P'ing Fan, Jen Ying-lun and Kuo Chien-fu, Li Ch'ang-sheng, and Hsüeh Ch'in in *CCCK*. Perhaps the most outspoken of these attacks on the Kuomintang is the piece written by Hsüeh Ch'in, which is entitled "Tang-shih hui-i" or "Party Matters in Retrospect" and features a drawing of a man weeping bitterly.

[31] *NCH*, Jan. 10, 1934, 44:3.

Yen must have foreseen Chiang Kai-shek's triumph over his rivals within the Kuomintang and lent him support because in March 1932, after regaining control of the central government, Chiang let Yen retain his title of Pacification Commissioner and subsequently appointed him chairman of the central government's Mongolian and Tibetan Affairs Commission. Yen responded by professing loyalty to the central government and in 1933 rejected Feng Yü-hsiang's overtures after Feng momentarily overthrew Nanking's authority in neighboring Chahar. A year later, the Shansi Army actually put down a rebellion against the central government in nearby Ninghsia.[32] Yen probably felt that these uprisings were unlikely to succeed and therefore must be discouraged or suppressed lest Nanking use them as an excuse for sending its own troops into northwest China. Nonetheless, his actions, together with the persuasiveness of H. H. K'ung, caused Chiang Kai-shek to seek a reconciliation. In November 1934 Chiang flew to Taiyuan, where he praised Yen's administration of Shansi and otherwise treated him like a trusted friend and ally.[33] This was tantamount to admitting that Yen remained the undisputed ruler of Shansi and consequently the most important man in northwestern China.

These events illustrate vividly some of the formidable obstacles which Chiang Kai-shek encountered in the course of his efforts to bring all of China under his own domination. Because of the vastly superior resources at his disposal Chiang invariably defeated militarists who challenged his control of the central government, but usually he was obliged to let them retain their regional power and for this reason his military victories did not contribute appreciably to the political unification of China. In addition to fearing that if he tried to destroy a beaten rival other warlords would become alarmed and join forces against him, he also was frustrated by the unwillingness of most Chinese to be governed by anyone from outside their own province. All of this suggests that in spite of the nominal unity which Chiang Kai-shek imposed on the Chinese after 1928, warlordism persisted in much of China throughout the 1930's.

[32] *NCH*, April 11, 1934, 8:4.
[33] *NCH*, Nov. 28, 1934, 328:5, and *CWR*, Dec. 17, 1934, p. 391.

CHAPTER NINE

THE INITIATION OF THE TEN YEAR PLAN

Genesis of the Ten Year Plan

AFTER RETURNING to Shansi and reestablishing his power there, Yen Hsi-shan found himself confronted with problems which, according to the newspaper *I-shih pao*, afflicted not only Shansi but likewise all of China during the 1930's.[1] Most of these problems were an outgrowth of Shansi's exceedingly adverse balance of trade. By 1932, specie was flowing out of Shansi in great quantities, largely in exchange for narcotics and a host of other foreign-made goods, including kerosene, matches, leather products, paper, textiles, and cigarettes. Yen blamed this situation on the world depression, which he said was compelling the more economically advanced nations to dump the surplus products of their factories on markets in underdeveloped countries.[2] As an ever increasing quantity of cheaper and better-made foreign commodities appeared in Shansi, that province's once flourishing handicraft industries collapsed altogether, reducing appreciably the income of the peasants, who had operated such industries. For example, after 1930 the sale of homespun made in Shansi almost stopped, the province's once flourishing candle-making industry was all but destroyed, and the number of families engaged in the manufacture of copper utensils in Tatung fell from 800 to 100.[3] Meanwhile, bumper harvests, together with an influx of foreign cereals, caused the price of farm products to fall by as much as two thirds. This occurred at a time when other prices were rising steeply on account of the collapse of Yen's currency, which by 1932 was worth less than 10 percent of its original value.[4] At the same time, because of the growing

[1] The Tientsin *I-shih-pao* as quoted in *Lectures*, I, p. 467 (Dec. 1934).

[2] *Lectures*, IV, pp. 41, 50 (March 1932 and April 1933), III-A, pp. 330, 333 (Dec. 1932 and May 1933). His opinion was shared by the *NCH*, Oct. 5, 1932, 4:1, and Jan. 10, 1934, 44:1.

[3] *Lectures*, IV, p. 51 (April 1933), *Industrial Gazetteer*, p. 411-szu, and *CEB*, Aug. 3, 1935, pp. 66-67.

[4] Chao Shu-li, *op.cit.*, pp. 8-12, Tuan Liang-ch'en, *op.cit.*, pp. 14-15, and *Industrial Gazetteer*, p. 86-hsin.

scarcity of specie, interest rates also soared, with the result
that instead of borrowing in order to offset the decline in their
purchasing power, most peasants simply stopped buying. Consequently, the depression quickly spread from agriculture to
commerce and industry. Between 1927 and 1935 half of the
pawnshops in rural Shansi went out of business, along with
several textile mills, all of the province's match factories, its
only distillery, and thousands of other commercial and manufacturing enterprises.[5] Within the course of a single year,
nine tenths of the business establishments in Taiyuan failed.[6]
In addition, the output of Shansi's coal mines fell off appreciably and the sale of pins manufactured in Shansi declined by
nearly 50 percent.[7]

The result of all this was that unemployment soon became
the most serious problem confronting Yen and his followers.
By 1934 fully one third of the working force in Taiyuan were
without jobs,[8] while in the countryside there existed an apparently staggering amount of disguised unemployment in the
form of millions of underemployed tenants, agricultural laborers, and landless vagabonds.[9] According to a Japanese writer,
Shansi had become a four-class society, made up of "the
capitalists, the peasantry, the workers, and the unemployed."[10]
In 1933 a writer for the *North China Herald* spoke of widespread and increasing poverty among the mass of Yen's subjects.[11] Two Chinese investigators agree that after 1929 peasants in Shansi often were unable to live off what they grew
on the land and had to borrow in order to survive.[12] "Their

[5] Tuan Liang-ch'en, *op.cit.*, pp. 8-12, *Industrial Gazetteer*, pp. 82-
86-hsin, *Shansi Report*, p. 116, and *NCH*, Jan. 1, 1934, 44:1.
[6] Ch'ü Chih-sheng, *op.cit.*, p. 1. Another writer says that in 1934
two thirds of the commercial enterprises in Shansi went bankrupt. See
Ch'i T'ien-shou, "Lün nung-ts'un hsin-yung ho-tso ch'üan" ("A Discussion of Village Credit Cooperative Certificates"), p. 2, *CCCK*.
[7] *CEB*, Feb. 24, 1934, pp. 118-119, and *Industrial Gazetteer*, p.
548-szu.
[8] Tuan Liang-ch'en, *op.cit.*, p. 23, and Chen Ming-t'ing, "Lün
wu-ch'an cheng-ch'üan" ("A Discussion of Product Certificates"), pp.
2-3, *CCCK*.
[9] *Lectures*, I, pp. 392-393 (Oct. 1935), and Ying Ch'iu, "I-nien-lai
chih ta-shih shu-p'ing" ("A Discussion of Important Events in Shansi
during the Past Year"), p. 31, *CCCK*.
[10] Fukada Yuzō, *op.cit.*, p. 372.
[11] *NCH*, June 12, 1933, 49:2.
[12] Anonymous, "Plight of the Shansi Peasantry," *PT*, Jan. 16, 1932,
p. 135 and Chang Chiao-fu, "Living Conditions of Peasants in Middle
Shansi," *Agrarian China* (Shanghai, 1938), p. 199.

food consists chiefly of the cheapest kinds of grain such as kaoliang and millet flour," says one of these writers. "Even this flour is limited to one meal a day and only given to members of the family doing hard field work."[13] In much of Shansi, young women and girls could be purchased at prices ranging from CH$2 to CH$25 a head.[14] So many impoverished parents killed their female infants at birth that by 1935 women comprised less than 44 percent of the population.

By 1936, when Communist armies invaded Shansi, most of the peasants living in villages near Taiyuan felt that any change would be for the better;[15] however, as early as 1931, before the Communists threatened his power, Yen warned that discontent provoked by massive unemployment was undermining the stability of his regime. The desperate poverty and consequent disorderliness of his subjects explains why the number of crimes committed in Shansi rose significantly during the 1930's. By 1936 there were in Shansi two and a half times as many workhouses as in 1929.[16] Among the more than 30,000 people arrested for crimes in 1934, well over 23,000 had little or no property. In 1935 the warden of a prison in Tatung blamed the economic depression for a twelvefold increase in the population of his prison since 1928.[17] Yen was alarmed especially by the impact of unemployment on the always unruly intelligentsia of Shansi. So many middle school and college graduates were out of work that students took up the cry of "graduate and join the jobless" (*pi-yeh chi shih shih-yeh*), causing Yen to voice the fear that his government would be overthrown unless jobs were found for unemployed intellectuals.[18] There also was much unem-

[13] Chang Chiao-fu, *op.cit.*, p. 201.
[14] "Plight of the Shansi Peasantry," p. 133.
[15] Ch'i Chih-chin, " 'T'u-ti ts'un-yu' hsia chih Chin-pei nung-ts'un" ("Peasant Villages of Northern Shansi under [Yen's] 'All Land to the Village Scheme' "), *KWCP*, March 23, 1936, p. 26. Ch'i was a native of northern Shansi but apparently was attending school in Nanking at the time he wrote this article. His observations were an outgrowth of talks with peasants living in his own village, as well as in neighboring communities. Besides being unusually well informed, he seems to have been very objective, since although he held the rich responsible for the suffering of the peasants, he also was sympathetic to Yen Hsi-shan and afraid of the Communists.
[16] *Industrial Gazetteer*, pp. 696-699-chi.
[17] Anonymous, "Prison Life in Shansi," *China Today*, hereafter referred to as *CT*, April 1935, p. 134.
[18] *Lectures*, VI, p. 125 (Aug. 1935).

ployment and considerable unrest among discharged soldiers and retired officers of the Shansi Army.

These are some of the reasons why beginning in 1932 Yen undertook to modernize the underdeveloped economy of Shansi by carrying out a Provincial Ten Year Plan of Economic Reconstruction (*Shan-hsi sheng-cheng shih-nien chien-she chi-hua*); he also aspired to the power to be gained from control of a fully developed economy. The defeats he suffered at the hands of Chiang Kai-shek in 1930 left him convinced that without economic strength comparable to Chiang's he could not keep his rival's armies out of Shansi. He consequently elected to build heavy industries capable of producing a wide range of modern weapons, including aircraft. At the same time, he dreamed of making Shansi the industrial heart of a vast commercial empire which would take in all of northwestern China and extend as far as Szechwan, on the fringes of Tibet.[19] Shansi was ideally fitted for such a role because of its immense reserves of coal and its proximity to substantial deposits of iron ore, located in neighboring Chahar and Suiyuan. Sparsely populated Suiyuan, with nearly three times as much iron as Shansi, also had unusually fertile soil, which if irrigated adequately would yield more food than Shansi. Therefore, the development of Suiyuan's economy was a primary objective of Yen's Ten Year Plan. "Shansi and Suiyuan are mutually dependent," he claimed, "and would be lost without each other."[20] He began mining Suiyuan's iron, reorganized its finances, and by 1936 had brought under cultivation in western Suiyuan more than 4,000 acres of formerly untilled land.[21] Much of this land was being farmed by ex-soldiers from Shansi, who continued to train under the command of retired army officers and thus formed a kind of army of occupation. All of this caused a visiting reporter to refer to Suiyuan as a "colony" of Shansi.[22]

Yen's experiences in Manchuria after his defeat by Chiang Kai-shek in 1931 were another reason for his subsequent pre-

[19] *Lectures*, IV, p. 41 (March 1932), *CWR*, Dec. 12, 1931, p. 60, *Shansi Report*, pp. 4-5, and the advertisement of the Northwestern Industrial Company opposite page 140 of *Industrial Monthly*.

[20] *Lectures*, III-C, p. 152 (March 1937).

[21] *SMR Survey*, p. 237.

[22] Fan Ch'ang-chiang, "Shan-hsi chi-hsing" ("Recollections of a Trip through Shansi"), *KWCP*, March 29, 1937, p. 26.

occupation with industrializing Shansi. While living in Dairen, he formed a close friendship with Kōmoto Daisaku, a key figure in the Japanese-owned South Manchurian Railroad Company, and after returning to Shansi he employed as an advisor on economic matters a former director of the Peking-Mukden Railroad. On several occasions he praised Japan's economic achievements and held them up as models for China and Shansi.

It appears, however, that his Ten Year Plan was inspired chiefly by the success of Russia's first five year plan. Beginning in 1931 Yen and his supporters again and again lavished praise on the Soviet Union for its spectacular accomplishments in the field of industrial development and repeatedly advocated adopting Russian methods in order to achieve similar results.[23] They were impressed especially by the rapidity with which the Communists were modernizing Russia's formerly backward economy. "The Soviet Union accomplishes in one year what it takes other countries five years to achieve," remarked Yen in 1936.[24] In April 1937 he delivered a speech in which he eulogized the results of Russia's second five year plan and hailed in the most extravagant terms the goals of the third five year plan. Appended to this speech is an elaborate chart contrasting the productivity of the Soviet economy in 1936 with the output of China's economy as a whole and that of Shansi in particular.[25] Much of his admiration for the Soviet Union sprang from a belief that the Communists had succeeded in eradicating unemployment in Russia.[26] Is it possible that whereas in the 1920's Chinese support for the Russian Revolution came largely from radically inclined intellectuals, during the 1930's the spectacle of Soviet Russia forging ahead economically while the economies of other industrialized countries stagnated caused even warlords and other normally anti-Communist Chinese to look toward the U.S.S.R. for a solution to China's economic difficulties? Perhaps this new admiration for the Soviets on the part of Chinese conservatives helped lay a

[23] For example, see *Lectures*, I, p. 27 (March 1931), as well as Li Ch'ang-sheng, "P'o-ch'an te Chung-kuo ching-chi chih ch'u-lu" ("The Way Out for the Bankrupt Chinese Economy"), pp. 4-6, *CCCK*, and Tuan Liang-ch'en, *op.cit.*, p. 23.
[24] *Lectures*, III-A, p. 521 (Sept. 1936).
[25] *Lectures*, IV, pp. 126-136 (April 1937).
[26] *Lectures*, I, p. 359 (June 1938).

foundation for cooperation between Soviet Russia and Chiang
Kai-shek's government after Japan invaded China in 1937.

The Mechanics of the Ten Year Plan

Yen returned from Dairen believing that in the past he had
failed because his various schemes were ill-planned. He now
tried to introduce planning into all phases of economic life
in Shansi. In every village he set up an Economic Reconstruction Committee (*ts'un ching-chi chien-she tung-shih hui*),
made up of prominent villagers who each year drafted an
economic development plan for their own community. District
reconstruction committees used these village plans to formulate
district plans, which in turn were integrated into the provincial
plan by a central reconstruction committee, sitting in Taiyuan.
Thus, planning began at the lowest level and proceeded upward, on the assumption that what resulted would be realistic
and feasible inasmuch as those responsible for planning were
familiar with local conditions and therefore not inclined to set
unattainable goals.[27] On many occasions, Yen warned against
initiating impractical schemes that would squander precious
resources and alienate the public. He emphasized the importance of making a thorough investigation and having reliable
and comprehensive statistical data before undertaking any
project. In addition to creating the Association for the Promotion of Statistical Investigation of the Economies and Societies
of Shansi and Suiyuan (*Chin-Sui she-hui ching-chi tiao-ch'a
t'ung-chi hui*),[28] he also published each year two 400-page
volumes containing statistics on virtually every aspect of life
in Shansi.[29] Furthermore, a number of public and semiofficial
organizations were set up for the purpose of making certain
that plans submitted by the village reconstruction committees
actually were put into effect. These included the Village In-

[27] *Shansi Report*, pp. 20, 321, *Lectures*, III-A, p. 317 (Dec. 1932),
III-B, pp. 219-221 (July 1933), and Ch'ü Chih-sheng, *op.cit.*, p. 4.
[28] Chin-Sui she-hui ching-chi tiao-ch'a t'ung-chi hui (Association
for the Promotion of Statistical Investigation of the Economies and
Societies of Shansi and Suiyuan), pub., *Chin-Sui she-hui ching-chi
tiao-ch'a t'ung-chi she nien-kan* (*Annual of the Association for the
Promotion of Statistical Investigation of the Economies and Societies of
Shansi and Suiyuan*) Dec. 1935, hereafter referred to as *CSSH*.
[29] Shan-hsi sheng cheng-fu (Provincial Government of Shansi), pub.,
Shan-hsi Sheng t'ung-chi nien-chien (*Shansi Statistical Annual*) (Taiyuan, 1935), hereafter referred to as *Statistical Annual*, I, and II.

spection Committees (*ts'un chien-ch'a wei-yuan-hui*), which operated under the supervision of the newly established Provincial Political Planning Committee (*sheng cheng-chih she-chi wei-yuan-hui*) in Taiyuan, and the Shansi People's Political Supervisorial Association (*Shan-hsi min-chung chien-cheng yün-tung hui*). In 1935 there were more than 11,000 village inspection committees, having a total membership of about 46,400.[30] Members of the committees audited village accounts and otherwise scrutinized the behavior of local gentry and officials, whose misdeeds or lack of enthusiasm for economic reconstruction were publicized in the pages of a magazine issued weekly by the Supervisorial Association. By 1935 this periodical, entitled *Supervisorial Weekly* (*Chien-cheng chou-k'an*), had publicly exposed several hundred persons, including twenty district magistrates, the heads of twenty-three district finance bureaus, fifteen tax collectors, the chief of the Military Telegraph Bureau, and the entire municipal government of Taiyuan.[31] Most of the individuals accused had misappropriated public funds or evaded their responsibilities under the Ten Year Plan. Although powerful officials like the chief of the Military Telegraph Bureau often escaped punishment, Yen dismissed from office many of the local officials exposed by the association and in 1935 imprisoned all of the persons involved when the association revealed that many of the officials in charge of building railroads in Shansi were conspiring with dishonest contractors to cheat the provincial government.[32] According to one of its leaders the Supervisorial Association was modeled after the old imperial censorate; however, the association also spent much of its time promoting economic modernization by studying and publicizing economically significant developments that occurred elsewhere in China and abroad.

Two other semiofficial organizations, the Society for National Salvation Through Production (*tsao-ch'an chiu-kuo she*) and the Committee for the Consumption of Locally Made Goods (*fu-yung t'u-huo wei-yuan-hui*), encouraged merchants to stock goods manufactured in Shansi rather than articles

[30] See *ibid.*, I, p. 170.
[31] Li Ch'ang-sheng, "Pen-hui kung-tso chih hui-ku yü ch'an-wang," ("The Work of Our Association in Retrospect and its Possibilities for the Future"), pp. 6-17, *CCCK*.
[32] *NCH*, Sept. 11, 1935, 421:5.

imported from foreign countries. Their activities were supplemented by the provincial government's Bureau of Economic
Controls (*ching-chi t'ung-chih chü*), which attempted to
license imports in such a way as to keep foreign-made commodities out of Shansi. Yen maintained that buying and selling
foreign goods was unpatriotic, that foreigners living in China
demonstrated their patriotism by consuming only products
made in their own countries, and that since the Chinese were
unable to raise tariff barriers against foreign imports, they
must emulate Mohandas Gandhi and his followers by refusing
to use goods manufactured abroad.[33]

Besides trying to prevent his subjects from buying foreign
commodities, he also discouraged the sale of products made
in other parts of China if they competed with goods manufactured in Shansi. As part of this effort, he insisted that employees of the provincial government wear only uniforms made
in Shansi and use for the most part locally manufactured
commodities. He dismissed those who did not, and in order
to make doubly certain that government personnel in Taiyuan
obeyed his directive he paid them a part of their salary in the
form of scrip, which could be exchanged for goods only at the
Shansi Marketing Cooperative for Locally Made Goods (*Shan-
hsi t'u-huo ch'an-hsiao ho-tso shang-hang*). This was a large
and modern department store that Yen built in Taiyuan for
the purpose of selling merchandise turned out in Shansi. He
wanted to secure a monopoly of retail trade in Shansi by
obliging manufacturers to sell all of their wares and farmers
most of their produce through this and other government-
operated stores.[34] One of his supporters admitted that as a
result the merchant class in Shansi would cease to exist but
said that otherwise the destruction of Shansi's industries owing
to foreign competition was inevitable.[35]

The ignorance, inefficiency, conservatism, lethargy, and

[33] *Lectures*, VI, p. 119 (May 1933), III-A, pp. 301, 329-333 (June-
Dec. 1932), and IV, pp. 51-55 (April-May 1933).

[34] *SMR Survey*, p. 238, Chen Han-seng, *op.cit.*, p. 376, Sterling
Fisher, "Shansi Tries Out Radical Reforms," *NYT*, Feb. 2, 1936, 7:6,
Stanton Lautenschlager, *With Chinese Communists* (London, 1941),
p. 23, and Hsin San, "Chen-hsing Shan-hsi shang-yeh ch'u-i" ("My
Humble Opinion about How to Promote Commercial and Industrial
Prosperity in Shansi"), *Industrial Monthly*, pp. 9-10.

[35] Shun Wu, "I-nien-lai Shan-hsi chih chien-she" ("Economic Reconstruction in Shansi during the Past Year"), p. 19, *CCCK*.

short-sightedness of most businessmen in Shansi already have been described. After the advent of the world depression in 1930 reduced appreciably the market for goods manufactured in Shansi by provoking an influx of foreign-made commodities, these vices resulted in the ruin of many privately operated enterprises, including the province's largest flour mill and one of its leading cotton mills.[36] In addition to indulging in sharp practices which had the effect of destroying popular confidence in their products, local businessmen usually marketed their goods in a haphazard fashion, without taking into consideration such things as changes in demand, prices on the world market, the monetary policies of foreign governments, and fluctuations in the value of foreign currencies. They habitually overproduced and often were victimized by speculators having a more sophisticated knowledge of economic conditions.[37]

Private enterprises in Shansi during the 1930's were virtually all small, undercapitalized, and inefficient, while at the same time engaged in savage and mutually ruinous competition with one another.[38] This was especially true with respect to the rich coal fields in eastern Shansi, where ferocious competition between a multitude of small producers drove prices steadily downward. In an effort to reduce their costs, the mines stepped up their output, which, of course, simply caused prices to sink even lower. Since many also were tempted to undercut their competitors by adulterating their coal with grades of lesser quality, coal mined in Shansi acquired an unsavory reputation in much of China. Because the mines likewise competed with each other for the use of carts and boats, moreover, the cost of transporting their coal to market became so prohibitive that often after arriving it failed to earn a profit.[39] The same kind of conditions, together with chronic mismanagement, were characteristic of privately owned iron works, water-control projects, and flour mills.[40] All of this

[36] *Shansi Report*, pp. 122, 126-129.

[37] *Lectures*, IV, pp. 115-116 (July 1936). See also Hsin-san, *op.cit.*, pp. 9-12.

[38] See *Industrial Gazetteer*.

[39] Chang Chih-chieh, "Yang-ch'üan mei-yeh pu chen chih wang-yin yü ch'ao-su ho-tso chih pi-yao" ("The Principal Causes of the Depression Afflicting the Coal Industry in Yang-ch'üan and the Necessity of Speedy Cooperation"), *Industrial Monthly*, pp. 1-4.

[40] *Shansi Report*, pp. 64, 302, and Oliver J. Todd, *op.cit.*, p. 566.

explains why after 1931 Yen set out to create in Shansi an economy like that of the Soviet Union, where all industries were run by the government.[41] Besides fixing prices and standards of quality for goods made in Shansi, he also forced manufacturers to employ modern methods in their shops and factories and compelled many enterprises to merge in order to achieve the economies inherent in large scale production. For example, although they protested loudly, he made all of the privately owned mining companies operating in and around Tatung sell their output through a single, government-managed marketing cooperative.[42] Formation of a government-controlled corporation, the Northwestern Industrial Company (*Hsi-pei shih-yeh kung-szu*), to undertake the development of heavy industry in Shansi was another step in the direction of state socialism. In 1937 Yen bluntly equated economic modernization with government control of commerce and industry.[43] Several observers agree that by that time he owned most of the industries in Shansi and rapidly was monopolizing its commerce.[44]

Yen pursued similar policies with respect to banking. In spite of opposition on the part of private banks and pawnbrokers, the state banks he set up to finance his Ten Year Plan came to dominate the fiscal resources of Shansi.[45] He reorganized the Provincial Bank of Shansi, bringing it completely under his own control, and by 1936 had created three more government-operated banks, the Northern Shansi Salt Industry Bank (*Chin-pei yen-yeh yin-hao*), the Shansi-Suiyuan Railroad Bank (*Chin-Sui t'ieh-lu yin-hao*), and the Western Suiyuan Land Reclamation Bank (*Sui-hsi k'en-yeh yin-hao*). These banks possessed assets worth almost CH$13 million, whereas their largest private competitor had only CH$300,000 and most of the other banks in Shansi less than CH$100,-

---

[41] Tuan Liang-ch'en, *op.cit.*, p. 19, and *Lectures*, IV, p. 104 (Feb. 1936).

[42] Wu Pao-san, "Ch'a-Sui-Chin lü-hsing kuan-kan" ("Observations Made during a Trip through Chahar, Suiyuan, and Shansi"), Part I, *Tu-li p'ing-lün* (*Independent Commentary*), Nov. 10, 1935, hereafter referred to as *Wu Pao-san*, I, p. 18.

[43] *Lectures*, III-C, p. 150 (March 1937).

[44] Chen Han-seng, *op.cit.*, p. 377, and Haldore Hanson, *Humane Endeavour* (New York, 1939), p. 35.

[45] *Industrial Gazetteer*, pp. 5-hsin, 38-39-ping, and *Shansi Report*, pp. 315-321.

000.[46] Another CH$2,294,000 was invested in privately owned pawnshops, but it appears that Yen intended to tax these out of existence and replace them with publicly operated enterprises.[47]

His ruthless determination to place his regime on a sound financial footing also led him to repudiate more than CH$70 million worth of unbacked paper currency issued by his government during its war with Chiang Kai-shek in 1930;[48] however, this measure backfired inasmuch as it had the effect of creating a permanent lack of confidence in Yen's banks and currency. In a desperate effort to reassure the public, he promised that money issued by his banks would not be used to finance military expenditures and would be backed with specie to the extent of 80 percent of its face value. When this failed to bring about monetary stability, he offered to redeem in full every note presented at the Provincial Bank of Shansi in Taiyuan. So many people demanded payment that within less than two days his supply of silver was exhausted and he had to withdraw his offer.[49]

After Communist armies invaded Shansi early in 1936, popular confidence in his currency declined even further, with the result that in the fall of 1936 there occurred in Shansi a serious financial crisis. Thus, monetary instability continued to be one of Yen's worst headaches. Because of it he was unable to expand significantly the supply of money in Shansi, since he dared not issue currency having a value much greater than the limited amount of gold and silver in his banks. He overcame this disadvantage to some extent by debasing most of the copper coins in Shansi and minting several million dollars worth of new ones,[50] but nevertheless it hampered severely his efforts to finance his Ten Year Plan.[51] In 1935, moreover, there appeared in Shansi for the first time a large quantity of banknotes issued by the central government. For several years

[46] *Industrial Gazetteer*, pp. 38-39-ping, 159-hsin, and chart opposite page 156-hsin.

[47] See *ibid.*, pp. 87-88-hsin.

[48] *SMR Survey*, p. 244, and *NCH*, Jan. 10, 1934, 44:1.

[49] Haldore E. Hanson, "Chinese War Lord Dreams of Russia," *CWR*, Feb. 8, 1936, p. 356.

[50] *Lectures*, I, p. 4 (March 1931), and Henry Lieberman, "State Industries of Shansi Grow but Benefit to People is Delayed," *NYT*, Feb. 14, 1947, 14:3.

[51] *Shansi Report*, p. 325.

the postal authorities in Shansi, as well as the management of the recently nationalized Cheng Tai Railroad, had refused to accept Yen's currency, and now he retaliated against the central government by trying to keep its money out of his domain.[52] Following the Communist invasion, however, the value of his currency vis-à-vis notes issued by the central government declined so rapidly that early in 1937 he conceded defeat and stopped printing his own money.

Foreign investment seems to have played an unimportant role in the implementation of Yen's Ten Year Plan. Although there circulated many rumors that the Japanese were putting up much of the money for Yen's scheme, Higuchi Hiromu's scholarly and comprehensive study of Japanese economic policy in China prior to 1938 indicates that Japan's financial stake in Shansi was exceedingly small and consisted largely of investments made before 1930.[53] According to another study published under the auspices of the Japanese-owned South Manchurian Railroad Company, by September 1933 the Japanese had loaned Yen's regime a meager CH$1,106,000.[54] A perusal of the official checklist of documents in the archives of the Japanese Foreign Office (*Gaimushō*) indicates that the Japanese government stopped lending money to Shansi after May 1931.[55] Perhaps, as one scholar suggests, Yen received covert assistance from Japanese financiers who wanted to extend their influence into Shansi but nonetheless were not in sympathy with the Japanese Army's aggressive designs in North China.[56] At least two of Yen's banks maintained branch offices in Tientsin for the purpose of soliciting foreign capital, and a Japanese writer contends that mining operations in and around Tatung were being financed by Japanese entrepreneurs.[57] On the other hand, a usually well-informed and objective investigator says that Yen raised all of the capital for

[52] Li Ch'ang-sheng, *op.cit.*, p. 11, *NCH*, June 27, 1934, 463:3, and Feb. 18, 1936, 477:4, and Haldore Hanson, *op.cit.*, p. 356.

[53] Higuchi Hiromu, *Nippon no tai Shina tōshi kenkyū* (*A Study of Japanese Investments in China*) (Tokyo, 1939).

[54] *SMR Survey*, p. 207 and chart opposite p. 382.

[55] Cecil H. Uyehara, comp., *Checklist of Archives in the Japanese Ministry of Foreign Affairs, Tokyo, Japan, 1868-1945* (Washington, 1954), especially pp. 62, 233.

[56] Interview with Professor James T. C. Liu, Stanford University, Nov. 1, 1962.

[57] Kojima Seiichi, *op.cit.*, pp. 57-58.

his Ten Year Plan in Shansi, which he calls "the only genuinely independent province in North China."[58] His opinion is shared by an American newsman who visited Yen's domain in 1946.[59] During the 1930's, moreover, Yen's relations with the Japanese became increasingly acrimonious, for reasons discussed in Chapter 16.

Since Yen was unable or unwilling to borrow much outside Shansi, he had to exploit to the utmost every source of capital available in his domain. His new industries were given a monopoly over the domestic market and charged for their products whatever the traffic would bear. He sold for between CH$6.00 and CH$7.00 a barrel of cement that cost him only CH$4.20 a barrel to manufacture and realized a profit of more than 75 percent off the sale of alcohol produced by his new distillery.[60] Together with the earnings of other industries and part of the revenue collected each year by the provincial government, this money was used to underwrite losses incurred by Yen's heavy industries. He felt that such losses were inevitable until progress in other sectors of the economy caused the demand for things like machine tools, locomotives, and agricultural machinery to grow substantially.[61] In an effort to procure additional revenue for his hard-pressed regime, he brought more closely under his control the activities of salt merchants in Shansi and began replacing them with officials, who he hoped would be less inclined to engage in smuggling or otherwise cheat the government.[62]

In the past Yen had fought hard against drug addiction, but he proceeded to make the manufacture and sale of opium in Shansi an official monopoly, under the guise of selling medicine to addicts.[63] District magistrates received this "medicine" in lots weighing as much as 600 pounds and were dismissed from office if they failed to dispose of it. A foreigner who subjected some of it to chemical analysis found that it consisted of 90 percent opium and 10 percent "preventative."[64] Yen tried to justify his actions by claiming that under the new system the

[58] *Shansi Report*, pp. 132, 78.
[59] Henry Lieberman, *op.cit.*, 17:3.
[60] *Shansi Report*, pp. 108, 116-117.
[61] *Industrial Monthly*, pp. 128-129.
[62] Ying Ch'iu, *op.cit.*, pp. 28-29.
[63] *NCH*, Dec. 14, 1932, 415:3.
[64] Haldore E. Hanson, "Leaks in the Opium Barrel," *CWR*, March 7, 1936, p. 20.

amount of opium consumed by addicts would be regulated and diminished gradually until their need for drugs vanished; however, in 1935 one of his supporters revealed that each year the provincial opium monopoly earned CH$2 million, which Yen invested in economic reconstruction.[65] According to a foreign observer, most of the opium Yen sold to his subjects came from Suiyuan, and taxes in the form of fines levied against those who grew and transported it yielded another 6 or 7 million dollars a year.[66] But Yen was still unable to stop the influx of foreign-made heroin and morphine, popularly known as *chin-tan*, which each year resulted in the loss of more than CH$30 million worth of specie.[67] Yen complained about this situation repeatedly, and after 1932 he executed at least 600 persons caught smuggling *chin-tan* into Shansi, but the traffic persisted and he dared not oppose it too vigorously for fear of provoking the Japanese, who were behind much of the smuggling.

After initiating the Ten Year Plan, Yen taxed his subjects unmercifully. He raised existing taxes and imposed a host of new ones,[68] including taxes on virtually every kind of business transaction, a 50 percent tax on alcohol, a 30 percent tax on cigarettes, and, if we can believe the Communists, taxes on births, weddings, and funerals.[69] Instead of farming taxes out to merchants, he began employing professional collectors, whose training and activities he supervised closely, with the result that during the 1930's taxes were collected in Shansi with unusual thoroughness.[70] This is why, at a time when most of Yen's subjects were becoming poorer and poorer, the income of his government increased enormously. Throughout the 1930's the land tax in Shansi was 25 percent higher than in the 1920's. Whereas in the 1920's the land tax accounted for all but 20 percent of the government's income, after 1932 other taxes brought in more than 45 percent of the money Yen collected from his subjects.[71] As one merchant put it,

[65] Wang Meng-chou and Chang Lan-t'ing, *op.cit.*, p. 4.
[66] *NCH*, Dec. 2, 1936, 358:1-2.
[67] *Shansi Report*, pp. 3, 307, and Ch'ü Chih-sheng, *op.cit.*, p. 2.
[68] *SMR Survey*, pp. 142-143, 243, and Chen Han-seng, *op.cit.*, p. 375.
[69] *Shansi Report*, pp. 116-117, and Hsi Jung, *op.cit.*, p. 4.
[70] *Lectures*, III-B, p. 206 (June 1932), and III-C, p. 157 (April 1937).
[71] Ch'i T'ien-yü, "I-nien-lai Shan-hsi chih ts'ai-cheng" ("Fiscal Administration in Shansi during the Past Year"), p. 3, *CCCK*, and Kojima Seiichi, *op.cit.*, p. 72.

"You can't do business in . . . [Shansi]. They tax a man's excrement."[72] Consequently, in spite of the awful poverty in Shansi, Yen succeeded in raising a substantial amount of capital for his Northwestern Industrial Company; more than US$2 million in 1932 and roughly US$22.5 million during the four years that followed.[73] By 1936 the inhabitants of Shansi were among the most heavily taxed people in China.[74] Furthermore, Yen conscripted not only the peasants but also other elements of the population for free labor on public enterprises and requisitioned what he needed whenever regular taxes failed to yield enough revenue.[75] As a result, popular dissatisfaction with his regime mounted rapidly. "The average person living in Shansi thinks the 'Ten Year Plan' is a 'Ten Year Famine,' " charged one of his critics.[76] Yet in the 1920's, before Yen became preoccupied with economic modernization, taxes in Shansi had been comparatively light.[77]

In his eagerness to achieve rapid economic development, Yen even risked alienating his army. He cut back its size to 50,000 and diverted to industry much of the money normally spent on the army, with the result that his troops often lacked adequate food and clothing.[78] To their dismay, most of his soldiers were put to work building railroads in return for wages lower than those paid ordinary coolies.[79] The officers too must have resented being retrained and employed as foremen in railroad section gangs. All of this helps to explain why the Shansi Army fought so feebly when the Chinese Communists invaded Shansi in the winter of 1936.

Yen was indifferent to the dissatisfaction aroused by his demands. When his subjects clamored for lower taxes he threatened to exact even more from them, saying that unless they

[72] Edgar Snow, *Red Star over China* (New York, 1944), p. 394.
[73] Wang Ch'ien, *op.cit.*, p. 20b, A. Doak Barnett, *op.cit.*, p. 254, *CWR*, Dec. 12, 1931, p. 60, and *Industrial Monthly*, pp. 128-129.
[74] Himeno Tokuichi, *Hoku Shi no seijō (Political Conditions in North China)* (Tokyo, 1936), p. 152, and *NCH*, Feb. 6, 1935, 211:2.
[75] Ch'i T'ien-yü, *op.cit.*, p. 11, *Shansi Report*, p. 189, and *NCH*, Dec. 20, 1933, 449:4.
[76] Ch'ü Chih-sheng, *op.cit.*, p. 5.
[77] Ch'i T'ien-yü, *op.cit.*, pp. 3-11, and Chen Han-seng, *op.cit.*, p. 374.
[78] Ying Ch'iu, *op.cit.*, p. 29, and Hatano, *History of the C. C. P.*, 1936, p. 46.
[79] Hatano Ken'ichi, *op.cit.*, p. 7, Haldore E. Hanson, "Toy Railway Thrives in Shansi," *CWR*, Feb. 22, 1936, p. 421, and *Shansi Report*, p. 189.

and other Chinese made enormous sacrifices China would never become a great power. This preoccupation with the need for unlimited sacrifice was characteristic of Yen's thought after 1930. It grew out of his admiration for the people of the Soviet Union, whose own sacrifices he repeatedly extolled. "We Chinese must imitate the Russians by making enormous sacrifices in order to import foreign machinery so that eventually we will be industrially self-sufficient," wrote one of his followers in 1934.[80] In keeping with this outlook, Yen compelled his subjects to get along on very little salt, which he exported in large quantities as part of an effort to raise funds for his Ten Year Plan.[81] He quoted Stalin to the effect that lack of bread is not likely to result in the destruction of the nation but that without steel mills a country is lost.[82] Like the leaders of the Soviet Union, he was bent on making everybody participate in the drive for greater productivity. His speeches are filled with exhortations to produce and denunciations of indolence.[83] As part of a massive campaign against idleness, he made gambling a crime and each year arrested thousands of persons for indulging in this previously almost universal pastime. Both his speeches and the testimony of foreigners living in Shansi reveal that during the 1930's his emotional and often irrational commitment to industrial progress developed into an obsession and that he readily sacrificed anything likely to interfere with his efforts to increase output.[84]

Education under the Ten Year Plan

Yen's attempts to modernize the economy of Shansi affected profoundly the young people attending schools in his domain. In order to secure for his new factories enough engineers and other skilled personnel he revamped the existing system of education in such a way as to emphasize technical training.[85]

[80] Li Ch'ang-sheng, "P'o-ch'an te Chung-kuo ching-chi chih ch'u-lu," p. 4, *CCCK*.

[81] Hsü Ying, *op.cit.*, p. 50.   [82] *Lectures*, II, p. 299 (July 1937).

[83] For example, see *ibid.*, pp. 187, 289 (April, July 1937), I, p. 343 (April 1937), III-A, pp. 364, 534 (July 1935, Sept. 1936), and IX, p. 53 (Nov. 1936).

[84] *Lectures*, IV, pp. 48-49 (Oct. 1932), I, pp. 221-222 (March 1931), *NCH*, July 8, 1936, 80:2-3, and *SMR Survey*, p. 244.

[85] An excellent discussion of technical and vocational education in Shansi during the 1930's can be found in Ma Shao-po and Ts'ao Tzu-chung, *op.cit.*, *CCCK*.

Significantly, one of his supporters held up the educational system of the U.S.S.R. as a model for Shansi and the rest of China.[86] Yen even sent his own son abroad to study science and engineering, along with at least a score of other students, and subsequently employed him as a translator of technical literature. Most of Shansi's schools, including the People's Normal School in Taiyuan and one of the women's normal schools, became technical colleges or vocational institutions.[87] In addition, new laboratories, shops, and other training facilities were erected and there appeared a great many periodicals dealing with science and technology. Perhaps the most outstanding of these was the *Chinese Industrial Monthly* (*Chung-hua shih-yeh yueh-k'an*), published by the semiofficial Chinese Industrial Association (*Chung-hua shih-yeh hsieh-hui*), which also maintained a department for the translation into Chinese of technical works written in foreign languages. In September 1935 the *Chinese Industrial Monthly* contained articles dealing with a variety of technical subjects, ranging from coal mining, cottage industry, and well-digging to the construction of steel-making facilities, conditions in the Japanese chemical industry, boiler-making, the operation of different kinds of precision machinery, and how to manufacture speedier locomotives.[88] After 1931 Yen treated with contempt anything that he regarded as "unscientific." He called the mastery of natural science the key to economic progress and repeatedly denounced educated Chinese for being indifferent to science.[89] He and his followers wanted to rid Chinese intellectuals of the notion that literature, history, philology, and art were the only subjects worth studying. They charged that the traditional system of education in China had produced nothing but useless learning, useless books, and useless men.[90] "Too often, teachers don't

[86] Chang Wei-lu, "Shan-hsi chih-yeh chiao-yü chih chien-t'ao chi ch'i chiang-lai ying ch'ü chih t'u-ching" ("An Examination of Vocational Education in Shansi and the Road It Ought to Take in the Future"), *Hsin nung-ts'un* (*New Village*), hereafter referred to as *HNT*, May 15, 1936, pp. 65-66.

[87] Ma Shao-po and Ts'ao Tzu-chung, *op.cit.*, pp. 4-12, and *Lectures*, VI, pp. 123-127 (April-Aug. 1935).

[88] *Industrial Monthly*.

[89] *Lectures*, III-A, p. 422 (Sept. 1935), I, p. 346 (April 1937), and VI, pp. 120, 123-124 (April 1934 to Aug. 1935).

[90] *Lectures*, VI, p. 116 (March 1933), III-A, p. 495, 597 (Sept. 1936, Feb. 1937), Huang Li-ch'üan, "Hsü" ("Introduction"), *HNT*,

care what their students study and make no effort to teach them anything they will find useful in the future," complained Yen. "The result is that many students are attending school simply for the purpose of providing a living for scholars (*hsüeh-che*)."[91] He compared a government filled with persons trained in the impractical subjects which most Chinese took up in college and middle school to a man who hires a carpenter to build a house, only to find that the carpenter spends his time painting pictures and perfecting his handwriting.

Besides compelling students in Shansi to interest themselves in science and technology, Yen made them combine theory with function by obliging them to put into practice the principles they were studying. In every technical school there was a workshop or factory where the students constructed with their own hands the machines and other devices they had learned about in their classrooms.[92] Similarly, students being trained in agriculture spent many hours laboring in the fields, side by side with the peasants. "Technical knowledge must be acquired on the job," maintained Yen. "It cannot be gotten simply by reading books."[93] One of his supporters advocated turning the schools into factories (*hsüeh-hsiao kung-ch'ang-hua*) and said that students and teachers should spend a third of their time actually manufacturing goods or working in the fields.[94] Yen even wished to call persons attending his schools "apprentices" rather than "students" and wanted to deny them diplomas, lest otherwise they become too proud to work with their hands and insist on being officials instead of scientists and engineers.[95] Not only manual labor but athletics and physical culture were an important part of the curriculum of Yen's schools. Writing in a semiofficial periodical, one of his supporters warned students that in order to carry out the tasks of economic reconstruction they first must build up their bodies, preferably through organized athletics.[96]

---

pp. 1-2, Ma Shao-po and Ts'ao Tzu-chung, *op.cit.*, p. 6, and Li Ch'ang-sheng, *op.cit.*, p. 5.

[91] *Lectures*, VI, p. 124 (Aug. 1935).

[92] *Statistical Annual*, II, p. 145, and Ma Shao-po and Ts'ao Tzu-chung, *op.cit.*, pp. 4-6.

[93] *Lectures*, III-C, p. 233 (June 1937).

[94] Chang Wei-lu, *op.cit.*, pp. 65-67.

[95] *Lectures*, VI, p. 126 (Aug. 1935).

[96] Ma Shao-po and Ts'ao Tzu-chung, *op.cit.*, p. 11.

Thus, Yen's aim was to create in Shansi an entirely new intelligentsia, made up of physically vigorous people having both technical training and a practical orientation and capable of serving as the driving force behind economic modernization. As a professional soldier, he appreciated keenly the importance of military modernization and consequently the imperative need for economic reconstruction. Because of his modern education and comparative lack of training in the Chinese classics, moreover, he was not indoctrinated with loyalty to China's nonfunctional educational tradition. Therefore, he repudiated that tradition upon realizing that it ran counter to the requirements of economic reconstruction and military modernization by obstructing the achievement of a high level of technical development.[97]

Yen's attempts to remodel the educational system in Shansi must have yielded results. By 1937 many of the engineers and technicians employed on his modernization projects were graduates of his own schools.[98] He expressed the hope that his Ten Year Plan would end unemployment among intellectuals by creating well-paid jobs for all those having higher education. His speeches, together with the writings of his supporters, leave the impression, however, that many students continued to emerge from the schools with what he scornfully referred to as an old-fashioned and "bureaucratic" education which disqualified them from doing anything more useful than paper work. Others took up the study of science and technology, but upon graduating refused to work for the government ex-

[97] Yen was not altogether hostile to China's traditional learning. Many of his speeches are set down in a flowery, semipoetic style reminiscent of the kind normally used when writing the famous *pa-ku-wen* or "eight-legged essay," so popular in China among scholars during the Ch'ing dynasty. He also continued to quote from the Confucian classics and served as chairman of the Shansi Archival Committee (*Shan-hsi wen-hsien wei-yüan-hui*). In this capacity he composed in 1936 a laudatory introduction for a five-volume collection of essays written in classical Chinese by or for Chao Tai-wen and dealing with the careers of outstanding officials who had served in Shansi under dynasties extending all the way back to the Han. See Chao Tai-wen, *Shan-hsi hsien-cheng* (*Archival Compilations of Shansi*) (Taiyuan, 1936), I, pp. 1-2. Thus it would appear that he retained a considerable respect for China's old learning but was unwilling to let it interfere with his efforts to modernize Shansi's economy.

[98] Oliver J. Todd, *op.cit.*, pp. 4, 157, 535, 538, 549, 554, *NCH*, April 5, 1933, 11:1, and May 29, 1935, 300:4, and *Shansi Report*, p. 188.

cept in a bureaucratic capacity.[99] The outcome was paradoxical. Although Yen's industries remained sorely in need of
trained personnel, intellectual unemployment in Shansi persisted throughout the 1930's, because the nonfunctional orientation of educated Chinese frequently made them unemploy-
able by modern standards.

Yen continued to talk about the need for universal primary
schooling. He and his followers warned that unless the masses
were adequately educated they would be unable to participate
effectively in the Ten Year Plan; in other words, he wanted to
give his subjects enough schooling to make them more efficient and productive workers. With this aim in mind, he
altered the curriculum of the people's schools in such a way
as to virtually convert them into vocational training schools.[100]
Enrollment in the people's schools fell off rapidly, however,
until by 1936 no more than 30 percent of the children of
primary school age in Shansi were attending school.[101] Yen's
supporters blamed this situation on the agricultural depression,
which they said compelled farmers to work longer hours and
therefore made them less willing to spare the labor of their
children. But it was shown in Chapter 5 that Yen was largely
responsible for the decline because after 1931 he invested in
economic reconstruction or allocated to middle schools, technical colleges, and other institutions of higher education much
of the money formerly spent on the people's schools.[102] He
stepped up his efforts to promote adult education by creating
the Association in Charge of the Movement for Putting into

[99] *Lectures*, VI, pp. 116, 126 (March 1933, Aug. 1935), and Ma
Shao-po and Ts'ao Tzu-chung, *op.cit.*, pp. 6-7.
[100] Liu Po-ying, "Hu-yen nung-ts'un chiao-yü shih-yen hsüeh-hsiao
san-nien-lai chih ching-kuo lüeh-shu" ("A Résumé of Events during the
Past Three Years at the Hu-yen Experimental School for Village Education"), *HNT*, pp. 19-20, 43-49, 51-53.
[101] Hsü Tso-hsin, "Shan-hsi nung-ts'un hsien-chuang chi ch'i kai-chin
fang-fa" ("Present Conditions in the Villages of Shansi and Methods
of Improving Them"), p. 2, *CCCK*.
[102] *SMR Survey*, p. 33. The statistics on pages 316-317 of *Statistical
Annual*, II, indicate that in 1934 middle schools and institutions of
higher education in Shansi received well over 60 percent of the money
Yen spent on education. Significantly, while enrollment in the village
primary schools was declining, the number of students attending middle
schools in Shansi increased considerably. See Ma Shao-po and Ts'ao
Tzu-chung, *op.cit.*, p. 4. Thus it seems that Yen did not have sufficient
resources to provide universal primary schooling and at the same time
train the technicians he needed in order to implement his Ten Year Plan.

Effect Mass Education in Shansi (*Shan hsi min-chung chiao-yü shih-shih yün-tung hui*). The association had its headquarters in Taiyuan, where Yen built for it a library, a lecture hall, a clubhouse, an athletic field, and even a public tea garden and ice-skating rink. Besides operating a school for illiterates, the association published a weekly magazine, posted wall newspapers, and sent out traveling exhibits.[103] Furthermore, in most parts of Shansi there were public reading rooms stocked with materials written in easily understood language and classes for adults, where many learned at least the rudiments of literacy.[104] Significantly, in 1933 and again in 1935 China's leading authority on mass education, James Yen, visited Taiyuan for the purpose of discussing with the authorities ways of combatting illiteracy in Shansi. Nonetheless, much of the progress Yen made in his campaign to educate the masses in Shansi was more apparent than real. For example, the Association in Charge of the Movement for Putting into Effect Mass Education in Shansi confined its activities to Taiyuan and many of the public reading rooms Yen set up remained empty except for piles of stale, unused newspapers.[105] Nevertheless, his efforts yielded results. After 1931 the number of printing establishments in Shansi almost doubled, owing to what an objective and usually unimpeachable source calls "the development of popular education and culture."[106] By 1935 there were published in Shansi eight daily newspapers and a multitude of periodicals, including eight weeklies, three fortnightlies, five bimonthlies, seven monthlies, and three quarterlies. Titles of the periodicals ranged from *Reconstruction Weekly* (*Chien-she chou-k'an*), *New Education* (*Hsin chiao-yü*), *Resurrection Monthly* (*Fu-sheng yüeh-k'an*), and the *Student's Weekly* (*Hsüeh-sheng chou-k'an*) to *The Masses* (*Min-chung*), *The People's Livelihood* (*Min-sheng*), *The Peasants' Bell* (*Nung-to*), and the *Young People's Cultural Monthly* (*Ch'ing-nien wen-hua yüeh-k'an*). Most of these publications were issued under the auspices of the provincial government for the benefit of the semiliterate and with the

[103] Ma Shao-po and Ts'ao Tzu-chung, *op.cit.*, pp. 7-8.

[104] *NCH*, Feb. 8, 1933, 212:2, and *Statistical Annual*, II, p. 329.

[105] Ta Pei, "I-nien-lai Shan-hsi chih ch'u-pan chieh" ("Publishing in Shansi during the Past Year"), p. 8, *CCCK*, and *NCH*, March 15, 1933, 412:3.

[106] *Industrial Gazetteer*, pp. 665-szu, and pp. 666-667-szu.

aim of arousing popular enthusiasm for Yen's Ten Year Plan.[107] In an effort to persuade his subjects of the advantages of economic modernization, Yen employed a number of devices usually associated with the Chinese Communists. These included dramas performed by troupes of student actors who traveled from town to town,[108] as well as songs, promoting his ideas but often set to the melody of the popular "seedling song" (yang-ko).[109] For example, in 1936 he composed the following song, expressing the hope that in the future:

> There will not be a mountain without trees
>   or a field without water.
> There will be no village without factories
>   and no area without vocational schooling.
> There will not be a man who has not served in
>   the army or attended school.
> There will be no one who is idle or unfair.[110]

Yen threatened to punish severely persons who neglected to learn his songs or failed to display his slogans, which he expected his subjects to substitute for the usual New Year's greetings upon meeting their friends and neighbors.

Perhaps the most important objective of Yen's propaganda was to dispel the fears and suspicions which traditionally had caused the public to remain aloof from anything involving officialdom. In 1933 he complained that popular unrest caused by arrogance on the part of the officials in charge was interfering with the construction of railroads in Shansi.[111] He repeatedly urged the common people (lao-pai-hsing) to help his government implement its policies and especially desired their cooperation against elements opposed to modernization, such as officials who neglected to carry out their responsibilities under the Ten Year Plan.[112] "Only the force of public opinion can turn China into a modern and powerful state," said Yen.[113]

107 Ta Pei, op.cit., pp. 1-12. The writer adds that all of this publishing activity represents a sharp break with the past, when the people of Shansi were noted for their "voluntary silence." See p. 12.

108 Statistical Annual, II, p. 329, Lectures, II, p. 183 (March 1937), and Liu Po-ying, op.cit., pp. 22-23.

109 Lectures, IX, pp. 32-34, 39 (Aug.-Nov. 1936).

110 See ibid., p. 68 (Nov. 1936).

111 Lectures, III-B, p. 223 (Dec. 1933).

112 For example, see Lectures, III-A, pp. 296-297, 303, 327, 332 (April, Oct., Dec. 1932, May 1933), and IX, p. 54 (Nov. 1936).

113 Lectures, III-A, p. 492 (Aug. 1936).

Thus Yen continued to favor educating the masses and became increasingly enthusiastic about having them participate more actively in public affairs. Soviet achievements caused him and his supporters to feel this way by making them acutely conscious of the immense power which might be unleashed if the energies of China's vast population were liberated.[114]

The Gentry and the Ten Year Plan

Yen's already stormy relations with the old privileged class in Shansi became even worse as a result of his efforts to implement his Ten Year Plan. The gentry certainly must have resented the exhortations to arouse and organize the masses which fill his speeches and the writings of his followers.[115] By 1935 he had set up, at least on paper, more than a hundred organizations for the purpose of mobilizing the common people behind his program.[116] The most important of these were the village inspection committees and the People's Political Supervisorial Association, whose activities already have been described. Other bodies he organized included the Youth Cultural Movement (Ch'ing-nien wen-hua yün-tung) and the Mass Organization (min-chung t'uan-t'i).[117] Later he created the village assistance committees (ts'un-cheng hsieh-chu yüan-hui) and the Movement for the Revival of Responsibility (hui-fu tse-jen hsin yün-tung),[118] as well as farmers' associations, labor associations, and a women's association.[119] Although in most instances these groups were ineffectual, owing to popular indifference and opposition on the part of the privileged classes, they represented, nevertheless, an earnest attempt by a supposedly old-fashioned warlord to organize his subjects outside the framework of the traditional family system.

[114] Tuan Liang-ch'en, op.cit., p. 23, and Lectures, I, p. 320 (Sept. 1935).

[115] Hsü Tso-hsin, op.cit., p. 5, Li Ch'ang-sheng, "Peh-hui kung-tao chih hui-ku yü ch'an-wang," p. 2, P'ing Fan, "Min-chung yün-tung chih tso-jih chin-jih yü ming-jih" ("The Mass Movement in Shansi: Yesterday, Today, and Tomorrow"), p. 6, CCCK, and Lectures, III-A, pp. 363, 499 (July 1935, Aug. 1936), and I, p. 246 (1919).

[116] Statistical Annual, I, p. 34.

[117] Ta Pei, op.cit., pp. 8-9, and Ma Shao-po and Ts'ao Tzu-chung, op.cit., p. 7.

[118] Lectures, III-B, p. 270 (Dec. 1936), and III-A, p. 526 (Sept. 1936).

[119] George E. Taylor, The Struggle for North China (New York, 1940), p. 35.

Another campaign that Yen undertook as part of his Ten Year Plan also must have aroused considerable dissatisfaction among the gentry. During the 1920's he had attempted to reduce the autonomy normally enjoyed by local officials in Shansi. The need for economic controls created by the Ten Year Plan reinforced his determination to concentrate authority in his own hands; he brought district and subdistrict magistrates even more closely under his control, summoning them to Taiyuan for several months of retraining and dismissing many who failed to measure up to his standards.[120] Headmen and other village officials were made salaried employees of the provincial government, no doubt in the hope that their new status would inhibit them from acting independently.[121] By mid-1937 thousands of headmen and their assistants had attended training courses in Taiyuan.[122]

If Fenyang was typical of most districts in Shansi, after 1932 district magistrates acquired unprecedented power vis-à-vis village officials. This was accomplished in Fen-yang by dividing each subdistrict into sections (*tuan*). The section chiefs (*tuan-chang*) helped the subdistrict magistrates scrutinize and regulate the behavior of village officials, who thus lost much of their autonomy.[123] Foreigners who investigated a village in another district say that whereas throughout the 1920's the post of headman was occupied by one person, belonging to the richest family in the village, in 1933 the district magistrate forbad his reelection and limited future headmen to a single term of three years.[124] According to a well-informed American observer, by 1936 most of the villages in Shansi were dominated completely by Yen's district magistrates.[125] Speeches made by Yen, as well as the writings of his followers and other sources, all suggest that he was bent on reducing the villages of Shansi to utter subservience in order to mobilize their resources behind his Ten Year Plan.

[120] *Lectures*, III-C, p. 203 (March 1932), IV, p. 54 (May 1933), IX, p. 70 (Dec. 1936), and *NCH*, April 14, 1937, 57:1.
[121] *Lectures*, I, p. 438 (Dec. 1935), and III-A, p. 625 (July 1937), and *PT*, Nov. 1, 1936, p. 184.
[122] Fukada Yuzō, *op.cit.*, p. 372.
[123] Ch'i T'ien-yü, *op.cit.*, p. 11.
[124] Sidney D. Gamble, *North China Villages* (Berkeley, 1963), p. 288.
[125] Haldore E. Hanson, "Chinese War Lord Dreams of Russia," *CWR*, Feb. 8, 1936, p. 356.

Yen was convinced of the need for more authoritarianism in Shansi. "Our politics are permeated by indifference and our people are lazy and irresponsible," he charged. "With such politics and a people like ours it will be difficult to achieve results in the field of economic development without employing unusual methods of enforcement."[126] Besides maintaining an army of special investigators, he also used the police to intimidate recalcitrant villages and otherwise coerce his subjects. In an effort to turn Shansi into a police state comparable to the U.S.S.R., he reorganized and retrained the police along Soviet lines.[127] His aim was to make them agents of the provincial government, who he hoped would work assiduously to uphold its interests, even if this involved bullying local gentry and officials. By 1934 in each district of Shansi there was a Peace Preservation Bureau (*kung-an chü*), which operated under the supervision of the Provincial Peace Preservation Bureau (*Shan-hsi sheng-hui kung-an chü*) in Taiyuan. The bureaus employed more than 11,000 persons,[128] and Yen's goal was a policeman for every 25 families.[129] In addition, he recruited thousands of civilian volunteers into an auxiliary police force known as the Peace Preservation Corps (*kung-an t'uan*). He accused the public of being too conservative to accept the changes necessary in order to realize the objectives of his Ten Year Plan and conceded that he might have to carry out a "reign of terror" before his subjects lent him their support.[130] According to foreigners who traveled in Shansi during the 1930's, Yen's police force was large, well-organized, and seemed to be keeping everybody under continual surveillance.[131] A Chinese writer even quotes the chief of the Japanese Army's Special Service to the effect that Japanese agents in Shansi were unable to make much headway because police control in Yen's domain was "rather minute."[132]

[126] *Shansi Report*, p. 18.
[127] *Lectures*, III-B, p. 224 (Dec. 1933), and Wu Ch'i-an and Ku P'ei-ying, "Shan-hsi ching-cheng chih t'an-t'ao" ("An Investigation of Police Administration in Shansi"), p. 4, *CCCK*.
[128] *Statistical Annual*, I, pp. 222-226.
[129] *Lectures*, III-B, p. 201 (April 1932).
[130] *Lectures*, III-A, pp. 310, 313 (Dec. 1932).
[131] *NCH*, Aug. 23, 1933, 291:3, Sept. 27, 1933, 493:5, and Jan. 10, 1934, 45:1.
[132] C. Y. W. Meng, "Japan's Plans to Attack China's 'First Line of Defense,'" *CWR*, June 19, 1937, p. 90.

Yen's intense concern with economic development also explains his sudden enthusiasm for the principles of equality. In the past he had more or less accepted the inequity of the existing social system; however, after 1930 he insisted on everybody being equal in the eyes of the law. Again and again he and his followers denounced those with wealth and power for behaving as if they were above the law.[133] "Even respectable members of the gentry think it is fashionable to disregard the law," he complained, "while less reputable elements among the rich delight in breaking the law."[134] Involved here is a feeling that arbitrary indifference to the law on the part of the elite is incompatible with the uniformity and impersonality required for economic modernization. Significantly, he attributed much of the strength enjoyed by the industrialized countries of the West to their uncompromising enforcement of the law. His favorite example was the arrest of Mrs. Coolidge for violating a traffic ordinance while peddling a bicycle in Boston.[135]

Yen was annoyed with the gentry not only on account of their contempt for the law but also because many of them opposed his Ten Year Plan. In speech after speech he denounced "bad gentry," "old men," and village officials for hampering his efforts to reconstruct Shansi's economy.[136] Village headmen were among his worst enemies and disliked especially his policy of forbidding the sale in Shansi of goods manufactured abroad.[137] They generally had wealth[138] and obviously were upholding the interests of the rich, who consumed a large percentage of the foreign-made commodities sold in Shansi. Many of the accusations hurled at Yen must have originated with the gentry, since they charged that by stirring up the masses he was disrupting the status quo and indicted him for ignoring the Confucian injunction to *hsiu-yang sheng-hsi* or "nourish and pacify" the people.[139] Foreigners living in

[133] *Lectures*, III-B, pp. 203, 258 (April 1932, Dec. 1936), III-A, p. 490 (Aug. 1936), and Wang Ch'i-an and Ku P'ei-ying, *op.cit.*, pp. 3-4.
[134] *Lectures*, III-A, p. 335 (May 1933).
[135] See *ibid.*, p. 470 (Aug. 1936).
[136] *Lectures*, III-A, pp. 299-300, 487 (June 1932, Aug. 1936), III-B, p. 225 (Jan. 1934), and IV, pp. 80-81 (Jan. 1934).
[137] *Lectures*, III-A, pp. 299-300 (June 1932).
[138] Chang Chiao-fu, *op.cit.*, p. 203.
[139] *Lectures*, III-A, pp. 304, 322 (Oct., Dec. 1932).

Shansi, who it would seem associated for the most part with persons belonging to the privileged class, say there was much criticism of Yen's Ten Year Plan.[140]

Yen and his followers also complained that the abuse and exploitation which the masses suffered at the hands of the rich alienated them from the government, making it difficult to mobilize popular support for his policy of rapid economic development.[141] For example, merchants and unscrupulous members of the gentry compelled the peasants to labor without pay on their own projects under the guise of conscripting them for work on Yen's railroads.[142] If the wealthy continued to dominate the countryside, however, Yen at least made earnest attempts to prevent them from misusing their power. A reporter who accompanied Communist armies into Shansi in 1937 says that in every village he passed through, the walls of the houses were covered with placards urging the population not to tolerate evil gentry and officials.[143] Even a pro-Communist writer, otherwise hostile to Yen, commended him for attempting to restrain the gentry in Shansi.[144] Yen also continued to wage a campaign against lawsuits. In 1934, such litigation cost his subjects more than CH$3 million.[145] He and his followers accused magistrates of deliberately prolonging lawsuits in return for bribes from wealthy litigants, who stood to gain if suits dragged on until poorer contestants ran out of money.[146] In addition to speeding up considerably the process of appeal,[147] he used the village schools to disseminate among the peasants a broader knowledge of the law[148]

[140] *NCH*, Jan. 10, 1934, 44:1-2, and July 8, 1936, 80:2. According to one writer, early in 1936 Yen broke into tears while talking about the indifference of many provincial leaders with respect to his program. See *NCH*, Jan. 29, 1936, 175:1.

[141] *Lectures*, III-A, pp. 406, 409 (Sept. 1935), VIII, p. 57 (June 1936), and IX, p. 38 (Nov. 1936), Ying Ch'iu, *op.cit.*, p. 23, Hsü Tso-hsin, *op.cit.*, pp. 1-2, and Li Hsi-chen, "Wo hsien chiao-yü ying yu te hsin tao-hsiang" ("The New Direction which our District Education Ought to Take"), *HNT*, p. 83.

[142] Li Ch'ang-sheng, *op.cit.*, p. 13.

[143] *TPLC*, p. 220.

[144] Fan Ch'ang-chiang, *et al.*, *Hsi-pei hsien* (*Northwestern Front*) (Shanghai, 1938), hereafter referred to as *HPH*, p. 147.

[145] *Statistical Annual*, II, pp. 249-283.

[146] *Lectures*, IX, pp. 16-17 (Oct. 1935).

[147] See *ibid.*, p. 55 (Nov. 1936).

[148] Liu Po-ying, *op.cit.*, pp. 20-21.

and redoubled his efforts to have disputes arbitrated at the village level as soon as they arose.[149]

It would appear, moreover, that a chief function of the Village Inspection Committees was to ferret out and denounce persons guilty of oppressing the common people.[150] In 1935 Yen went even further by creating the Force for the Promotion of Justice (*Chu-chang kung-tao t'uan*), for the avowed purpose of competing with the social reforms advocated by the Chinese Communists, who invaded Shansi early in 1936. In reality the Justice Force was an outgrowth of the Village Inspection Committees and the culmination of Yen's growing antagonism to the conservative gentry. It was organized along the lines of the Communist Party, with a cell in virtually every village and a membership which ran into the hundreds of thousands.[151] During the first year of its existence, it indicted more than 5,000 merchants, gentry, and officials. The accused came from the higher as well as the lower echelons of the privileged class and were charged with a multitude of crimes, ranging from corruption and rapacity to abusiveness and mere arrogance.[152] Among those singled out for criticism by the Justice Force were the family of Yen's chief lieutenant, Chao Tai-wen, who had appropriated for their exclusive use a temple erected in their native village with funds contributed by all of the villagers and were otherwise mistreating their poorer and less influential neighbors.[153] All of Yen's actions were taken under the pretext of destroying the popular appeal of Communism by eliminating the worst grievances of the peasantry; however, Yen's motives were also economic, inasmuch as he gave to the Justice Force a large part of the responsibility for implementing his Ten Year Plan.[154] Then too, many of the offenses exposed by the Justice Force involved the embezzlement of public funds, tax evasion on the part of the rich, and

[149] *Statistical Annual*, II, p. 170, and *Lectures*, IX, p. 57 (Nov. 1936), and II, p. 182 (Feb. 1937).

[150] Li Ch'ang-sheng, *op.cit.*, pp. 1-3, 6-19.

[151] Fukada Yuzō, *op.cit.*, pp. 336-352, and Fan Ch'ang-chiang, "Shanhsi chi-hsing," *KWCP*, March 29, 1937, p. 22.

[152] Fukada Yuzō, *op.cit.*, pp. 357-358, and *Lectures*, III-A, p. 580 (Jan. 1937), and III-C, p. 239 (June 1936).

[153] Fukada Yuzō, *op.cit.*, p. 359.

[154] *Lectures*, IV, p. 112 (June 1936), and Fukada Yuzō, *op.cit.*, pp. 338-345, 356-357.

other activities likely to slow up the pace of economic development.[155]

Although a Japanese writer maintains that Yen succeeded in freeing the peasants in Shansi from exploitation at the hands of the rich,[156] according to persons who witnessed the Justice Force in action, its efforts on behalf of the poor were sincere but not very effective.[157] If members of the Justice Force criticized village officials too harshly, they got into trouble with their superiors. When the Justice Force in one village accused the headman of taxing the rich less heavily than the poor, it was attacked, presumably by local bullies in the employ of the wealthy. In 1932 Yen warned that it was necessary to enlist the cooperation of the masses without alienating the privileged classes, whose backing the government also needed in order to achieve its economic objectives,[158] which perhaps accounts for the timidity of the Justice Force. At any rate it failed to win much support among the peasants, who, in spite of its attempts to reassure them, regarded it as merely another device for conscripting men into the army.[159] Many of them readily sided with the rich against it, and others were coerced or deceived into doing so. Furthermore, undesirable elements inevitably found their way into the ranks of the Justice Force and helped make it unpopular by leveling false charges and using their power to advance their own interests. Yen complained that in the rural areas members of the Justice Force often were ill-trained, while personnel recruited in the cities refused to spend even a part of their time working in the countryside.[160] In February 1937 he expressed his dissatisfaction with the Justice Force by dismissing thousands of its leaders and more than 100,000 of its members. On the other hand, if the Justice Force was unable to prevent the rich from taking advantage of the poor, it enhanced considerably the authority enjoyed in Shansi by the provincial government.[161] In fact, according to a well-informed Japanese writer,

[155] Fukada Yuzō, op.cit., p. 347.
[156] S. Washio, as quoted in CWR, July 20, 1935, p. 251.
[157] Fukada Yuzō, op.cit., pp. 359, 361, and TPLC, p. 276.
[158] Lectures, III-B, pp. 203, 209 (April, June 1932).
[159] Lectures, III-C, p. 218 (1933).
[160] See ibid., pp. 143-145 (1935).
[161] Fan Ch'ang-chiang, op.cit., p. 23, and Fukada Yuzō, op.cit., pp. 352-353.

the activities of the Justice Force had the effect of giving Yen Hsi-shan the "dictatorial powers of a Stalin."[162]

The rich especially disliked the financial sacrifices which Yen demanded from them in order to advance his economic objectives. Merchants and manufacturers, who in many instances also were wealthy landowners,[163] resented bitterly his monopolies and the controls he imposed on trade and private business. Some of his critics went so far as to accuse him of leaning toward bolshevism.[164] Furthermore, in an effort to secure capital for his new industries, he levied heavy taxes against the gentry. As already indicated, by 1934 the land tax in Shansi was 25 percent higher than in the 1920's. The bulk of this extra income must have come from the gentry because after the onset of the depression most of the population was too poor to pay existing taxes, much less additional ones.[165] Yen likewise raised substantially the taxes paid by pawnshops and other commercial enterprises from which the gentry drew much of their wealth.[166] Together with the economic depression, these new taxes compelled so many pawnshops to close their doors that in 1935 the pawnbrokers of Shansi formed an association for the purpose of resisting the government's demands for money.[167] In 1935 Yen rejected a plea for lower taxes on the grounds that easing the tax burden would not help the poor because in Shansi the rich paid most of the taxes.[168]

Proceeds from all of the taxes Yen raised or levied after 1931 went to the provincial government. On the other hand, he persistently tried to lower the taxes owed to village and district governments. Such taxes frequently were three times as great as the land tax and[169] were pocketed for the most part by the gentry, who dominated the village governments and the local finance bureaus (ts'ai-cheng chü).[170] Yen com-

[162] Fukada Yuzō, op.cit., p. 333.
[163] Chang Chiao-fu, op.cit., p. 203, and Anonymous, "Plight of the Shansi Peasantry," PT, Jan. 16, 1932, p. 134.
[164] NCH, Jan. 10, 1934, 44:1-2.
[165] Chang Chiao-fu, op.cit., p. 201, "Plight of the Shansi Peasantry," pp. 134-135, SMR Survey, p. 240, NCH, Oct. 5, 1932, 14:2, and Feb. 6, 1935, 211:2, Ch'i T'ien-yü, op.cit., pp. 4-5, and Tuan Liang-ch'en, op.cit., p. 17.
[166] Industrial Gazetteer, p. 88-hsin.   [167] Ibid.
[168] Lectures, III-A, p. 374 (Aug. 1935).
[169] Tuan Liang-ch'en, op.cit., p. 15.
[170] Ch'i T'ien-yü, op.cit., p. 14.

plained that often gentry and officials responsible for collecting local taxes took from the peasants as much as four times the amount due.[171] According to him, unscrupulous gentry even invited soldiers from neighboring provinces to raid villages in Shansi because this gave them an excuse for extorting additional money from the villagers under the guise of raising funds for local defense. One of his followers accused members of the gentry and village officials of stealing or misappropriating public funds to the extent of CH$10 million a year.[172]

Inasmuch as the land tax was millions of dollars in arrears by 1935,[173] Yen no doubt concluded that until the poor were freed from the burden of paying exorbitant taxes to local authorities they would be unable to meet their obligations to the provincial government. He sought, therefore, to reduce local taxes by curtailing local expenditures. Besides competing with the gentry for control of the finance bureaus,[174] he demanded from each village an annual budget[175] and periodically sent experts to audit local accounts.[176] As a result, local taxes in Shansi declined appreciably until by 1936 they were among the lowest in China.[177] Tax evasion by the rich was another problem that preoccupied Yen and his followers throughout the 1930's. Again and again they denounced the wealthy for not paying their taxes.[178] In 1931, during the fighting against remnants of Feng Yü-hsiang's Kuominchün in southern Shansi, Yen refused to punish an army commander who executed prominent members of the local gentry because they failed to meet his demands for money.[179] Although he urged his tax collectors to remain on friendly relations with the gentry, he told them not to let the gentry evade their taxes under any

[171] *Lectures*, III-C, p. 211 (1932).

[172] Ch'i T'ien-yü, *op.cit.*, pp. 9-12.

[173] See *ibid.*, p. 4.   [174] See *ibid.*, p. 14.

[175] See *ibid.*, pp. 12-13, Ying Ch'iu, *op.cit.*, pp. 25-26, and Li Shu-hua, "Shan-hsi ts'un-cheng te kuo-ch'ü yü hsien-tsai" ("Past and Present Village Administration in Shansi"), 3, *Chien-cheng chou-k'an*, Jan. 1, 1935.

[176] Li Ch'ang-sheng, *op.cit.*, p. 6.

[177] Ch'i T'ien-yü, *op.cit.*, pp. 15-21, Ying Ch'iu, *op.cit.*, p. 26, Himeno Tokuichi, *op.cit.*, p. 33, and Li Fei, "So-wei 't'u-ti ts'un-yu'" ("The so-called 'All Land to the Village Scheme'"), *Hsin wen-hua (New Culture)*, Feb. 1, 1936, p. 14.

[178] For example, see Ch'i T'ien-yü, *op.cit.*, pp. 17-21, Ying Ch'iu, *op.cit.*, p. 26, and *Lectures*, IX, p. 16 (Oct. 1935), and III-A, pp. 475, 490, 515 (Aug., Sept. 1936).

[179] *NCH*, Nov. 29, 1933, 331:1-2.

circumstances.[180] Beginning in 1933 he repeatedly talked about introducing a graduated income tax in order to make the rich shoulder their share of the tax burden.[181] His determination to restrain and milk the wealthy explains why during the first year of its existence the Justice Force indicted 900 members of the gentry for conspiring with local officials to embezzle public funds and accused another 725 of evading their taxes.[182]

Yen's own speeches, as well as the writings of reporters who accompanied Communist armies into Shansi in 1937, indicate that he failed to stop the rich from evading taxes, usually by collecting from the poor most of what the government demanded. According to a Chinese investigator, however, Yen achieved an unprecedented degree of fiscal centralization in Shansi during the 1930's.[183] He attributes much of the sharp decline in land values that occurred in Shansi after 1931 to the government's more effective collection of the land tax.[184] A Japanese writer also says the revenue yielded by taxes in Shansi increased substantially during the 1930's and largely because for the first time severe punishments were meted out to those who tried to evade taxes.[185] Apparently the rich turned to the central government in Nanking for protection against Yen's rapacity. In spite of its much greater capital, his Provincial Bank of Shansi attracted considerably less money, in the form of deposits, than the provincial branch of the central government's Bank of China.[186] Between 1932 and 1934, moreover, the amount of money which persons living in Shansi deposited with the postal savings system operated by Nanking rose from CH$723,954 to CH$1,131,471.[187] Nevertheless, Yen succeeded in wresting away from the rich a substantially larger proportion of the agricultural surplus than had been the case before 1930. Two fifths of the capital used to endow his Northwestern Industrial Company was extracted from wealthy landowners in the form of forced loans.[188]

[180] *Lectures*, III-B, p. 208 (June 1932).
[181] See *ibid.*, pp. 208, 214-215 (April, May 1933), and III-A, pp. 380, 534, 622 (Aug. 1935, Sept. 1936, April 1937).
[182] *Lectures*, III-C, p. 239 (1934).
[183] Chen Han-seng, *op.cit.*, p. 378.
[184] See *ibid.*, p. 374.   [185] *SMR Survey*, p. 242.
[186] *Industrial Gazetteer*, chart opposite page 156-hsin.
[187] See *ibid.*, p. 59-jen.
[188] Henry Lieberman, *op.cit.*, 14:3.

The rich also had to bear most of the cost of building railroads in Shansi.[189] Furthermore, each year Yen obliged businessmen to invest in his own enterprises a sizable percentage of their profits, giving them in return almost worthless, noninterest-bearing securities.[190] Many firms went bankrupt; however, he refused to let them close their doors until they paid their taxes in full.[191] A visiting American charged that Yen's aim was to acquire a monopoly over commerce and industry in Shansi by taxing private enterprise out of existence,[192] and his indifference to the interests of the rich is illustrated vividly by his habit of quartering his troops free of charge in the business establishments of wealthy merchants.[193]

Yen's euthusiasm for economic progress also brought him into conflict with the gentry over the issue of moneylending. Because of the severe depression which afflicted agriculture in Shansi throughout the 1930's, all but the richest peasants were compelled to borrow money, usually from the gentry, in order to support themselves and their families.[194] A native of Shansi recalled that by 1937 96 percent of the families living in his village were in debt.[195] Since this clamor for loans coincided with a growing shortage of specie, interest rates rose rapidly, until by 1936 they averaged 50 to 60 percent, and frequently for loans of only six months' duration.[196] No wonder one writer spoke of the poorer peasants being perpetually in debt.[197] Another described the hysteria of debtors at the end of the year when their creditors ordered them to either meet their obligations or give up their land.[198] Thus usury was a problem of overriding importance to virtually every peasant living in Yen's domain. In fact, there seems to have existed in Shansi a great deal of "disguised" tenantry, in the form of millions of

189 *NCH*, June 21, 1933, 449:3-4.
190 Wu Pao-san, "Ch'a Sui Chin lü-hsing kuan-kan," Part II, *Tu-li p'ing-lün*, Nov. 17, 1935, hereafter referred to as *Wu Pao-san*, Part II, p. 20.
191 Ch'ü Chih-sheng, *op.cit.*, p. 1.
192 Haldore E. Hanson, *op.cit.*, p. 356.
193 *NCH*, July 8, 1936, 80:1.
194 Chang Chiao-fu, *op.cit.*, pp. 201, 203.
195 Hsü Fan-t'ing, *Letter*, p. 11.
196 Tuang Liang-ch'en, *op.cit.*, p. 4, and *Shansi Report*, pp. 316, 326. In at least one village interest rates were as high as 80 percent by 1936. See Ch'i Chih-chin, *op.cit.*, p. 25.
197 Chang Chiao-fu, *op.cit.*, p. 203.
198 Ch'i Chih-chin, *op.cit.*, p. 25.

nominally independent yet in reality permanently indebted peasants, whose suffering at the hands of moneylenders was comparable to the exploitation endured by most tenant farmers. This is why the peasants remained unenthusiastic about Yen's efforts to initiate land reform but often rioted when banks and moneylenders tried to collect the sums owed to them.[199] The political and social instability that resulted from this situation was a source of continual concern to him and his followers.

Soaring interest rates also meant that on occasions when Yen found it necessary to borrow for the purpose of financing economic modernization he had to pay exorbitant prices.[200] In 1932 he complained that the government was in dire need of money but could raise it locally only by paying interest at the rate of 10 percent a month.[201] Since he had to pay dearly for whatever he borrowed in order to construct railroads in Shansi, he tried to hold down these obligations by using narrow gauge track and cheap but inferior building materials, with the result that his railroads were much less efficient than would otherwise have been the case.[202] At the same time, because usury was so profitable it absorbed capital which in the absence of high interest rates might have gone to support his Ten Year Plan.[203] As early as 1933 the Supervisorial Association indicted several persons, including the president of the semiofficial Farmers Bank, for charging interest in excess of 30 percent.[204] Following its creation in 1935, moreover, the Justice Force called for a crusade against high interest rates on the grounds that they promoted communism.[205] Yen also tried to destroy usury in Shansi by taxing away the profits of moneylenders.[206]

[199] Tuan Liang-ch'en, *op.cit.*, p. 11.

[200] *Lectures*, III-A, p. 318 (Dec. 1932).

[201] *Lectures*, IV, p. 46 (Oct. 1932).

[202] *Shansi Report*, pp. 250, 256.

[203] *Lectures*, IV, p. 45 (Oct. 1932), Ch'i Chih-chin, *op.cit.*, p. 24, and Hsü Tso-hsin, *op.cit.*, p. 4.

[204] Li Ch'ang-sheng, *op.cit.*, pp. 16-17. In a speech delivered in 1932, Yen denounced the Suiyuan-Shansi Land Reclamation Bank, which I assume is the bank referred to as the Farmers' Bank in Li's article, for compelling needy farmers to pay extortionate rates of interest in return for government loans. See *Lectures*, III-C, p. 211 (1932). This suggests that he was in agreement with, if not responsible for, the Supervisorial Association's indictment of the bank's president.

[205] Fukada Yuzō, *op.cit.*, p. 372.

[206] *Lectures*, I, p. 104 (March 1931), and III-A, p. 379 (Aug. 1935) and Haldore E. Hanson, *op.cit.*, p. 356.

On several occasions Yen or his supporters expressed the fear that owing to high interest rates the peasants would be unable to secure enough capital to introduce the improvements he was urging upon them as part of a campaign to increase agricultural productivity.[207] In an effort to combat this situation, Yen set up a network of district banks (*hsien yin-hao*) and rural credit cooperatives (*hsiang-ts'un hsin-yung ho-tso she*). The district banks received a part of their capital from the government, in the form of a low-interest loan extended to them by the Provincial Bank of Shansi, but were expected to raise most of it locally, in many instances by squeezing the rich.[208] The sole function of the district banks was to lend money to the credit cooperatives. By 1935 there were in Shansi 184 credit cooperatives, operating in more than seven hundred villages and located in sixteen different districts.[209] Each was in the process of issuing credit cooperative certificates (*hsin-yung ho-tso chüan*). These were forced on landowners, who in return had to mortgage to the cooperatives all of their land to the extent of 10 percent of its officially assessed value. Yen hoped that because they were backed with land the certificates would circulate like money and thus constitute a "loan" to their recipients. Interest on the certificates was 10 percent a year, the entire obligation to be retired at the end of twelve years without any repayment of principal. In other words, holders of the certificates received from the cooperatives what amounted to a virtually interest-free, long-term loan, simply by putting up a part of their land as collateral.[210] Yen urged debtors to pay off their obligations with credit cooperative certificates[211] and professed to believe that if enough certificates were issued interest rates in Shansi would sink to almost nothing.[212] Nor was this his only effort to organize cooperatives. After 1931 he and his supporters frequently talked about the need for stepping up farm output by encouraging

---

[207] *Lectures*, III-A, p. 318 (Dec. 1932), Tuan Liang-ch'en, *op.cit.*, p. 4, and Hsü Tso-hsin, *op.cit.*, pp. 4-5.

[208] Tuan Liang-ch'en, *op.cit.*, p. 18, and *Industrial Gazetteer*, p. 158-hsin.

[209] Ch'i T'ien-shou, *op.cit.*, p. 5, *SMR Survey*, p. 69, and *Statistical Annual*, II, p. 194.

[210] *Lectures*, IV, pp. 60-74 (Nov. 1933), *Shansi Report*, pp. 323-337, *Industrial Gazetteer*, p. 71-i, Ch'i T'ien-shou, *op.cit.*, pp. 2-7, and *SMR Survey*, pp. 187-189.

[211] *Lectures*, IV, p. 72 (Jan. 1934).

[212] See *ibid.*, p. 62 (Nov. 1933) and Ch'i T'ien-shou, *op.cit.*, pp. 3-5.

the peasants to pool their resources and work together. His aim was to create in every village a producers' and consumers' cooperative.[213] By 1937 thousands of peasants engaged in the growing of cotton in Shansi had been organized into producers' cooperatives,[214] there were at least a score of consumers' and marketing cooperatives,[215] and even officials of the normally unsympathetic central government in Nanking predicted "a bright future in the development of the rural cooperative enterprise in Shansi."[216]

Yet, in spite of all these activities, Yen failed to destroy the power of the rural moneylenders. The district banks fell under the control of the gentry,[217] with results that he had anticipated when he warned against letting the gentry use the banks "to enrich themselves and impoverish the district."[218] Owing to mismanagement and the indifference of local officials, the banks were unable to accumulate sufficient specie to underwrite transactions made between members of the credit cooperatives and persons living in areas having no credit cooperatives, destroying public confidence in the credit cooperatives, which came to be regarded as merely another device for circulating unbacked paper currency. Nor did the operations of the credit cooperatives affect the poorer and more needy elements of the population, who either had no land or not enough land to obtain credit cooperative certificates. Therefore, only about CH$500,000 worth of certificates were issued,[219] interest rates in Shansi remained exorbitant,[220] and private capital continued to be channeled largely into old-fashioned and comparatively unproductive short-term loans.

Yen held the gentry responsible, moreover, for much of the monetary instability which afflicted his regime throughout the 1930's. His speeches are filled with complaints about wealthy speculators, whose manipulations undermined public confidence in his currency.[221] He likewise accused the rich of

213 *Lectures*, II, p. 258 (Aug. 1937), and *Shansi Report*, p. 26.
214 Kojima Seiichi, *op.cit.*, p. 4.   215 Li Shu-hua, *op.cit.*, p. 4.
216 *CEJ*, Dec. 1936, p. 663.   217 Ying Ch'iu, *op.cit.*, p. 24.
218 *Lectures*, IV, p. 80 (Jan. 1934).
219 *SMR Survey*, p. 90, and *Wu Pao-san, Part II*, p. 19.
220 *TPLC*, p. 186, and Agnes Smedley, *China Fights Back* (New York, 1938), p. 162.
221 *Lectures*, IV, pp. 99-100 (Feb. 1936), and III-C (1932), and Ch'en Fang-t'ung, "T'ai-yüan lüeh-ying" ("Fleeting Impressions of Taiyuan"), *KWCP*, Dec. 7, 1936, p. 20.

hoarding or squandering specie.[222] Merchants and gentry seem to have been the most frequent violators of his ban against purchasing foreign-made narcotics and other goods manufactured outside Shansi.[223] This had been a cause for concern before 1930; however, Yen's subsequent commitment to rapid modernization intensified his desire for monetary stability by confronting him with the necessity for increasing substantially the amount of currency in circulation without provoking more inflation. The problems created by the growing shortage of specie in Shansi were so grave that he contemplated doing away with money altogether. He advocated using "product certificates" (*wu-ch'an cheng-chüan*) in lieu of currency. Instead of being redeemable in silver, these certificates would be backed by foodstuffs and other commodities stored in government warehouses.[224] The monetary structure of the Soviet Union was the inspiration for this scheme. Yen attributed the success of the Soviet Union's first five year plan to Russia's use of the so-called paper ruble, which was not backed with specie.[225] "Because the U.S.S.R. no longer is enslaved by its monetary system, it is free to use its enormous human resources to develop its immense material resources," he maintained.[226] He contended that using gold and silver as media of exchange caused men to exaggerate the value of these metals and hoard them, with the result that money passed out of circulation, the demand for goods remained inadequate, and output lagged. "Money comes first and productivity is a poor second," he declared.[227] Yen's critics say that his "product certificates" were nothing but unbacked paper currency, which he hoped to foist on his subjects under the guise of introducing economic reforms. In reality, his scheme had considerably broader implications. He wanted to set up in each town or city a government-run producers and consumers cooperative organization (*wu-ch'an ch'an-hsiao ho-tso chi-kuan*). Every-

[222] *Lectures*, III-A, p. 335 (May 1933).
[223] Ch'en Fang-t'ung, *op.cit.*, p. 29, and *CWR*, May 22, 1937, p. 306.
[224] For a comprehensive description of this scheme see Yen Hsi-shan, *Wu-ch'an cheng-ch'üan yü an-lao fen-p'ei* (*Product Certificates and Distribution According to Labor*) (Taiyuan, 1939) as well as *Lectures*, I, pp. 1-245 (March 1931).
[225] *Lectures*, I, pp. 148-149, 358 (March 1931, Jan. 1938).
[226] See *ibid.*, p. 320 (Sept. 1935).
[227] See *ibid.*, p. 5 (March 1931).

body, including peasants from the surrounding countryside, would be obliged to sell to these cooperatives whatever they produced for market and accept in return "product certificates," which, of course, had no value unless exchanged for goods sold by the cooperatives.[228] Thus, product certificates were chiefly a means of bringing every aspect of economic life in Shansi completely under the control of the provincial government. Yen boasted that their use would allow the government to set prices, regulate output, and prevent the sale of foreign-made goods in Shansi.[229]

Yen's scheme enjoyed much notoriety outside Shansi, perhaps because in spite of its absurdities, it reflected a realistic awareness that inadequate consumption was the principal cause of China's economic difficulties. Even *The New York Times* devoted an editorial to it and Chinese newspapers published in places as remote from Shansi as Peiping, Shanghai, and Kwangtung expressed a critical but nonetheless sympathetic interest in Yen's proposal.[230] Although Yen conceived of product certificates as early as March 1931, he did not begin issuing them until the fall of 1935, when he used popular unrest aroused by Communist victories in neighboring Shensi as an excuse for initiating more changes aimed at remodeling Shansi's economy along Soviet lines. By February 1936 well over 2 percent of the currency circulating in Shansi, or about CH$2 million, was in the form of product certificates.[231] An American reporter speaks of "docile concurrence" on the part of Yen's subjects with respect to his efforts to promote the use of product certificates.[232] On the other hand, Yen's speeches, as well as the testimony of a visiting Chinese newsman, indicate that much of the population of Shansi distrusted his product certificates, refused to accept them, and continued to hoard specie. As part of a desperate attempt to

[228] See *ibid.*, pp. 465-490 (Dec. 1934, Jan. 1935).
[229] See *ibid.*, p. 45 (March 1931).
[230] Peiping *I-shih-pao*, Dec. 17, 1934, *Kuang-chou min-kuo jih-pao* (*The Kuangchou Republican Daily*), Dec. 16, 1934, *Shen-pao*, Jan. 15, 1935, and Shanghai *Chung-hua pao* (*The China News*), March 13, 1935, as quoted in *Lectures*, I, pp. 478-481 (Dec. 1934), 484-486 (Jan. 1935), 503, 526 (Jan., March 1935) respectively.
[231] United States Department of State, pub., *Papers Relating to the Foreign Relations of the United States, The Far East, 1936* (Washington, 1954), hereafter referred to as *U.S. Foreign Relations Papers, 1936*, p. 72.
[232] Randall Gould, *China in the Sun* (New York, 1946), p. 11.

stabilize the value of his currency by stockpiling foodstuffs, Yen set up in many villages commodity storehouses (*shih-wu chün-pei k'u*). Along with his state banks, these store-houses exchanged provincial bank notes, rather than product certificates, for grain and other farm products. This gave rich speculators an opportunity to send food prices soaring, how-ever, so that eventually the government had to dispose of its stocks for fear that otherwise the price of food would rise beyond the reach of the masses.[233]

Yen's Ideology after 1930

In his eagerness to promote economic growth in Shansi, Yen considered making even more radical changes in the existing social and economic system. Beginning in 1931 he called for "distribution according to labor" (*an-lao fen-p'ei*). His objec-tive was to get rid of parasites and stimulate productivity by turning Shansi into a society much like that of the U.S.S.R.[234] "He dreams of creating a little Russia in Shansi," observed a visiting American newsman.[235] Writing in 1934, one of Yen's supporters pointed to the absence of unemployment in the Soviet Union and its massiveness in other nations, including Japan, as proof that socialism is infinitely superior to capitalism. "If we want to match the Soviet Union's achieve-ments, we must mirror the Soviet Union," he contended.[236] Yen said much the same thing,[237] and apparently *Das Kapital* inspired his scheme for "distribution according to labor."[238] Whereas before 1930 he was unfamiliar with Communist theory, speeches he delivered after 1931 reveal a broad al-though sometimes inaccurate knowledge of Marxism, which he probably acquired from reading while an exile in Manchuria. As late as 1935, when Chinese Communist armies menaced Shansi, he warned against classing the Communists with other bandits and called them courageous and self-sacrificing fa-natics, whose challenge must be met not only by raising armies but also with a dynamic program of social and economic re-

---

[233] Ch'i Chih-chin, *op.cit.*, p. 25.
[234] *Lectures*, I, pp. 50-70, 90-102 (March 1931).
[235] Haldore E. Hanson, *op.cit.*, p. 356.
[236] Li Ch'ang-sheng, *op.cit.*, p. 4.
[237] *Lectures*, IV, p. 88 (May 1935).
[238] Henry Lieberman, *op.cit.*, 17:1.

form that would get rid of the conditions responsible for communism.[239]

Like Marx, Yen wanted to nationalize the means of production and do away with unearned profits by rewarding only persons who worked. He reinterpreted Marxism, however, in such a way as to eliminate what he regarded as its chief flaw: namely, the Marxist belief in the inevitability of class warfare. He professed to believe that in China economic progress was impossible unless all classes worked together. He praised Marx for analyzing correctly the material side of human life, with its many apparent contradictions, but accused him of ignoring the underlying spiritual and moral unity of mankind, which, in Yen's opinion, militated in favor of harmony rather than conflict. His own theories provided for the gradual and orderly expropriation of the rich.[240] The result would be a socialist state, patterned after the U.S.S.R., but free from the disunity and violence provoked in Russia by the Bolshevik revolution. Yen likewise attacked the Marxist notion that human beings are products of their physical environment and for this reason completely at its mercy. He talked about the spiritual forces animating mankind, which he said transcended matter and gave men the power to alter their physical environment. In other words, he rejected economic determinism in favor of morality and free will. According to Yen, moreover, although the Soviet economy was considerably more productive than the economies of other countries, its output would be dwarfed by China's if his proposals were put into effect on a nationwide scale. He claimed that under his scheme people would work harder than in a society organized along Marxist lines because instead of being distributed according to need, goods would go chiefly to those who put forth the greatest effort.[241] His avowed purpose was to create in China a society more productive and less violent than communism, while at the same time avoiding the exploitation and human misery that he felt were the inevitable result of capitalism.[242]

[239] *Lectures*, ix, p. 7 (Oct. 1935).
[240] *Lectures*, i, pp. 68-69, 98, 216 (March 1931).
[241] See *ibid.*, pp. 71-76 (March 1931), 345-350 (April 1937).
[242] See *ibid.*, pp. 234 (March 1931), 343 (April 1937), and R. W. Swallow, *op.cit.*, 196:3.

Yen's contempt for capitalism antedated the 1930's, but was aggravated enormously by the economic decline which took place in the United States and Europe after the onset of the world depression. In 1931 he likened capitalism to theft and accused capitalists of murdering people by exploiting them and destroying their means of livelihood. "The capitalists are curtailing production, eliminating jobs, and creating unemployment and starvation," he charged.[243] Although he acknowledged the economic gains made under capitalism, he said that in a socialist economy, like the U.S.S.R.'s, output was much greater, owing to the absence of private profits, which made possible a higher rate of reinvestment.[244] It has been suggested that by seeming to demonstrate the moral bankruptcy of the West the First World War enabled conservative Chinese to reassert the myth of China's spiritual supremacy.[245] Perhaps the Great Depression afforded such men an opportunity to go further and deny even the material superiority of much of the West. After 1931 Yen began to promote antiimperialism along Leninist lines. He and his followers repeatedly accused the foreign powers of turning China into a "semicolonial" country and exploiting the Chinese unmercifully in order to offset the effects of overproduction and unemployment at home.[246] Children attending village schools in Shansi were reminded continually of the humiliations suffered by China at the hands of other nations.[247] Yen and his supporters condemned especially the so-called unequal treaties, which gave Japan, France, England, and the United States special privileges in China, including virtual exemption from the Chinese tariff. In a speech delivered in 1937, Yen denounced France for seizing Annam and Great Britain for occupying Burma. A year earlier, one of his followers referred

[243] *Lectures*, I, p. 121 (March 1931).

[244] See *ibid.*, pp. 113 (March 1931), 344 (April 1937).

[245] For example, see Joseph Levenson, *Liang Ch'i-ch'ao and the Mind of Modern China* (Cambridge, 1953), pp. 198-204, as well as my own description of Yen's reaction to the First World War in Chapter IV.

[246] For example, see *Lectures*, I, pp. 36-40, 242 (March 1931), 331 (July 1936), II, p. 31 (Sept. 1936), III-A, p. 594 (Feb. 1937), and IV, pp. 49-51, 79 (Jan. 1932, April 1933, Jan. 1934), as well as Shun Wu, *op.cit.*, p. 1, Li Ch'ang-sheng, *op.cit.*, p. 5, and Ying Ch'iu, *op.cit.*, p. 29. In Jan. 1938 Yen said that only the U.S.S.R. dared advocate international peace because only Russia had full employment. See *Lectures*, I, p. 359.

[247] Liu Po-ying, *op.cit.*, p. 47.

to England and the United States as capitalist societies in the final stage of decay.[248] As part of a campaign to drive foreign-made goods out of Shansi, Yen tried, with considerable success, to prevent the British-American Tobacco Company from selling cigarettes in his domain. He also complained about the sale in Shansi of American kerosene and flour, which, together with the availability of cotton grown in the United States, was helping to destroy the market for the products of Shansi's own farms and industries.[249] In 1937 and again in 1938 he accused the United States of using its Open Door doctrine as a pretext for helping other countries plunder China.[250] Several of his followers deplored the impact on China's economy of President Franklin Roosevelt's devaluation of the American dollar in 1933. They said that this had the effect of draining silver out of China and blamed Roosevelt for the acute shortage of specie in Shansi.[251]

On the other hand, Yen was heartily in favor of totalitarianism as practiced in Germany and Italy. He found the accomplishments of the Germans and the Italians less impressive than those of the Russians but praised the Fascists too for attacking the economic problems created by the depression. His preoccupation with combatting the depression also caused him to conceive a warm admiration for President Franklin Roosevelt. In spite of Roosevelt's policy with respect to silver, Yen and his supporters often lavished praise on the New Deal. "The New Deal is an effective way of stopping communism," said Yen, "by having the government step in and ride roughshod over the interests of the rich."[252] His own public works program, which he initiated for the purpose of reducing unemployment, may have been inspired by the New

[248] Wang Ta-san, "Lün Chung-kuo hsü-yao ho-chung chih-yeh chiao-yü" ("A Discussion of What Kinds of Vocational Training are Needed in China"), *HNT*, p. 10.

[249] *Lectures*, IV, p. 50 (April 1933), and III-A, pp. 328-330 (Dec. 1932). Yen's charges are supported by the *Industrial Gazetteer*, p. 97-teng, and *NCH*, Sept. 27, 1933, 493:5.

[250] *Lectures*, III-A, p. 598 (Feb. 1937), and I, p. 359 (Jan. 1938).

[251] Ying Ch'iu, *op.cit.*, p. 14, and Hsü Hsin, "Mei-kuo pai-yin cheng-ts'e chih yen-chiu" ("A Study of American Silver Policy"), *CSSH*, pp. 1-6. Chen Ming-t'ing, *op.cit.*, pp. 1-2, infers that Yen initiated his "product certificate" scheme in order to deal with the catastrophic situation created in Shansi by Roosevelt's devaluation of the dollar.

[252] *Lectures*, III-A, p. 443 (Dec. 1935).

Deal, together with his avowed belief that public investment would create an environment favorable to the growth of private enterprise.[253] Speeches he delivered in 1935 leave the impression that he favored borrowing from fascism as well as the New Deal, on the grounds that both were effective methods of stopping communism. He warned against slavishly imitating any foreign country, however, and claimed that the best solution for China's current problems was a return to the primitive kind of agrarian socialism which he professed to believe had existed in China before its conquest by Ch'in in 221 B.C. Thus he was equally attracted by communism, fascism, Confucianism, and American liberalism. At one point he reinforced a plea for rapid industrialization by quoting from the writings of Stalin, Hitler, and a prominent member of the nineteenth century Confucian reform movement known as the T'ung-chih Restoration.[254] Because he was not concerned about intellectual consistency he readily borrowed whatever seemed likely to help him advance his political, social, and economic interests.

Yen's treatment of missionaries and other foreigners in Shansi during the 1930's is an example of how invariably he brushed aside ideological considerations when they threatened to interfere with his pursuit of more practical objectives. Throughout his life he was indifferent and at times hostile to religion. "A Heaven which cannot be found among men is too remote to be of any use," he remarked late in the 1920's.[255] In 1935 he came out in favor of confiscating all of the land owned by the great Buddhist temples in Shansi.[256] His followers attacked not only Buddhism but also Christianity, which they said was being used by the foreigners to drug and delude the Chinese people.[257] Nevertheless, Christian missionaries continued to work and preach in Shansi and Yen still cultivated their friendship. Besides teaching in his technical schools and serving as members of his Water Conservancy Commission, missionaries in Shansi also carried out a program of mass education and rural economic reconstruction that supplemented

[253] Lectures, IV, p. 88 (May 1935).
[254] Lectures, II, pp. 299-301 (July 1937).
[255] Yen Hsi-shan, pub., Chin Shan hui-i lu, p. 7.
[256] Lectures, I, p. 435 (Oct. 1935).
[257] Jen Ying-lun and Kuo Chien-fu, op.cit., p. 2.

Yen's own efforts along these lines.[258] Whereas there are in-
dications that in the past Yen's officials discouraged young
people from attending Christian schools, in 1934 the number
of students who applied for admission to schools maintained
in Shansi by Oberlin College and the China Inland Mission
increased substantially. Similarly, in spite of his hostility to
imperialism, Yen sent students to study science and engineering
in Japan, England, and the United States, while at the same
time employing English and Japanese technicians.[259]

Germany was Yen's principal source of technical assistance,
however, and also supplied most of the machinery he purchased
abroad for his new industries. The Germans must have given
him better terms than other foreign manufacturers, since he
patronized them after likewise soliciting bids from British,
French, and American concerns. Much of the machinery he
bought in Germany was produced by the Siemens Company
machine-making firm.[260] Its representative in China was
Werner Jannings, an ardent Fascist, whose apparently close
friendship with Yen may account for Yen's favorable impression of what the Nazis were doing in Germany.[261] The
Germans, however, frequently took advantage of Yen. Some
of the supposedly new locomotives they sold him had been
used by the German Army in the First World War and broke
down shortly after arriving in Shansi.[262] Another expensive
apparatus that he ordered in Germany with the aim of dis-
tilling petroleum from coal turned out to be little more than
a small boiler and refrigerator, linked together with a few
pipes and worth less than a fifth of the CH$300,000 he paid
for it. According to a usually well-informed writer, a large
part of the machinery Yen purchased abroad after 1930 was
flawed and otherwise defective, owing to the fact that he had
too few qualified technicians and not enough equipment to
test machinery adequately before buying it.[263]

[258] For example, see NCH, July 8, 1936, 57:1, Nov. 11, 1936,
228:3, and April 14, 1937, 57:1.
[259] Japanese Steel Survey, 405:2, 407:2-408:2, Himeno Tokuichi,
op.cit., p. 33, Shansi Report, pp. 125, 170, and NCH, Jan. 10, 1934,
45:2.
[260] Hsüeh Hui-tzu, op.cit., p. 28.
[261] Benjamin Welles, "Japanese Soldiers Are Still in Shansi," NYT,
Feb. 10, 1947, 18:3-4.
[262] Haldore E. Hanson, "Toy Railway Thrives in Shansi," CWR,
Feb. 22, 1936, p. 421.
[263] Shansi Report, p. 148.

Yen's uninhibited eclecticism is illustrated still more vividly by his ambivalence with respect to Confucianism. He endorsed Chiang Kai-shek's attempts to revive Confucianism under the guise of promoting the New Life Movement, and cast in neo-Confucian terms the complicated ideology he devised in the hope of providing an acceptable metaphysical sanction for modernization. Yet his actions often ran counter to the fundamental principles of Confucianism. Although he accused the Communists of wanting to destroy the family, he maintained that family life was less important than participation in village or municipal activities.[264] His efforts to organize the population outside the framework of the traditional family system already have been described. In a speech delivered in 1933 he urged his subjects to stop habitually placing the interests of their families ahead of the welfare of the state. Two years later he initiated a program of land reform which would have destroyed much of the authority traditionally enjoyed by the average Chinese father with respect to the other members of his family. This authority was in part the result of the land belonging to the father, who could disinherit his sons if they displeased him; however, Yen wanted to transfer ownership of all land to the state and thus do away with hereditary tenure.[265] In his eagerness to step up agricultural productivity he even advocated reburying the dead in village cemeteries so that land formerly set aside for family graveyards could be brought under cultivation.[266] And finally, in April 1937, he publicly urged young people to marry whom they wanted rather than someone picked out for them by their parents.[267]

After 1930 Yen also demonstrated a new interest in emancipating women. Whereas in the 1920's he had been only moderately concerned about the plight of women in Shansi, now he and his supporters frequently spoke out in favor of giving them equal rights.[268] During the year 1934 the num-

[264] *Lectures*, I, pp. 1-2 (March 1931).
[265] See *ibid.*, pp. 424-425 (Oct. 1935).
[266] See *ibid.*, p. 445 (Dec. 1935).
[267] *Lectures*, VI, p. 137 (April 1937).
[268] For example, see *Lectures*, VIII, p. 61 (March 1937), *CSSH*, p. 82, and Han Mei, "Ts'ung fu-nü wen-t'i shuo tao Shan-hsi fu-nü te yün-tung" ("The Question of Women and the Women's Movement in Shansi"), pp. 1-5, *CCCK*.

ber of women enrolled in Yen's schools increased by 8,951.[269]
By 1935 well over one third of the students attending primary,
secondary, and normal schools in Shansi were women.[270] According to an apparently well-informed writer, women also
comprised a large percentage of the adults taking part in
Yen's mass education movement.[271] Yen enrolled thousands
more in vocational training courses at institutions like the
Shansi Women's Vocational Training Factory (*Shan-hsi nü-
tzu chih-yeh kung-ch'ang*) and the women's vocational middle school in Tai-hsien. There they learned everything from
weaving to medicine and electrical engineering. Yen's aim
was to increase productivity by getting women out of the
home and into the factory or shop.[272] "The evils currently
afflicting China are not the result of inadequate efforts on
the part of the male working force but instead are caused by
the parasitical idleness of Chinese women," charged one of his
followers.[273] Significantly, Yen attributed much of the success
of the Soviet five year plans to the efforts of Russian women.[274]
During the 1930's he also created several mass organizations
for the purpose of arousing anti-Japanese feeling among wom-
en in Shansi and enlisting their aid in his fight against foreign-
made goods. At the same time, he continued to fulminate
against foot-binding, sadistic mothers-in-law, female infanticide,
prostitutes, and concubines. His enthusiasm for stamping out
prostitution must have been more apparent than real, however, since in 1937 there still was in Taiyuan a large red-
light district inhabited by well over one thousand "broken
shoes."[275]

If Yen's determination to accelerate the productivity of
Shansi's economy caused him to champion women's rights, it
also blinded him to the need for another reform affecting wom-
en, namely population control. During the 1930's Shansi's

[269] *Statistical Annual*, I, p. 323.   [270] See *ibid.*, p. 35.
[271] Ma Shao-po and Ts'ao Tzu-chung, *op.cit.*, p. 8.
[272] *Lectures*, I, p. 113 (March 1931), Shih I-hsiang, "Chung-kuo
nung-ts'un te chia-shih chiao-yü" ("Home Handicraft Training in the
Villages of China"), *HNT*, pp. 417-420, and Han Mei, *op.cit.*, p. 1.
[273] Kuo Hung-shih, "Mu hsiao (Hu-yen nung-ts'un chiao-yü shih-yeh
hsüeh-hsiao) ch'eng-li i-nien-lai" ("The First Year of Our School (the
Hu-yen Experimental School for Village Education)"), *HNT*, p. 326.
[274] *Lectures*, I, p. 113 (March 1931), and VIII, p. 61 (April 1937),
and Han Mei, *op.cit.*, p. 1.
[275] Hsüeh Hui-tzu, *op.cit.*, p. 32.

population increased significantly.[276] Yet, although he warned the poor against having children they could not support, Yen continued to outlaw abortion and on several occasions expressed the hope that in the future Shansi's population would grow even more rapidly, since this would result in a larger working force.[277] Most of the families in Shansi had five members; Yen's goal was to provide each family with an income large enough to support eight persons.[278] In other words, he wanted to increase by more than 50 percent the number of people living in his already overcrowded domain.

Yen's behavior with respect to women and his attitude toward the family are not the only examples of his iconoclasm. Even in his nominally Confucian ideology there were many elements out of keeping with orthodox Confucianism. Despite his appeals for universal harmony, he tacitly denied this Confucian ideal when he admitted that in the modern world man must struggle or die.[279] He and his followers were obsessed with the need for incessant struggle, although not between classes but only against the forces of nature or among nations.[280] Writing in 1934, one of his supporters said that instead of accepting the natural order, men should struggle with nature and try to subjugate it through the use of natural science.[281] Another condemned the Communists for advocating class warfare when the real struggle was against foreign imperialism. "Men struggle with each other for what they want and war is a means of resolving this struggle," remarked Yen in 1937. "Since war is unavoidable, brute force inevitably will triumph, which means that morality is less important than national defense and economic reconstruction."[282]

---

[276] *Statistical Annual*, I, p. 122. Several writers attributed the growing poverty of Shansi to its mushrooming population. For example, see Ch'i T'ien-shou, *op.cit.*, p. 7, and the reporter Hsü Ying, on pp. 236-237 of *TPLC*. Writing in 1937, Hsü Ying said that everywhere in Shansi one saw young people.

[277] *Lectures*, III-A, p. 316 (Dec. 1932), and I, p. 460 (Dec. 1935).

[278] *Lectures*, II, p. 212 (June 1937), and Chang Chiao-fu, *op.cit.*, p. 201.

[279] *Lectures*, I, p. 462 (Dec. 1935).

[280] See *ibid.*, pp. 133-135, 150-154, 172 (March 1931) and IV, p. 91 (May 1935).

[281] Li Ch'ang-sheng, "Shan-hsi te ch'ien-t'u," *CCCK*.

[282] *Lectures*, II, p. 288 (June 1937). Yen expressed the same view even earlier. See *Lectures*, I, pp. 312-313 (June 1935), and III-A, p. 532 (Sept. 1936). It would appear that the Japanese menace and

He even argued that under the feudal lords who ruled China before its unification by Ch'in in 221 B.C. conditions had been ideal because the struggle for power between these lords compelled them to practice good government and develop to the utmost the material resources of their domains. He likened the international situation to this so-called Period of the Warring States (*chan-kuo shih-tai*) and urged his countrymen to reembrace the competitive outlook and other values of that era.[283]

After 1932 he stopped fulminating against materialism and in several speeches asserted the overriding importance of the material environment as a force shaping human thought and behavior.[284] He urged upon his subjects the notion that their chief objective must be survival and that in the struggle to survive victory depends on how successfully men adapt to changes in their physical environment.[285] In other words, he wanted them to behave according to the dictates of expediency rather than morality. Although he continued to profess admiration for China's "spiritual civilization," he said that the Chinese had gone much too far in this direction and must slough off their prejudices against materialism or perish.[286] One of his followers even reinterpreted Confucianism in such a way as to make the sage an advocate of science and economic progress.[287] In keeping with this philosophy, Yen rejected "moral character" (*tzu-ke*) as a criterion for selecting officials and other government personnel.[288] He confessed to wanting men having administrative and technical ability, irrespective of whether or not their character measured up to

other aspects of the international situation after 1932 revived his earlier faith in Social Darwinism.

[283] *Lectures*, III-A, pp. 457-476 (July-Aug. 1936), 596-599, 622 (Feb., April 1937).

[284] *Lectures*, I, p. 241 (March 1931), and pp. 308-309 (Feb. 1931), and III-A, pp. 350-351 (May 1935), 558, 571 (Dec. 1936).

[285] *Lectures*, IV, p. 41 (March 1932), and pp. 50-53 (April 1933), and Ch'en Po-ta, *Yen Hsi-shan p'i-p'an*, p. 9.

[286] *Lectures*, III-B, p. 222 (Nov. 1933), VI, p. 121 (April 1935), and II, p. 44 (Oct. 1936).

[287] Li Ch'ang-sheng, "Pen-hui kung-tso chih hui-ku yü ch'an-wang," pp. 3-4, *CCCK*.

[288] *Lectures*, III-A, p. 641 (Feb. 1938), and Ma Shao-po and Ts'ao Tzu-chung, *op.cit.*, pp. 2-3.

Confucian standards.[289] He was rapidly moving away from the Confucian view that in the conduct of government human factors should outweigh all other considerations. He talked a great deal about personal responsibility, but placed much of his faith in institutional changes. It seems, then, that Yen's sudden departure from the basic tenets of Confucianism was a result of his determination to create in Shansi an environment favorable to economic growth.

All of this reveals how profoundly the Ten Year Plan affected Yen's relations with the rich. Besides taking their wealth, he injured them as well by undermining established values and institutions which traditionally had contributed to their power and prestige. This is why a large part of the privileged class refused to cooperate with him. On the other hand, he enjoyed much support among younger members of the gentry, especially those having a modern education. Two thirds of the bureaucrats he gathered around him in Taiyuan were less than forty years old, and virtually all had attended colleges or middle schools, generally in Shansi.[290] Yen also used the students themselves in a variety of semiofficial capacities. Organizations like the Justice Force recruited their members largely from the schools and students frequently served as propagandists or agitators on behalf of the Ten Year Plan.[291] In most villages the headquarters of the Justice Force was near the people's school and its secretary was the village schoolteacher. Like Yen, the young people who supported his regime admired the industrial accomplishments of the Soviet Union and were determined to achieve a comparable degree of economic modernization in China. Their leader seems to have been Yen's own nephew, Liang Hua-chih, whose influence over his uncle was profound.[292] A Japanese writer has accused Liang of being a Communist before the outbreak of the Sino-Japanese War in 1937.[293] Certainly some of the

[289] *Lectures*, I, p. 226 (March 1931), and III-A, pp. 335-343 (May 1933).

[290] *Statistical Annual*, I, pp. 8-11.

[291] Fukada Yuzō, *op.cit.*, pp. 346, 355, *Lectures*, VI, p. 118 (April 1933), and III-A, p. 438 (Dec. 1935), Himeno Tokuichi, *op.cit.*, p. 34, and Liu Po-ying, *op.cit.*, pp. 9 and 12.

[292] Ch'en Fang-t'ung, *op.cit.*, p. 31, and the biography of Liang Hua-chih in *Kuomintang Biographies*.

[293] Hirano Reiji, *Chūkyō ryoshū ki* ("I Was a Prisoner of the Chi-

views held by Yen's adherents were exceedingly radical and obviously borrowed from Marxism.[294] They suggest that after 1930 young men belonging to the privileged class in Shansi demonstrated a willingness to demolish much of the existing social and economic system in order to create an industrialized power state. A comparison of Yen's speeches with the writings of his younger followers reveals that although the young men surrounding Yen were loyal to him and shared his antagonism toward Chinese communism, he was more conservative than many of them but probably tolerated their radicalism because of their enthusiasm for economic modernization. Inasmuch as not only a large part of the gentry but likewise much of the bureaucracy were indifferent or opposed to the Ten Year Plan, Yen found it necessary to make concessions to the only other element in the population having sufficient education to oversee the implementation of his scheme. These concessions to the educated youth of Shansi had the effect of giving his policies, if not always the actions of his regime, a revolutionary coloration.

---

nese Communists") (Tokyo, 1957), hereafter referred to as Hirano, *Prisoner*, p. 68.

[294] For example, see Shun Wu, *op.cit.*, pp. 1-2, 30, Ying Ch'iu, *op.cit.*, pp. 17-21, Ch'i Chih-chin, *op.cit.*, pp. 21-26, P'ing Fan, *op.cit.*, pp. 7-9, and Chang Wei-lu, *op.cit.*, pp. 65-67. All of these writers use Marxist arguments to attack the West, as well as the existing social and economic structure of China, but nevertheless are exceedingly hostile to the Chinese Communists and lavish praise on Yen. The ambivalence of Yen's younger followers with respect to communism is illustrated vividly by the article entitled "T'u-ti wen-t'i chih shih te yen-chiu" ("An Historical Investigation of the Land Question") by Chi Sheng in *CSSH*, pp. 21-64. It is an orthodox Marxist denunciation of the rich in general and the landed gentry in particular, but at the same time is liberally punctuated with anti-Communist statements, such as those on pp. 39 and 63. The same journal contains an eight-page article written by or for Yen which discusses ways of defeating communism in China.

CHAPTER TEN

 ## THE IMPLEMENTATION OF THE TEN YEAR PLAN

Some Obstacles

IN SPITE of Yen's efforts to recruit the services of young, educated men who sympathized with the objectives of his Ten Year Plan, he was thwarted repeatedly by indifference and lack of cooperation on the part of local officials. For example, when he asked district magistrates what they felt should be the chief goals of the Ten Year Plan, many did not reply, while others submitted ridiculous answers or implied that the plan was of little importance. Again and again, Yen accused local officials of evading their responsibilities under the Ten Year Plan.[1] He charged that many were in the habit of gambling all night, with the result that during the day they were too exhausted to perform their duties. "Gambling is their vocation and everything else merely their avocation," he complained.[2] He admitted that often directives issued by the provincial authorities were so ill-conceived and unrealistic that officials charged with putting them into effect found this impossible and became demoralized and apathetic. "It is better to aim low and accomplish something rather than aim too high and achieve nothing," he warned his planners.[3] On the other hand, instead of asking for help when they encountered difficulties which prevented them from implementing Yen's orders, local officials frequently turned in false statistics and otherwise tried to deceive the government into believing that its goals were being met.

Officials in charge of economic modernization often neglected to coordinate their activities. This was true with respect to not only the construction of railways but also the operation of industry. Because each of the factories Yen built employed a different system of weights and measures, in many instances machinery constructed in one plant could not be used in the

---

[1] For example, see *Lectures*, III-A, pp. 312 (Dec. 1932), 345 (April 1935), and 463 (Aug. 1936), and III-C, pp. 249, 254 (Feb., April 1937).

[2] *Lectures*, III-C, p. 228 (Jan. 1936).

[3] *Lectures*, IV, p. 105 (Feb. 1936).

others. Factory managers refused to exchange technical information or take advantage of opportunities for cooperation and specialization. Consequently, discoveries made in one factory frequently were not communicated to other plants, and there was much inefficiency and wasteful duplication.[4] Thus, Yen's efforts to industrialize his domain were hampered by the persistence among officials in Shansi of two attitudes traditionally characteristic of Chinese bureaucrats: an inclination to conceal their difficulties for fear that otherwise their superiors would remove them from office and the assumption that an official post is a piece of property, belonging to its current holder and therefore not to be shared with anyone else.

In speech after speech, Yen stressed the need for better planning, especially at the local level. "All the hard work in the world will be fruitless if there is no method in it," he contended.[5] He charged that officials responsible for building railroads in Shansi often failed to make an adequate survey before laying down track. Others left projects unfinished or neglected to maintain them after they were completed; and there were officials who carried out their orders slavishly without taking into account weather, terrain, popular customs, and other local conditions. For example, officials responsible for railroad construction attempted to transport building materials during rain storms, with catastrophic results. In an effort to meet Yen's demands for increased output, moreover, factory managers generally ignored costs and often turned out goods of inferior quality.

Another major problem was lack of technical and managerial skill on the part of local officials and others responsible for implementing the Ten Year Plan. "Proper organization and administration is just as important as having good machinery," Yen told his factory managers.[6] He maintained that China was in the process of absorbing the lessons of the first Industrial Revolution, but accused his countrymen of ignoring the second Industrial Revolution, which he said was aimed chiefly at promoting scientific management of industry.[7] He

4 *Shansi Report*, pp. 147-148.
5 *Lectures*, III-B, p. 266 (Dec. 1936).
6 *Lectures*, IV, p. 139 (May 1937).
7 *Ibid.*

reiterated the need for a more rational, methodical, and less subjective approach to economic development. This is why he wanted, in addition to the already existing bureaucracy, another official hierarchy made up of persons having technical training who would do nothing except carry out his Ten Year Plan. An account written in 1936 by an informed and objective investigator leaves the impression that Yen rapidly was creating such a body.[8]

Much of the incompetence in the administration of Yen's Ten Year Plan was the result of widespread nepotism. "Economic progress is being obstructed because local officials are appointing unqualified friends and relatives to important posts," complained one of his followers.[9] Official corruption was another perennial headache. For example, in 1935 more than a dozen officials in charge of railroad construction were arrested for helping unscrupulous contractors defraud the provincial government. In many instances, moreover, local officials discredited Yen's Ten Year Plan by using it as a device for exploiting the public. In addition to embezzling funds set aside for the payment of masons and other artisans working on government projects, they neglected to compensate peasants for the use of their carts and donkeys. "Corruption is the worst evil afflicting the bureaucracy," declared Yen.[10] He praised the Soviet practice of executing government employees who stole from the state and talked about making dishonest officials commit suicide. On the other hand, he continued to pay his officials such meager salaries that corruption in his regime was inevitable. In 1934, he reduced administrative expenses, including official salaries, by more than 20 percent.[11] In fact, it would seem that thereafter many local officials received hardly any wages at all.[12]

The inadequate salaries which he generally paid government employees hampered severely his efforts to improve the quality of the police in Shansi. His aim was to create a modern police force—well trained and effective but at the same time

---

[8] *Shansi Report*, p. 132. The author dismisses Yen's efforts to promote industrialization during the 1920's and cites bad management as a major reason for their failure, but says that after 1931 the management of Yen's new industries was "highly efficient and very orderly."

[9] Shun Wu, *op.cit.*, p. 25.

[10] *Lectures*, III-A, pp. 419-420 (Sept. 1935).

[11] Ch'i T'ien-yü, *op.cit.*, p. 7, and Himeno Tokuichi, *op.cit.*, p. 33.

[12] Fukada Yuzō, *op.cit.*, p. 372.

enjoying the respect and even the affectionate regard of the public. Besides erecting training schools where the police were taught more up-to-date methods, he outlawed the use of corporal punishments by policemen and in other ways tried to prevent them from abusing their authority. He did not raise their wages, however, and in rural areas they continued to be recruited chiefly from among discharged soldiers and unemployed vagabonds, whose ignorance, corruption, and vicious exploitation of the peasantry caused the masses to fear and despise them.[13] Officials in charge of prisons in Shansi also were ill paid and frequently embezzled funds that should have been used to provide food and medical care for the prisoners. As a result, prisoners often sickened and died; many even starved to death.[14]

Yet although Yen wanted his officials to live simply and not amass wealth, he kept on adding to his own fortune. In 1934 there circulated rumors that he had stopped a run on the Provincial Bank of Shansi by lending the bank three truckloads of silver from his private hoard.[15] When Mongol forces allied with the Japanese invaded Suiyuan in 1936, he gave its defenders CH$870,000, which he said was a bequest from his once impoverished father.[16] After the Japanese occupied Hopients'un in 1937, they found another CH$300,000-worth of silver buried on the grounds of Yen's palatial estate, whose magnificence was described as "feudal" by one of their sympathizers.[17] The CH$300,000 uncovered by the Japanese probably comprised only a minute fraction of Yen's wealth. According to one writer, as soon as the Japanese invaded Shansi, Yen removed the bulk of his fortune to Shensi, in the form of eighty carts filled with 520 tons of opium and silver.[18]

Not only Yen but also his chief lieutenants possessed great wealth. During the fighting in Suiyuan, Fu Tso-i, Chao Tai-wen, Hsü Yung-ch'ang, Yang Ai-yüan, and others each contributed tens of thousands of dollars to Yen's cause.[19] Non-Communist as well as Communist observers say that high-

13 Wen Ch'i-an and Ku P'ei-ying, *op.cit.*, pp. 5-6.
14 Li Ch'ang-sheng, *op.cit.*, p. 7, *CWR*, May 1, 1937, p. 333, and Anonymous, "Prison Life in Shansi," *CT*, April 1935, p. 134.
15 *NCH*, June 27, 1934, 463:3.
16 *CWR*, Dec. 21, 1936, p. 406.
17 Hsüeh Hui-tzu, *op.cit.*, p. 23.
18 *San Man Po*, Nov. 14, 1958, p. 2.
19 Ch'en Fang-t'ung, *op.cit.*, p. 31.

ranking officers in Yen's army had enormous wealth and lived extravagantly.[20] All of this caused Yen's enemies to charge that the sole purpose of his Ten Year Plan was to enrich himself and his followers by bringing under their control every aspect of economic life in Shansi. "You see," said one of his critics, "everything in Shansi is run for profit."[21] "Shansi is Yen Hsi-shan and Yen Hsi-shan is Shansi," remarked another.[22] "Power, power, monopoly, monopoly, authority, authority: these are the sole objectives of Mr. Yen's life," charged a third.[23]

Achievements of the Ten Year Plan: Mining and Communications

In spite of the obstacles he encountered and the difficulties created by his own failings, Yen's accomplishments in the realm of economic modernization were numerous and impressive. By investing CH$1.5 million in the development of new mines, while at the same time compelling existing ones to coordinate their operations, he succeeded in nearly doubling the output of coal in Shansi.[24] Between 1930 and 1934 the amount of coal mined each year in Shansi rose from 2,204,617 tons to 4,127,305 tons.[25] Owing to the high cost of transportation, however, coal from Shansi could not be sold at competitive prices in the principal markets of North China, notwithstanding its excellent quality and the fact that at the pithead it was perhaps the cheapest coal in China. Whereas in 1934 the average price of coal in China was CH$4.61 a ton, coal mined in Shansi usually sold at the pithead for $2.52 a ton.[26] Since coal from Shansi was also the best in North China, it was in great demand in Hankow, Shanghai, and the Peiping-

[20] Hsü Fan-t'ing, Letter, p. 10, NCH, Dec. 15, 1937, 398:4, and Fan Ch'ang-chiang, et al., Hsi-hsien hsieh-chan chi (An Account of the Bloody Fighting on the Western Front) (Shanghai, 1937), hereafter referred to as HHHCC, p. 39.
[21] James M. Bertram, First Act in China (New York, 1938), p. 58.
[22] NCH, July 8, 1936, 80:2.   [23] Ch'en Po-ta, op.cit., p. 10.
[24] Kojima Seiichi, op.cit., p. 42, CEB, Nov. 24, 1934, p. 353, and CWR, Nov. 17, 1934, p. 411.
[25] Statistical Annual, II, p. 135. These are provincial statistics. According to statistics in SMR Survey, p. 254, and Hsueh Hui-tzu, op.cit., p. 27, the output of Shansi's mines rose by 75 percent. On the other hand, the objective and apparently well-informed author of Shansi Report says on p. 37 that production increased by well over 100 percent.
[26] Shansi Report, p. 42.

Tientsin area. Yet in 1933 Shansi's mines sold considerably less than they produced, with the result that many went bankrupt, output plunged to 2,686,046 tons a year, and the provincial government's income from the coal tax dwindled to almost nothing.[27] This occurred because the expense of transporting coal from Shansi to Hankow and cities along the coast was so great that by the time it reached these markets it cost between CH$18 and CH$30 a ton.[28] Yen and his followers blamed this situation on the management of the Cheng-Tai Railroad, which in 1932 became the property of the central government. In addition to maintaining the exorbitant rates charged by their French predecessors, the officials Nanking sent to operate the Cheng-Tai line refused to follow the customary practice of demanding less for long hauls.[29] Therefore, to get their coal to markets outside Shansi mines in eastern Shansi had to pay rates that were two to four times greater than those charged by railroads in other parts of China.[30] This is why in 1933 the Cheng-Tai Railroad earned profits equal to 32.8 percent of the capital originally invested in its construction.[31] To the north, the Peiping-Suiyuan Railroad demanded less for transporting coal mined in and around Tatung but also charged unusually high rates and reaped enormous profits.[32] When Yen complained about the exorbitant profits earned by the Cheng-Tai Railroad and asked the Ministry of Railroads in Nanking to lower its rates, he was told that the operating expenses of the Cheng-Tai lines were too great to justify a reduction in rates. One writer accuses the Cheng-Tai and Peiping-Suiyuan railroads of ignoring Nanking's orders to reduce their rates,[33] which suggests that the central government's control over its own railroads was more apparent than real. On the other hand, if the Cheng-Tai Railroad really wanted to maximize its profits, it would have lowered its

[27] *NCH*, Oct. 4, 1933, 11:2, and April 11, 1934, 8:4, *SMR Survey*, p. 255, Tuan Liang-ch'en, *op.cit.*, p. 9, *Statistical Annual*, II, p. 135, and Ch'i T'ien-yü, *op.cit.*, p. 5.

[28] Tuan Liang-ch'en, *op.cit.*, p. 21, and *Shansi Report*, p. 48.

[29] The Tientsin *I-shih-pao*, April 21, 1932, as quoted in *Archives*, April 1932, pp. 289-290.

[30] Kojima Seiichi, *op.cit.*, p. 41, *Shansi Report*, pp. 44-48, 241-242, and *CEB*, Jan. 20, 1934, pp. 37-38.

[31] *Shansi Report*, pp. 246-248.

[32] See *ibid.*, p. 242, *Industrial Gazetteer*, p. 29-jen, and *CEB*, Nov. 7, 1925, p. 272.

[33] *Shansi Report*, p. 46.

charges, because in 1934, after competition from Yen's new railroads compelled it to reduce its rates, its profits increased by more than one third, owing to the greater demand for its services.[34] Furthermore, coal mined in neighboring Hopei and transported on the Cheng-Tai Railroad paid charges that were four times lower than the rates demanded for hauling coal from Shansi.[35]

It is possible that in order to curtail the power of his rival Chiang Kai-shek deliberately used his authority over the railroads in North China to prevent Yen from exploiting successfully Shansi's immense reserves of coal. This suspicion is strengthened by the central government's failure to build a railroad linking Shihchiachuang on the Cheng-Tai line with the Ch'in-Pu Railroad at Ts'angchou. Construction of such a railroad had been contemplated for decades and would have reduced by almost 50 percent the cost of transporting coal and other commodities from Shansi to markets along the coast.[36] Yet the central government refused to put up the money needed in order to build this short and relatively inexpensive line, with the result that, as a Japanese writer puts it, "the possibility of developing Taiyuan into an industrial center remains distinctly limited."[37] Obviously, the use of railroads as instruments of political and economic warfare is a subject of the utmost importance in the history of modern China.

All of this provoked Yen into building his own railroad— a 600-mile-long narrow-gauge affair, which ultimately extended the length of the province, making cheap rail transportation available to almost every important city and mine. Because it began at Tatung in the northeast and terminated in the extreme southwest near the city of Puchou, this line came to be known as the T'ung-Pu Railroad. Yen started constructing it in the summer of 1932 and virtually had completed it, together with at least a hundred miles of branch line, when the Japanese invaded Shansi in the summer of 1937.[38] Besides wanting to provide cheap transportation for

[34] See *ibid.*, p. 267, and *Industrial Gazetteer*, p. 19-jen.
[35] *Shansi Report*, pp. 241-242, and Tuan Liang-ch'en, *op.cit.*, p. 21.
[36] *Shansi Report*, pp. 273-274, and *CEB*, Feb. 16, 1924, pp. 1-2.
[37] Takagi Rikurō, *op.cit.*, p. 101.
[38] See *ibid.*, pp. 69, 71, Higuchi Hiromu, *op.cit.*, p. 149, and Haldore E. Hanson, *op.cit.*, p. 356. A Chinese writer generally hostile to Yen

Shansi's coal, he felt that a rail network would give his new factories access to raw materials, as well as a means of getting their products to market. "Communications are the hub of economic reconstruction," he declared.[39]

The T'ung-Pu Railroad was built for the most part by Yen's soldiers; however, villages in districts which presumably would benefit from the operations of the railroad had to supply tools, carts, mules, and, if required, additional workers. Furthermore, Yen virtually confiscated land for the right-of-way; owners were given in return promissory notes which he said would be redeemed out of the railroad's future earnings. Together with the excessive use of corvée labor, this aroused enormous unrest among the mass of Yen's subjects. He warned his officials against conscripting peasants for work on the railroad when their labor was needed in the fields and urged them to explain to the common people the advantages of having a railroad. Not only the peasantry but also village headmen opposed construction of the T'ung-Pu Railroad, on the ground that it would deprive coolies, mule skinners, and carters of their livelihood.[40] Their dismay must have been shared by the wealthy merchants and gentry who operated the bus lines and trucking companies in Shansi. These concerns enjoyed a monopoly and charged so much for their services that in spite of Yen's attempts to fix their rates, each year they earned profits of between 300 and 400 percent.[41] Now, their business fell off rapidly, owing to the much lower rates demanded by the T'ung-Pu Railroad.[42] Besides following the route of the principal motor roads, occasionally the railroad even employed a stretch of highway as a road bed, rendering it useless to motor traffic.[43] Consequently, the T'ung-Pu Railroad is another example of how Yen's efforts to promote eco-

says that at the time of the Japanese invasion only 10 miles of track remained to be laid in order to complete the T'ung-Pu Railroad. See Hsü Ying, "Chiu-hua Shansi," *KWCP*, Nov. 22, 1937, p. 50.

[39] *Lectures*, III-A, p. 318 (Dec. 1932).

[40] See *ibid.*, p. 299 (May 1932).

[41] *Shansi Report*, pp. 280-281, Oliver J. Todd, *op.cit.*, p. 538, and Haldore E. Hanson, *op.cit.*, p. 432.

[42] *NCH*, Feb. 10, 1937, 234:1, *Shansi Report*, p. 86, *Industrial Gazetteer*, p. 34-jen, and Haldore E. Hanson, "Chinese War Lord Dreams of Russia," *CWR*, Feb. 8, 1936, p. 356.

[43] *Shansi Report*, pp. 184-185, 271-277, and *NCH*, July 8, 1936, 80:3.

nomic modernization in Shansi hurt the interests of the rich.

Some of Yen's most loyal supporters felt that the T'ung-Pu Railroad was too ambitious and expensive an undertaking. He disregarded their warnings but nonetheless was preoccupied with holding down the cost of building his railroad. Although he purchased in Germany most of the steel rails he needed, as well as 45 locomotives and other equipment, he manufactured locally all of the wooden sleepers used by the railroad and assembled in his own factories its more than 460 freight cars.[44] He also laid down narrow-gauge track having a weight of only 32 pounds per yard. This was lighter by far than the track used by any other railroad in China and permitted all kinds of economies, such as cheaper sleepers, smaller and therefore less expensive locomotives, cars, and tunnels, lighter, generally wooden bridges, less stone ballast for the track, and smaller curves, which made it possible for the railroad to follow the contour of the land so closely that costly fills and cuts seldom were necessary.[45] Other savings resulted from the use of manual signals and couplings instead of automatic ones and hand brakes rather than air brakes. The low wages Yen paid his soldiers and construction workers, as well as his policy of more or less confiscating land for a right-of-way, also explain why the 600-mile-long T'ung-Pu Railroad cost less than CH$20 million or about twice as much as a 60-mile long railroad built in a neighboring province by the central government.[46]

In his eagerness to get his railroad into operation, moreover, and retire as soon as possible the obligations he had incurred for the purpose of financing its construction, Yen laid down track at the unheard-of rate of 150 miles a year.[47] On the other hand, because the track was inadequately ballasted, trains could not go faster than 20 miles an hour and even then swayed dangerously from side to side, frequently jumping the rails. Cuts, embankments, and bridges were equally flimsy and unreliable. A foreigner recalled traveling for 5 miles through a cut having walls that towered 100 feet above the carriages but nevertheless rose within eight inches of the car

---

[44] *Shansi Report*, p. 189.

[45] See *ibid.*, pp. 250-251, and *NCH*, Feb. 15, 1933, 411:3.

[46] *Shansi Report*, p. 189, Wang Ch'ien, *op.cit.*, p. 19b, and *NCH*, Jan. 10, 1934, 45:2.

[47] *Shansi Report*, p. 188.

windows on either side, causing much loose dirt and gravel to shower down upon the train as it passed below; he called this ride an "unpleasant experience."[48] In addition to being dangerous, travel on Yen's railroad was exceedingly uncomfortable. Most of the coaches were renovated box cars, which had ill-fitting doors and windows, wooden benches instead of seats, and virtually no heat. An Australian who spent a winter night riding in one of them called it the coldest night of his life. According to another foreigner, everyone who studied Yen's railroad doubted that it would be standing at the end of fifteen years.

Yen was confident, however, that the profits earned by his railroad during the first years of its operation would be great enough to finance the improvement of its right-of-way and the purchase of more and better equipment.[49] By the summer of 1935 trains were running at regular intervals between Taiyuan and Fenlingtu, in the extreme southwestern corner of Shansi.[50] Profits exceeded CH$1 million a year[51] and soon jumped to more than CH$200,000 a month,[52] with the result that Yen was able to order additional locomotives and improve appreciably the service on his railroad.[53] An informed and objective investigator estimated that when completed the T'ung-Pu Railroad would have a carrying capacity of 120 million ton-kilometers a year.[54] According to him, Yen was planning to spend another CH$25 million for the construction of more than 1,500 miles of branch line.[55] A foreigner living in Shansi said that in districts serviced by the T'ung-Pu Railroad the price of coal plummeted.[56] For the first time, moreover, coal mined in Shansi had access to the Lung-Hai Railroad in neighboring Shensi. This line junctured with the T'ung-Pu Railroad opposite Fenlingtu, where Yen built a steel railroad

[48] Haldore E. Hanson, "Toy Railway Thrives in Shansi," *CWR*, Feb. 22, 1936, p. 421.
[49] *Lectures*, iv, pp. 57-58 (May 1933).
[50] *Shansi Report*, p. 192, and *NCH*, Feb. 10, 1937, 234:1.
[51] *Shansi Report*, p. 225.
[52] Haldore E. Hanson, *op.cit.*, p. 421.
[53] *NCH*, July 8, 1936, 80:1-2, and Feb. 10, 1937, 234:1.
[54] *Shansi Report*, p. 194.
[55] See *ibid.*, pp. 268-271. The *NCH*, April 21, 1937, 100:2, also speaks of plans for extending the T'ung-Pu line into southeastern Shansi.
[56] *NCH*, Oct. 10, 1934, 52:1.

bridge across the Yellow River.[57] Its rates were considerably lower than those demanded by the Cheng-Tai Railroad and its use shortened appreciably the distance which commodities from Shansi had to travel in order to reach Shanghai, Hankow, and other markets in central China.

Yen intended to place his domain in an equally advantageous position with respect to the Tientsin-Peiping area by constructing branch lines that would link up with other railroads to the southeast of Shansi.[58] He must have felt confident that the demand for coal from Shansi would grow rapidly because he erected another large colliery in eastern Shansi—the CH$360,-000 *Hsi-pei mei-k-'uang ti-i ch'ang* or Northwestern Colliery Number One.[59] It went into operation in August 1934, shortly after competition from its new rival compelled the Cheng-Tai Railroad to reduce its rates by 20 percent.[60]

Not only mining but likewise agriculture in Shansi benefited enormously from the construction of the T'ung-Pu Railroad. Whereas in the past carters and trucking companies had charged between seven and sixteen cents a ton-mile for hauling farm produce, now grain and other foodstuffs could be transported over the T'ung-Pu Railroad at a cost of less than two cents a ton-mile.[61] "From the farmers' viewpoint the new railroads are an unquestionable blessing," admitted a foreigner otherwise hostile to Yen's regime.[62] He said that the rates charged by Yen's railroad were "ridiculously cheap" and spoke of a "tremendous" volume of traffic and a "phenomenally" rapid increase in the movement of grain from Shansi to the coast.[63] Another informed and usually temperate foreigner called for the creation of a vast water control system as "the logical next step" toward making Shansi the breadbasket of North China.[64] Other foreign and Chinese observers agreed that the T'ung-Pu Railroad was affecting profoundly almost every aspect of economic life in Shansi.[65] Besides having an im-

[57] *CWR*, Nov. 28, 1936, p. 472, and *Industrial Gazetteer*, p. 3-jen.
[58] *Shansi Report*, p. 272.
[59] See *ibid.*, p. 25, *CEB*, Dec. 14, 1935, p. 375, and *SMR Survey*, p. 239.
[60] *Shansi Report*, p. 46.
[61] See *ibid.*, pp. 240-241, and Haldore E. Hanson, *op.cit.*, p. 432.
[62] Haldore E. Hanson, *op.cit.*, p. 432.
[63] See *ibid.*, pp. 421, 432.
[64] Oliver J. Todd, *op.cit.*, p. 546.
[65] For example, see *Wu Pao-san, Part II*, p. 19, and *NCH*, Oct. 10,

pact on Shansi's economy, Yen's railroad probably altered considerably the political situation in his domain, since it enabled him to reduce still further the autonomy of local gentry and officials. Significantly, its construction was accompanied by a more than threefold increase in the size of the telephone system in Shansi.[66] Yen's goal was to extend his railroad into neighboring Suiyuan and eventually knit together much of northwestern China by erecting there a network of railroads and telecommunications.[67]

Achievements of the Ten Year Plan: Industry

Yen's efforts to realize the objectives of his Ten Year Plan also resulted in the creation of many new industries, located for the most part in and around Taiyuan. Beginning in 1932, he expanded his arsenal and machine-tool works into a complex of eight factories, whose products included not only weapons and machine tools but also locomotives, railroad cars, and steel rails, as well as electric motors, iron boilers, agricultural machinery, and hydraulic equipment of all kinds.[68] By the winter of 1935 these plants had well over 5,200 machines and employed more than 5,000 persons.[69] Although crude and somewhat old-fashioned, the machines they turned out were serviceable and, in the opinion of an informed and unbiased observer, "adequate in every respect."[70] By purchasing a new electric furnace,[71] Yen succeeded in raising the output of steel to 20 tons a day,[72] while at the same time the

---

1934, 52:1, Jan. 16, 1935, 88:5, and Nov. 6, 1935, 230:5. The author of the last article cited says that "people are rejoicing about the convenient and cheap transportation supplied by the T'ung-Pu Railroad."

[66] *Industrial Gazetteer*, pp. 63-69-jen.

[67] *CWR*, April 3, 1937, p. 190.

[68] *Shansi Report*, pp. 23-25, 80-95, *NCH*, Nov. 29, 1933, 331:2, Wang Ch'ien, *op.cit.*, p. 20a, and Anonymous, "Hsi-pei yü-ts'ai lien-kang chi-ch'i ch'ang," *Industrial Monthly*, Sept. 1, 1935, pp. 119-123. A brief official description of these factories and their products can be found on p. 152 of *Statistical Annual*, II, and photographs of them, throughout the pages of *Industrial Monthly*, Sept. 1, 1935.

[69] *Shansi Report*, p. 144, and "Hsi-pei yü-ts'ai lien-kang chi-ch'i ch'ang," p. 120.

[70] *Shansi Report*, pp. 80, 22-23. A foreign observer also was impressed with the quality of the machinery turned out by Yen's factories. See *NCH*, Nov. 29, 1933, 331:2.

[71] *NCH*, Nov. 23, 1932, 288:2.

[72] Kojima Seiichi, *op.cit.*, p. 240.

production of iron at the Pao Chin Foundry in eastern Shansi trebled.[73] He also erected a CH$400,000 plant for the manufacture of electrolic salts[74] and by the summer of 1935 virtually had finished building a CH$10 million factory capable of turning out each day 10 tons of sulphuric acid, together with 44,000 pounds of nitric acid and a comparable quantity of other chemicals.[75] In addition, there were shops for the repair of automobiles and electric motors.[76]

Yen even contemplated building his own aircraft and motor vehicles,[77] but invested much of his energies and capital in the construction of a modern steel mill, worth more than CH$5 million and comparable in size to the Japanese-operated Pen-chi-hu mill in Manchuria.[78] When completed it would manufacture each day 240 tons of coke, 160 tons of cast iron, 240 tons of open-hearth steel, and 150 tons of steel rails for the T'ung-Pu Railroad.[79] About 80 percent of this mill was standing at the time Shansi fell to the Japanese, who were much impressed by it.[80] In fact, a part of it already may have been in operation, because in 1937 Yen claimed that during the preceding year Shansi produced more than 43,000 tons of steel.[81]

Chiefly in order to provide paper, alcohol, and other commodities for his heavy industries, Yen built a CH$200,000 tannery, a CH$500,000 paper mill, a CH$150,000 distillery, a CH$500,000 printing plant, a CH$400,000 factory for the manufacture of fire-resistant bricks, and a CH$500,000 cement works. By the end of 1935 these enterprises were turning out each month 3,000 feet of leather belting, as well as 1,500 pairs of shoes, between 100 and 125 tons of newsprint, 1,500 40-pound barrels of 95 proof alcohol, electroplates, lithographic plates, photolithographic plates, and reams of printed material, 2,000 tons of silicon and fire-resistant brick, together with 200,000 ordinary bricks, and 175,000

[73] *Shansi Report*, p. 72. [74] See *ibid.*, p. 118.
[75] See *ibid.*, pp. 105-106. [76] See *ibid.*, pp. 85-86.
[77] *CWR*, Aug. 26, 1933, p. 555, and Ch'ü Chih-sheng, *op.cit.*, p. 5.
[78] Hsüeh Hui-tzu, *op.cit.*, p. 28, *Shansi Report*, pp. 70-78, *NCH*, Jan. 10, 1934, and *SMR Survey*, p. 239.
[79] *Shansi Report*, p. 73.
[80] Hsüeh Hui-tzu, *op.cit.*, p. 28, and *Japanese Steel Survey*, pp. 405-408.
[81] *Lectures*, IV, chart opposite p. 136 (April 1937).

tons of cement.[82] Visitors to Taiyuan agreed that the quality
of many of these products was exceptional.[83]

Although preoccupied with the problems created by the
collapse of Shansi's old-fashioned handicraft industries, Yen
and his followers regarded the production of consumer goods
as less important than the development of heavy industry.[84]
They justified their indifference to light industry by citing
the example of the Soviet five year plans, which emphasized
the construction of capital goods.[85] Nevertheless, Yen erected
match and cigarette factories worth CH$750,000 and capable
of manufacturing each day 150,000 cigarettes and 24,000
boxes of matches. This was enough to meet the demands of
the entire province.[86] He also built a CH$450,000 woolen
mill, which turned out what appears to have been excellent
beige and wool shirting at the rate of 360,000 yards a year,
not to mention 6,000 lengths of wool carpet and 60,000
pounds of "woven goods" (*chen-chi-wu*).[87] By 1937 Taiyuan was the site of an industrial complex consisting of no
less than 21 large factories. Meanwhile, the already existing
cotton mills had expanded their facilities enormously, at a cost
of well over CH$7 million.[88]

Electric power for Yen's factories came from generating
plants having a capacity of 21,835 kilowatts. This represented
a ninefold increase since 1929 and was accomplished by building 10 new generating plants.[89] Several foreigners speak of a

[82] *Shansi Report*, pp. 24-25, 100-130, *SMR Survey*, pp. 228-229, 238,
and *Industrial Gazetteer*, pp. 369-370-jen.

[83] For example, see *Shansi Report*, pp. 22-23, *SMR Survey*, p. 238,
NCH, July 8, 1936, 80:3, *CEB*, Dec. 14, 1935, p. 375, Ch'en
Fang-t'ung, *op.cit.*, p. 28, and Fan Ch'ang-chiang, "Shan-hsi chi'hsing,"
KWCP, March 29, 1937, p. 24. Writing on page 239 of *TPLC*, the
pro-Communist writer Hsü Ying refers to Yen's cement plant as "world
famous."

[84] For example, see Li Ch'ang-sheng, *op.cit.*, pp. 18-19.

[85] *Lectures*, II, p. 296 (July 1937), and Li Ch'ang-sheng, "P'o-ch'an
te Chung-kuo ching-chi chih ch'u-lu," pp. 5, 7, *CCCK*.

[86] *Shansi Report*, pp. 129-130, and *SMR Survey*, pp. 228-229.

[87] *Shansi Report*, pp. 123-125. Ch'en Fang-t'ung, *op.cit.*, p. 28, *SMR
Survey*, p. 240, and *NCH*, Oct. 14, 1936, 52:1, all agree that the
woolens produced by Yen's new mill were of excellent quality and
reasonably priced.

[88] *Industrial Gazetteer*, pp. 7-16-szu, and *Shansi Report*, p. 121.

[89] I arrived at this conclusion by comparing the statistics in *CWR*,
May 9, 1931, p. 361, with those in Takagi Rikurō, *op.cit.*, p. 232.
The author of *Shansi Report* mentions a fourteenfold increase (see pp.
88-90), and the *Industrial Gazetteer* says that the number of kilowatt

steady growth in the number of cities having electricity.[90] At the time Japan invaded Shansi, moreover, Yen was preparing to build a CH$6,500,000 hydroelectric station, situated at the Hu-k'ou Falls on the banks of the turbulent Yellow River and large enough to generate 50,000 horsepower or 326,748,-000 kilowatt hours a year.[91] Most of the surveys necessary were completed and an 80-mile-long motor road had been laid down for the purpose of transporting cement and other building materials to the construction site.[92] As part of an effort to exploit additional sources of power, Yen invested another CH$200,000 in the refinery he had built during the 1920's with the aim of extracting petroleum from shale rock.[93] This was in keeping with the experimental orientation of the Ten Year Plan, which found expression in the large number of laboratories attached to Yen's factories. According to a usually reliable observer, technicians employed in these laboratories were engaged in serious and often significant research aimed at lowering costs and improving quality.[94] Owing to their labor, by 1936 Shansi was producing its own potassium chloride and potassium carbonate.[95] They also developed a charcoal-burning engine for use in buses and other motor vehicles.[96] Yen was so pleased that in 1937 he set aside CH$1 million for the creation of an Academy for Research into the Natural Sciences (*k'o-hsüeh yen-chiu yüan*).[97]

It would appear that not only were the products of Yen's new industries serviceable and reasonably priced, but the process of industrial growth in Shansi became to some extent self-sustaining. In other words, demands arising out of the operation of one factory created a market for goods turned out by another plant whose own needs had to be met by still

---

hours generated by plants serving the Northwestern Industrial Company almost doubled within the course of a single year (see p. 676-szu). According to Yen, in 1936 Shansi produced 172,800,000 kilowatt hours of electricity or about 3.5 percent of China's total output. See *Lectures*, IV, chart opposite p. 136 (April 1937).

[90] *NCH*, Feb. 28, 1933, 491:2, and Oct. 11, 1933, 49:4.
[91] Oliver J. Todd, *op.cit.*, p. 563, and *NCH*, Dec. 21, 1932, 449:2.
[92] Oliver J. Todd, *op.cit.*, p. 159.
[93] *Shansi Report*, pp. 169-180.
[94] See *ibid.*, pp. 64-65, 81, 109, 112-113, 114-115, 134-136.
[95] See *ibid.*, p. 116.
[96] *NCH*, Sept. 27, 1933, 493:5.
[97] *Lectures*, III-A, p. 624 (April 1937), and *PT*, April 1, 1937, p. 73.

other factories.[98] Yen was unable to sell much of the machinery produced by his heavy industries, however, owing largely to the high cost of transporting such machines to markets outside Shansi.[99] This is why in 1935 the machine-tool works, locomotive factory, and several other plants belonging to the Northwestern Industrial Company were operating at half their capacity. Furthermore, although the T'ung-Pu Railroad discriminated against commodities not produced in Shansi and Yen threatened to execute merchants who sold them, competition from more cheaply priced, foreign-made goods virtually destroyed the market for silk and cotton textiles manufactured in Shansi and probably was responsible for the difficulties encountered by Yen's cigarette factory and some of his other new industries.[100] For all of these reasons, Yen's factories lost almost CH$700,000 in 1934[101] and still were operating at a loss a year later.[102] This in turn accounts for the persistence of Shansi's annual trade deficit, which was CH$7,683,000 in 1934 and only slightly less in 1935.[103] No wonder an American who interviewed Hsü Yung-ch'ang in 1936 found Hsü preoccupied with Shansi's finances.[104]

These disappointments were offset to a certain extent by the enormous demand for some of the products being turned out by Yen's new industries. In 1934 the Ta I Woolen Mills earned a profit of almost CH$700,000 off the sale of its textiles in not only Shansi but also parts of North China.[105] Matches and industrial alcohol manufactured in Shansi were equally popular, and Yen was exporting paper, bricks, and

[98] For example, see *Shansi Report*, pp. 49, 114, 134.

[99] *NCH*, July 8, 1936, 80:3.

[100] *Industrial Gazetteer*, pp. 7-8-szu, 13-17-szu, Li Teh-hsien, "Kai-chin Shan-hsi nung-yeh chih wo chien" ("My Views On How to Improve Agriculture in Shansi"), *Industrial Monthly*, Sept. 1, 1935, p. 13, and *Shansi Report*, p. 24. Most of the foreign goods entering Shansi or competing with the products of Yen's industries in markets outside Shansi were made in Japan, and their impact on the Ten Year Plan will be discussed in Chapter 11.

[101] *Statistical Annual*, II, p. 144. I am assuming that the term *nien-ch'an tsung-chih* is used here to mean annual cost, although in most Chinese-English dictionaries *tsung-chih* is translated as worth or value.

[102] Sterling Fisher, *op.cit.*, p. 7:6.

[103] Tuan Liang-ch'en, *op.cit.*, p. 15, and *Industrial Gazetteer*, pp. 147-148-hsin.

[104] *U.S. Foreign Relations Papers, 1936*, p. 72.

[105] *Statistical Annual*, II, p. 144, Shun Wu, *op.cit.*, pp. 14-15, *Shansi Report*, pp. 125-126, and *Industrial Gazetteer*, p. 19-szu.

cement to neighboring provinces.[106] His machine-tool works likewise received orders from outside Shansi, with the result that by 1936 its productivity was increasing rapidly.[107] As early as 1934, the number of bankruptcies in Taiyuan fell off sharply, employment rose, and the city experienced what must have been by contemporary standards an economic boom.[108] Between 1932 and 1936 its population almost doubled, rising from 76,472 to 143,625.[109] This occurred because persons from other parts of Shansi flocked into the city, seeking employment in Yen's new factories,[110] whose workers received what a visiting American newsman infers were comparatively high wages, ranging from US6¢ to US12¢ a day.[111] A Communist writer says that by 1937 one of the "distinguishing features" of the Taiyuan Basin was its "large numbers of industrial workers."[112] The prosperity of Taiyuan may be why in 1934 two of China's leading insurance companies opened branch offices there.[113] By 1936 Yen was in the process of raising money for the construction of a sugar refinery, as well as a rayon factory,[114] and must have been planning to erect other industries, since the dam and power plant which he intended to build on the Yellow River at Hu-k'ou Falls would produce considerably more power than was necessary in order to meet Shansi's current needs.[115] Foreigners and others from outside Shansi who visited Taiyuan marveled at Yen's achievements.[116] One said that although in the past

[106] *Industrial Gazetteer*, pp. 247-szu, 354-358-szu, 383-szu, 402-szu, and *SMR Survey*, pp. 117, 226, 239.

[107] *Industrial Gazetteer*, p. 489-szu, *Shansi Report*, pp. 22-23, 84-85, 146, and "Hsi-pei yü-ts'ai lien-kang chi-ch'i ch'ang," p. 120.

[108] Tuan Liang-ch'en, *op.cit.*, pp. 13-14.

[109] *Industrial Gazetteer*, p. 5-ping.

[110] *Ibid.*, and Ch'i Chih-chin, *op.cit.*, p. 26.

[111] Sterling Fisher, *op.cit.*, p. 7:6. This would have been in keeping with Yen's behavior during the 1920's, when he paid skilled workers employed in his arsenal unusually good wages. See Anonymous, "Labor Conditions in Shansi," *CEM*, June 1925, p. 22. Apparently his enthusiasm for stepping up the quantity and improving the quality of industrial output in Shansi outweighed even his stinginess.

[112] Israel Epstein, *The Unfinished Revolution in China* (Boston, 1947), p. 111.

[113] *Industrial Gazetteer*, p. 36-ping.

[114] *Shansi Report*, pp. 132, 135, and Ch'ü Chih-sheng, *op.cit.*, p. 3.

[115] *Shansi Report*, p. 104.

[116] For examples, see *Wu Pao-san, Part II*, p. 20, *SMR, Survey*, p. 240, *Japanese Steel Survey*, p. 405:1, and Hatano Ken'ichi, *Gendai Shina no seiji to jimbutsu (Politics and Outstanding Men in Contemporary China)* (Tokyo, 1937), p. 117.

Yen's regime was indifferent to industry and harassed it, now the prospects for industrial development in Shansi were "unlimited."[117]

Probably because he wanted to deceive Chiang Kai-shek, Yen did not publicize his efforts to create a complex of heavy industries in Shansi. When his Northwestern Industrial Company registered with Nanking's Ministry of Industry in 1931, it stated that its aim was to promote coal mining, animal husbandry, leather tanning, and the manufacture of cotton textiles.[118] Whereas in the 1920's Shansi's economy was the subject of many articles in the *Chinese Economic Bulletin*, after 1931 this publication of the central government seldom mentioned Shansi. Moreover, in an otherwise exceedingly comprehensive statistical report issued by the provincial authorities in 1934 there is virtually no information about the factories operated by the Northwestern Industrial Company. A reporter from Peiping who visited Shansi in 1934 gained the impression that for some reason Yen's regime was concealing its achievements in the realm of industrialization, which he says were considerably more spectacular than persons outside Shansi generally assumed.[119]

Yet in spite of the secrecy that surrounded it, Yen's Ten Year Plan won for Shansi acclaim in other parts of China. In 1935, after making an exhaustive investigation of Yen's

[117] *Shansi Report*, pp. 22, 131. The author of this volume ridicules Yen's economic policies in the 1920's and is by no means uncritical of the Ten Year Plan, but nevertheless says that by Oct. 1935 it succeeded "beyond the original expectations of its creators" (see page 26).

[118] *CWR*, Dec. 12, 1931, p. 60.

[119] *Wu Pao-san, Part II*, p. 20. All of this raises the question of whether after 1930 other warlords in China also tried to industrialize their domains but likewise kept their progress a secret for fear of alarming Chiang Kai-shek. Although scholars have not investigated them, there exist many examples of industrial development under other warlords. On p. 128 of his book *Nippon no tai Shina tōshi kenkyū*, Professor Higuchi Hiromu mentions an ambitious "three year plan" undertaken in 1933 by the provincial government of Kwangtung, which resulted in the construction of 24 factories, including an arsenal, an iron foundry, and several chemical factories. The same warlord regime intended to build a sugar refinery, a distillery, a cement factory, and a plant for the manufacture of agricultural machinery. According to Higuchi, the provincial governments of Shantung, Hunan, Kwangsi, and Szechwan also were in the process of erecting modern industries. Significantly, Szechwan, as well as Shensi and Kansu, purchased many of the machines turned out by Yen's machine tool works. See *Shansi Report*, pp. 22-23, 84-85, and *Industrial Monthly*, Sept. 1, 1935, p. 120.

new industries, an engineer from Shanghai held them up as
a model for the rest of China and called on the central government to emulate Yen instead of continuing to indulge in empty
talk about economic planning.[120] His feelings were shared by
the *Peking and Tientsin Times*, which charged that while
Nanking talked and wrote endlessly about its elaborate plans
for economic development, "Shansi has said little and done a
great deal."[121] No wonder Nanking ignored Yen's appeals for
financial assistance, especially since persons writing in a
publication issued under Yen's auspices likewise boasted that
economically his regime was more progressive than the central
government.[122] In 1932 Yen tried without success to persuade
the central government to help finance the construction of his
T'ung-Pu Railroad by turning over to him the enormous profits annually earned in Shansi by the recently nationalized
Cheng-Tai Railroad.[123] Subsequent pleas for aid from Nanking
were equally fruitless,[124] and when Yen retained for his own
use the tax on salt which the central government normally
collected in Shansi, Chiang Kai-shek retaliated by inundating
northwest China with salt obtained along the coast, which he
sold at prices so low that neighboring provinces virtually
stopped buying salt mined in Shansi.[125] Nanking also must
have been responsible for the articles deriding Yen's Ten Year
Plan that occasionally appeared in pro-Kuomintang newspapers.[126] Nevertheless, Chiang Kai-shek may have had in
mind Yen's efforts to industrialize Shansi when in 1935 he
initiated his own "five year plan," with the aim of creating in
and around Nanking a complex of heavy industries capable of
producing everything from chemicals to steel.[127]

[120] *Shansi Report*, pp. 26, 52, 132.

[121] Oliver J. Todd, *op.cit.*, p. 596.

[122] Li Ch'ang-sheng, *op.cit.*, p. 20, and Tuan Liang-ch'en, *op.cit.*, p. 22.

[123] Tientsin, *I-shih pao*, April 21, 1932, as quoted in Hatano, *Archives*, April 1932, p. 288.

[124] Wang Ch'ien, *op.cit.*, pp. 19a-19b, speaks of Yen asking Nanking's Ministry of Railroads to pay for half the cost of building the T'ung-Pu Railroad. Ying Ch'iu, *op.cit.*, p. 27, seems to be asking the central government to help finance the construction of the dams and water control works Yen wished to erect in Shansi.

[125] Higuchi Hiromu, *op.cit.*, p. 129, and Tuan Liang-ch'en, *op.cit.*, pp. 21-22.

[126] Shun Wu, *op.cit.*, p. 23.

[127] Li Ch'ang-sheng, *op.cit.*, p. 20, strongly infers that Chiang was imitating Yen. A brief description of Chiang's plan can be found in

Achievements of the Ten Year Plan: Agriculture

If Yen achieved considerable success in the field of industrialization, however, he was unable to overcome the problems bedeviling agriculture. In the countryside his attempts to combat unemployment took the form of establishing small factories where jobless peasants and artisans could find work. After 1930 he set up at least ten and perhaps as many as fourteen "model textile factories" (*mo-fan chih-pu kung-ch'ang*), at a cost of no less than CH$100,800.[128] According to one of his followers, he invested another CH$500,000 in the creation of "common peoples' factories" (*p'ing-min kung-ch'ang*).[129] Instead of wishing merely to revive old-fashioned handicraft industries, he wanted to modernize the rural economy by introducing mechanization and the factory system. He did not blame machines for the problems afflicting China's economy; he praised them for increasing productivity and called on his fellow Chinese to adapt their society to the machine age.[130] But although his workshops survived, they did not flourish and failed to undo the damage wrought by the depression.

Yen's campaign to encourage greater specialization among farmers was more successful. Between 1931 and 1936 the amount of land devoted to the growing of cotton in Shansi increased almost sixfold.[131] In 1936 Yen sowed 31,439 acres with cotton and reaped a harvest of 496,000 piculs.[132] He accomplished this by punishing farmers who did not grow cotton, while at the same time guaranteeing an income to those who did. In addition, he built ten more "cotton experimental stations" and redoubled his efforts to irrigate formerly unproductive land.[133] Besides wanting to bring under cultivation at least 121,000 acres of unused land,[134] Yen was eager to stop the floods which annually devastated much of Shansi,

Higuchi Hiromu, *op.cit.*, pp. 129-130, and a more detailed discussion, in F. F. Liu, *A Military History of Modern China* (Princeton, 1956), pp. 97-101.

[128] *Industrial Gazetteer*, pp. 33-37-szu, and Li Shu-hua, *op.cit.*, p. 3.
[129] Shun Wu, *op.cit.*, p. 17.
[130] *Lectures*, I, pp. 38 (March 1931), 330 (July 1936).
[131] Kojima Seiichi, *op.cit.*, p. 89, and *CEB*, Nov. 1936, p. 17.
[132] *Ibid.*
[133] Kojima Seiichi, *op.cit.*, p. 107.
[134] *Shansi Report*, p. 297, Ch'ü Chih-sheng, *op.cit.*, p. 3, and *NCH*, April 25, 1934, 99:1.

causing millions of dollars worth of damage. In 1932 and again in 1933 and 1934 these floods were especially disastrous. Many farmers lost their entire crop for the second or third successive year, Yen's new paper mill sustained heavy damage, and his Ten Year Plan was set back substantially. Consequently, early in 1933 he enlisted the aid of the China International Famine Relief Commission and at the suggestion of its chief engineer, Oliver J. Todd, formed the Shansi Water Conservancy Commission. Under Todd's leadership the Chinese engineers employed by the Water Conservancy Commission carried out an exhaustive investigation of Shansi's rivers and other water resources. This survey cost Yen US$50,-000 and resulted in a report which recommended spending another US$4 million for the construction of a large dam across the upper reaches of the Fen River, smaller dams on the Sang-kan and Hu-t'o rivers, and a host of other water control works, including a 70-mile-long concrete channel for the Fen River south of Taiyuan.[135] Significantly, Yen built his new cement plant only a short distance from the banks of the Fen.

Beginning in 1933 he replaced the earthen dams formerly used to control the waters of that river with two masonry sluices, costing US$300,000.[136] These diverted enough river water to irrigate more than 7,800 acres of previously uncultivated land.[137] To the south, new pumping stations erected at a cost of CH$217,000 provided water for another 212 acres.[138] By the summer of 1935, moreover, Yen was in the process of constructing a concrete channel for the Fen River, as well as a CH$550,000 dam across the Sang-kan River, which he hoped would irrigate more than 16,500 additional acres.[139] He also renewed his campaign to dig wells and plant trees; however, it continued to yield disappointing results, owing to official mismanagement and popular indifference. On the other hand, impressive strides were made with respect to improving the quality of cotton, wool, and some other farm

[135] Oliver J. Todd, op.cit., pp. 76, 84, 155, 535-555.

[136] See ibid., p. 156, and NCH, April 25, 1934, 99:1.

[137] Shansi Report, p. 300.

[138] See ibid., p. 301, and NCH, Dec. 21, 1932, 449:1, and May 17, 1933, 248:4.

[139] Oliver J. Todd, op.cit., pp. 158-159, and Shansi Report, pp. 302-304.

products. Most of the wool processed by Yen's new woolen mill came from Merino sheep,[140] and his efforts to promote the raising of chickens[141] also must have paid dividends because after 1931 there occurred an almost threefold increase in the number of albumen factories operating in Shansi.[142] As for cotton, in addition to encouraging the use of better strains, Yen brought ginning completely under the control of the state.[143] This was done in order to end the practice of adulterating cotton and must have been resented by the local merchants and gentry, who owned most of the cotton gins in Shansi.[144]

Yen and his followers deplored the ignorance of the peasants, and his regime continued to promote scientific agriculture. For example, it maintained an elaborate weather forecasting service.[145] In the statistical annual published by the provincial government in 1935 no less than 34 pages are given over to a detailed analysis of the climate in various parts of Shansi at different times of the year.[146] As part of his Ten Year Plan, Yen also built a large agricultural laboratory (*nung-shih shih-yen ch'ang*) and established schools for the training of agricultural experts.[147] If the Experimental School for Village Education (*nung-ts'un chiao-yü shih-yen hsueh-hsiao*) at Hu-yen was typical of these schools, they were attended by not only farm boys but also well-born young men recruited from the student class, who nevertheless were compelled to live humbly and spend much of their time in the fields, working side by side with the local peasants.[148] Apparently, Yen hoped to break down the prejudices which in

[140] *Shansi Report*, p. 125.

[141] *Lectures*, III-A, p. 320 (Dec. 1932).

[142] *Industrial Gazetteer*, pp. 285-286-szu.

[143] *Lectures*, II, p. 183 (Feb. 1937), Ying Ch'iu, *op.cit.*, p. 22, and *Industrial Gazetteer*, p. 96-ting.

[144] *CEB*, March 28, 1925, p. 185.

[145] *Industrial Gazetteer*, p. 3-ping.

[146] *Statistical Annual*, II, pp. 1-34.

[147] See *ibid.*, pp. 321-322, 329, and *Shansi Report*, p. 135.

[148] For a vivid description of life at the Hu-yen school see Chao Lien-ch'eng, "Tsai Hu-yen nung-ts'un chiao-yü shih-yen hsüeh-hsiao i'nien-lai sheng-huo chung te chi-ko p'ien-tuan" ("Some Snatches of Life during the First Year at the Hu-yen Experimental School for Village Education"), and Liu Po-ying, "Hu-yen nung-ts'un chiao-yü shih-yen hsüeh-hsiao san-nien-lai chih ching-chi kuo lüeh-shu" ("An Economic Summary of the Past Three Years at the Hu-yen Experimental School for Village Education") in *HNT*, pp. 178-198, 1-66, respectively.

the past had caused educated Chinese to scorn manual labor and those who performed it.

In 1933 he urged middle school graduates to enter professions like the science of animal husbandry and denounced them for thinking that farming was beneath them.[149] At Hu-yen, the students cultivated the fields barefooted and stripped to the waist and hauled their produce to market on their own backs. When not laboring in the fields or on the public roads, they studied animal husbandry, veterinary medicine, tree culture, agronomy, and food processing, as well as biology and practical medicine, mathematics, simple physics and mechanics, literature, accounting, and law. Much of their training consisted of putting into practice the agricultural principles and techniques they read about in their text books.[150] Students attending the school at Hu-yen also went out of their way to cultivate the friendship of peasants living in the surrounding countryside. This was necessary because graduates of schools like the one at Hu-yen were responsible for teaching and advising the peasants, directing their activities, and otherwise helping them fulfill their obligations under the Ten Year Plan. "They must revolutionize the countryside by . . . acting as spearheads for the organization of the masses—as basic cadre for the implementation of economic reconstruction at the village level," said one of them.[151] Another of Yen's followers accused Kuomintang members in Shansi of remaining in the cities and disseminating empty propaganda instead of going out among the rural masses in an effort to understand them and their predicament.[152] Besides taking part in village festivals and staging plays for local farmers, students attending the school at Hu-yen also ran a free clinic and operated a consumer cooperative, which they hoped would free the population of neighboring villages from exploitation at the hands of village merchants.[153]

[149] *Lectures*, VI, p. 116 (March 1933).

[150] Liu Po-ying, *op.cit.*, pp. 19-22, 37-45, and Kuo Hung-shih, "Mu hsiao (Hu-yen nung-ts'un chiao-yü shih-yen hsüeh-hsiao) ch'eng-li i-nien-i-lai" ("The First Year of Our School, the Hu-yen Experimental School for Village Education"), pp. 151-173.

[151] Liu Po-ying, *HNT*, *op.cit.*, pp. 58-59.

[152] Li Ch'ang-sheng, *op.cit.*, p. 2.

[153] Liu Po-ying, *op.cit.*, pp. 57-58, and Chao Lien-ch'eng, *op.cit.*, pp. 185-186. Chao even refers to the local farmers as *nung-yu*, or "peasant friends."

Yet they were staunchly anti-Communist and very loyal to Yen.[154] He and Chao Tai-wen headed the committee in charge of the school at Hu-yen and in May 1936 his photograph adorned the frontispiece of the school's official journal, *New Village* (*Hsin nung-ts'un*).[155] By that time, the school at Hu-yen had been in existence for three years and was preparing to graduate its first class of seventy-two students. One of these students says that Yen intended to create a multitude of schools like the one at Hu-yen.[156] On the other hand, most of the seventy new schools he set up in rural areas for the training of village school teachers foundered and had to be closed.[157] Yen was unable to recruit qualified students or instructors for them because in Shansi persons with schooling generally were not willing to spend their lives in the countryside teaching ignorant farmers. An American observer recalled that during the 1930's Yen sent a number of first-rate students to the University of Nanking and financed their training in agriculture there, only to have them join the faculty of the university instead of returning to Shansi.[158] Most likely the social and economic significance of the school at Hu-yen is not significant, but its creation underlines vividly the extent to which Yen's enthusiasm for economic development caused him to depart from the policies traditionally pursued by men who ruled in China.

In spite of Yen's efforts, the depression in the countryside persisted. According to non-Communist as well as Communist writers, farm income remained low, and most of the peasants living in Shansi continued to be desperately poor.[159] "The

[154] For example, see Li Hsi-chen, *op.cit.*, p. 82, and *HNT*, pp. 86-150.

[155] Other official and semiofficial publications in Shansi beamed exclusively at farmers included *Nung-to* (*The Farm Bell*), which was published by the Agricultural Technical College in Taiyuan, *Hsing-nung* (*Farmers Awake*), the bimonthly organ of the *Shan-hsi nung-min tzu-ch'iang hsieh-hui* (Shansi Association for the Promotion of Self-Strengthening among the Rural Population), and a weekly magazine put out by the *Shan-hsi chiao-yü hsüen-yüan chiao-yü hsüeh-hui* (Educational Association of the Shansi Graduate School of Education) and entitled *Hsin chiao-yü* (New Education). See Ta Pei, *op.cit.*, pp. 5-7.

[156] Liu Po-ying, *op.cit.*, p. 64.

[157] *Ibid.*

[158] Interview with John L. Buck, Stanford University, Jan. 30, 1963.

[159] *Shansi Report*, pp. 316-317, *CWR*, March 14, 1936, p. 57. Hsü Tso-hsin, *op.cit.*, p. 6, *TPLC*, p. 225, and Tanaka Ryūkichi, as quoted on p. 172 of Maruyama Shizuo, *Ushinawaretaru kiroku* (*The Story of Defeat*) (Tokyo, 1950).

peasants of the north[ern part of Shansi] marry early, work incredibly hard, and then die having lived out their tortured and muddled lives without any hope for the future," wrote one of them in 1937.[160] This was admitted by a supporter of Yen's regime, who contrasted the growing misery of the rural population with the burgeoning prosperity of Taiyuan.[161] The ills besetting agriculture in Shansi were chiefly the result of dumping by Japan and other foreign powers. This was destroying the market for Shansi's foodstuffs and textiles in North China by causing commodity prices there to decline sharply. Nevertheless, Yen must bear some of the responsibility for the increasingly miserable plight of farmers in his domain. On several occasions, he or his followers maintained that rehabilitating agriculture was less important than building heavy industries.[162] In 1934 banks in Shansi operated by the provincial authorities practically ignored agriculture and sank their money into the development of industry. That year Yen's banks accounted for more than 68 percent of the bank loans made in Shansi; well over 50 percent of these loans went to industry, while farmers received less than 4 percent of them.[163] Furthermore, the government-supported Industrial Technical College in Taiyuan was given considerably more money than its agricultural counterpart.[164] Even a student enrolled in the school at Hu-yen acknowledged the greater importance of industrial training.[165] Yen's failure to erect a single plant for the manufacture of fertilizer is another example of how he neglected agriculture and favored industry. In 1937, moreover, Shansi still had virtually no hospitals, only a few well-trained doctors, and a public health program hardly worthy of the name, since it was confined to the cities and consisted of little more than arresting persons caught urinating in the streets. As a result typhoid, cholera, and other diseases continued to kill thousands of persons in Shansi every year. "The Ten Year Plan is being carried out at the expense of the proper development of Shansi," remarked a

[160] *TPLC*, p. 84.
[161] Tuan Liang-ch'en, *op.cit.*, p. 13.
[162] *Lectures*, III-A, p. 297 (April 1932), and Wang Ta-san, *op.cit.*, pp. 1-25, and especially p. 7.
[163] *Industrial Gazetteer*, p. 176-hsin.
[164] *Statistical Annual*, II, p. 390.
[165] Wang Ta-san, *op.cit.*, pp. 22, 25.

foreign observer, ". . . everything else takes a back seat to industrial development."[166] Thus Yen's determination to create in Shansi a complex of modern industries destroyed completely the bias in favor of agriculture which occasionally permeates speeches he delivered before 1930.

On the other hand, inasmuch as agriculture was a major source of wealth in Shansi, the deterioration of the countryside severely limited the amount of capital available for investment in other sectors of the economy, with the result that Yen's new industries and his other enterprises were plagued by a chronic shortage of funds. The impact of this situation on the construction of the T'ung-Pu Railroad already has been described. Work on vitally needed water control projects also was held up for lack of funds,[167] and Yen's campaign to bring about the mechanization of agriculture suffered because although he built in Taiyuan a factory which manufactured agricultural machinery, he did not have enough money to erect in other parts of Shansi shops for the maintenance and repair of such machinery.[168] Raising capital for economic modernization in Shansi became still more difficult after 1934, when for three successive years drought and floods destroyed a large part of the crops in central and southern Shansi. Together with plunging commodity prices, this compelled Yen to reduce substantially the amount of money he was spending abroad for machinery and scientific apparatus needed by his industrial enterprises.[169] Late in 1935 a visiting engineer found the T'ung-Pu Railroad operating at considerably less than its optimum capacity, chiefly because Yen could not afford to buy twenty additional locomotives.[170] A promising experiment looking toward the smelting of better iron had been discontinued, the petroleum refinery was all but closed down, and the chemical works remained unfinished, although most of its machinery was on hand and simply had to be installed.[171] Meanwhile, a critical shortage of rolling stock complicated and delayed construction of the northern

[166] *NCH*, July 8, 1936, 80:3.

[167] *NCH*, Dec. 21, 1932, 449:1, and *Shansi Report*, p. 301.

[168] *Shansi Report*, p. 150, and Ku Chi-kang, "Farm Settlements in the Rear Loop," in *Agrarian China*, p. 48.

[169] *Shansi Report*, pp. 316-318.

[170] See *ibid.*, pp. 194-195.

[171] See *ibid.*, pp. 64-65, 107, 177, 180.

part of the T'ung-Pu Railroad.[172] No wonder in 1937 Yen called for a 20 to 30 percent increase in agricultural output during the forthcoming year.[173]

Yen's Land Reform Program

Instead of acknowledging his own blame, Yen held the foreign powers responsible for the depression in agriculture, but he likewise charged that in Shansi farming was ill-organized, primitive, and inefficient. In 1935 he set out to refashion the entire structure of rural society. He announced that he intended to do away with private ownership of land by transferring to the villages control of all the arable land in Shansi. Although the land would be divided equally among able-bodied cultivators, it was to remain the property of the village, which reserved the right to dispossess anyone who failed to work it efficiently. Landlords were to be compensated for the loss of their rents out of the proceeds of a 10 percent tax levied annually against the yield from their former holdings.[174]

Yen's proposal to nationalize and redistribute all the farmland in Shansi aroused nationwide interest,[175] but generally was regarded as a desperate attempt to compete with the land reforms advocated by the Chinese Communists, whose forces had recently established themselves in neighboring Shensi. In reality Yen had formulated his program of "All Land to the Villages" (*ts'un-yu t'u-ti*) as early as 1931, when the menace of communism was remote.[176] This means that in addition to fearing the Communists, he also used their sudden proximity as a pretext for promoting a policy which he already wished to undertake for entirely different reasons. Communist writers accuse him of wanting to protect rich landowners in Shansi from the effects of rapidly falling land values.[177] Owing to the agricultural depression, after 1931

[172] Tuan Liang-ch'en, *op.cit.*, p. 17.
[173] *Lectures*, IV, p. 109 (Feb. 1936).
[174] For a complete exposition of Yen's land-reform scheme see "T'u-ti ts'un-kung yu wen't'i" ("Questions Having to Do with the Villagization of Land") in *Lectures*, I, pp. 385-465 (Sept.-Dec. 1935).
[175] *CWR*, March, 14, 1936, p. 56, and Chung-kuo ti-cheng hsüeh-hui (Chinese Land Policy Study Association), pub., *T'u-ti ts'un-yu wen-t'i* (*The All Land to the Villages Question*) (Nanking, 1935), pp. 1, 59.
[176] *Lectures*, I, pp. 100-106 (March 1931).
[177] Chen Han-seng, *op.cit.*, pp. 378-380, and Li Fei, *op.cit.*, pp. 15-16.

the price of land in Shansi declined by 80 percent.[178] The noninterest-bearing bonds which Yen proposed to give land-lords in return for their land would have a value about 50 percent greater than its real worth.[179] Yen complained, how-ever, that although this valuation angered tenants, landlords found it outrageously low,[180] and the fact remains that under Yen's scheme landlords received each year only a tenth of the crop,[181] whereas currently their share was two thirds or more.[182] Then too, in the opinion of informed and unbiased observers, the water control projects Yen was building or planned to build in Shansi would increase enormously the value of the surrounding farmland.[183] Yen likewise intended to tax usurers to the extent of 30 percent of their profits and use the proceeds to help compensate landlords for the termina-tion of their rents.[184] Since in most cases landlords also were moneylenders, this was tantamount to having them make up their own losses.

According to no less than four impartial observers, land-lords in Shansi were incensed by Yen's attempts to take their land away from them.[185] Yen himself anticipated encountering opposition from the gentry,[186] but must have been dismayed when "village elders" boycotted a meeting he held for the purpose of getting his land reforms underway in his own village of Hopients'un.[187] Even other families in Hopients'un having the surname Yen refused to follow his example by de-manding less rent from their tenants.[188] Meanwhile, the Hankow newspaper Ta Kuang Pao accused him of advocating communism,[189] and the central government urged him to

[178] Industrial Gazetteer, p. 9-i.
[179] Ch'i Chih-chin, op.cit., p. 22.
[180] Lectures, I, pp. 388-389 (Sept. 1935).
[181] See ibid., p. 406, and NCH, Jan. 29, 1936, 175:1.
[182] Chen Han-seng, op.cit., p. 377, and TPLC, p. 83.
[183] Oliver J. Todd, op.cit., p. 545, and Shansi Report, pp. 302-304.
[184] T'u-ti ts'un-yu wen't'i, p. 54, and Fukada Yuzō, op.cit., pp. 370-371.
[185] Ch'i Chih-chin, op.cit., pp. 23-24, NCH, Jan. 29, 1936, 175:1, CWR, March 14, 1936, p. 56, and Ta Kung Pao as quoted in "P'ing-lün" ("Commentary") of KWCP, March 16, 1936, p. 1.
[186] For example, see Lectures, I, p. 407 (Oct. 1935).
[187] Haldore E. Hanson, op.cit., p. 356, and NCH, Jan. 29, 1936, 175:1.
[188] NCH, Oct. 2, 1935, 13:3, and Hsu Ying, op.cit., p. 51.
[189] Li Fei, op.cit., p. 14.

abandon his plans,[190] apparently on the ground that they were not in keeping with the principles of Sun Yat-sen.[191] Together with popular indifference or hostility and the vigorous resistance offered by landlords in Shansi, this prevented Yen from implementing his land reforms in all but a handful of villages.[192]

Several apparently unbiased observers maintain that tenant farmers and agricultural labors in Shansi welcomed Yen's land reforms and were bitterly disappointed when they failed to materialize.[193] Yet, although widespread in parts of central Shansi, tenantry was not a serious problem in most of Yen's domain. In 1935 almost 60 percent of the peasants in Shansi owned all of the land they cultivated, while another 21 percent were semiindependent.[194] This caused an American investigator to conclude that in Shansi "agricultural problems evidently are primarily not those of land tenure."[195] Consequently, if Yen risked alienating his more conservative sup-

[190] U.S. Foreign Relations Papers, 1936, p. 70.

[191] T'ang Ch'i-yü, "P'ing Yen Hsi-shan shih chin 'T'u-ti ts'un-yu' " ("A Criticism of Mr. Yen Hsi-shan's 'All Land to the Village Scheme' "), Tung-fang tsa-chih, Nov. 1, 1936, pp. 7-8. In 1943 Chiang Kai-shek tacitly condemned Yen's land-reform scheme by rejecting as "too disruptive" the so-called well-field (ching-t'ien) system of land tenure, an institution that supposedly existed in antiquity and which Yen repeatedly hailed as the inspiration for his own proposals with respect to land reform. See Joseph R. Levenson, "Ill Wind in the Well Field: The Erosion of the Confucian Ground of Controversy," in Arthur F. Wright, ed., The Confucian Persuasion (Stanford, 1960), p. 284. Thus, it would seem that in the realm of land reform Yen was considerably to the left of the Nanking regime.

[192] Ch'i Chih-chin, op.cit., p. 26, Yen Hsi-shan, op.cit., pp. 412-437 and Vol. III Hsia, p. 218, CWR, March 14, 1936, p. 56, and Ta Kung Pao as quoted on page 1 of "P'ing-lün," KWCP, March 16, 1936. The last two sources say that opposition on the part of landlords was chiefly responsible for the failure of Yen's reforms.

[193] Ch'i Chih-chin, op.cit., pp. 23-24, and CWR, March 14, 1936, p. 56.

[194] Industrial Gazetteer, p. 56-i. Another authoritative source states that in 1934 fully independent peasants and their families comprised 66 percent of the rural population in Shansi. See Monthly Review of Economic Statistics, Sept. 1935, p. 8. A third set of statistics, which indicates that only 40 percent of the peasants in Shansi were tenants or partial tenants, can be found in T'ang Ch'i-yü, op.cit., p. 7. After visiting Shansi in the winter of 1935, the American writer Haldore Hanson said that no less than 70 percent of the farmers there were completely independent and a mere 3 percent exclusively tenants. See Haldore E. Hanson, op.cit., p. 356. A Japanese study also indicates that in Shansi tenantry was not widespread. See Kojima Seiichi, op.cit., p. 68.

[195] U.S. Foreign Relations Papers, 1936, p. 70.

porters by trying to nationalize all of the land in Shansi, he must have had reasons other than merely the desire to end tenantry. One of these was his antagonism toward usury, which he claimed would become unprofitable as soon as the land belonged to the villages and therefore could not be used as collateral.[196] Significantly, in areas where he prepared to carry out his land reforms, panic-stricken usurers stopped lending money.[197] After his reforms went into effect, moreover, the government would collect the entire land tax from cultivators and compel former landlords and other wealthy persons to pay a progressive income tax.[198] In a speech advertising the merits of his land reform program, Yen said that in Shansi taxes were too low, that the peasants paid out ten times as much in the form of rents and interest, and that heavier taxes must be levied against the rich.[199] All of this suggests that to some extent his scheme was simply an effort to tax the rich more effectively and otherwise wrest away from them a larger proportion of the agricultural surplus.[200]

Yen and his followers maintained that in addition to counteracting the popular appeal of communism, the abolition of private land ownership would result in an enormous increase in farm output by making possible the rationalization and mechanization of agriculture.[201] Since they repeatedly praised

[196] *Lectures,* I, p. 429 (Oct. 1935).

[197] Ch'i Chih-chin, *op.cit.,* pp. 24-25.

[198] *Lectures,* I, p. 419 (Oct. 1935), and Fukada Yuzō, *op.cit.,* pp. 370-371.

[199] *Lectures,* III-A, pp. 374-379 (Aug. 1935).

[200] Even Li Fei, *op.cit.,* p. 14, and Chen Han-seng, *op.cit.,* p. 378, admit that Yen was less interested in protecting large landowners than in securing additional revenue for his regime, although they say that he was bent on victimizing the peasants rather than the rich. A Chinese reporter who visited Taiyuan in 1935 was told that the aim of Yen's land-reform program was not only to lessen the burden of the farmers but also to "limit and control the further expansion and *movement* [the italics are mine] of the money of the rich." See C. Y. W. Meng, " 'Model Governor' Yen Hsi-shan Advocates Abolition of Private Ownership of Land," *CWR,* Sept. 21, 1935, p. 88. In other words, Yen wanted to get his hands on the wealth of the rich.

[201] For example, see *Lectures,* I, pp. 113-114 (March 1931), 432 (Oct. 1935), 461-462 (Oct.-Dec. 1935). On p. 432 he says "After the land has been nationalized if a farmer does not improve his land, it will be repossessed, . . . and this certainly will encourage him to make improvements." At the age of fifty-eight every cultivator had to give up his land and thereafter was supported by the village, so that only the youngest, strongest, and therefore most productive members of the rural population would be working the land. Yen's follower, Chi

the kind of farming practiced in the Soviet Union, it is likely that their real aim was to collectivize agriculture in Shansi along Russian lines.[202] A number of persons from outside Shansi who visited Yen's domain came away with the impression that his land reform scheme was inspired by the Soviet collectives.[203] In response to a question asked by an American visitor, moreover, Yen said that the goal of his land reform program was identical with that of the Russians, namely, the mechanization of agriculture.[204] In January 1935 one of his semiofficial publications carried an article calling for the collectivization of agriculture.[205] According to a Japanese writer, Yen stipulated that if a majority of the villagers concurred, all the land in the village was to be consolidated into a "concentrated farm" (chi-t'uan nung-ch'ang).[206] Another writer says the same thing but refers to the new farms as "cooperative farms" (ho-kuo nung-ch'ang).[207] In his speeches Yen expressed the hope that frequently several villages would agree to form one such cooperative farm.[208] As a matter of fact, by proposing to get rid of private land ownership altogether Yen went beyond the Soviets and anticipated the more radical agrarian policies of the Chinese Communists. He even wanted communal housing (lien-huan chu-chai)[209] and expected the villages to care for persons too old to work.[210]

Sheng, op.cit., p. 64, also said that Yen's land reforms would result in the mechanization of agriculture and an increase in farm output. And on p. 154 of T'u-ti ts'un-yu wen-t'i a writer critical of Yen maintains that his land reforms were designed to increase the productivity of agriculture as well as equalize land ownership.

[202] For example, see Lectures, III-A, p. 318 (Dec. 1932), and Chi Sheng, op.cit., pp. 32-34. Writing in 1935 a visiting reporter from Peiping expressed the belief that Yen's credit cooperative scheme would be unsuccessful as long as most of the farm land in Shansi continued to be divided up into small, individually worked plots. See Wu Pao-san, Part II, p. 20. When Yen's land reforms went into effect, each cultivator would receive as much land as he could work with his own labor, so that the size of individual holdings would increase greatly. See Lectures, I, p. 423 (Oct. 1935).

[203] For example, see Fukada Yuzō, op.cit., pp. 334-335, and T'u-ti ts'un-yu wen-t'i, pp. 27, 143, 147.

[204] Lectures, I, p. 356 (Jan. 1938).

[205] Tuan Liang-ch'en, op.cit., p. 24.

[206] Fukada Yuzō, op.cit., p. 369.

[207] Hsüeh Mu-ch'iao, op.cit., p. 44.

[208] Lectures, I, p. 462 (Dec. 1935).

[209] Ibid., p. 463.

[210] See ibid., pp. 103, 105 (March 1931), 430 (Oct. 1935).

The implication of all this is that in his eagerness to mobilize the agricultural resources of Shansi behind his Ten Year Plan, Yen at least contemplated overhauling drastically the existing peasant-gentry relationship in such a way as to eliminate much of the economic power traditionally enjoyed by the privileged class. Writing in a semiofficial publication late in 1935, one of his followers denounced landlords and moneylenders in terms normally used by Communists and praised the Bolsheviks for expropriating them in Russia, while at the same time calling Yen's land reforms the only alternative to communism and the best cure for the economic ills afflicting the countryside.[211] Although more restrained, Yen spoke about the need for having the villages support impoverished landlords after they lost their land.[212] He set out to collectivize agriculture, incidentally, under the guise of putting into effect a perennial ideal of Confucian-minded reformers, namely the so-called well-field system (*ching-t'ien*) of land tenure.[213] Nothing illustrates more vividly the profound impact of the Soviet Union or the thinking of Chinese leaders after 1930 than the spectacle of this violently anti-Communist warlord invoking an ancient tradition to justify adopting perhaps the most revolutionary feature of Russian communism.[214]

[211] Chi Sheng, *op.cit.*, pp. 21-64, esp. pp. 31, 63-64.

[212] *Lectures*, I, pp. 430-431 (Oct. 1935), and T'ang Ch'i-yü, *op.cit.*, p. 8.

[213] *Lectures*, I, pp. 308-310 (Feb. 1931) and C. Y. W. Meng, *op.cit.*, p. 88.

[214] Yen's enthusiasm for the "ching-t'ien" system may have been inspired by the views of Chiang K'ang-hu, the founder of China's short-lived Socialist Party (*she-hui tang*). Chiang founded the Socialist Party in 1911, after being ousted from his professorship at Peking University because of his radicalism. In 1913 the socialists were forced to dissolve their party; however, Chiang continued to write and otherwise promote his views. (See Kiang Kang Hu, *China and the Social Revolution* [San Francisco, 1914], pp. 23-24, 30.) Later he joined the faculty of McGill University in Montreal, where he acquired international notoriety by stating, in a review of Pearl Buck's *The Good Earth*, that although coolies, peasants, and other humble persons formed the vast majority of China's population, they "are certainly not representative of the Chinese people." (See *CWR*, Oct. 13, 1934, p. 244.) Chiang had the reputation of being a "Socialistic Confucian." Like Yen, he tried to provide a traditional sanction for nationalizing agriculture by arguing that in antiquity there existed in China a socialist utopia but that this vanished after Ch'in conquered the rest of China and did away with the public ownership of land, meaning the existing ching-t'ien system of land tenure. Besides wanting to get rid of private property, Chiang likewise advocated rapid industrialization under the control of the state, as much local self-government as possible, universal

schooling, and the emancipation of women. Not only Chiang's ideas but his methods were remarkably like Yen's. According to the French sinologist Fr. Leon Wieger, in 1922 Chiang visited Taiyuan three times, with the aim of winning over Yen Hsi-shan. Yen rejected Chiang's overtures, but Wieger infers that Yen was much impressed by some of Chiang's ideas. (See Leon Wieger, *Chine Moderne*, Vol. IV, p. 344.) Significantly, after Yen announced his land reform scheme in 1935, Chiang came to Taiyuan for the purpose of discussing it and subsequently wrote an article lavishing praise on Yen, whom he called "practical rather than a theoretical socialist." (See *Lectures*, I, p. 408 [Oct. 1935], and *T'u-ti ts'un-yu wen-t'i*, pp. 42-44.) Is it possible that Yen borrowed many of his notions from Chiang K'ang-hu and that Chiang's Confucian-oriented socialism appealed to other reforming warlords who wished to initiate fundamental changes in the existing social and economic system without seeming to indulge in radicalism? Yen's relationship with Chiang also raises the question of to what extent anarchism influenced Yen's thinking. Chiang and other members of his Socialist Party subscribed to many anarchist beliefs (see Robert Scalapino and George Yu, *The Chinese Anarchist Movement* [Berkeley, 1961], p. 38), and perhaps he communicated some of these to Yen. I have in mind Yen's glorification of the village, his dislike for a money economy, his feeling that the state must preempt functions hitherto performed for individuals by their families, and his hatred of parasites, together with his conviction that practice, in the form of manual labor, is an inseparable part of learning. After Chiang K'ang-hu broke with them, the anarchists accused him of being "hopelessly confused" (see *ibid.*, p. 43); however, his confusion was not apparent to Mao Tse-tung, who confessed that as a student he was profoundly impressed by Chiang's writings. (See Edgar Snow, *op.cit.*, p. 138.)

CHAPTER ELEVEN

THE GATHERING STORM

Yen and the Japanese

SINCE his graduation from the Imperial Military Academy in 1909, Yen Hsi-shan had enjoyed friendly relations with the Japanese, and it would seem that their intervention on his behalf is one of the reasons why Chiang Kai-shek let Yen retain control of Shansi after his defeat at Chiang's hands in 1930.[1] As late as 1935 the Japanese lavished praise on Yen and tried to create the impression that he was willing to serve as the ruler of an "autonomous," Japanese-dominated North China.[2] In an effort to win him over to their side, they exploited his friendship with high-ranking Japanese army officers and may have benefited as well from pro-Japanese feeling on the part of some of the men around him.[3] Although rumors

[1] Hsi Jung, *op.cit.*, p. 3. Hsi Jung is a Communist and therefore not altogether reliable; however, a writer in the non-Communist *NCH*, July 8, 1936, 80:2, says much the same thing. Moreover, in Aug. 1931, when Yen returned to Shansi after a period of exile in Manchuria, he was flown there in an airplane provided by the Japanese Army and, according to Mr. Uno Shigeaki of the Japanese Foreign Ministry, the pilot of this airplane has said that Yen was allowed to come back at the behest of the Japanese. (Interview with Mr. Uno Shigeaki, Stanford, Nov. 27, 1962.) The *CWR*, Nov. 28, 1931, p. 503, on the other hand, maintains that Chiang Kai-shek permitted Yen to return for fear that otherwise he and his supporters would conspire with the Japanese against the Nanking government. Perhaps Chiang was aware of overtures which the Japanese made to Yen after he fled to Manchuria in 1930. An American newspaperman who visited Yen's headquarters in 1944 was told that six months before their conquest of Manchuria the Japanese invited Yen to become the head of the projected puppet state of Manchukuo. See Harrison Forman, *Report from Red China* (New York, 1945), p. 27. Although Forman often is ill-informed, there must be an element of truth in his story because a writer intimately associated with Yen's regime also says that while Yen was living in Manchuria the Japanese sought to entice him into becoming their puppet. See Wang Ch'ien, *op.cit.*, p. 18a.

[2] For example, see *CWR*, July 20, 1935, pp. 250-251, and Sept. 7, 1935, p. 5.

[3] For example, in 1935 General Tanaka Ryūkichi visited Shansi for the purpose of inducing Yen to join Japan's so-called North China Autonomy Movement. Tanaka's friendship with Yen dated back to 1928 when he had called on him to assure him of Japanese support in his race with Feng Yü-hsiang for the possession of Peking. See Maruyama Shizuo, *op.cit.*, pp. 171-172. In addition, Yen had many friends among

that the Japanese were financing Yen's Ten Year Plan are not borne out by an examination of the evidence available, much of the coal and iron mined in Shansi during the 1930's went to Japan,[4] presumably in exchange for the electrolyc salts plant, the cement factory, and other machinery Yen purchased from the Japanese.[5] It is less certain whether, as Yen's enemies charge, his campaign to promote the growing of cotton in Shansi was initiated at the behest of Japan.[6] In order to reduce their dependence on cotton imported from the West the Japanese encouraged its cultivation in North China and probably bought a part of what Shansi produced. According to a usually authoritative source, however, most of the cotton exported from Shansi was purchased by mills in Tientsin, Shanghai, and Hankow.[7] Furthermore, because the Japanese flooded the Tientsin-Peiping area with cheap Manchurian coal, Shansi's coal mines sustained heavy losses.[8] A similar fate overtook Shansi's cotton mills, whose products were driven off the market in neighboring provinces by less expensive Japanese-made cloth and yarn.[9]

Japanese army officers who had been his fellow cadets at the Imperial Military Academy in Tokyo. As for pro-Japanese feeling on the part of his supporters, according to the Communist leader Po I-po, Yen's uncle and brother-in-law consistently promoted Japanese interests in Shansi. See Anonymous, "Po I-po t'ung-chih hsieh-lu Yen Hsi-shan t'ung-ti p'an-kuo nui-mu" ("Comrade Po I-po Reveals the Inside Story of Yen Hsi-shan's Treason"), pp. 4-5 in Ch'en Po-ta, *Yen Hsi-shan p'i-p'an.* It would seem that at least one of Yen's chief lieutenants, Su T'i-jen, also inclined toward Japan, since he subsequently headed the Japanese puppet regime in Shansi.

    [4] Takagi Rikurō, *op.cit.*, p. 181, *Shansi Report*, p. 52, and *CEJ*, April 1933, p. 433.

    [5] *Shansi Report*, p. 118, and *Industrial Gazetteer*, p. 589-szu.

    [6] Chen Han-seng, *op.cit.*, p. 377, Hsüeh Mu-ch'iao, *op.cit.*, p. 46, Nieh Jung-chen, as quoted in Evans F. Carlson, *op.cit.*, p. 218, and Po Li, *Chin Ch'a Chi pien-ch'ü yin-hsiang chi* (*Impressions of the Shansi-Chahar-Hupei Border Region*) (Hankow, 1938), pp. 41-42. Po Li admits that there is no proof that Yen was raising cotton for the Japanese but assumes this to be the case.

    [7] *Industrial Gazetteer*, p. 96-ting.

    [8] *CWR*, March 7, 1936, p. 24, and *CEB*, Jan. 20, 1934, p. 37. According to the *NCH*, April 11, 1934, 8:4, there circulated rumors that "Japanese representing industrial interests are making frequent trips to Shansi to negotiate for the taking over of the mines and works at Yangch'uan." Is it possible that the Japanese were trying to coerce Yen into turning over to them his bankrupt coal mines?

    [9] *Industrial Gazetteer*, pp. 17-szu, 32-szu.

Yen was eager to develop Shansi's cotton textile industry.[10] Yet by 1936 both the privately owned Chin Sheng mill and the government-operated Chin Hua mill were bankrupt.[11] Writing in 1934, one of Yen's supporters complained bitterly about not only the textiles but also the host of other commodities, ranging from beer to paper, which the Japanese were pouring into China.[12] Besides depriving Yen's new factories of markets in other parts of North China, goods produced in Japan comprised a large percentage of the foreign-made merchandise smuggled into Shansi after 1930.[13] As early as 1933 Yen charged that cheap Japanese cloth was destroying the local market for textiles made in Shansi.[14] Thus Japanese efforts to acquire a monopoly over the sale of manufactured goods in China were ruining the industries Yen had erected in an attempt to rehabilitate Shansi's badly depressed economy. This is why in 1932 he came out strongly in favor of an antiforeign boycott[15] and apparently encouraged students to help him keep Japanese goods out of Shansi.[16] In 1935 he publicly denounced the Japanese for indulging in "economic aggression" against China and accused them of being responsible for most of China's social and economic distress because in order to stave off a depression and unemployment in Japan they were dumping their surplus manufactures in China, to the detriment of China's own infant industries.[17] Since most of the narcotics entering Shansi also were manufactured by the Japanese or made under their auspices,[18] Yen came to feel that Japan menaced the well-being of his regime.

Fear of the Japanese Army is another reason why after 1930 Yen became increasingly antagonistic to Japan. It would

[10] *Lectures*, IV, p. 49 (Nov. 1932), and II, p. 236 (July 1937), Ying Ch'iu, *op.cit.*, p. 22, and *NCH*, Jan. 16, 1935, 88:5.

[11] Ch'i Chih-chin, *op.cit.*, p. 26, and *Industrial Gazetteer*, p. 97-ting.

[12] Ying Ch'iu, *op.cit.*, p. 18.

[13] According to a usually reliable writer, most of the contraband that entered northern Shansi during the 1930's came from Japan. See *HHHCC*, p. 39.

[14] *Lectures*, III-A, p. 333 (May 1933).

[15] *Lectures*, IV, p. 44 (May 1932).

[16] In 1932 the Supervisorial Association indicted two students for accepting bribes in return for allowing merchants to bring Japanese goods into Shansi. These students had been given the job of *chien-ch'a jih-huo*, "watching out for Japanese goods." See Li Ch'ang-sheng, *op.cit.*, p. 6.

[17] *Lectures*, IV, pp. 92-94 (1935).

[18] Ying Ch'iu, *op.cit.*, pp. 27-28, and Wang Meng-chou and Chang Lan-t'ing, *op.cit.*, pp. 5-6.

appear that while he was living in Manchuria he received overtures from the Japanese and feigned collaborating with them in order to frighten Chiang Kai-shek into letting him return to Shansi; however, Japan's subsequent occupation of Manchuria must have terrified him because speeches which he delivered early in 1932 indicate that a major purpose of his Ten Year Plan was to strengthen Shansi's defenses against the Japanese.[19] In December 1931 he supported, and may have been responsible for, the anti-Japanese riots which destroyed the authority of the central government in Shansi and made it possible for him to regain control of his province. He proclaimed his solidarity with the demonstrators by publicly appealing to the central government to throw an immense force of crack troops into the battle for Chin-chou, a city located in Liaoning about 100 miles northeast of the border between Manchuria and Hopei.[20] In addition to describing the Japanese occupation of Manchuria as "barbarous" and "evil," he warned that it was simply a prelude to the invasion of North China so that by not resisting in Manchuria the government was committing suicide.[21] Significantly, there were reports that the Taiyuan Arsenal was turning out ammunition for use by Chinese volunteers fighting the Japanese in Manchuria.[22] Immediately after returning to Shansi, moreover,

[19] *Lectures*, III-A, pp. 287, 292-295 (Nov. 1931, Feb.-April 1932) and *Shansi Report*, p. 2. Writing several years after the Japanese conquest of Manchuria, supporters of Yen, as well as Yen himself, said that the decision to create a complex of modern industries in Shansi was inspired by fear of Japan. See Liu Kuan-san, "Pen she ch'eng-li chih ching-kuo" ("The Experiences of Our Association since its Creation"), *CSSH*, p. 5, Wang Ch'ien, *op.cit.*, p. 18a, and *Lectures*, II, p. 293 (July 1937), as well as Jen Ying-lun and Kuo Chien-fu, *op.cit.*, p. 5. An American who interviewed Yen in 1944 says that while in Dairen Yen was informed of Japan's plans for the conquest of Manchuria by the Japanese, who expected him to cooperate with them against Chiang Kai-shek; instead, Yen fled and communicated his knowledge to Chiang, who expressed his gratitude by letting Yen return to Shansi. See Harrison Forman, *op.cit.*, p. 27. This story sounds far-fetched but may contain an element of truth, since Yen left Manchuria suddenly and on the very eve of the Japanese takeover. Apparently, the Japanese expected him to go from Dairen to Japan and were surprised when he did not. See Peip'ing *Ch'en-pao*, Dec. 22, 1930, as quoted in *Archives*, Dec. 1930, p. 292, and Gaimushō, *Honpō no chihō-seifu oyobi kojin ni taisuru shakkan kankei zakken: Sansei oyobi kyōsei shō no bu, ji Shōwa gogatsu shidō roku-nen gogatsu.*

[20] *Hua-pei jih-pao*, Dec. 25, 1931, as quoted in *Archives*, Dec. 1931, pp. 337-339.

[21] *Ibid.*, and *Lectures*, IV, p. 37 (Dec. 1931).

[22] *CYB*, *1934*, p. 298.

Yen founded at least two anti-Japanese organizations: The Blood and Iron National Salvation Corps (*T'ieh hsieh chiu-kuo t'uan*) and the Revenge Corps (*Fu-ch'ou t'uan*).[23]

Japan's conquest of Manchuria, together with the Japanese occupation of neighboring Jehol in the spring of 1933, completed the destruction of Shansi's once flourishing commercial empire. In Manchuria and Jehol, Shansi's bankers and merchants had continued to do business, but now they were driven out by the Japanese, with the result that remittances to Shansi almost ceased, causing additional bankruptcies and misery in Yen's already impoverished domain.[24] Yen's behavior during Japan's invasion of Jehol suggests that he was dissuaded from coming to the defense of Jehol only by the knowledge that the central government would not support him.[25] As early as December 1931 he had warned that having acquired control of Manchuria, the Japanese next would invade Inner Mongolia, with the aim of seizing Chahar and Suiyuan.[26] In addition to being under the rule of Yen's subordinate, Fu Tso-i, and consequently what might be called a "satellite" of Shansi, Suiyuan was a source of iron and other raw materials urgently needed by Yen's new industries, as well as a market for many of the goods manufactured in Shansi.[27] As for Chahar, much of its trade with the rest of China was in the hands of merchants from Shansi,[28] and undoubtedly Yen intended to exploit its rich deposits of iron for the benefit of his steel mill. Whereas Shansi has less than 8 percent of the iron in China, Chahar has 24 percent, which is more iron than in any province south of the Great Wall.[29] Northeastern Shansi is peculiarly vulner-

[23] Jen Ying-lun and Kuo Chien-fu, *op.cit.*, p. 4.

[24] *Lectures*, III-A, p. 369 (July 1935), *Industrial Gazetteer*, pp. 86-87-hsin, *Shansi Report*, p. 242, and Ch'i T'ien-shou, *op.cit.*, p. 7.

[25] *CWR*, March 4, 1933, p. 13 and *NCH*, April 5, 1933, 11:1.

[26] *Hua-pei jih-pao*, Dec. 25, 1931, as quoted in *Archives*, Dec. 1931, p. 338. He reiterated this view in Feb. 1932. See *Lectures*, III-A, p. 291.

[27] *CEB*, Dec. 26, 1925, p. 360, *NCH*, Oct. 4, 1933, 11:2, and Takagi Rikurō, *op.cit.*, p. 98. For example, the large distillery which Yen built in Tatung was making industrial alcohol out of sweet potatoes grown in Suiyuan. See *Wu Pao-san, Part I*, p. 18.

[28] *CEB*, Aug. 29, 1925, p. 121. Until 1929 Chahar and Suiyuan were one province. See Hata Ikuhiku, *Nitchū sensō shi* (*A History of the Sino-Japanese War*) (Tokyo, 1961), p. 115.

[29] Ho Lien, "Hua-pei Chi Lü Chin Ch'a Sui wu-sheng ching-chi tsai cheng-ko Chung-kuo ching-chi chih ti-wei" ("The Position Occupied by the Economies of the Five Provinces of North China, Honan, Shantung, Shansi, Chahar, and Suiyuan, in the Economy of China, as a

able to attack by an enemy in possession of southern Chahar, moreover, since both regions are part of the Sang Kan River basin and therefore not separated by geographical barriers.[30] For these reasons Yen resented bitterly Japan's attempts to extend her authority into first Chahar and then Suiyuan, under the guise of creating an autonomous Inner Mongolia.

Because they were being exploited and mistreated by the Chinese around them, Mongols living in Chahar and Suiyuan generally did not want to remain under China's rule.[31] For decades, merchants from Shansi had waxed rich at the expense of the Mongols, who, according to one writer, often were gulled into exchanging a valuable horse or sheep for a strip of cotton cloth, a few pieces of brick tea, or perhaps simply a wooden comb.[32] Chinese traders also enriched themselves by lending money to Mongol princes, from whom they demanded interest, in the form of livestock, at the rate of 50 to 70 percent a year.[33] The Mongols must have been equally outraged by Yen's policy of encouraging Chinese farmers to settle in Suiyuan, where they not only plowed up vast stretches of grassland which the Mongols needed for their herds but likewise provided Yen with an excuse for depriving Mongol princes of much of their power on the grounds that they were not capable of governing Chinese settlers.[34] Since in Manchuria and Jehol the Japanese prevented Chinese merchants from exploiting the Mongols and upheld the authority of the Mongol princes, Mongols living in Chahar and Suiyuan became increasingly receptive to Japanese propaganda aimed at encouraging the Mongols to separate from China and establish an independent Mongol state, which the Japanese chose to call "Mengkukuo."[35]

Whole"), *Tung-fang tsa-chih*, April 1, 1936, pp. 8-9, and *CEB*, Nov. 30, 1935, p. 339.

[30] *HHHCC*, p. 50.

[31] Hattori Takushirō, *Dai-Tōa sensō zenshi* (*The Complete History of the War for Greater East Asia*), I (Tokyo, 1953), p. 35, and Ho Tung, "Sui-yüan tsai kuo-fang te ti-wei" ("Suiyuan's Position with Respect to National Defense"), *KWCP*, Nov. 2, 1936, p. 5.

[32] *CEB*, Aug. 29, 1925, p. 122.

[33] *Ibid.*

[34] Ku Chi-kang, *op.cit.*, p. 50, and Anonymous, "China's Great Northwest," *PT*, March 1, 1934, p. 281.

[35] Chang Tso-hua, "Nui-Meng wen-t'i yü kuo-fang" ("The Inner Mongolian Question and National Defense"), *KWCP*, Sept. 7, 1936, pp. 2-3.

In order to counteract Japan's growing influence over the Mongols, in the spring of 1934 the central government created the Inner Mongolian Autonomous Political Council (*Nuimeng ti-fang tzu-chih cheng-wu hui*), with headquarters at Pailingmiao in northern Suiyuan. This organization was made up of prominent Mongols and supposedly governed Chahar and Suiyuan; in reality, Fu Tso-i harassed the council and frustrated its efforts to establish its authority in southern Suiyuan and western Chahar.[36] This caused most of its members to advocate collaboration with the Japanese, especially after January 1935, when Manchurian troops armed with Japanese weapons and in many instances under the command of Japanese officers invaded Chahar for the avowed purpose of freeing Mongols there from the domination of the Chinese.[37] By the winter of 1936 the Manchurians were in possession of northeastern Chahar, and in February the leading figure on the Council, Prince Teh, entered into an alliance with them. Thus Japan's advance into Inner Mongolia threatened to shatter Yen's dream of bringing all of northwestern China under his control. In retaliation, he engineered the defection of anti-Japanese elements from the Inner Mongolian Autonomous Political Council and virtually declared war against Japan's ambitions in the Northwest by accepting an appointment as "advisor" (*chih-tao chang-kuan*) to the rival Suiyuan Mongolian Political Council (*Sui-yüan meng cheng hui*), which the Central Government organized from among Mongols opposed to the Japanese.[38]

Yen's antagonism toward Japan was reinforced by the knowledge that the Japanese undoubtedly wanted Shansi as well as Inner Mongolia. According to many writers, the Japanese wished to exploit Shansi's natural resources, especially its immense deposits of coal, and therefore were financing the construction of railroads in North China which would give them direct access to Shansi.[39] Significantly, they often ex-

[36] *CWR*, Sept. 8, 1934, pp. 58-60, and Sept. 22, 1934, p. 119.

[37] Chang Tso-hua, *op.cit.*, pp. 4-5.

[38] See *ibid.*, p. 5, and p. 3 of "P'ing-lün" ("Commentary"), as well as pp. 7-8 of "Ta-shih shu-yao" ("Résumé of Important Events"), *KWCP*, March 2, 1936.

[39] C. Y. W. Meng, *op.cit.*, p. 90, James Bertram, *op.cit.*, p. 35, and *CWR*, March 17, 1934, p. 8, July 27, 1935, p. 287, Aug. 24, 1935, p. 439, Sept. 26, 1936, p. 126, and March 23, 1940, p. 120. Apparently Japan coerced the central government into giving the South Manchurian

pressed a willingness to participate in the economic development of Shansi,[40] and after ousting Yen in 1937 they spent
approximately US$62.5 million developing coal mines in north-
ern Shansi, which one writer says "dominated Japan's plans
for an increase in coal production in China."[41] Certainly the
Japanese must have perceived the military usefulness of the
railroads and industries Yen was building and perhaps they
also regarded his Ten Year Plan as a menace to their economic
interests in China. For example, China bought much of its
steel from Japan;[42] however, because Shansi possessed an
abundant supply of cheap coal, steel manufactured in Taiyuan and transported over the new T'ung-Pu Railroad probably
would sell for considerably less than Japanese-made steel in
the markets of North China.[43] All of this explains why throughout the 1930's Shansi teemed with Japanese agents seeking
information about its economy and its defenses.[44] No wonder
Yen and his supporters feared an attack on Shansi when
Japan seized Jehol in 1933.[45] Early in 1934 Yen protested

Railroad Company and Mitsubishi interests the exclusive right to build
a railroad linking Shihchiachuang on the Cheng-Tai line near the border
between Hopei and Shansi with the Tientsin-P'uk'ou line at Ts'angchou
in Shantung. See Higuchi Hiromu, *op.cit.*, p. 149. According to *NCH*,
Jan. 10, 1934, 45:2, the construction of such a railroad would reduce
appreciably the cost of hauling coal from Shansi to the coast.

[40] *CWR*, July 20, 1935, p. 250, Oct. 5, 1935, p. 154, and March 7,
1936, p. 24.

[41] *CWR*, May 7, 1938, p. 288.

[42] *Shansi Report*, pp. 69-70.

[43] See *ibid.*, p. 77. According to Mr. Uno Shigeaki of the Japanese
Foreign Ministry, when Japanese forces attacked China in 1937 they
were ordered to bypass Shansi; however, the Japanese high command
disregarded these instructions from Tokyo on the grounds that because
of its new industries Shansi was the most important part of North
China and consequently had to be taken immediately. (Interview with
Mr. Uno Shigeaki, Stanford University, Nov. 27, 1962.) Significantly,
after occupying Taiyuan the Japanese hastily completed Yen's steel
mill and put it into operation. See *Japanese Steel Survey*, 406:2.

[44] *CWR*, Oct. 7, 1933, p. 221, and May 5, 1935, p. 187, and Haldore
E. Hanson, "Chinese War Lord Dreams of Russia," *CWR*, Feb. 8, 1936,
p. 356. Japan must have been keeping a watchful eye on events in
Shansi, since Yen's Ten Year Plan is the subject of several chapters
in a study of economic conditions in North China published in 1935
under the auspices of the Japanese-owned South Manchurian Railroad
Company. With the exception of Hopei, which the Japanese were in the
process of annexing, no other province in North China interests the
author of this book as much as Shansi, and he warns that Yen's efforts
to industrialize his domain merit close attention. See *SMR Survey*,
especially p. 240.

[45] *NCH*, March 15, 1933, 411:3.

against what he called "Japan's invasion of the Northwest"[46] and in January 1935 there appeared in a semiofficial publication of the provincial government several articles denouncing the central government for not resisting the Japanese. One called for the recovery of Manchuria and other territory lost to Japan;[47] another warned that a Japanese invasion of Chahar would imperil the security of Shansi.[48] Consequently, Yen must have been terrified by the fighting in northeastern Chahar, especially since it took place at a time when Japan was pressing for the creation of a nominally autonomous but in reality Japanese-dominated state comprising all of North China and including Shansi.

The Japanese began promoting autonomy for North China late in the summer of 1935. Apparently they felt that although occasionally obliged to indulge in anti-Japanese oratory in order to appease Chinese nationalism, Yen and other warlords in the North were fundamentally pro-Japanese and therefore willing to subordinate themselves to Japan in return for protection against Chiang Kai-shek.[49] Yen promptly shattered this illusion. In an open letter he published in September, he warned that Japan intended to conquer all of China within the next two decades.[50] A month later, he demonstrated his opposition to autonomy by going to Nanking and accepting

[46] *Lectures*, I, p. 311 (Jan. 1934).

[47] Li Ch'ang-sheng, *op.cit.*, p. 18. Li says that Manchuria has been cast into hell, that its people cry out in vain, and that their helplessness is a source of agony for them. Significantly, he complained that the loss of Manchuria eliminated a valuable source of employment for persons fleeing from the depression-ridden countryside of North China. He likewise attacked the central government and the Kuomintang for suppressing anti-Japanese demonstrations and called the so-called T'ang-ku Truce an abject surrender to Japanese imperialism (pp. 2-3). His contempt for Nanking's policy of appeasing Japan at the expense of Manchuria and North China was shared by other writers in the Jan. 1, 1935 issue of *Chien-cheng chou-k'an*. See Jen Ying-lun and Kuo Chien-fu, *op.cit.*, pp. 4-5. These writers go on to say that although Shansi has no choice but to follow the central government's policy of "keeping quiet" in the face of Japanese aggression, throughout the province "activist elements" are carrying out "educational and political work" aimed at stirring up popular resistance to Japan. All three of these writers were very anti-Communist and enthusiastic supporters of Yen Hsi-shan.

[48] Shun Wu, *op.cit.*, p. 25. Ying Ch'iu, *op.cit.*, p. 3, denounces what he calls "Japan's invasion of Inner Mongolia." In fact, this whole issue of *Chien-cheng chou-k'an* is permeated with anti-Japanese feeling.

[49] For example, see Hata Ikuhiku, *op.cit.*, pp. 60-61, and Maruyama Shizuo, *op.cit.*, pp. 172-173.

[50] *Lectures*, III-A, pp. 417-418 (Sept. 1935).

from Chiang Kai-shek an appointment to the Central Executive Committee of the Kuomintang. In November, when the Japanese imposed autonomy on eastern Hopei, a periodical issued under the auspices of Yen's regime and bearing his photograph on its frontispiece accused them of wanting to destroy the Chinese people.[51] Students in Taiyuan were allowed to demonstrate against Japan's actions in Hopei, and in January Yen drew even closer to the central government by assuming the vice-chairmanship of the National Military Affairs Commission (*kuo-fu chün wei-hui*).[52] Thereafter the Japanese regarded Yen as an enemy and stepped up their efforts to oust him from Inner Mongolia.

The Chinese Communists subsequently charged that Yen actually favored autonomy for North China along the lines proposed by the Japanese, yet dared not express his views for fear of outraging public opinion in Shansi.[53] According to Japanese writers, Yen entered into negotiations with the Japanese[54] and perhaps, as one scholar believes, he offered to cooperate with them if they allowed him to rule all of North China and treated him as an ally rather than a puppet, but rejected their overtures upon perceiving that this was not their intention.[55] Japanese writers also leave the impression, however, that Yen never expressed much enthusiasm for autonomy.[56] Most likely he flirted with the Japanese largely for the purpose of frightening Chiang Kai-shek into committing

[51] *CSSH*, p. 1.

[52] P. 1 of "I-chou chien-p'ing" ("Weekly Commentary"), *KWCP*, Feb. 3, 1936, interprets Yen's acceptance of this post as an anti-Japanese move on his part and tantamount to rejection of Japan's invitation to join its North China Autonomy Movement.

[53] For example, see Hsi Jun, *op.cit.*, p. 3.

[54] Hata Ikuhiku, *op.cit.*, pp. 60-61, and Maruyama Shizuo, *op.cit.*, p. 173.

[55] Interview with Professor James T. C. Liu, Stanford University, Nov. 1, 1962. It would seem that Yen continued to negotiate with the Japanese as long as the chief proponent of autonomy for North China was Japan's so-called North China Army and broke off relations with the Japanese only after the leadership of the autonomy movement passed into the hands of General Kenji Doihara and the Kwantung Army, stationed in Manchuria. See Hata Ikuhiku, *op.cit.*, pp. 60-61. If Professor Liu is correct about Yen's motives, this suggests that whereas Doihara and the Kwantung Army regarded autonomy as merely a device for bringing North China under Japanese control, the North China Army advocated genuine autonomy and therefore an alliance with warlords like Yen. This whole subject merits further investigation.

[56] Hata Ikuhiku, *op.cit.*, p. 61, and Maruyama Shizuo, *op.cit.*, p. 173.

his Central Armies to the defense of Shansi, since it would appear that Yen feared Chiang was preparing to sacrifice Shansi and the rest of North China in order to appease Japan.[57] This is probably why Yen went to Nanking only after Chiang visited Taiyuan, where he must have assured Yen that in the event he was attacked by the Japanese the central government would come to his assistance. The Communists are correct in saying that Yen was under considerable popular pressure to resist Japan, inasmuch as most of the students and educated youth of Shansi, who made up the bulk of Yen's following by 1935 and on whom he was depending for the implementation of his Ten Year Plan, were exceedingly anti-Japanese.[58] On the other hand, the charge that Yen opposed Japan merely because he feared that otherwise he would lose the support of his youthful followers is belied by the fact that as early as 1933 he was encouraging students fleeing from Japanese-occupied territory to attend schools in Shansi.[59] All of this may explain why in 1935 his once trusted but very pro-Japanese lieutenant Su T'i-jen resigned from the provincial government.

The Communist Invasion

Notwithstanding his admiration for their economic accomplishments, Yen professed to fear the Russians almost as much as the Japanese. In 1932 he warned that because of its growing strength within ten years the U.S.S.R. would be a serious menace to China.[60] Undoubtedly he held the Soviet Union responsible for the collapse of Shansi's once flourishing trade with Outer Mongolia and Sinkiang, where Russian influence was paramount after 1930. On several occasions he

57 Ying Ch'iu, op.cit., p. 20.
58 Both J. W. Phillips, "The Rising Tide in North China," CT, July 1936, p. 195, and Tan Shin She, "The Policy of the C. P. of China and the Chinese Red Army," International Press Correspondence, hereafter referred to as IPC, May 16, 1936, p. 630, say that students in Shansi were exceedingly anti-Japanese. According to H. P. Tasmania Wu, "Chinese Red Army in Shansi," China Today, Jan. 1937, p. 39, some of the "youth rich" in Shansi were intensely anti-Japanese. Several of Yen's supporters, who expressed a loathing for communism, also detested Japan and wanted to resist Japanese aggression. For example, see P'ing Fan, op.cit., pp. 3-4, and Ying Ch'iu, op.cit., pp. 11-15. The latter is violent in his condemnation of Japan but extravagant in his praise of Yen.
59 NCH, June 21, 1933, 449:3.
60 Lectures, III-A, p. 296 (April 1932).

and his followers denounced the Soviets for ousting the Chinese from Outer Mongolia and accused them of having designs on Suiyuan and the rest of Inner Mongolia.[61] As for the Chinese Communist Party, in addition to persecuting unmercifully its adherents in Shansi, Yen also sent troops to fight the Communists in Kiangsi and subsequently in neighboring Shensi, which became the chief Communist stronghold in China in the summer of 1935 when the bulk of the Red Army established itself there after completing its "Long March" from South China. Since 1927 there had been many Communist sympathizers among the students attending middle schools and colleges in Shansi, but by 1935 Yen was considerably more alarmed about the increasingly radical outlook of the peasants who made up the vast majority of his subjects. Early in 1936 a well-informed and apparently unbiased Chinese investigator encountered widespread enthusiasm for the Communist cause among peasants living in northern Shansi, which he attributed to their dissatisfaction with the existing social and economic system. He felt that because of their desperate poverty they would welcome the Communists in the hope that any change would be for the better.[62] Undoubtedly peasant unrest explains why in the fall of 1935 small bands of Communist infiltrators succeeded in virtually taking over several districts in Shansi lying along the southwestern border opposite Shensi. Yen admitted that the Communists enjoyed the sympathy of 70 percent of his subjects and warned that if the Red Army entered Shansi, it could recruit well over a million men from among the poor peasants and the unemployed.[63]

In order to combat this threat to his power, Yen organized the younger members of the gentry into what he called *fang-kung pao-wei t'uan*, the "anti-Communist militia"; however, the speeches Yen delivered during the fall of 1935 reveal that he was less frightened by the military strength of the Communists than by the probability that the radical social and economic reforms which the Communist Party advocated

[61] For example, see *Lectures*, I, p. 311 (Jan. 1934), Shun Wu, *op.cit.*, p. 25, and Heng San, " 'K'ai-fa Hsi-pei wen-t'i' chih shang-chiao" ("What About the so-called 'Problem of Developing the Northwest' "), pp. 2-3, *CCCK*.

[62] Ch'i Chih-chin, *op.cit.*, p. 26.

[63] *Lectures*, III-A, pp. 386 (Aug. 1935), and 439 (Dec. 1935).

would cause his own people to join forces with the Red Army against him.[64] "The job of suppressing communism is 70 percent political and only 30 percent military, while the job of preventing its growth altogether is 90 percent political," he remarked.[65] Consequently, he initiated a propaganda campaign aimed at discrediting the Communists. He accused them of killing 100,000 people in northern Shensi and composed a number of anti-Communist songs like the following:

> The Communists cut down people like grass.
> Whether rich or poor, few escape.
> The rich must awake; the poor must be made
>   to realize that everyone will suffer if commu-
>   nism triumphs.
> Alas![66]

As part of an effort to counteract the popular appeal of the Communist Party's program, he created the Justice Force, whose members were responsible for protecting the poor against abuse and exploitation at the hands of persons having wealth and influence. By proposing to nationalize and redistribute all of the cultivated land in Shansi, he likewise tried to compete with the Communist Party's program of land reform, which he regarded as an important reason for its popularity. He inferred strongly that the Communists had survived Chiang Kai-shek's annihilation campaigns in South China because they retained the support of the masses, owing to Chiang's failure to introduce fundamental social and economic reforms.[67] Writing in the winter of 1936, an American observer says that under the guise of fighting communism many of Yen's followers were preaching doctrines remarkably like those professed by the Communists.[68]

These reforms came too late to ward off the catastrophe which Yen had foreseen. In February 1936, 34,000 Communist soldiers, led by Liu Chih-tan and Hsü Hai-tung, crossed the frozen waters of the Yellow River and invaded southwestern Shansi, where they enjoyed what must have been massive

---

[64] See *ibid.*, pp. 432-433 (Dec. 1935), I, p. 437 (Oct. 1935), and IX, p. 10 (Oct. 1935).

[65] *Lectures*, III-A, p. 414 (Sept. 1935).

[66] *Lectures*, IX, p. 13 (Oct. 1935).

[67] *Lectures*, III-A, p. 409 (Sept. 1935).

[68] *U.S. Foreign Relations Papers, 1936*, p. 71.

popular support, because although outnumbered and ill-armed, within less than a month they succeeded in occupying nearly a third of Yen's domain. Only two thirds of the Communist troops had rifles,[69] whereas Yen's 70,000-man army even commanded the services of warplanes supplied by the central government.[70] Nevertheless, Yen's forces suffered one defeat after another, largely on account of the vastly superior mobility of their opponents. Instead of concentrating for the purpose of fighting a pitched battle with the bulk of Yen's forces, the Communist armies struck out in all directions, moving so rapidly that the Shansi Army lost track of their whereabouts, with the result that it repeatedly fell victim to surprise attacks which left it confused and demoralized.[71] The Red Army could not have employed such tactics without the assistance of peasants living in the surrounding countryside, who in addition to concealing its presence from Yen's soldiers also must have kept the Communists informed about the movements of the Shansi Army, since the government admitted that the invaders always knew precisely where its own forces were located.[72] A foreign observer says that peasant support was one of the major reasons why the Communists advanced so rapidly into Shansi.[73] Later, when powerful armies sent by the central government compelled the Communists to withdraw from Shansi, a part of the Red Army escaped only by breaking up into small groups, which surely would have perished unless hidden and fed by the peasants.

The behavior of Yen and his followers during this invasion likewise suggests that the masses went over to the Communists. Yen was so alarmed by the ease with which Communist agitators infiltrated his territory and their subsequent effectiveness that he ordered his police to arrest all travelers who had not obtained from the authorities permission to leave their

[69] P. 1 of "Ta-shih shu-yao," *KWCP*, April 6, 1936. Another account states that only one third had rifles and that the Communists were without cannon of any kind. See *NCH*, July 8, 1936, 80:3.

[70] Hatano, *History of the C.C.P., 1936*, p. 47.

[71] See *ibid.*, pp. 14, 42, 46-47, *NCH*, May 6, 1936, 226:3, and Himeno Tokuichi, *op.cit.*, p. 152.

[72] Fukada Yuzō, *op.cit.*, p. 364. According to another source, initially Communist soldiers succeeded in disguising themselves as merchants, farmers, and laborers. This would have been impossible without the cooperation of the local population. See *NCH*, March 18, 1936, 477:4.

[73] *NCH*, April 1, 1936, 8:3-4.

native villages.[74] According to a Communist source, magistrates in districts still unoccupied by the Red Army executed as many as 150 persons a day on the ground that those killed were either Communists or guilty of collaborating with the Communists.[75] An anti-Communist writer speaks of "a holocaust of executions" carried out by Yen's soldiers in areas from which the Communists had withdrawn.[76] When the American reporter Edgar Snow talked with Communist leaders in 1936, he was told that while in Shansi the Communist armies recruited 8,000 soldiers, and a total of 15,000 volunteered for the Red Army.[77] Several anti-Communist sources agree that a large number of the young men living in areas occupied by the Communists accompanied the Red Army when it returned to Shensi in April 1936.[78]

Many who joined the Red Army during its invasion of Shansi were from Yen's own Shansi Army, whose troops surrendered without a fight on several occasions. Foreign observers say that most of Yen's soldiers were demoralized and unwilling to resist the Communists.[79] Besides resenting the brutality of their officers, they disliked building railroads and otherwise working like coolies in return for meager wages.[80] In fact, according to one writer, for some time before the Communists invaded Shansi Yen's troops were not paid at all.[81] This explains why after suffering a few defeats they retired into the cities, which the Red Army was unable to capture owing to its lack of artillery, and allowed the Communists to move unmolested through the countryside. Subsequently, Yen more or less admitted that his soldiers had fought badly,[82] and in an effort to improve their morale he raised their wages.[83]

The apathetic behavior of the Shansi Army caused Japanese newspapers to charge that Yen's troops had concluded a truce with the Red Army, whose real destination was Suiyuan and

[74] Himeno Tokuichi, *op.cit.*, p. 153.
[75] Chao Shu-li, *op.cit.*, p. 51.
[76] *NCH*, July 8, 1936, 80:4.
[77] *CWR*, Nov. 21, 1936, p. 430.
[78] *NCH*, May 6, 1936, 266:3, and July 8, 1936, 80:3.
[79] Himeno Tokuichi, *op.cit.*, p. 153, and Hatano, *History of the C.C.P., 1936*, p. 46.
[80] Haldore E. Hanson, *op.cit.*, p. 356.
[81] *NCH*, April 1, 1936, 8:3-4.
[82] *Lectures*, III-C, pp. 231-234 (June 1936), and v, pp. 63-64 (July 1936).
[83] *NCH*, May 6, 1936, 226:5.

Hopei, where, presumably, it would attack the Japanese and their allies.[84] This is doubtful because of the vigor with which the Shansi Army resisted Communist efforts to seize P'ingyao, Hungt'ung, and other cities.[85] Nevertheless, the existence of intense antagonism toward Japan on the part of those who governed Shansi undoubtedly encouraged the Communists to hope that if they entered Shansi for the avowed purpose of fighting the Japanese, they would be welcomed by Yen and his followers. As early as January 1935 there appeared in one of Yen's semiofficial publications an article calling for the creation of a Chinese People's Anti-Imperialist Front (*Chung-hua min-ts'u te fan-ti chan-hsien*).[86] In December 1935 Yen warned against trying to eradicate communism while at the same time appeasing Japan, on the ground that such a policy would "drive the strong into the hands of the Communists and invite the weak to collaborate with the Japanese."[87] A foreign reporter who visited Taiyuan a month later says that Yen's only hope lay in Nanking's willingness to lead a national crusade against the Japanese.[88] All of this explains why Communist leaders left off denouncing Yen as a traitor and offered to help him resist Japan. For example, in December 1935 the former secretary-general of the Chinese Communist Party, Wang Ming, conspicuously omitted Yen's name from a list of Kuomintang leaders and warlords whom he stigmatized as traitors and agents of Japanese imperialism.[89] The following month, after calling for the establishment of an anti-Japanese united front, he warned that Chiang Kai-shek was preparing to make war on "Yang Si-chang,"[90] which indicates that the Communists were trying to entice Yen into

[84] The Shanghai *Nichinichi*, as quoted in *CWR*, April 18, 1936, p. 225. Hatano, *History of the C.C.P., 1936*, p. 12, and the Dairen *Manchu Pao*, as quoted in Tan Shin She, *op.cit.*, p. 630.

[85] Himeno Tokuichi, *op.cit.*, p. 153, and *NCH*, March 18, 1936, 477:3, May 6, 1936, 226:3, and July 8, 1936, 80:4. P. 2 of "I-chou chien-p'ing," *KWCP*, March 9, 1936, says that Communist gains in Shansi were confined entirely to the countryside and that although the Red Army tried to seize cities, it failed to capture a single one.

[86] Jen Ying-lun and Kuo Chien-fu, *op.cit.*, p. 5.

[87] *Lectures*, III-A, p. 428 (Dec. 1935).

[88] Haldore E. Hanson, *op.cit.*, p. 356.

[89] Wan Min, "The New Situation and the New Tactics in Soviet China," *IPC*, Dec. 8, 1935, p. 1659.

[90] Wan Min, "Replies to Chief Arguments Against the Anti-Imperialist Front in China," *IPC*, Jan. 11, 1936, p. 40.

allying with them by taking his side against not only Japan's but also Chiang Kai-shek's efforts to gain control of Shansi. Upon entering Shansi the Communists asked Yen to join forces with them or at least allow the Red Army to pass through so that it could attack Japanese forces to the east.[91] Even after his troops had occupied much of Shansi, Mao Tse-tung expressed a willingness to make peace with any army willing to call off hostilities and oppose Japan.[92]

The Red Army's avowed determination to resist Japan gained for the Communists considerable backing from intellectuals in Shansi. According to an American newspaperman, educated people living in Taiyuan and other cities were intensely anti-Japanese and sympathized with Communist demands for a united front.[93] Shortly after the Communists entered Shansi, students in Taiyuan staged a series of anti-Japanese demonstrations. Both Western and Japanese observers say that initially the provincial authorities encouraged the demonstrators, who tried to stop the sale of Japanese goods in Taiyuan and surrounding districts.[94] As the Red Army approached Taiyuan, however, Yen arrested the demonstrators by the hundreds and shot at least a score of them for collaborating with the Communists.[95] The demonstrations were taking on a pro-Communist coloration[96] and he must have been terrified by the class warfare which his followers subsequently accused the Communists of fomenting in the countryside.

Speaking in the fall of 1935, Yen implied that Communist appeals for all-out resistance to Japan were the least impor-

[91] Chie Hua, "A Further Step towards the Annexation of North China," *IPC*, June 13, 1936, p. 917.

[92] *IPC*, March 14, 1936, p. 377. Mr. Uno Shigeaki of the Japanese Foreign Ministry, who has examined much of the Japanese material pertaining to the Communist invasion of Shansi, feels that Communist leaders sent their armies into Shansi, not with the intention of overthrowing Yen Hsi-shan, but rather in the hope that a show of strength would induce Yen to accept their offer of an anti-Japanese alliance. (Interview with Mr. Uno Shigeaki, Stanford, Nov. 27, 1962.)

[93] Earl Leaf, as quoted in Tan Shin She, *op.cit.*, p. 630.

[94] *NCH*, Jan. 29, 1936, 175:2, and March 18, 1936, 477:4, and Hatano, *History of the C.C.P., 1936*, p. 16. Hatano expresses amazement at the provincial government's willingness to sponsor anti-Japanese demonstrations at a time when Communist armies were invading Shansi.

[95] *Tung-fang tsa-chih*, April 16, 1936, p. 96, and H. P. Tasmania Wu, *op.cit.*, p. 39.

[96] *NCH*, March 18, 1936, 477:4.

tant source of the party's popularity in Shansi.[97] An experienced foreign observer says that after the Communists entered Shansi, the peasants aided the Red Army in order to free themselves from exploitation at the hands of Yen's officials.[98] Following their withdrawal from Shansi, Communist leaders claimed that while there the Red Army forswore revolution and gained the support of the masses simply by opposing Japan, but in 1947, when the Communist Party no longer was obliged to conceal its real aims for the sake of preserving its alliance with Chiang Kai-shek, a well-informed Communist writer declared that in Shansi people had welcomed the Red Army because they believed the Communists would destroy the rich.[99]

Much of the propaganda which the Communist Party disseminated among peasants in Shansi before its armies invaded Yen's domain was aimed at exploiting the social and economic grievances of poorer farmers. In the villages of northern Shansi, Communist leaflets appeared at the end of the year when peasants were trying to elude bailiffs sent out to collect sums owed to moneylenders and other creditors. These leaflets must have preached revolution, because peasants exposed to their contents spoke of nothing else.[100] On the eve of the Communist invasion, moreover, a semiofficial Communist periodical carried an article attacking Yen's program of land reform and calling for the confiscation and redistribution of land in Shansi along lines followed by the Communists in Kiangsi and later in northern Shensi.[101] In the same issue of this journal there appeared an article on the united front, written by perhaps its most outspoken Communist advocate, Wang Ming, who probably realized how many of his comrades held different views, since in another Communist publication he accused the Chinese Communist Party of pursuing radical policies out of keeping with the spirit of the united front.[102]

A contemporary Communist account says that during its

[97] *Lectures*, III-A, pp. 432-433 (Dec. 1935).

[98] *NCH*, April 1, 1936, 8:3-4.

[99] Chao Shu-li, *op.cit.*, pp. 51-55.

[100] Ch'i Chih-chin, *op.cit.*, p. 26.

[101] Li Fei, *op.cit.*, pp. 13-15.

[102] Wang Min, "For a Change in All Spheres of Our Work," *IPC*, Feb. 8, 1936, p. 223.

invasion of Shansi the Red Army actually redistributed land belonging to the rich,[103] but eyewitnesses state that while in Shansi the Communists were too busy searching for food to carry out a systematic program of land reform.[104] Their pre-occupation with foraging may mean that their invasion of Shansi was merely a raid, undertaken with the aim of feeding tens of thousands of newly arrived Communist soldiers, fresh from their Long March, who were starving in the wilds of northern Shensi.[105] Yet although circumstances kept them from dividing the land, the Communists continued to behave like revolutionaries in other respects. Yen, foreign mission-aries, and Japanese observers all maintain that wherever it went in Shansi the Red Army plundered and abused the rich while at the same time treating the poor with the utmost con-sideration and often sharing with them what it took from the wealthy.[106] Everyone having wealth who refused to co-operate with the Communists was killed, along with many of Yen's officials and virtually every army officer taken prisoner by the Red Army.[107] According to an American reporter, Com-munist soldiers frequently announced that they were invading

[103] H. P. Tasmania Wu, *op.cit.*, p. 39.

[104] Pp. 1-2 of "Ta-shih shu-yao," *KWCP*, April 6, 1936.

[105] This was the opinion of the newspaper *Ta Kung Pao*, as quoted on p. 2 of "I-chou chien-p'ing," *KWCP*, Feb. 24, 1936. It is shared by Hatano, *History of the C.C.P., 1936*, pp. 4-6, and Wan Ya-kang, a reporter who spent several years in the Communist capital of Yenan after the outbreak of the Sino-Japanese War in 1937. See Wan Ya-kang, *Chung-kuo kung-ch'an-tang chien-shih* (*A Brief History of the Chinese Communist Party*) (Hong Kong, 1951), p. 48.

[106] The testimony of Yen Hsi-shan and his supporters can be found in *Lectures*, III-A, p. 448 (March 1936), Fukada Yuzō, *op.cit.*, pp. 362-363, and p. 5 of "Ta-shih shu-yao," *KWCP*, May 18, 1936. Re-ports written by English and American missionaries stationed in Shansi appeared in the *NCH*, May 6, 1936, 226:3, and July 8, 1936, 80:4. For a revealing Japanese narrative, which maintains that the Com-munists confiscated the wealth of even the rich peasants, see Himeno Tokuichi, *op.cit.*, p. 152. Another Japanese account merely says that not-withstanding its demands for an anti-Japanese united front, in Shansi the Communist Party pursued orthodox Communist fiscal and economic policies. See Otsuka Reizo, "The Red Influence in China," in *Data Papers, Sixth Congress, Institute of Pacific Relations* (Tokyo, 1936), VII:49. This is corroborated by at least one Communist writer, H. P. Tasmania Wu, *op.cit.*, p. 39.

[107] Yen, Himeno, and the missionaries all speak of officials and wealthy persons being killed. Only Hatano Ken'ichi, *History of the C.C.P., 1936*, p. 43, mentions the execution of captured officers; how-ever, he seems to be exceptionally knowledgeable with respect to the actual fighting and conditions within the various armies.

not only in order to fight Japan but also for the purpose of "exterminating" Yen Hsi-shan.[108]

As a result of all this, in Shansi most of those who supported the Communists in 1936 came from the rural poor and especially from among the millions of unemployed or under-employed vagabonds, whose idleness and consequent poverty and disorderliness had been for years perhaps the most perplexing problem confronting Yen.[109] The extent to which such people were motivated by hatred of the existing social and economic system can be determined from the answers Edgar Snow received when he asked men who had joined the Red Army in Shansi why they elected to throw in their lot with the Communists. One spoke simply about helping to carry out the revolution; another said that he had followed the Red Army back to Shensi because it offered him an opportunity to learn how to read, and a third replied: "The Communist Party fights for the poor. No wonder everybody is eager to join it."[110] Others who encountered the Red Army during its invasion of Shansi also must have been attracted chiefly by its revolutionary program, since many peasants hailed it as the army of the poor when it returned to Shansi in the fall of 1937 and expected it to champion their interests against the rich.[111]

The peasants of Shansi supported the Communists so vigorously that, in the opinion of Japanese observers, without the help of the central government Yen would have suffered an overwhelming defeat.[112] Beginning in March, tens of thousands of troops belonging to Chiang Kai-shek's Central Army entered Shansi for the avowed purpose of driving out the Communists,[113] who hastily retreated into Shensi, not only because

[108] Earl Leaf, as quoted in J. W. Phillips, *op.cit.*, p. 195.

[109] *NCH*, May 6, 1936, 22:3, and July 8, 1936, 80:4.

[110] Edgar Snow, as quoted in Hatano Ken'ichi, *Chūgoku kyōsantō shi, ichi ku san shichi nen* (*A History of the Chinese Communist Party during 1937*) (Tokyo, 1961), pp. 680-682.

[111] *HPH*, pp. 146-147.

[112] Hatano, *History of the C.C.P., 1936*, p. 47.

[113] Several Japanese writers charged that the Communist invasion of Shansi was the result of an agreement between Chiang Kai-shek and the Communists, who promised to withdraw from Shansi after remaining there long enough to give Chiang an excuse for sending his own troops into the province, but that the Communists doublecrossed Chiang by attempting to retain the areas they occupied. See Himeno Tokuichi, *op.cit.*, p. 151, Hatano, *History of the C.C.P., 1936*, p. 12, and *CWR*,

they were hopelessly outnumbered but also on account of the vastly superior fire power of Chiang's forces, which were equipped with heavy artillery and supported by aircraft.[114] It is uncertain, however, whether Yen wanted Chiang's soldiers in Shansi; probably he asked the central government for money and arms but was obliged to let it send troops as well.[115] In addition to feeling that the Shansi Army was unable or not willing to resist the Communists, Chiang undoubtedly wished to establish his own authority in Shansi. As one of his soldiers put it: "Hugh! we didn't come to fight the Reds, we came to throw out old Yen."[116] It would seem, nevertheless, that although many of Chiang's soldiers remained in Shansi after the Communists fled, Yen continued to govern there without much interference from Nanking.[117] Maybe Chiang needed Yen's support owing to the rebellion of the Kwangsi generals in the summer of 1936; more likely, he feared antagonizing the Japanese, who warned him against trying to acquire control of Shansi under the guise of fighting the Communists.[118]

Yen and the United Front

Perhaps, as one writer maintains, the defeat of their armies in Shansi impressed upon Communist leaders the wisdom of making peace with Chiang Kai-shek before he destroyed their movement.[119] Throughout the remainder of 1936, the Communists repeatedly offered to support Chiang if he fought Japan, with the result that more and more of Chiang's nor-

May 16, 1936, p. 376. The Communists, on the other hand, accused Chiang of intervening in Shansi at the behest of the Japanese Army, which they said dared not become involved in the fighting in Shansi for fear of outraging Chinese nationalism and thus enhancing Communist appeals for a united front against Japan. See Tan Shin She, *op.cit.*, p. 631. Evidently, Chiang was in league with neither the Communists nor the Japanese, although both were convinced that he was the ally of the other.

[114] Fukada Yuzō, *op.cit.*, p. 364, *NCH*, April 15, 1936, 97:3, *CWR*, May 16, 1936, p. 376, and *NYT*, April 6, 1936, 13:1.

[115] This is the opinion of Hatano, *History of the C.C.P., 1936*, p. 51, Otsuka Reizo, *op.cit.*, p. 47, and *NYT*, April 6, 1936, 13:3.

[116] *NCH*, July 8, 1936, 80:5.

[117] *NCH*, June 3, 1936, 394:5, and *CWR*, Oct. 3, 1936, p. 145.

[118] *NYT*, March 3, 1936, 15:1, and *U.S. Foreign Relations Papers, 1936*, pp. 74-75. This also was the opinion expressed by a writer in *NCH*, July 8, 1936, 80:2.

[119] Wan Ya-kang, *op.cit.*, p. 48. Mr. Uno Shigeaki is of the same opinion. (Interview with Mr. Shigeaki, Stanford, Nov. 27, 1962.)

mally conservative followers pressed him to form an anti-
Japanese alliance with the Red Army. Yen, on the other hand,
feared another Communist invasion of Shansi. After the
Communists withdrew from Shansi, he executed or imprisoned
hundreds of persons suspected of having sided with them and
built a network of stone blockhouses in districts adjoining
Shensi.[120] In the hope that if their worst grievances were
satisfied the poor would be less receptive to Communist propaganda aimed at fomenting class warfare, the Justice Force
redoubled its efforts to expose corrupt, unjust, or exploiting
gentry and officials.[121] Yen's followers accused the Communists of trying to seize power under the pretext of resisting
Japan and called for the creation of a movement which would
be anti-Japanese but also opposed to communism.[122] The fight
against communism continued to preoccupy members of the
Justice Force until late in 1936 when Yen apparently yielded
to Communist demands for a united front.[123]

Yen turned to the Communists because Japan's actions during the summer and fall of 1936 caused him to fear the Japanese more than the Red Army. From their enclave in northeastern Chahar, the Japanese smuggled into Shansi additional
quantities of cheaply priced goods, which threatened to ruin
many of Yen's new industries by destroying entirely the market for their products.[124] In June Yen told a Japanese reporter
that dumping by Japanese manufacturers was responsible for
most of the troubles besetting China's economy. "It is the
greatest obstacle to the achievement of economic cooperation
between China and Japan," he declared.[125] Subsequently, he
threatened to put to death anyone caught smuggling,[126] and
by November he was encouraging his subjects to boycott
everything made in Japan, urging them to purchase from

[120] Chao Shu-li, *op.cit.*, p. 56, and *NCH*, July 8, 1936, 80:4, and
Feb. 10, 1937, 234:1.
[121] *Lectures*, III-C, p. 239 (July 1936), and Fukada Yuzō, *op.cit.*,
pp. 357-358, 365-366.
[122] Fukada Yuzō, *op.cit.*, p. 363, and Chang Wei-lu, *op.cit.*, p. 67.
[123] Fan Ch'ang-chiang, "Shan-hsi chi-hsing," *KWCP*, March 29,
1937, p. 23.
[124] Chie Hua, *op.cit.*, p. 745, and *NCH*, July 8, 1936, 57:2, Oct.
7, 1936, 11:2.
[125] Himeno Tokuichi, *op.cit.*, pp. 176-177.
[126] *Lectures*, IV, p. 118 (July 1936).

Europe and the United States whatever goods they needed which were not manufactured in Shansi or the rest of China.[127] Moreover, after his police arrested several Japanese for peddling drugs in Shansi, he warned that "foreigners" were seeking to destroy the Chinese people by flooding China with narcotics.[128]

But Yen's mounting antagonism toward Japan was chiefly the result of Japanese attempts to overthrow his rule in neighboring Suiyuan. In March Manchurian troops from northeastern Chahar invaded northern Suiyuan and seized the city of Pailingmiao, where the pro-Japanese Inner Mongolian Autonomous Political Council maintained its headquarters. Three months later, the leader of the council, Prince Teh, proclaimed himself the ruler of an independent Mongolia and organized his own army, which was equipped and trained by the Japanese.[129] In August a part of this force tried to advance into eastern Suiyuan, but was driven back by troops under the command of Fu Tso-i. While Prince Teh prepared to launch another invasion of eastern Suiyuan, this time in cooperation with his Manchurian allies, Shansi swarmed with Japanese agents, who sketched or photographed its defenses and treated Yen's police and officials with the utmost contempt.[130] No wonder there circulated rumors to the effect that after taking Suiyuan the Japanese would attack Shansi.[131]

Yen sought to meet this challenge by insisting that his officials, members of the Justice Force, and students attending middle schools and colleges in Shansi undergo several months of military training. A reporter who visited Taiyuan in October says that at least half of the people he encountered on the streets wore uniforms.[132] Yen wanted to expand his army to 100,000 men and create a militia three times that size, as well as a "reserve officers corps" (*p'a-ch'ien chün-kuan tui*) consisting on 15,000 students.[133] As part of a campaign to

127 Ch'en Fang-t'ung, *op.cit.*, p. 29.
128 *NCH*, Oct. 14, 1936, 52:2, and *Lectures*, IX, p. 43 (Sept. 1936).
129 Hata Ikuhiku, *op.cit.*, pp. 114-115, Chang Tso-hua, *op.cit.*, p. 6, Lawrence Hearn, "Suiyuan—Heart of Eastern Asia," *CT*, Dec. 1936, p. 21, and *CWR*, Nov. 28, 1936, p. 443, Dec. 21, 1936, p. 495.
130 *CWR*, March 14, 1936, p. 50, and *NCH*, Nov. 4, 1936, 178:4.
131 *CWR*, Aug. 29, 1936, p. 463.
132 Ch'en Fang-t'ung, *op.cit.*, pp. 27-28.
133 *Lectures*, III-A, pp. 528-529 (Sept. 1936).

win popular support for this program, he composed songs like the following:

> To fight we must mobilize the people.
> Everyone shall go to the front.
> Students will form the vanguard which
>   breaks through the enemy's lines.
> Therefore, students must learn to be soldiers.[134]

Beginning in July, he repeatedly urged his subjects to prepare for war against an enemy having vastly superior material resources, including a powerful air force. Writing from Taiyuan in October, a foreign resident says that for months the authorities had been excavating caves in neighboring cliffs for use as air raid shelters.[135] In August Yen warned that China was in danger of becoming like Korea and professed to be astonished by the ease with which Japan bullied a country ten times its size. A month later, he called the loss of Manchuria a national disgrace and demanded nationwide mobilization in order to repel the invaders.[136] By October Taiyuan seethed with anti-Japanese feeling, largely on account of the fighting in Suiyuan. Officials suspected of being pro-Japanese were expelled from the provincial government, the police began harassing Japanese living in Taiyuan, and Yen allowed his soldiers to take part in anti-Japanese demonstrations staged by the new League for National Salvation through Sacrifice (*Hsi-sheng chiu-kuo t'ung-meng hui*).[137]

Yen created the Sacrifice League (*Hsi meng hui*) in September and recruited its members from students living not only in Shansi but also in the Peiping-Tientsin area. Its leaders included Po I-po and Sung Shao-wen, both returned students from Peiping where Sung had been arrested for engaging in anti-Japanese activities, and Yen's nephew and personal secretary, Liang Hua-chih, who, according to the Communists, enjoyed Yen's complete confidence.[138] Whereas the Justice Force remained primarily an anti-Communist organization, at

[134] *Lectures*, IX, p. 33 (Aug. 1936).
[135] *NCH*, Oct. 14, 1936, 52:1-2.
[136] *Lectures*, II, p. 10 (Sept. 1936), and III-A, p. 503 (Sept. 1936).
[137] Ch'en Fang-t'ung, *op.cit.*, pp. 29-30, and *NCH*, Nov. 4, 1936, 178:4, 214:3.
[138] Biography of Liang Hua-chih in *Kuomintang Biographies*.

least until the end of October,[139] the chief function of the Sacrifice League was to promote the boycott against Japanese goods and otherwise enlist popular support for Yen's efforts to resist Japan. On the other hand, in 1938 Sung Shao-wen told a foreign reporter that Yen organized the Sacrifice League in cooperation with the Chinese Communists after secretly concluding a truce with them in June 1936.[140] According to Po I-po, in October Yen promised to form a united front with the Communist Party if Po returned to Shansi and assumed the leadership of the Sacrifice League.[141] Communist writers, as well as Japanese intelligence reports and Kuomintang adherents in Shansi, also say that Yen entered into an alliance with the Communists during the summer or fall of 1936.[142] "In 1936 Yen gave sanctuary to a few who advocated the 'united front' when the phrase was enough to land you in jail in Nanking," comments an American reporter.[143] All of this suggests that although Yen continued to fight communism in Shansi, he was ready to ally with the Communists against Japan for several months before events at Sian compelled Chiang Kai-shek to yield to Communist demands for a united front.

Subsequently, the Communists implied that from the beginning Yen distrusted the Sacrifice League and merely used it to ward off the anger of his youthful followers, who wanted him to oppose Japan more vigorously. Yet two of his most trusted supporters, Liang Hua-chih and Liang Tun-hou, were leaders of the Sacrifice League,[144] and the league's preoccupation with stopping the sale of Japanese goods in Shansi indicates that he exercised considerable influence over its activities. A Chinese reporter who visited Taiyuan in November found the Sacrifice League operating under Yen's personal supervision and came away feeling that Yen was largely

139 Ch'en Fang-t'ung, op.cit., p. 31.

140 Haldore E. Hanson, Humane Endeavour, p. 245.

141 Anonymous, "Po I-po t'ung-chih hsieh-lu Yen Hsi-shan t'ung-ti p'an-kuo nui-mu," p. 9, Ch'en Po-ta, Yen Hsi-shan p'i-p'an.

142 Biography of Yen Hsi-shan in Kuomintang Biographies, and Koain seimu pu (Asia Development Board, Political Affairs Bureau), pub., "Shin-Satsu-Ki henku no jōkyō" ("The General Situation in the Chin-Ch'a-Chi Border Region"), Jōhō (Intelligence), No. 35 (Feb. 1, 1941), p. 1. Also see Anonymous, Shan-hsi ch'ing-tang ch'ien-hou chi-lüeh, p. 5.

143 Edgar Snow, The Battle for Asia (New York, 1941), p. 254.

144 The biographies of Liang Tun-hou and Liang Hua-chih in Kuomintang Biographies, and CWR, Aug. 14, 1937, p. 395.

responsible for its efforts to arouse popular antagonism toward Japan.[145] One writer infers that Yen also used the Sacrifice League to attack the Kuomintang.[146] Perhaps Yen hoped to strengthen himself against Japan, while at the same time maintaining his independence from the central government by allying with the Communists, who appeared to be weaker and therefore less menacing than his other enemies. "Yen was adroit and refused to fade away gracefully," remarks an American investigator.[147]

An examination of Yen's speeches, however, suggests that he turned to the Communists for assistance chiefly because he needed help in Suiyuan and feared that the central government intended to let Suiyuan, and maybe Shansi as well, fall to the Japanese without a struggle. As early as July he complained that although the present government was not to blame for China's military weakness, this did not relieve Chinese soldiers of the responsibility of resisting an invasion.[148] In September, after returning from Sian where he conferred with Chang Hsüeh-liang, he accused the central government of pursuing an "inadequate and tortuous" policy with respect to national defense.[149] He urged it to publicize rather than minimize instances of foreign aggression and called on it to stop pretending that China enjoyed friendly relations with its enemies.[150] The same month he offered to place all the troops at his command under the control of the central government, warned that the loss of Suiyuan would be a national disaster, promised to give all the aid possible to its defenders, and asked Nanking to do the same.[151] Significantly, in 1947 Po I-po referred to Yen's "dissatisfaction with Chiang Kai-shek's continued appeasement of Japan" as a primary reason why before the Japanese invasion Po was invited to organize anti-Japanese movements among students in Shansi.[152]

Probably in response to Yen's entreaties, late in October Chiang Kai-shek sent into northeastern Suiyuan 20,000 troops belonging to his own army and armies allied with the

[145] Ch'en Fang-t'ung, op.cit., p. 30.
[146] "Party Purification in Shansi," p. 5.
[147] Paul Elmquist, op.cit., p. 43.
[148] Lectures, v, p. 75 (July 1936).
[149] Lectures, III-C, p. 241 (Sept. 1936).
[150] See ibid., p. 242.   [151] CWR, Sept. 19, 1936, p. 85.
[152] Jack Belden, op.cit., p. 51.

central government, but, according to a Japanese writer, these soldiers were under orders to attack the Communists rather than the Mongol and Manchurian forces to the west.[153] Apparently their presence did not frighten Prince Teh, because early in November he presented Fu Tso-i with what amounted to an ultimatum. When Fu responded by calling him a puppet of "certain quarters" and exhorted him to submit to the central government, Mongol and Manchurian armies based at Pailingmiao launched another, and this time more ambitious, invasion of eastern Suiyuan. The more than 15,000 Mongol and Manchurian soldiers who took part in this campaign were armed with Japanese weapons, supported by Japanese aircraft which bombed numerous towns in Suiyuan, and on many occasions led by Japanese officers.[154] Yen and his followers were convinced that Japan was preparing to attack Shansi,[155] and the invaders contemplated assaulting Tatung, where members of the Special Service (*tokumu kikan chō*) of Japan's Kwantung Army destroyed a large supply dump and committed other acts of sabotage.[156] This is why Yen placed under Fu's command many of his best troops, led by two of his most able generals, Chao Ch'eng-shou and his own son-in-law, Wang Ching-kuo.

There ensued almost a month of sporadic but often savage fighting which resulted in the death of more than 400 of Yen's soldiers and a much larger number of Mongols and Manchurians. After turning back the outnumbered and comparatively ill-trained invaders, Fu's troops counterattacked and on November 24 recaptured Pailingmiao.[157] There immediately circulated rumors that Yen intended to pursue the defeated Mongol and Manchurian forces into northern Chahar and perhaps as far as the Manchurian border.[158] This caused the

[153] Hata Ikuhiku, *op.cit.*, p. 116. In an interview with me at Stanford University, April 10, 1963, Claude Buss, formerly an American diplomat in China, said that in the opinion of many foreigners in Nanking, Chiang Kai-shek had no intention of attacking Mongol forces invading Suiyuan.

[154] Hata Ikuhiku, *op.cit.*, p. 116, *CWR*, Nov. 28, 1936, pp. 443-444, Dec. 5, 1936, p. 11, and Chu Ch'eng, "Sui chü chieh-k'ai" ("What's Happening in Suiyuan"), *KWCP*, Nov. 30, 1936, p. 4.

[155] *NYT*, Nov. 23, 1936, 9:4.

[156] Hata Ikuhiku, *op.cit.*, pp. 115-116.

[157] See *ibid.*, p. 116, and p. 1 of "Ta-shih shu-yao," *KWCP*, Dec. 7, 1936.

[158] Hata Ikuhiku, *op.cit.*, p. 118.

Kwantung Army to issue a statement warning that if the fighting in Suiyuan spread into areas "contiguous" to Man-churia, Japanese troops would be obliged to intervene on be-half on Prince Teh's forces.[159] Meanwhile, at the behest of the Japanese, the remnants of Prince Teh's army repeatedly tried to drive the Chinese out of Pailingmiao; however, this only provoked Fu Tso-i into sending his troops northward, where they seized the last of Prince Teh's Suiyuan bases and virtually annihilated his army.[160] A Japanese caught serving with the Mongols was shot,[161] and for the first time Yen publicly ac-cused Japan of helping the invaders.[162]

The fighting in Suiyuan persuaded Yen that it was neces-sary to mobilize the entire population of Shansi behind his efforts to resist Japan. Early in December he warned his sub-jects that Suiyuan and Shansi were in danger of being de-stroyed and called on everyone who loved Shansi to come to its defense. He urged the central government to initiate uni-versal conscription along lines practiced in Turkey and the U.S.S.R. Already, he was obsessed with the need for encourag-ing the normally apathetic peasants (*lao-pai-hsing*) to take a personal and active interest in the war effort. For their benefit, he formed the Village Mutual Assistance Association (*ts'un-cheng hsieh-chu hui*). He also enlisted the help of vil-lage school teachers, who he said were closer to the common people than most of his officials and therefore more likely to be trusted and believed by the lao-pai-hsing.[163] He even per-suaded a large number of women, generally from wealthy fam-ilies in Taiyuan, to serve at the front as nurses.[164] In response to his summons, moreover, students attending colleges and middle schools in neighboring provinces flocked into Shansi, where they were enrolled in officer training schools like the Shansi Cadre Training Force (*Shan-hsi min-hsun kan-pu chiao-lien t'uan*).[165] According to one of them, students in all

---

[159] *Ibid.*

[160] P. 4 of "Ta-shih shu-yao," *KWCP*, Dec. 21, 1936, and Hattori Takushirō, *op.cit.*, p. 35.

[161] Hata Ikuhiku, *op.cit.*, p. 117.

[162] *NYT*, Nov. 23, 1936, 1:7.

[163] *Lectures*, III-A, p. 557 (Dec. 1936).

[164] *Lectures*, VIII, p. 61 (March 1937), and IX, pp. 71-72, 92 (Dec. 1936, Jan. 1938), and *HPH*, p. 46.

[165] *Lectures*, III-A, pp. 561, 582-584 (July 1936, Jan. 1937), *CWR*, Nov. 28, 1936, p. 446, and *HPH*, p. 18.

parts of North China looked upon Yen as a "flicker of light
in an otherwise unlit sea of darkness."[166] This raises the
question of whether Yen hoped that by resisting Japan and
thus endearing himself to patriots everywhere he could regain
the position of leadership in North China which he had lost as
a result of his defeat at the hands of Chiang Kai-shek in 1930.

The victories won by Yen's armies in Suiyuan aroused
great enthusiasm throughout much of China. For example, on
December 6 the influential Peiping newspaper *Ta Kung Pao*
called the recapture of Pailingmiao a triumph for the entire
country.[167] Beginning in mid-November, delegations from
places as far away as Hankow, Shanghai, and Canton regularly
made their way to Taiyuan, where they assured Yen that by
resisting in Suiyuan he was defending all of China and
urged him to go on fighting.[168] Most carried with them large
sums of money, collected as part of a nationwide Aid Suiyuan
Movement (*yüan Sui yün-tung*) and often under the slogan
"Donate One Day's Wages for the Boys at the Front."[169] In
addition, Yen received hundreds of telegrams, many of them
from other warlords and political leaders, which praised him
for defying the Japanese. According to the *China Weekly
Review*, the whole nation mobilized in support of the defenders of Suiyuan.[170] "Many believe that a greater mass of
Chinese has been swayed by Yen's campaign against the Japanese in Suiyuan than ever before in History," remarked the
North China Herald.[171]

The fighting in Suiyuan affected profoundly China's subsequent relations with Japan. Writing in June 1937, Nathaniel
Peffer warned that their recent victories in Suiyuan had made
the Chinese overconfident, reckless, and impatient to exploit
their triumphs by regaining their lost territories.[172] Shortly
after Yen's troops drove the Mongols from Pailingmiao, the
Ta Kung Pao called for the reconquest of northern Chahar,
and a week later one of its correspondents referred to this

[166] Hsü Fan-t'ing, *Letter*, p. 2.
[167] *Ta Kung Pao*, Dec. 6, 1936, as quoted in "I-chou chien-p'ing,"
p. 1, *KWCP*, Dec. 14, 1936.
[168] *CWR*, Nov. 28, 1936, p. 446, and James Bertram, *op.cit.*, p. 35.
[169] *CWR*, Nov. 28, 1936, p. 461.
[170] *CWR*, Dec. 5, 1936, p. 30, Dec. 12, 1936, p. 44.
[171] *NCH*, Dec. 16, 1936, 470:4.
[172] *CWR*, June 26, 1937, p. 121.

as "the very least" that ought to be done.[173] Speaking early in December, Chiang Kai-shek hailed the recapture of Pailingmiao as "the starting point of national regeneration" and proof that "if only the nation be unified and present a unified front in a determined effort to struggle to the finish, we should not lose a single inch of national territory."[174] About this time, an English reporter was told by an official of the central government that having defended Suiyuan the Chinese would retake northern Chahar and perhaps Manchuria as well.[175] A Japanese historian also claims that the outcome of the fighting in Suiyuan caused China's leaders to doubt the strength of the Kwantung Army and attributes to this their increasingly belligerent attitude toward Japan.[176] Significantly, late in November Nanking broke off negotiations looking toward a new Sino-Japanese agreement, on the grounds that Japan was behind the invasion of Suiyuan.

Yet it appears that in spite of its bellicosity, the central government avoided becoming involved in the war in Suiyuan. On November 18 Chiang Kai-shek flew to Taiyuan, where he assured Yen and Fu that the invasion of Suiyuan was a matter of national and not purely local concern; however, instead of promising to come to their aid, he merely said that he had plans for dealing with the situation and urged them to keep calm and work toward greater unity.[177] Yen, on the other hand, dwelt upon the seriousness of the situation in Suiyuan, while Fu emphasized that in Suiyuan he was acting as an agent of the central government.[178] Earlier, Yen had virtually withdrawn his own currency from circulation in Shansi and therefore from competition with Nanking's money "in order to express his loyalty to the central government."[179] Nevertheless, both Chinese and foreign observers say that Chiang's soldiers did not take part in the campaign against the Mongols, nor did his air force attack Japan's warplanes, which inflicted most of the casualties suffered by Fu's troops.[180] According

---

[173] P. 1 of "I-chou chien-p'ing," *KWCP*, Dec. 14, 1936.
[174] *CWR*, Dec. 5, 1936, p. 13.
[175] James Bertram, *op.cit.*, p. 21.
[176] Hattori Takushirō, *op.cit.*, p. 35.
[177] Chu Ch'eng, *op.cit.*, p. 2.
[178] See *ibid.*, pp. 2-3.
[179] *CWR*, Nov. 7, 1936, p. 348.
[180] "I-chou chien-p'ing," p. 1, and "Ta-shih shu-yao," p. 2 in *KWCP*, Dec. 7, 1936, *Ta Kung Pao*, Nov. 26, 1936, as quoted in "P'ing-lün,"

to Edgar Snow, moreover, Chiang rebuffed commanders of
the Manchurian and provincial armies stationed in Shensi who
wanted to stop fighting the Communists and go to Yen's assistance in Suiyuan.[181] As for the amount of financial aid
which Yen received from the central government, he got only
a tenth of what he requested[182] and later admitted that treaty
obligations, presumably to Japan, prevented Nanking from
giving him more.[183] All of this may be why in December he
more or less cautioned his subjects against depending on the
central government for help and warned that Shansi might be
compelled to fight alone.[184]

Chiang Kai-shek probably did not feel strong enough to
fight the Japanese and was unwilling to antagonize them by
seeming to oppose their ambitions in Inner Mongolia; however, he may have feared that if he allowed the conflict in
Suiyuan to develop into a national war of resistance, Yen's
prestige soon would be comparable to his own. Even before
the recapture of Pailingmiao, the *Ta Kung Pao* referred to
Yen in terms which suggest that the newspaper regarded him
as equal in importance to Chiang.[185] "Chiang and Yen [*Chiang
Yen erh kung*] are leading the drive for national salvation,"
observed the nationally circulated Peiping journal *Kuo-wen
chou-pao* on December 21.[186] Early in 1937 the deputy leader
of the Kuomintang, Wang Ching-wei, expressed the same
opinion in an article written for the semiofficial *People's
Tribune*.[187] Certainly Chiang's reaction to the invasion of
Suiyuan differed strikingly from the behavior of the Chinese
Communists, who promptly called on the central government
to end the civil war and reinforce Yen's troops in Suiyuan.[188]

---

p. 2 of the same issue of *KWCP*, *CWR*, Dec. 5, 1936, pp. 12-13, and
James Bertram, *op.cit.*, p. 22.

[181] Edgar Snow, *The Battle for Asia*, p. 441.

[182] *CWR*, Dec. 5, 1936, pp. 13, 16, and Dec. 12, 1936, p. 47.

[183] *Lectures*, III-C, p. 154 (March 1937). Yen had assured his followers that the central government would bear the entire cost of the war
in Suiyuan. See *NYT*, Nov. 23, 1936, 1:7.

[184] *Lectures*, IX, p. 74 (Dec. 1936).

[185] *Ta Kung Pao*, Nov. 19, 1936, as quoted in "P'ing-lün," *KWCP*,
Nov. 30, 1936.

[186] P. 5 of "Ta-shih shu-yao," *KWCP*, Dec. 21, 1936.

[187] Wang Ching-wei, "Suiyuan as a Symbol of National Unity,"
PT, April 1, 1937, pp. 1-13, esp. pp. 4-6.

[188] James C. Thomson, Jr., "Communist Policy and the United Front

Perhaps in response to this gesture, late in November Yen inferred that ideological differences must not stand in the way of mobilizing the nation against a foreign invader.[189] Since he subsequently referred to this statement as an appeal for the policy which the central government actually put into effect after the resolution of the so-called Sian Incident[190]—in other words, a united front against Japan—the Communists must have had him in mind when they expressed the belief, late in the fall of 1936, that they could form an alliance with "certain military leaders . . . in Shansi."[191]

This is the situation that confronted Chiang Kai-shek early in December when he flew north to confer with Chang Hsüeh-liang at the latter's headquarters in Sian. He was greeted by crowds of students, who petitioned him to end the civil war and help Fu Tso-i fight the Japanese in Suiyuan.[192] When he refused, Chang arrested him and detained him in Sian. Immediately after "kidnapping" Chiang, Chang sent a telegram to Taiyuan explaining his actions and asking for Yen's support.[193] In a politely worded reply, Yen expressed the fear that Chang's rashness would weaken rather than strengthen China by provoking a disastrous civil war and urged him to liberate his captive. A week later, he reiterated his demand for Chiang's release, but in the same breath declared that Chinese must reconcile their differences and achieve an enduring unity.[194] Meanwhile, he converted his *fang-kung pao-wei t'uan* or anti-Communist militia into an anti-Japanese force and otherwise stepped up his campaign to mobilize his subjects against what he called "the invading enemy."[195] He likewise publicly denounced those who felt that Japan's conquest of Manchuria and Jehol was of little consequence to the rest of the country and warned that the invasion of Suiyuan and Shansi were imminent and that their loss would be the

in China, 1935-1936," Harvard University, Committee on International and Regional Studies Seminar, *Papers on China*, XI (1957), p. 130.

[189] *Lectures*, III-A, p. 548 (Nov. 1936).

[190] See *ibid.*, p. 572.

[191] Edgar Snow, *Random Notes on Red China (1936-1945)* (Cambridge, 1957), p. 109.

[192] *CWR*, Dec. 26, 1936, p. 142.

[193] P. 3 of "Ta-shih shu-yao," *KWCP*, Dec. 21, 1936.

[194] P. 3 of "Ta-shih shu-yao," *KWCP*, Jan. 1, 1937. Yen made this statement on Dec. 21, 1936.

[195] *Lectures*, III-A, pp. 551-552 (Dec. 12, 1936).

beginning of the end for China.[196] Thus he condemned Chang Hsüeh-liang's actions but tacitly endorsed his objectives.

Although Yen continued to denounce Chang for refusing to let Chiang Kai-shek leave Sian, he was instrumental in preventing the central government from sending troops to attack Sian and lent his support to Madame Chiang and her relatives, who hoped to save Chiang's life and avoid a civil war by negotiating with Chang.[197] He must have been deeply involved in the bargaining that followed, because he sent at least one emissary to Sian and on several occasions Chang's representatives flew to Taiyuan.[198] "All through the Sian affair Yen Hsi-shan played the traditional part of middleman between the Northwest and Nanking, and he probably did very well out of it," comments an Australian observer.[199] He adds that during Chiang's imprisonment Shansi would seem to have been a regular route through which Chang Hsüeh-liang's agents and sympathizers made their way in and out of Sian. Among those who passed through Shansi en route to Sian was an ultraradical named Miao Chien-ch'iu, who expressed the belief that in reality Yen approved of Chang's actions.[200] His opinion was shared by Hsü Fan-t'ing, an emissary of Chang's ally, Yang Hu-ch'eng, the warlord of Shensi, who says that when he approached Yen on Yang's behalf Yen remained noncommittal but voiced doubts about the wisdom of releasing Chiang and letting him return to Nanking.[201]

Yen's reaction to the alliance with the Communists which Chiang was obliged to enter into at Sian also indicates that his sympathies lay with Chiang's kidnappers. On the day of Chiang's release, Yen publicly deplored China's casual abandonment of Manchuria, called the loss of northern Chahar a catastrophe of equal importance, and declared that if the question of whether to resist remained an academic one for much of China that was no longer the case in Shansi.[202] A week later he denounced arguments over abstract concepts of

[196] See *ibid.*, p. 556 (Dec. 14, 1936).

[197] *CWR*, Dec. 26, 1936, p. 115, and Harry Gannes, *When China Unites* (New York, 1937), p. 260.

[198] Fan Ch'ang-chiang, *op.cit.*, p. 26, and James Bertram, *op.cit.*, p. 34.

[199] James Bertram, *op.cit.*, p. 33.

[200] See *ibid.*, pp. 31, 37-38.

[201] Hsü Fan-t'ing, *Letter*, *op.cit.*, p. 1.

[202] *Lectures*, III-A, p. 568 (Dec. 25, 1936).

right and wrong, saying that they were mutually suicidal and that the actual differences between those who professed the "People's" or *jen-min* line and those who followed the "National" or *kuo-min* line were insignificant.[203] In January 1937 he condemned quarrels between Left and Right, socialists and capitalists, and Bolsheviks and anti-Bolsheviks on the ground that such disputes did not involve basic issues of right or wrong and only weakened China's unity against the common enemy.[204]

It is possible that Yen's clandestine rapprochement with the Communists, which a Japanese writer infers was common knowledge in Nanking,[205] and his euphemistically worded but unmistakable demands for a nationwide united front were major reasons why at Sian Chiang Kai-shek yielded to Communist appeals for an alliance against Japan. Perhaps he feared that otherwise Yen would go over to the Communists along with other warlords in North China who wanted to resist the Japanese. For example, Shang Chen, whose troops controlled much of Honan, was Yen's former subordinate and very opposed to Japan.[206] By 1936 Yen also was friendly with Han Fu-chü, the warlord of Shantung, and the Japanese charge that after recapturing Pailingmiao he repeatedly urged Han's counterpart in Hopei, Sung Che-yüan, to help him oust the Japanese and their allies from northern Chahar.[207] In July 1936 the Communists told Edgar Snow that the generals commanding Chiang's troops in and around Shansi likewise were dissatisfied with Chiang's policy of appeasing Japan and were ready to support a united front.[208] Consequently, Chiang may have decided that much of North China would join forces with the Communists unless he called off the civil war and fought Japan.

Yen Mobilizes against Japan

The destruction of Prince Teh's army, together with grow-

[203] See *ibid.*, p. 573 (Dec. 30, 1936).
[204] See *ibid.*, pp. 587, 590-591 (Jan. 18, 23, 1937).
[205] Hata Ikuhiku, *op.cit.*, p. 116.
[206] *CWR*, Dec. 21, 1935, p. 81, and Dec. 30, 1935, p. 445.
[207] Hata Ikuhiku, *op.cit.*, p. 118.
[208] Edgar Snow, *Random Notes on Red China*, p. 59. Snow's informant was Chou En-lai, and the Nationalist commanders mentioned were Ch'en Ch'eng and Hu Tsung-nan.

ing tension in the Peiping-Tientsin area, caused the Japanese to abandon momentarily their efforts to acquire control of Suiyuan; however, they helped Prince Teh establish his authority in Chahar, and by the summer of 1937 he was preparing to reinvade Suiyuan. Meanwhile, besides openly engaging in espionage, Japanese living in Shansi attacked Yen's police and otherwise behaved as if they were above the law.[209] Yen undoubtedly was equally alarmed when a party of Japanese engineers visited Shansi for the avowed purpose of exploring the possibility of exploiting its coal resources.[210] In February 1937 he reiterated his charge that dumping by Japanese manufacturers was bankrupting China's industries and said that, economically speaking, China was in mortal danger.[211] Perhaps he had in mind the catastrophe which overtook Shansi's cotton growers in 1937 when competition from foreign, presumably Japanese, cotton caused the price of cotton to decline by more than 50 percent, with the result that most peasants were unwilling to put forth the effort necessary to harvest their crop, but instead left it standing in the fields.[212] Yen also warned that "the enemy" was using drugs to destroy the Chinese people and threatened to return to a policy of shooting addicts.[213] According to *The China Weekly Review*, during the spring of 1937 the price of narcotics in Shansi fell from CH\$60 an ounce to CH\$10 an ounce, largely because the Japanese were smuggling into the province massive quantities of morphine and heroin, manufactured in the Japanese concession at Tientsin.[214]

No wonder a reporter who traveled through Shansi in February found the authorities using the traditional New Year's celebrations as vehicles for disseminating anti-Japanese propaganda.[215] In March, for the first time since 1932, Yen publicly accused Japan of wanting to conquer China.[216] Thereafter, his speeches were permeated with the notion that Shansi was China's first line of defense and that what happened there

[209] *CWR*, July 31, 1937, p. 312 and C. Y. W. Meng, *op.cit.*, p. 90.
[210] Higuchi Hiromu, *op.cit.*, p. 168.
[211] *Lectures*, III-A, p. 598 (Feb. 1937).
[212] Hsü Ying, *op.cit.*, p. 50.
[213] *Lectures*, VIII, pp. 64, 66 (April 1937, Aug. 1938), and IX, p. 87 (Jan. 1937).
[214] *CWR*, May 15, 1937, p. 431, May 22, 1937, pp. 455-456.
[215] Fan Ch'ang-chiang, *op.cit.*, p. 23.
[216] *Lectures*, V, pp. 94, 97-98 (March 1937).

would decide the fate of the nation. Under the slogan "Defend and Resist" (*shou-t'u k'ang-chan*) he urged his subjects to "find life in death and be ready for sacrifice in the imminent struggle which shall decide whether the province will survive."[217] "We should not abandon an inch of territory," he declared, "no matter what the consequences."[218] In order to frighten the normally apathetic masses into supporting his cause, he warned that whereas in the past wars had resulted only in the destruction of the defeated government, Japan's aim was to exterminate the Chinese people in order to secure living space for its excess population.[219] Yet although he executed Chinese for serving as Japanese agents,[220] he did not attack northern Chahar, for fear of provoking a Japanese invasion of Shansi. This aroused considerable dissatisfaction among his younger followers, especially student volunteers from other provinces in North China, who wanted to regain China's lost territories as soon as possible and therefore urged him to counterattack immediately. He rebuked them for indulging in "irresponsible heroics" and warned that trying to regain the lost territories before China was better prepared would be suicidal. "We must fight rather than surrender more territory," he declared, "but until we are stronger we cannot retake what already is lost."[221] He was accused of being unconcerned about what happened to the rest of China so long as Japan did not attack Shansi or Suiyuan; however, his activities during the winter and spring of 1937 indicate that he was stalling for time in order to strengthen Shansi's defenses against an invasion which he obviously regarded as inevitable.

Yen reorganized and began retraining his army immediately after the Communists withdrew from Shansi in the spring of 1936. The physical condition of his troops was poor, owing to malnutrition and disease, and many of his soldiers were addicted to narcotics.[222] In addition, a large number of his officers could not read and few of them knew anything about

---

[217] *CWR*, July 24, 1937, p. 299.
[218] *CWR*, June 26, 1937, p. 120.
[219] *Lectures*, III-A, p. 556 (Dec. 1936).
[220] For example, see *CWR*, July 3, 1937, p. 160.
[221] *Lectures*, III-A, p. 604 (Feb. 1937).
[222] See *ibid.*, p. 550 (Dec. 1936), and IV, p. 121 (July 1936), and Hatano, *History of the C.C.P., 1936*, p. 46.

modern warfare.[223] "They are unable to place artillery properly," he complained, "and do not know how to calculate range
and trajectory or what weapons should be used together."[224]
He likewise accused his officers of stealing military supplies
and charged that generally they were indifferent to their responsibilities. Furthermore, higher ranking officers quarreled
continually and habitually abused their subordinates, who in
turn treated the enlisted men so cruelly that company commanders were compelled to surround themselves with guards
for fear that otherwise their soldiers would shoot them.[225] Yen
especially deplored the army's relations with the civilian population. Whereas in the 1920's his soldiers had been relatively
well-behaved and not unpopular in Shansi, their defeat in 1930
and their subsequent wretchedness destroyed their morale and
discipline, with the result that they began to prey on the
public, which came to fear and detest them.[226] Peasants also
resented bitterly the unscrupulousness of many recruiting
officers who conscripted luckless farmers into the army after
district magistrates lured them into the cities by promising to
stage free theatrical performances.

As part of a campaign to modernize his officer corps, Yen
ordered higher ranking officers in the Shansi Army to study
the latest methods of warfare by serving for two months in
the Staff Officers Training Regiment (*ts'an-mou hsun-lien
t'uan*). At the same time he stepped up his efforts to recruit
junior officers from among the students of Shansi.[227] "Only
persons having education can achieve proficiency in modern
technology and military science," he declared.[228] This is why
he wanted to make the army such a respectable profession
that it would attract first-class men.[229] He called on his officers
to stop quarreling and urged them to establish a democratic
relationship with their soldiers by respecting enlisted men,

[223] *Lectures*, v, p. 71 (July 1936).
[224] See *ibid.*, p. 73.
[225] See *ibid.*, pp. 60, 110, 106 (July 1936, Jan. 1937).
[226] See *ibid.*, pp. 61-62, 66 (June, July 1936), and iii-C, p. 247
(Feb. 1937).
[227] *Lectures*, vi, pp. 129-130 (Dec. 1936).
[228] *Lectures*, iii-A, p. 583 (Jan. 1937).
[229] *Lectures*, v, p. 68 (July 1936). As early as 1935 Yen urged his
troops to disprove the old idea that "one does not use good iron to
make nails, nor good men for soldiers" by displaying courage, tenacity,
and a willingness to endure suffering in order to win. See *Lectures*, i,
pp. 400-401 (Oct. 1935).

sharing their daily lives, and even listening to their advice and criticism. He expressed his feelings in a song which he composed for his army:

> The ties which bind soldiers together
> are stronger than family loyalties.
> When ill or wounded, they care for one
> another.
> No matter what their rank, they depend
> on each other and share the triumphs
> and disappointments of battle.
> They work together in a spirit of mutual
> affection.[230]

He was equally concerned about the unpopularity of his army. He castigated Chiang Kai-shek for using Central Army troops to terrorize the local population while fighting the Communists in Kiangsi and warned that an army feared by its own people could not defeat the Japanese.[231] According to Yen, soldiers inspired by loyalty to a cause were infinitely superior to politically apathetic troops who fought simply because they feared their officers.[232] "We must stop using our army as an instrument of terror and turn it into a force capable of killing the enemy," he asserted.[233] He ordered his officers to punish severely soldiers who committed crimes against the civilian population and told them to preoccupy themselves with improving the character of their troops. As usual, he composed a song setting forth his views:

> Good soldiers cooperate with the people.
> Then, because they have the help of the
> masses, they triumph easily.
> Do not behave properly only when your
> officers are near.
> Acquire the spirit of self-discipline.[234]

Besides repeatedly haranguing his troops, Yen placed political commissars (*cheng-shun chu-jen*) in virtually every unit of his army and gave members of the Justice Force the right to

[230] *Lectures*, V, p. 92 (July 1936).
[231] See *ibid.*, pp. 82-83.
[232] See *ibid.*, p. 105 (Aug. 1937).
[233] See *ibid.*, p. 88 (July 1936).
[234] See *ibid.*, p. 92.

investigate the conduct of army officers and recommend their impeachment.[235] He also spoke of conscripting for three years of military service all men between the ages of twenty and twenty-five; however, he cautioned his officers and noncommissioned officers against treating conscripts harshly and urged them to win the respect and confidence of the new recruits. Although subsequent events indicate that most of his innovations were ineffectual and that his army did not heed his exhortations to reform, his statements illustrate vividly not only his determination to oppose Japan but likewise his realization that in order to resist the Japanese he must enlist the active support of the mass of his subjects.

Yen professed to want an ideologically motivated army like Soviet Russia's, which he called the best indoctrinated and therefore the most powerful army in the world.[236] Perhaps his real aim was to reconstruct his army along the lines of the Chinese Communist armies, whose performance in Shansi must have impressed him. Beginning in the summer of 1936 he urged his commanders to use tactics which resemble strikingly those employed by the Red Army during its invasion of Shansi. He told them to avoid engaging the bulk of the enemy's army in what he referred to as "futile and suicidal" positional battles and ordered them to fight instead a war of rapid movement over an extended and shifting front—in other words, a protracted war consisting largely of feints, ambushes, and sudden attacks on numerically inferior enemy forces. He described this kind of fighting in another marching song:

> Do what is unexpected; that is good strategy.
> Attack along the flanks or in the rear, and
>   the enemy will give way.
> If an attack fails, then wait for the enemy
>   [to advance] and ambush him.
> Attack at night and make use of the terrain.[237]

Although Yen was enthusiastic about tactics used by the Red Army and later compared the Russian Army favorably to

---

235 See *ibid.*, p. 105 (Aug. 1937), James Bertram, *Unconquered* (New York, 1939), p. 203, and Fukada Yuzō, *op.cit.*, p. 349.

236 *Lectures*, V, pp. 111-112 (Jan. 1938).

237 See *ibid.*, p. 92 (July 1936).

the Japanese Army,[238] many of the reforms he tried to initiate in his army were inspired by his experiences in Japan. He repeatedly praised the Japanese people for treating soldiers like heroes and urged his subjects to emulate them. He also reminded his troops that in Japan soldiers did not abuse or steal from the civilian population. He recalled that while he was serving in the Japanese Army a fellow soldier angered an officer by picking leaves from a tree in a peasant's orchard; the officer called his men together, cited China as an example of what happens to a country when its people have no respect for their army, and warned his soldiers that if they behaved like thieves a similar fate would overtake Japan, since its people would come to detest soldiers, causing able and upright men to shun service in the army. Yen also commended the Japanese for conscripting everybody, no matter how much wealth or influence they possessed.[239] He especially liked Japan's practice of inducting middle school graduates into the armed forces.[240]

Much of his philosophy with respect to battle also must have been borrowed from the Japanese. For instance, he used Japan's victory over Russia in 1905 to illustrate how spirit inevitably triumphs over matter. He frequently exhorted his troops to "find life by seeking death" and told them that courage to the point of self-sacrifice was enough to demoralize an enemy having vastly superior material resources.[241] He called attention to a battle between two African countries in which troops belonging to one side marched forward until they plunged into a river and sank from sight; their courage and discipline caused the other side to lose heart and surrender. In keeping with this outlook, he ordered his soldiers to engage their foes in hand-to-hand combat whenever possible, so as to conserve ammunition and minimize the enemy's superiority with respect to artillery and other forms of fire power. "It is not practical for a materially underdeveloped country to wage long-range [*yüan-chan*] warfare," he declared, "and a developed nation which fights such a war is immoral."[242]

[238] See *ibid.*, p. 112 (Jan. 1938).
[239] *Lectures*, III-C, p. 235 (June 1936).
[240] *Ibid.*
[241] *Lectures*, V, pp. 70, 84, 108 (July 1936, Aug. 1937), and IX, p. 33 (Aug. 1936).
[242] *Lectures*, V, p. 76 (July 1936).

His preoccupation with courage and personal heroism was shared by Chiang Kai-shek and the tactics he urged on his troops are similar to those which Chiang subsequently employed against the Japanese during the first battle for Chengchow in 1938.[243] Inasmuch as both men were graduates of military academies in Japan, their attitude toward warfare may have been a result of the training they received there.

Perhaps Yen's belief that morale and proficiency in hand-to-hand combat are more important than firepower accounts for his ambivalence with respect to positional warfare. He continued to denounce positional tactics but at the same time held up the battles of Verdun and Tannenberg as models for the defense of Shansi. In August 1937 he said that although there were some who wanted to wage a prolonged war of attrition, others advocated fighting a decisive battle in the hope of gaining an immediate victory. "Each argument has its merits," he concluded, "and the choice will depend on the condition of the country."[244] His inclination to belittle the importance of Japan's superior firepower was tempered, however, by a profound respect for the enemy's air force. In July he declared that air power was more important than an army or a navy and predicted that defeat in the air would result in defeat on the ground and at sea.[245] He especially feared the effect of incendiary bombs and warned that the only defense against them was to abandon the cities and rebuild Shansi's industries underground.[246] This is why he constructed beneath the streets of Taiyuan a network of caves and tunnels. One of the largest caves was under his own headquarters, where hundreds of officials learned how to carry on the work of the provincial government from deep within the earth.[247] Meanwhile, the authorities staged mock air raids, enlisted civilians to serve as air raid wardens, and issued thousands of leaflets and pamphlets instructing the population to Taiyuan about what to do if enemy bombers attacked.[248] "War

[243] Theodore H. White, ed., *The Stilwell Papers* (New York, 1948), p. 66.
[244] *Lectures*, II, p. 314 (Aug. 1937).
[245] See *ibid.*, pp. 290-291 (July 1937).
[246] *Lectures*, v, p. 85 (July 1936).
[247] Agnes Smedley, *China Fights Back*, pp. 56-57.
[248] *NCH*, Feb. 17, 1937, 277:1.

in the air has become an integral part of modern warfare, but in China most people don't even know what the term antiaircraft [*fang-k'ung*] means," complained Yen.[249]

Yen's efforts to arouse the public to the danger of air raids was part of an earnest but, it would seem, not very successful campaign to mobilize as quickly as possible the entire population of Shansi. In November 1936 he ordered able-bodied males between the ages of twenty and forty-five who were not serving in the army to enroll in the People's Volunteers (*Kuo-min ping-i*), an organization which probably was inspired by the militia or so-called Red Guards maintained by the Chinese Communists. After undergoing from four to six months of intensive military training, members of the People's Volunteers were to return to their villages and pursue their regular occupations while at the same time training and holding themselves in a state of continual readiness.[250] Officers in the Volunteers were for the most part village school teachers, who received their training in Taiyuan as members of the Shansi People's Military Training Regiment (*Shan-hsi kuo-min ping chün-kuan chiao-tao t'uan*). In his eagerness to bolster his strength against Japan, Yen allowed Po I-po and other radical-minded students to form a guerrilla army, which they called the *ch'ing-nien k'ang-ti chüeh-szu tsung-tui*, the Corps of Youth Sworn to Resist the Enemy to the Death, otherwise known as the Dare-to-Die Corps.[251] He also celebrated Youth Army Day and organized a Youth Vanguard Corps (*shao-nien hsien-feng tui*) and Shansi Junior Middle School Boys' Army (*Shan-hsi ch'u-chung t'ung-tzu chün*). In his speeches he called on the youth of Shansi to model themselves after the students of Japan, whom he hailed as paragons of honesty and patriotism. Teachers spent much of their time preaching loyalty to the nation and their work was supplemented by numerous youth days, parades, and other officially sponsored demonstrations aimed at exciting anti-Japanese feeling among the young people of Shansi.[252] Yen even formed a small women's army corps and organized school girls into

---

[249] *Lectures*, IV, p. 120 (July 1936).

[250] *Lectures*, IX, p. 61 (Nov. 1936), and *CWR*, June 19, 1937, p. 83.

[251] Jack Belden, *op.cit.*, p. 51.

[252] *Lectures*, VI, pp. 131-143 (Jan. 1937-Aug. 1937).

paramilitary groups.[253] After praising the women of Russia for enlisting in the army and fighting side by side with men, he warned Chinese women to expect a fate worse than death if the enemy occupied their country.[254] He said that he wanted to give military training to all women between the ages of twenty and forty and urged them to find work in the factories so that more men would be free to serve in the army.[255]

Yen repeatedly expressed the hope that he could make his subjects more politically conscious and therefore less indifferent to the danger that menaced Shansi. "We must awaken the masses, give them a clear understanding of the situation that confronts their country, and by inculcating in them a spirit of patriotism induce them to unite and sacrifice themselves for the sake of the nation," he declared.[256] He complained that whereas in Japan and other foreign countries virtually everybody was well-informed with respect to national and international affairs, in China even schoolteachers frequently did not know or care about what was happening around them. "Modern warfare is mass warfare," he cautioned.[257] For this reason he ordered his army to fight a "peoples' war," which he also referred to as a "revolutionary war" and a "war of national liberation," by organizing the mass of the people, arming them, and persuading them to identify their interests with those of the government.[258]

In order to achieve these objectives Yen formed the Committee for the Dissemination of Information about the Difficulties Confronting the Nation (*kuo-nan chiao-hsün shih-shih wei-yüan-hui*). The Information Committee had a branch in each district and probably worked closely with the mobilization committees (*tung-yüan shih-shih wei-yüan-hui*), which Yen set up in almost every village.[259] Members of the mobiliza-

253 *NCH*, July 28, 1937, 137:1, and Fukada Yuzō, *op.cit.*, p. 355.
254 *Lectures*, VIII, pp. 61-62 (March 1937).
255 *Lectures*, IV, p. 119 (July 1936), and II, p. 322 (Aug. 1937).
256 *Lectures*, II, p. 311 (Aug. 1937).
257 See *ibid.*, p. 306 (July 1937).
258 *Lectures*, III-A, pp. 627-628 (Aug. 1937).
259 *Lectures*, VI, pp. 131-132 (Nov. 1937), and *Ti-pa lu Chün tsai Shansi-hsi* (*The Eighth Route Army in Shansi*) (Shanghai, 1938), p. 245. With respect to Communist activities in Shansi during the Japanese conquest, perhaps the most valuable sources of information are accounts written by Chinese newsmen who accompanied units of the Eighth Route Army. Many of these were edited by one Kao K'e-fu and published under the latter title above. The style in which these articles are written

tion committees were recruited from the Justice Force and the Sacrifice League. In addition, there was a Peoples' Self-Defense Corps (*jen-min tzu-wei chün*), as well as numerous antiaircraft detachments (*fang-k'ung hu tui*).[260] Even a writer sympathetic to the Communists admits that Yen began arming the peasants before the Red Army reentered Shansi following its invasion by the Japanese in the autumn of 1937.[261] Other mass organizations which Yen created for the purpose of enlisting popular support for his war effort included a Transportation Corps, the Women's Sewing Corps, and the Old Peoples' Prayer Group.[262] He also wanted to place a government-trained propagandist in each village and encouraged the schools to offer courses on current events particularly designed for local peasants and townspeople.[263]

In spite of all this, the bulk of Yen's subjects remained indifferent to his appeals for support against Japan. When they returned to Shansi in the summer of 1937, the Communists encountered considerable anti-Japanese feeling in Taiyuan and other cities but very little among the peasants, who generally still were unorganized and politically apathetic.[264] Yen blamed this situation on his bureaucracy. "The people don't care what happens to their government because their government never has cared what happens to them," he admitted.[265] In many instances local officials and members of the Youth Vanguard Corps antagonized the peasants by extorting money from them under the guise of raising funds for national defense. It is evident, however, that Yen dared not really try to organize and mobilize the masses, especially in the countryside, for

---

suggests that they were set down in great haste and not appreciably altered by the editor. Most of the reporters who composed these narratives were sympathetic to the Communists, but wrote regularly for the non-Communist newspaper *Ta Kung Pao*. Their writings also appear in a number of other books published early in 1938 under the auspices of *Ta Kung Pao*, along with articles by correspondents like the famous Fan Ch'ang-ch'iang, who were attached to Kuomintang and provincial armies fighting the Japanese in northwestern China. Hereafter Kao K'e-fu's anthology is indicated by the abbreviation *TPLC*.

[260] *TPLC*, p. 226.
[261] See *ibid.*, p. 84.
[262] Chao Shu-li, *op.cit.*, pp. 66-67.
[263] *Lectures*, III-C, p. 251 (March 1937), III-A, pp. 579-580 (Jan. 1937), and Liu Po-ying, *op.cit.*, pp. 46, 48.
[264] *TPLC*, pp. 257, 276, Edgar Snow, *The Battle for Asia*, p. 254, and *CWR*, March 5, 1938, pp. 12-13.
[265] *Lectures*, III-A, p. 559 (Dec. 1936).

THE GATHERING STORM

fear of unleashing a revolutionary force likely to undermine his own authority. Opposition on the part of the gentry also explains why Yen failed to arouse more enthusiasm in the countryside for his efforts to resist the Japanese.

The gentry must have resented not only his proposal to arm and organize the peasant masses but likewise his avowed determination to conscript the rich as well as the poor.[266] They also disliked the additional controls which he imposed on the economy. The gentry were outraged especially by the extra taxes he levied against them in order to finance his war effort.[267] He wanted to confiscate the profits of moneylenders, for example, on the grounds that their wealth was unearned and that their activities caused popular unrest. "Since they stand to lose the most if the enemy triumphs, property owners likewise should be taxed heavily," he argued, "and it would be unjust if persons with large incomes did not pay more than those who earn less."[268] In the fall of 1936 he initiated a Contribute Your Fortune to the Nation Movement (*hui-chia nan-shu yün-tung*) and subsequently called on the rich to bear the cost of the war because the poor could not.[269] Furthermore, in the hope of winning support among the masses, he abolished many taxes normally paid by the poor and outlawed interest rates greater than 10 percent.[270]

Yen's speeches, as well as the testimony of Communist observers, indicate that the rich resisted vigorously, and with considerable success, his attempts to obtain from them more money for the strengthening of Shansi's defenses.[271] "The wealthy feel that in the event of trouble they can take refuge in Hong Kong or in the foreign concessions until it blows over," he charged.[272] As early as September 1935 one of his followers voiced the fear that if Yen nationalized and redistributed the land in Shansi, the gentry would turn for help

[266] In June 1937 Yen said that he intended to conscript the rich and would coerce them into serving if necessary. See *Lectures*, II, pp. 282-283.

[267] See *ibid.*, p. 278 (Sept. 1937), and IX, p. 133 (Aug. 1938).

[268] *Lectures*, IX, pp. 58-59 (Nov. 1936).

[269] Ch'en Fang-t'ung, *op.cit.*, p. 31, and *Lectures*, IX, p. 141 (Aug. 1938).

[270] *TPLC*, p. 45.

[271] See *ibid.*, p. 75, and *Lectures*, IX, p. 40 (Nov. 1936), and III-A, pp. 618-621 (March 1937).

[272] *Lectures*, III-A, p. 624 (April 1937).

to the Japanese, whom he euphemistically referred to as "the second foreign invader."[273] Together with the resignation from Yen's government in 1934 of the outspokenly pro-Japanese Su T'i-jen, this suggests that after 1932 a part of the gentry in Shansi began leaning toward Japan in the hope that the Japanese would protect their class from exploitation and perhaps extinction at the hands of the younger, more radical men surrounding Yen Hsi-shan. Sympathy for Japan on the part of Yen's wealthier subjects became unusually pronounced after the summer of 1936, when he entered into an informal alliance with the Chinese Communists aimed at repulsing Japanese aggression in northwestern China. During the months immediately preceding the Japanese invasion, Yen repeatedly complained about the activities of *han-chien*, "disloyal Chinese." His words leave the impression that most of these traitors came from the rich.[274] According to a Chinese reporter, Japanese agents operating in Shansi before the war were especially intent on enlisting the aid of wealthy people.[275] Several writers mention rich men in Shansi who were pro-Japanese,[276] and others state that much of the upper class in Yen's domain favored Japan.[277] Significantly, the rich were the worse violators of Yen's laws forbidding the sale or purchase of narcotics and other Japanese-made goods.[278]

There is much evidence which indicates that many of Yen's officials and army officers also were unenthusiastic about his determination to oppose Japan. His estrangement from Su T'i-jen already has been mentioned. Su was a returned student from Japan who served for many years as Minister of Foreign Affairs in the provincial government of Shansi and later became Minister of Finance for Suiyuan. In 1927 Yen sent him to Peking to negotiate with Chang Tso-lin. When Yen declared in favor of the Kuomintang, Su was arrested by Chang but escaped with the assistance of the Japanese Army.

[273] *Lectures*, I, p. 387 (Sept. 1938).
[274] For example, see *Lectures*, III-A, p. 360 (June 1935), IX, p. 40 (Nov. 1936).
[275] C. Y. W. Meng, *op.cit.*, pp. 90-91.
[276] For example, see James Bertram, *op.cit.*, pp. 257-258, and George A. Hogg, *I See a New China* (Boston, 1945), p. 33.
[277] *NCH*, Jan. 29, 1936, 175:1, and Hsüeh Mu-ch'iao, *op.cit.*, p. 46.
[278] *CWR*, May 22, 1937, p. 456, *NCH*, June 27, 1934, 5:1, Chao Shu-li, *op.cit.*, p. 49, and Ch'en Fang-t'ung, *op.cit.*, p. 29.

Thereafter he served as Yen's chief intermediary with Japan.[279] Presumably his resignation from Yen's government in 1934 was provoked by Yen's increasingly anti-Japanese posture, since he subsequently became governor of Shansi under the Japanese.[280] According to a Chinese writer, by 1936 Japanese agents in Shansi were under orders to encourage factionalism within Yen's regime and buy over disaffected persons in his army and government.[281] On several occasions the *North China Herald* accused officials and other leaders in Shansi of being pro-Japanese or unexcited about Yen's efforts to mobilize against Japan.[282] Yen admitted that his army was filled with traitors.[283] A foreign writer says that most of its officers were too wealthy to have any desire to sacrifice for the sake of Shansi.[284] Much of the Buddhist clergy in Shansi likewise favored the Japanese and later collaborated with them.[285] "Everyone in league with the foreign enemy should be killed on the spot!" raged Yen.[286] In most instances, however, he was obliged to tolerate the activities of Japanese sympathizers for fear that if he arrested many of them, Japan would retaliate by invading Shansi.

Yen refused to provoke Japan because he felt that China needed time to strengthen its defenses and believed that although the younger officers in the Japanese Army wished to invade China immediately, Japan's civilian leaders were less confident of their country's readiness for such a war and consequently wanted to wait ten years before attempting to conquer China.[287] Perhaps he knew that the Japanese government disapproved of the Kwantung Army's threat to intervene if his troops attacked Prince Teh's forces in northern Chahar.[288] Subsequently, partisans of Chiang Kai-shek and the Chinese Communists accused Yen of entering into negotiations with the Japanese at the same time he professed to oppose them. This

[279] *Japanese Biographical Survey*, p. 278, and Maruyama Shizuo, *op.cit.*, pp. 173-174.
[280] *NCH*, June 28, 1938, 535:4.
[281] C. Y. W. Meng, *op.cit.*, pp. 90-91.
[282] *NCH*, Jan. 29, 1936, 175:1, Nov. 4, 1936, 178:4.
[283] *Lectures*, v, p. 89 (July 1936).
[284] *NCH*, Dec. 15, 1937, 398:4.
[285] *TPLC*, p. 183, and Hirano, *Komoto*, p. 198.
[286] *Lectures*, IX, p. 38 (Nov. 1936).
[287] *Lectures*, III-A, pp. 586, 602-603 (Jan., Feb. 1937).
[288] Hata Ikuhiku, *op.cit.*, pp. 118-119.

may explain why, as late as July 1937, Japan's leading authority on political conditions in North China called Yen's attitude toward Japan "ambivalent" and a month later referred to him as "the pillar of stability in North China."[289] In spite of his willingness to fight rather than allow Japan to acquire control of Shansi or Suiyuan, Yen possibly continued to seek a rapprochement with the Japanese in the hope of avoiding war and securing Japan's backing for his own ambitions in North China. On the other hand, Yen cited an article from a Japanese newspaper which charged that he was a major obstacle to the growth of Japan's power in China.[290] This opinion was shared by an otherwise unsympathetic foreigner who visited Shansi in 1937.[291] On several occasions, moreover, Japanese writers denounced Yen for surrendering completely to the Communists or the central government.[292]

A lingering fear that Chiang Kai-shek still intended to abandon Shansi without a struggle may be the chief reason for Yen's willingness to continue negotiating with the Japanese. In March 1937 he again warned his subjects against expecting the rest of the country to come to their aid in the event of an invasion.[293] Probably in order to reassure him, the central government sent into Suiyuan an additional 20,000 troops and loaned his regime more than CH$5 million. Yen reciprocated by allowing it to build in his domain a system of telephones, which linked most parts of Shansi directly with Nanking and therefore had the effect of bringing them more closely under Chiang Kai-shek's control.[294] Although Yen used the Justice Force to prevent the Kuomintang from resurrecting its political authority in Taiyuan and other cities, he also let the central government open another branch of its state bank in Shansi and permitted its currency to circulate freely, with the result that the value of his own banknotes rapidly depreciated.[295]

His policy with respect to the Chinese Communists was

[289] Hatano Ken'ichi, *Gendai Shina no seiji to jimbutsu*, pp. 117, 228.
[290] *Lectures*, III-A, p. 625 (April 1937).
[291] John Gunther, *op.cit.*, p. 279.
[292] For example, see *CWR*, Jan. 16, 1937, p. 261, and Kojima Seiichi, *op.cit.*, p. 165.
[293] *Lectures*, III-C, p. 150 (March 1937).
[294] *NCH*, April 21, 1937, 100:1, and *CEJ*, Dec. 1936, p. 665.
[295] Fukada Yuzō, *op.cit.*, pp. 352-353, and *NCH*, June 9, 1937, 409:1, and July 28, 1937, 137:1.

equally ambivalent. He rejected their demands for an immediate effort to retake the lost territories. In February 1937,
moreover, he referred to them as *kung-fei*, "Communist
bandits," and denounced what he termed "ideological aggression aimed at creating a utopia by means of thought control."[296] Two months later he warned that because of its
spectacular achievements in the realm of industrialization the
Soviet Union menaced not only underdeveloped countries like
China but likewise Europe and the United States. In May he
predicted that ultimately Russia and Japan would go to war
for possession of North China and turn most of it into a battlefield. Furthermore, he reiterated his determination to use land
reform in order to check the spread of "bolshevism" in Shansi
and restricted the activities of the increasingly pro-Communist Sacrifice League. He continued to promote the united
front, however, and allowed Communist organizers and propagandists to operate in Shansi as long as they did not preach
communism or challenge his authority.[297] Apparently, his aim
was to prevent the central government and the Communists
from usurping his power in Shansi, while at the same time ob-
taining from each of them as much help as possible against
the Japanese.

[296] *Lectures*, III-B, pp. 278-279 (Feb. 1937), III-A, p. 594 (Feb.
1937).

[297] *Lectures*, III-A, p. 623 (April 1937), and *CWR*, Nov. 27, 1937,
p. 400.

CHAPTER TWELVE

THE JAPANESE INVASION

Japan Invades

In July 1937, after Chinese resistance at Lukouch'iao, the
Marco Polo Bridge, in eastern Hopei provoked the Japanese
into attacking Chinese forces in and around Peiping, the
Japanese sent a large number of warplanes and Manchurian
troops to reinforce Prince Teh's army in northern Chahar.
This convinced Yen that an invasion of northwestern China
was imminent, and he retaliated by flying to Nanking, where
he conferred with Chiang Kai-shek about the situation in
North China and accepted from him an appointment as commander of the Second War Zone, which comprised Shansi,
Suiyuan, Chahar, and northern Shensi.[1] Upon returning to
Shansi, he encouraged the Sacrifice League to step up its
efforts to apprehend traitors[2] and ordered his troops to attack
northern Chahar, in conjunction with units of Sung Che-yuan's
29th Army, stationed in southern Chahar. His aim was to
surprise and overwhelm Prince Teh's army before it invaded
Suiyuan or Shansi.[3] While the Mongols and Manchurians
fell back before this unexpected onslaught, Japanese armies
trying to force their way through the strategic Nan-k'ou Pass
into southwestern Chahar suffered heavy losses at the hands
of troops belonging to Yen and the central government.[4] Besides
wanting to save their allies in northern Chahar from destruction, the Japanese wished to secure control of Shansi's rich
deposits of coal and use it as a base for aerial operations
against Chinese forces to the south.[5]

The vastly superior firepower of their opponents eventually
compelled the Chinese to surrender Nan-k'ou. They withdrew
in considerable disorder, closely pursued by the Japanese, who

[1] *CWR*, Aug. 7, 1937, p. 356.
[2] *CWR*, Aug. 14, 1937.
[3] *HHHCC*, pp. 22-25.
[4] See *ibid.*, pp. 25-28, *TPLC*, pp. 217-218, *HPH*, p. 2, and U.S. Army,
Forces in the Far East, *North China Area Operations Record*, July
1937-May 1941 (Tokyo: Military History Section; Headquarters, Army
Forces Far East, 1955), Japanese Monograph 178, hereafter referred to
as *Japanese Monograph 178*, pp. 32-33.
[5] Hata Ikuhiku, *op.cit.*, p. 278.

quickly occupied Suiyuan, seized Tatung, and invaded Shansi. "I tell you it was terrible," replied one of Yen's officers when asked to describe the fighting around Tatung. "We never saw the Japanese. The planes came again and again—bom, bom! and the big guns; they killed thousands of us. And the tanks, and the armored cars. . . ."[6] Although Japanese artillery inflicted many of the losses suffered by the Chinese armies, Japan's air force wreaked still greater havoc, not only at the front but also in the rear areas, where civilians became so hysterical with fear that the sound of aircraft was enough to make them flee in terror.[7] During the day Taiyuan and other cities virtually were deserted, with the result that industrial production declined appreciably.[8]

Another reason for the defeat of Yen's army was the ineptness of its commanders, who used obsolete maps, built inadequate fortifications, neglected to obtain proper intelligence, and were so indifferent to staff work that their defense was ill-organized and in many instances completely unplanned. "Officers above the rank of battalion commander were, with few exceptions, quite unfit to command," remarked a foreign observer.[9] In addition to lacking ability and modern training, many of Yen's commanders must have been rivals and inclined to distrust one another, since frequently they refused to cooperate. Divisional commanders did not coordinate their operations with those of other divisions, and lower-ranking commanders habitually disregarded or countermanded instructions from their superiors. On one occasion an important pass was lost to the enemy because the commander of neighboring forces declined to come to the assistance of its defenders, presumably for fear that his own losses would be too great.[10]

Yen expected his commanders to obtain his approval before issuing even the least significant orders. This is why they were unable to attack quickly or otherwise take immediate advantage of opportunities for decisive action. From his headquarters in Taiyuan, a hundred miles away, Yen attempted

[6] James Bertram, *op.cit.*, p. 147.

[7] *TPLC*, p. 90, Hsü Ying, *op.cit.*, p. 51, *HPH*, pp. 1-30, and Agnes Smedley, *The Great Road* (New York, 1958), p. 369.

[8] *HPH*, p. 45, and *HHHCC*, pp. 46-47.

[9] *NCH*, Dec. 15, 1937, 398:4.

[10] *TPLC*, pp. 194-205.

to dictate tactics at the front, with often catastrophic results.[11] As for his strategy, it consisted of little more than ordering his soldiers to defend to the death the cities and towns of northern Shansi, which the Japanese simply bypassed and then reduced to submission with artillery.[12] Subsequently, Communist military leaders criticized Yen for having his troops fall back on the defensive instead of counterattacking and charged that his forces did not make effective use of Shansi's mountainous terrain. The situation was made worse by the breakdown of the transportation system in Shansi, owing to Japanese air raids, the inadequacy of the narrow gauge T'ung-Pu Railroad, the chaotic misuse of motor trucks, and attacks by Japanese plain-clothes troops, who repeatedly infiltrated Yen's lines.

After the Japanese seized Nan-k'ou and invaded Shansi, much of Yen's army became too demoralized to fight effectively. Tatung was surrendered without a struggle by one of Yen's most trusted commanders, Li Fu-ying, whose panic-stricken troops retreated so hastily that they had to destroy or leave behind a large part of their irreplaceable equipment.[13] According to a foreigner who witnessed much of the fighting in Shansi, Yen's soldiers were ill-disciplined and lacked spirit. "Their faces were listless and their feet dragged as they marched," he recalled. "They knew not why they fought except that they had been ordered to do so."[14] Later, Yen complained that the efforts of his political commissars were being thwarted by other officers in the army, who feared and resented the commissars and for this reason denounced them in front of the troops and otherwise obstructed their activities.[15] A foreign observer says that Yen's officers rode apart from their men, swinging incongruous walking sticks, and that the fur coats they wore made an unpleasant contrast with the soldiers' cotton uniforms.[16] The officers also were better fed than the enlisted men, who subsisted largely on cereals, inasmuch as they were given scarcely any meat and

[11] Fan Ch'ang-chiang, *et al.*, *Hsi-pei chan-yün* (*War Clouds over the Northwest*) (Shanghai, 1938), hereafter referred to as *HPCY*, pp. 110-113.
[12] *TPLC*, pp. 189-190.
[13] See *ibid.*, pp. 234-235, and *HPH*, pp. 39-45.
[14] Evans Carlson, *op.cit.*, p. 120.
[15] *Lectures*, v, p. 118 (Jan. 1938).
[16] James Bertram, *op.cit.*, pp. 192-193.

not many vegetables.[17] Furthermore, because Shansi had only a handful of doctors and even fewer hospitals, soldiers wounded at the front suffered terribly. Many were obliged to make their way to the rear as best they could; those having serious wounds were taken to the rear in boxcars and then deposited at railroad stations or along the banks of the Fen River, where they lay for days without medical attention, blankets, or food. Inevitably, a large number of them died of their wounds or succumbed to the effects of cold and hunger.[18] The bodies of some were left in the streets, to rot or be eaten by wild dogs.[19]

The behavior of Yen's now thoroughly demoralized soldiers with respect to the civilian population explains why in spite of his efforts to mobilize popular support for his cause, the masses remained indifferent to the Japanese in areas where his army was active. As they retreated southward, his increasingly undisciplined troops robbed, raped, and abused the peasantry until people living in rural areas came to fear Chinese soldiers more than they did the Japanese.[20] Consequently, propagandists attached to the Shansi Army for the purpose of interesting villagers in the war effort found the peasants hostile and unresponsive.[21] On one occasion, after a damaged Japanese plane was forced to land behind the Chinese lines, local farmers stood around watching calmly while the enemy pilot repaired his craft and flew off.[22] The peasants also willingly dug trenches and built defense works for the Japanese, who paid excellent wages for this kind of work.[23] In areas near the front lines, moreover, villagers generally ran away from Chinese troops, refused to sell them food, and ignored wounded Chinese soldiers.[24] Frequently they even mobbed and beat to death small groups of Yen's soldiers.[25] Eyewitness

[17] *TPLC*, pp. 239-240.

[18] Agnes Smedley, "China's Silent Heroes—Wounded Soldiers of Shansi," *CWR*, Nov. 6, 1937, pp. 214-215, *HHHCC*, pp. 41-43, 48-49, 60, *HPH*, p. 107, and Fan Ch'ang-chiang, *et al.*, *Hsi-hsien feng-yün* (*Wind and Clouds on the Western Front*) (No date or place of publication, but probably Shanghai, 1938), hereafter referred to as *HHFY*, p. 214.

[19] *HHHCC*, p. 74.

[20] See *ibid.*, p. 71, *HPCY*, p. 29, and *TPLC*, 71, 137, 277.

[21] *HHFY*, pp. 219-220.   [22] *HHHCC*, p. 44.

[23] *Ibid.*

[24] *HHFY*, pp. 213-217, and *TPLC*, pp. 79-80, 96, 100-103.

[25] *Lectures*, v, p. 114 (Jan. 1938).

accounts of how the rural population behaved when the Japanese invaded northern Shansi suggest that most peasants were unaware of the fundamental difference between Chinese and Japanese and therefore regarded the war with Japan as simply another contest between rival warlords, from which they instinctively tried to remain aloof.[26] Many of Yen's officials also frustrated his attempts to arouse the masses against Japan by running away as soon as the enemy approached. He must bear much of the blame himself, however, since although he gave arms to the peasants and urged them to defend their homes, he was reluctant to let them organize, for fear that they would become rebellious.[27] As a result, the Sacrifice League and the mobilization committees were not very effective in rural areas.[28]

Finally, espionage and sabotage carried out by Chinese who sympathized with Japan or were in the pay of the Japanese played an important role in bringing about the defeat of the Chinese armies in Shansi.[29] Besides keeping the Japanese informed about the disposition of Chinese troops, these traitors set numerous fires, used signals to guide Japanese bombers to important objectives, and spread rumors which had the effect of arousing hysteria and despair. Many of the spies and saboteurs who undermined Chinese resistance in Shansi were Buddhist priests or persons so poor that they willingly sold their services to the Japanese,[30] but much of the gentry approved of their activities and obstructed Yen's efforts to suppress them.[31] Their lack of concern for Yen's cause often took the form of refusing to provide money and supplies urgently needed by his hard-pressed armies.[32] Instead of helping him combat wartime inflation, moreover, they indulged in an orgy of hoarding and speculation, which sent prices soaring upward.[33] All of this lends support to

[26] *HHFY*, pp. 170, 213-222, and *TPLC*, pp. 79-80, 96, 100-103.
[27] *HHHCC*, pp. 31-32, 44-45, 48-49, and Hsü Ying, *op.cit.*, p. 50.
[28] *TPLC*, p. 42, and Chao Shu-li, *op.cit.*, p. 67.
[29] For example, see *TPLC*, pp. 88, 183-184, 278, *HHHCC*, pp. 40-41, and *HPH*, pp. 55, 65.
[30] *TPLC*, p. 183, and *HHFY*, p. 218.
[31] *HPH*, pp. 34-35, and *Lectures*, III-A, p. 630 (Aug. 1937).
[32] *TPLC*, p. 235, *HHHCC*, pp. 42-44, and *HHFY*, p. 219.
[33] *HHHCC*, pp. 47-48, and *TPLC*, pp. 41, 112. According to a visiting reporter from Peiping, in 1936 wealthy speculators in Shansi took advantage of the Suiyuan crisis to drive up the price of foodstuffs. See Ch'en Fang-t'ung, *op.cit.*, p. 29. This may be why in July 1937 the

charges that in areas overrun by the Japanese, the rich frequently collaborated with the enemy.[34] According to a partisan but nevertheless well-informed American observer, prosperous merchants and well-to-do gentry organized themselves
into peace preservation committees (*wei-ch'ih hui*) and in
this capacity were used by the Japanese as instruments for
maintaining order, collecting taxes, and conscripting corvée
labor.[35] In Chao Shu-li's novel, the wealthiest landowner in
Li Village turned out to be its chief collaborator.[36] Thus in
many instances members of the moneyed class became allies
and puppets of the Japanese, who repaid them for their
services by allowing them to retain their economic power over
the masses.[37]

As the Japanese advanced southward toward the passes
leading into the Taiyuan Basin, Yen sought to terrorize his
generals into resisting by executing Li Fu-ying and other
commanders guilty of running away from the enemy.[38] He
ordered his army not to retreat under any circumstances and
promised to continue fighting until the Japanese had been
defeated. His soldiers were invited to kill him if he violated his
pledge.[39] In addition to letting the Sacrifice League expand
its Dare-to-Die Corps into a 15,000-man force, which came
to be known as Shansi's "New Army," he organized teenagers
into a Youth Anti-Traitor Corps (*shao-nien ch'u-chien t'uan*)
and told his commanders to shoot anyone caught spying for
the Japanese.[40] Early in October, after the passes to the north

---

provincial government threatened to execute anyone who disturbed the
stability of its currency. See *CWR*, July 31, 1937, p. 312.

[34] For example, see Lo Fu's comments in *HPCY*, p. 150, and Chu
Teh's statement to the reporter Hsü Ying in *TPLC*, p. 163. Another
Ta Kung Pao correspondent also calls the gentry a major source of
collaborators in Shansi. See *TPLC*, p. 136.

[35] Agnes Smedley, as quoted in Hatano Ken'ichi, *Chūgoku kyōsantō
shi, ichi ku san shichi nen*, p. 307. Jack Belden, *op.cit.*, p. 176, says
about the same thing.

[36] Chao Shu-li, *op.cit.*, p. 96.

[37] It was an established policy of the Japanese to guarantee property
rights and other privileges belonging to indigenous elites in return for
their cooperation in administering newly conquered territories. For
example, see George W. Barclay, *Colonial Development and Population in Taiwan* (Princeton, 1954), pp. 49-52.

[38] *HPCY*, pp. 24-25, 148.

[39] *Lectures*, v, pp. 108-109 (Aug. 1937).

[40] George A. Hogg, *op.cit.*, p. 25, Wang Ch'ien, *op.cit.*, p. 22a, and
Hsiao Lin, "Tsai T'ai-yüan te i t'ien" ("A Day in Taiyuan"), *KWCP*,
Dec. 27, 1936, p. 58.

were captured by the Japanese, he apologized to the central government for the ineffectualness of his army, asked it to assume paramount responsibility for the defense of Shansi, and agreed to share control of the provincial government with a representative of Chiang Kai-shek.[41]

Again the Communists

Meanwhile, in response to an invitation extended by Yen as soon as Japan invaded his domain, Communist troops re-entered Shansi. Chu Teh became vice-commander of the Second War Zone, Chou En-lai set up headquarters in Taiyuan, and Communist troops occupied a large part of northern and southeastern Shansi. According to a foreign observer, Yen asked the Communists to return to Shansi because he thought he could hold off the Japanese indefinitely and that the Communists "would be as lukewarm toward Nanking as he was and, in the settlement after the Japanese were smashed, they would be satisfied with what he would give them as their share."[42] This time, instead of molesting the rich or preaching revolution, the Eighth Route Army, as the Communists now called themselves, urged patriots of all classes to close ranks against Japan and behaved as if its only aim was to help Yen and Chiang Kai-shek repel the invaders. In an obvious bid for Yen's support, Chou En-lai told Yen's followers that by halting the flow of Japanese goods into China the war would create there conditions favorable to the growth of China's own industries.[43] Yen responded by welcoming the Communists warmly, and they were greeted with comparable enthusiasm by local officials and the officers of Yen's army.[44]

Units of the Eighth Route Army arrived at the front just in time to defeat decisively a powerful Japanese force trying to penetrate the important mountain pass P'ing-hsing-kuan. After the Japanese succeeded in outflanking them, however, and began marching southward in the direction of Taiyuan, the Communists avoided pitched battles and simply carried out hit-and-run attacks against Japanese communications and

[41] *NYT*, Oct. 15, 1937, 3:4.

[42] Walter Judd, as quoted in Agnes Smedley, *The Great Road*, p. 367.

[43] *TPLC*, p. 200.

[44] See *ibid.*, pp. 38, 99, 218-219, 231-233, and Agnes Smedley, *China Fights Back*, p. 154.

lines of supply. The Japanese suffered as a result of these
raids, but they virtually ignored the Eighth Route Army and
threw most of their strength into the advance toward Yen's
capital.[45] This gave the Communists time to recruit from the
peasantry tens of thousands of members for the peasant associations, militia units, guerrilla bands, and other mass organizations which the Eighth Route Army set up in Shansi
wherever it went.[46] Unlike Yen's soldiers, the men of the
Eighth Route Army were popular among the peasants, who
showered them with gifts[47] and eagerly attended theatrical
performances given by the Communists. In the past most
farmers had stayed away when the local authorities staged
equally anti-Japanese plays.[48] The behavior of the Eighth
Route Army with respect to the civilian population explains
why Communist and non-Communist troops were greeted so
differently in the countryside. Communist soldiers always paid
in full for whatever they needed, never molested women, and
treated the peasants like allies, whose aid and friendship they
deeply cherished. Farmers often asked the Eighth Route Army
to protect them against not only the Japanese but also Yen's
forces.[49] Their attitude toward the Communists is reflected
in the words uttered by an old woman after she learned that
the soldiers entering her village belonged to the Eighth Route
Army. "Right! Right! I know! I know!" she exclaimed, "You
are the Southern Army, the Eighth Route Army . . . the good
army that doesn't harm people or do evil things. . . . You
are the Red Army!"[50] Thus, the masses chose to follow the
Eighth Route Army because they found its conduct a welcome relief from the rapacity and brutality of other armies
fighting in Shansi.

Besides appreciating the discipline and thoughtfulness of
Communist soldiers, the peasants also supported the Eighth
Route Army in the hope that it would carry out social reforms
comparable to those initiated by the Communists during their
invasion of Shansi in the winter of 1936. A reporter who accompanied the Eighth Route Army into Shansi says that it
owed its instant popularity among the peasants to the reputation which the Communists had earned in Shansi the pre-

45 *NYT*, Oct. 12, 1937, 3:3.   46 *TPLC*, p. 41.   47 *HPH*, p. 146.
48 *TPLC*, p. 223.   49 See *ibid.*, p. 41.   50 *HPCY*, p. 40.

ceding year.[51] As one villager put it, "We know you're the Red Army, the army of us poor people."[52] Several eyewitness accounts leave the impression that most people were over-joyed by the arrival of the Eighth Route Army simply be-cause they thought it would attack the rich.[53] Significantly, when approached by propagandists serving with the Shansi Army, peasants often replied that in order to secure their aid against the Japanese, the provincial government must first reduce taxes, stamp out injustice, and put an end to economic exploitation.[54] This caused one of Yen's agitators to conclude that in the absence of social and economic reform the peasants would remain indifferent to the war. "We say to them 'Arise! Arise!' when we really have no way of making them actually stand up [to the Japanese]," he complained.[55]

Although the Communists refrained from openly redistrib-uting the land, they introduced a host of other reforms which revolutionized the existing social structure in Shansi by un-dermining profoundly the power of the rich. These changes must have contributed enormously to the popularity of the Eighth Route Army because its leaders attached the utmost importance to them. Late in 1937 the Communist general P'eng Te-huai told a reporter that social and economic re-forms aimed at improving the livelihood of the masses in Shansi should be given priority over such things as organiz-ing the population, political indoctrination within the army, creation of a unified command, and the development of a new strategy.[56] Mao Tse-tung himself said more or less the same thing in an interview with the Australian reporter James Bertram.[57] After Taiyuan fell to the Japanese, Mao denounced capitulationism in the Communist Party and issued what was tantamount to a call for intensification of the class struggle in Shansi.[58]

[51] *TPLC*, p. 37.   [52] *HPH*, p. 147.
[53] *TPLC*, pp. 203, 221, 226-229.   [54] *HHFY*, pp. 219-220.
[55] See *ibid.*, p. 220.   [56] *TPLC*, pp. 186-187.
[57] See *ibid.*, p. 159. A Communist account written early in 1938 calls on the Communists to exploit the resentment aroused among the peasants by the behavior of the Japanese Army, but says that lightening their economic burden is "the most important way of inducing the masses to organize for resistance." See Jen Pi-shih, "Shan-hsi k'ang-chan te hui-i" ("Recollections of the Fighting in Shansi"), *Chieh-fang* (*Liberation*), Jan. 28, 1938, p. 17.
[58] Mao Tse-tung, *The Situation and Tasks in the Anti-Japanese War after the Fall of Shanghai and Taiyuan* (Peking, 1956), pp. 9, 18.

Upon reentering Shansi, the Communists enlisted the aid of the radically inclined Sacrifice League, which persuaded the provincial government to release everyone imprisoned for political reasons during the Red Army's invasion of Shansi in 1936.[59] Some of those freed had served in the Red Army, while the rest are referred to simply as "revolutionaries."[60] Inasmuch as they had been jailed for being Communists or pro-Communist at a time when the Red Army was preoccupied with fomenting class warfare in Shansi, these former prisoners must have sympathized for the most part with the revolutionary aims of the Communist Party rather than with its policy of opposing Japan. Nevertheless, they were allowed to enter the armed forces or sent into the countryside to organize the peasants in the name of the Sacrifice League. In his novel, the Communist writer Chao Shu-li described how one such "anti-Japanese" organizer incited the inhabitants of Li Village to rebel against the local gentry by telling them that the rich acquired their power unjustly and should be overthrown.[61] As a result, the post of village headman was taken away from the wealthiest landowner and given to a poor peasant, under whose leadership the poor drove the gentry from the village.[62]

The validity of Chao Shu-li's narrative is confirmed by a more contemporary account which states that cadres representing the Eighth Route Army frequently tried to organize villagers without first consulting village headmen or other members of the gentry.[63] The war, however, generally prevented the Communists from sending troops along with their agitators. For this reason, when the local authorities retaliated against peasants cooperating with its cadre, the Eighth Route Army was compelled to employ less obvious methods of reducing the gentry to impotence. Instead of attacking the rich directly, the Communists worked through the "mobilization committees" which the provincial government had set up in each village to mobilize the population against Japan.[64] Local officials were under orders to obey these committees, and their members also wielded considerable military power, owing to the fact that they recruited and commanded the

---

[59] Chao Shu-li, *op.cit.*, pp. 56, 58.   [60] *HHHCC*, p. 53.
[61] Chao Shu-li, *op.cit.*, pp. 67-68.
[62] See *ibid.*, p. 94.   [63] *TPLC*, p. 279.
[64] See *ibid.*, pp. 44-45, 250-262.

local militia, commonly known as the People's Self-Defense Corps. In the hands of the Communists and their allies, the mobilization committees became instruments for carrying out in Shansi what amounted to a social revolution.

This revolution took the form of compelling the gentry to relinquish their economic power over the masses, on the assumption that the peasants would oppose mobilization unless exempted from exactions of all kinds, for fear that otherwise their families would starve if they deserted their fields in order to fight the Japanese. For example, the Communists adopted the slogan "Those having wealth must contribute money; those with muscle, their strength" (*yu-ch'ien ch'u ch'ien; yu-li ch'u li*).[65] In areas occupied by the Eighth Route Army, taxes were reduced drastically and frequently were abolished altogether.[66] This policy endeared the Communists to the average farmer, who was accustomed to paying exceedingly heavy taxes. Then, the mobilization committees requisitioned from the gentry whatever was needed in the way of supplies for the armed forces or funds to support their own operations.[67] This means that in areas where the Eighth Route Army was active the rich were forced to bear virtually the entire cost of the war against Japan.

The contributions demanded from the gentry must have been immense, as they repeatedly tried to evade them.[68] The Communists, however, easily overcame such opposition. Gentry who refused to sacrifice their wealth were denounced in public and subjected to intense pressure from mass organizations.[69] If they continued to resist, their belongings were seized by the armed peasants who made up the People's Self-Defense Corps.[70] The Communists confiscated much of the wealth possessed by the gentry; often the gentry lost everything, and there was a regulation providing for the public use of land owned by rich families when they were unable to meet the demands of the mobilization committees.[71] Furthermore, according to Chao Shu-li, the Communists justified their treatment of the gentry by accusing them of having obtained their wealth through exploitation.[72] Several observers

---

[65] See *ibid.*, p. 45. [66] See *ibid.*, pp. 46, 75, 136-137, 164.
[67] See *ibid.*, pp. 46, 75, 279-280. [68] See *ibid.*, pp. 46, 229.
[69] See *ibid.*, pp. 75, 280. [70] See *ibid.*, p. 271, and *HPCY*, p. 44.
[71] *TPLC*, p. 281. [72] Chao Shu-li, *op.cit.*, p. 66.

have described the intense enthusiasm which this policy of taxing the rich instead of the poor aroused among the peasants.[73] It was probably the chief reason for the enormous popularity of the Eighth Route Army in Shansi.[74]

The Communists also used taxation as a device for effecting changes in the existing system of land tenure in Shansi. If the rich ran off or for other reasons persistently failed to pay the taxes levied against them, their land was confiscated and given to poor peasants, who thereafter worked it rent free.[75] In view of the extortionate demands made upon the gentry under the pretext of collecting taxes, much land must have been redistributed in this fashion.

Nevertheless, although Communists spoke of the desirability of doing away with tenantry,[76] in most instances the Eighth Route Army merely imposed a 25 percent reduction in rent.[77] Besides wishing to reassure Yen Hsi-shan and other conservative allies, the Communists also may have perceived that in most of Shansi tenantry was not an especially serious problem. Usury, however, was a problem of overriding importance to virtually every peasant living in Shansi, and by practically banning it in the areas under their control the Communists carried out a social and economic revolution of the utmost magnitude. Interest rates were not allowed to exceed 10 percent a year.[78] Moreover, the Communists suspended for the duration of the war all debts owed by the families of soldiers fighting the Japanese.[79] Inasmuch as the Eighth Route Army recruited its troops largely from among the poor[80] and the mobilization committees construed the word "soldiers" to mean not only peasants conscripted into the regular armies but also irregulars, such as members of the Communist-organized Volunteer Corps (*i-yung tui*),[81] this policy had the effect of wiping out the chronic indebtedness of the vast majority of the population. Its impact on the popularity of the Communists in Shansi must have been immense.

Under the guise of helping the relatives of peasants serving in the armed forces, the Communists extended other privileges to the poor, including free education and medical care.[82] De-

[73] For example, see *TPLC*, p. 75.   [74] See *ibid.*, pp. 275-276.
[75] See *ibid.*, p. 281.   [76] *HHFY*, p. 222.   [77] *TPLC*, p. 274.
[78] See *ibid.*, p. 273.   [79] *Ibid.*   [80] *HPCY*, p. 31.
[81] *TPLC*, pp. 273, 277, 280.   [82] See *ibid.*, pp. 273-274.

pendents of men at the front even received a share of the wealth taken from the rich by the mobilization committees.[83] Then too, the gentry were obliged to humble themselves by personally visiting the homes of even the poorest soldiers for the purpose of comforting their families.[84] An eyewitness says that the common people rejoiced in the new equality which the Eighth Route Army imposed on the villages of Shansi in the name of wartime solidarity.[85]

Although Yen had tried without success to do much of what the Communists accomplished in Shansi after the Japanese invaded, he was reluctant to give the Eighth Route Army a free hand in his domain for fear that it would usurp his power. In spite of his determination to resist Japan and his conviction that mass mobilization was the key to effective resistance, he let the Communists operate without restraint only in territory immediately threatened by the Japanese or already behind enemy lines.[86] In areas further to the rear, like Taiyuan, the local officials dragged their heels and hindered as much as possible the work of the mobilization committees.[87] The Communists accused Yen and his followers of being afraid that the masses, if armed and organized, would overthrow the established social order and with it authority of the provincial government.[88] The gentry circulated rumors aimed at discrediting the Eighth Route Army[89] and, according to Chao Shu-li, resisted tenaciously the efforts of the organizers sent into the villages by the Sacrifice League.[90] The Communists repeatedly complained about the rich evading wartime taxes.[91]

The Eighth Route Army had at its disposal, however, a formidable weapon for use against its conservative opponents. One of the principal functions of the Communist-dominated mobilization committees was to track down and punish pro-Japanese elements intent on undermining Shansi's defenses. Although such people were referred to as "traitors," this

[83] See *ibid.*, p. 271.   [84] See *ibid.*, p. 274.
[85] See *ibid.*, pp. 75-76.   [86] *HPCY*, pp. 106, 146.
[87] *TPLC*, p. 278, and Agnes Smedley, *Battle Hymn of China* (New York, 1943), pp. 189-190.
[88] Agnes Smedley, *Battle Hymn of Red China*, p. 189, Chu Teh's statement in *TPLC*, p. 164, and Lo Fu's in *HPCY*, p. 146.
[89] *TPLC*, pp. 277-278.
[90] Chao Shu-li, *op.cit.*, pp. 61-62, 69-76, 83.
[91] See *ibid.*, p. 77, and *TPLC*, pp. 46, 229.

term apparently was applied to everyone who resisted the radical policies of the mobilization committees. An important Communist leader inferred strongly that most of the gentry in Shansi were traitors because they continued to exploit the peasants and refused to sacrifice their economic interests on behalf of the war effort. He said these interests were insignificant since the rich comprised only a small percentage of the population.[92] After expressing a similar opinion, Mao Tsetung implied that the suppression of traitors was an indispensable part of the Communist Party's campaign to improve the livelihood of the masses in Shansi.[93] In other words, if the gentry tried to retain their privileged economic status, they ran the risk of being branded as traitors and utterly ruined. In Chao Shu-li's novel, the inhabitants of Li Village seized for themselves land owned by the powerful Li clan, on the ground that the Lis had gone over to the Japanese.[94] Accounts written at the time of the Japanese invasion state that all land and other property belonging to persons accused of treason were confiscated and frequently divided up among the poor.[95] This must have resulted in a considerable redistribution of wealth, for the Communists repeatedly called attention to the large number of rich traitors living in Shansi.[96]

Many whose property was expropriated by the mobilization committees probably were singled out because they were anti-Communist rather than pro-Japanese. In areas occupied by the Communists and their supporters, all who ran off forfeited their wealth, including gentry who fled southward with the retreating Shansi and Central armies.[97] On the other hand, Communist attempts to overthrow the rich in Shansi without seeming to repudiate the united front against Japan were aided substantially by the sympathy which many of the gentry felt with respect to the Japanese and their consequent willingness to collaborate with the invaders. This means that much of what appeared to be popular antagonism toward the Japanese was simply dissatisfaction with the existing social and economic system, which had passed under the protection of the Japanese Army. Because Japan defended the status

[92] Statement by Lo Fu in *HPCY*, pp. 149-151.   [93] *TPLC*, p. 159.
[94] Chao Shu-li, *op.cit.*, p. 112.   [95] *TPLC*, pp. 136-137, 252.
[96] See *ibid.*, pp. 136-137, 163.   [97] See *ibid.*, p. 281.

quo in Shansi, anti-Japanese feeling and the desire for revolutionary change often were indistinguishable.

Thus, under the guise of resisting the Japanese, the Communists continued to carry out in Shansi a sweeping program of social and economic reform. These reforms account in large part for the mass following which the Eighth Route Army gained in Shansi during the first year of the war. By assuming an anti-Japanese stance, the Communists also won over many patriotically inclined intellectuals and secured unharried access to the peasantry, since conservatives hesitated to attack them for fear of seeming to be pro-Japanese. As one sympathetic reporter put it, "the peasants are more easily organized *under the pretext* of resisting Japan than under any other slogan."[98] Then too, atrocities subsequently perpetrated by the Japanese Army in the course of its efforts to rid Shansi of Communist-led guerrillas undoubtedly aroused the hatred of millions of peasants and caused them to turn to the Communists for leadership against the Japanese. All of this explains why within less than a year the Communists and their sympathizers acquired control of most of the territory in Shansi left unoccupied by the Japanese.

Yen's Defeat

By executing its commanders if they did not resist the Japanese Yen succeeded in making his army fight more vigorously. During the battle for P'ing-hsing-kuan, Shansi troops stationed in the pass threw back one enemy assault after another while the Eighth Route Army attacked the Japanese from the rear and along their flanks.[99] Other units of the Shansi Army defended with equal heroism the neighboring pass of Tuan-ch'eng-kuan.[100] After breaking into the Taiyuan Basin, the Japanese continued to encounter ferocious resistance on the part of Yen's troops, who were ordered to fight to the death in defense of the provincial capital. At Yüan-p'ing, a single brigade of Yen's soldiers held up the oncoming Japanese for more than a week, with the result that armies sent into Shansi by the central government had time to reinforce Yen's shattered forces, which took up positions in the Hsin-

[98] See *ibid.*, p. 84.   [99] *HHHCC*, p. 51.
[100] *TPLC*, pp. 190-205.

k'ou Mountains just north of Taiyuan.[101] Although Chu Teh and P'eng Teh-huai condemned him for employing what they called "suicidal tactics" against Japan, Yen was confident that the Japanese already were dismayed by the size of their losses and that his determination to defend Taiyuan to the last man would demoralize them completely and cause them to withdraw from Shansi.

In spite of the devastating superiority of their opponents' air force and artillery, the defenders of Hsin-k'ou withstood the might of Japan's crack Itagaki Division for nearly a month.[102] By the end of October, Japanese losses were four times greater than those suffered at P'ing-hsing-kuan and the Itagaki Division was perilously close to defeat.[103] A Communist account describes the fighting at Hsin-k'ou as "the most fierce in North China,"[104] while an authoritative Japanese study calls the battle a "stalemate" and speaks of enormous Japanese casualties.[105] In a desperate effort to save their forces at Hsin-k'ou, the Japanese invaded eastern Shansi, with the aim of assaulting Taiyuan from two sides. After a week of savage fighting against troops belonging to the Shansi and Central armies, they seized the Niang-tzu Pass, the gateway to eastern Shansi, and pushed rapidly westward, supported by massive amounts of artillery and aircraft.[106] Units of the Eighth Route Army were present during the battle for Niang-tzu-kuan, but their guerrilla tactics were ineffective and failed to slow up the Japanese advance.[107]

Upon finding themselves in danger of being outflanked, the Chinese armies in the Hsin-k'ou Mountains withdrew southward through Taiyuan, leaving behind a small contingent of Shansi troops to defend that doomed city. For three days

[101] *HHHCC*, pp. 70-71. Even the Communists lavished praise on Yen's troops for their heroic defense of Yüan-p'ing. See Jen Pi-shih, *op.cit.*, p. 16.

[102] *HHHCC*, p. 72.

[103] Haldore E. Hanson, *Humane Endeavour*, p. 108. This interpretation of the battle of Hsin-k'ou also is based on the account given in *HPCY*, pp. 109-115.

[104] Jen Pi-shih, *op.cit.*, p. 16.

[105] Hata Ikuhiku, *op.cit.*, p. 277. Another Japanese writer also says that the provincial and Central troops defending the Hsin-k'ou mountains put up "fierce" resistance and halted the advance of the Itagaki Division. See Horiba Kazuo, *Shina jihen sensō shidō shi* (*An Historical Guide to the China Incident*) (Tokyo, 1959), p. 103.

[106] *HPH*, pp. 51-53.   [107] See *ibid.*, p. 53.

these 6,000 men held off the entire Japanese Army, causing a Japanese spokesman to remark that "Nowhere in North China have the Chinese fought so obstinately."[108] When the Japanese finally occupied Yen's shattered capital on November 8, they were unable to advance further, owing to their extremely heavy losses. Well over 30,000 Japanese soldiers had been killed and perhaps an equal number wounded as a result of the fighting in northern Shansi.[109] A Japanese study states that the battles of P'ing-hsing-kuan, Hsin-k'ou, and Tai-yuan were responsible for more than half of the casualties sustained by the Japanese Army in North China. According to this account, by the time it occupied Taiyuan, the Itagaki Division had lost virtually all of its officers.[110] On the other hand, most of Yen's army was destroyed, along with a large part of the forces sent into Shansi by the central government.

Shortly before the fall of Taiyuan, Yen moved his headquarters to the city of Lin-fen in southwestern Shansi.[111] He enjoyed a respite of several months while the Japanese attempted to consolidate their hold on northern Shansi by hunting down bands of Communist troops operating behind their lines. Pamphlets which Japanese planes dropped on towns and villages in southern Shansi assured Yen and his supporters that Japan would treat them with consideration if they severed relations with the central government and helped the Japanese Army suppress the Communists.[112] The Japanese also brought up reinforcements, however, for use in a new drive against the Chinese armies to the south and warned Yen that unless he surrendered before the end of the year he and his army would be exterminated.[113] Yen responded by reiterating his promise not to surrender until Japan was defeated and prepared to wage a prolonged war against the Japanese.[114] "Japan

[108] *CWR*, Dec. 8, 1937, 74:2. A vivid description of the battle for Taiyuan can be found in Agnes Smedley, *China Fights Back*, pp. 201-208.

[109] These were the figures given to Agnes Smedley, *China Fights Back*, p. 211, by General Wei Li-huang, who commanded the armies despatched to Shansi by the central government.

[110] Hata Ikuhiku, *op.cit.*, p. 279.

[111] Yen left Taiyuan on the night of Nov. 4, only hours before the Japanese assaulted the city. See *HHHCC*, p. 79.

[112] *NCH*, Jan. 5, 1938, 7:5.   [113] *Ibid.*

[114] C. Y. W. Meng, "Nippon Conquest of Shansi Still a Distant Dream," *CWR*, Dec. 9, 1939, pp. 59-60.

is too small to absorb China, just as a man with a small stomach cannot swallow a piece of meat bigger than himself," he told an American reporter.[115] Probably because he had lost 90 percent of his army, he wanted to abandon positional warfare and instead rely on China's vast distances and great population to wear the enemy down.[116] He dwelt on the need for fighting behind the Japanese lines, as well as at the front,[117] and began teaching his soldiers how to wage this kind of warfare.[118] Most of his New Army, made up largely of students, remained in northern Shansi, where it used Communist tactics to harass the Japanese. Persons who volunteered to serve as cadre in areas occupied by the enemy were trained at the People's Revolutionary University (*min-tsu ke-ming ta-hsüeh*), which the Eighth Route Army helped Yen set up in Lin-fen.[119] In January Yen told its students that their chief task was to organize the population behind the Japanese lines and cautioned them against believing that individual heroism is an adequate substitute for the creation of effective mass organizations.[120] "This is a big step for this old militarist to take," admitted a pro-Communist and unsympathetic American reporter. "It shows his determination to fight to the end and it shows that his mind is still capable of absorbing ideas and methods to which he was never before accustomed."[121]

Yen also removed from office most of the district magistrates and other high-ranking officials in northern Shansi. He replaced them with members of the Sacrifice League, whom he regarded as better patriots, less selfish, more enthusiastic, and therefore best qualified to lead a guerrilla war against the Japanese.[122] For example, Sung Shao-wen became the magistrate of Yen's native district of Wu-t'ai, Hsü Fan't'ing was appointed commander of the New Army, and Po I-po

[115] Anna Louise Strong, "An Interview with General Yen Hsi-shan," *CT*, April 1938, p. 8.

[116] *Lectures*, II, pp. 330-331 (Jan. 1938).

[117] *Lectures*, III-A, pp. 633-634 (Jan. 1938).

[118] *Lectures*, I, p. 355 (Jan. 1938), James Bertram, *op.cit.*, p. 233, and Evans Carlson, *op.cit.*, p. 120.

[119] Evans Carlson, *op.cit.*, pp. 61-62, and *Lectures*, II, pp. 329-341 (Jan. 1938).

[120] *Lectures*, II, pp. 335-336 (Jan. 1938).

[121] Agnes Smedley, *China Fights Back*, p. 190.

[122] Wang Ch'ien, *op.cit.*, pp. 22b-23a, and George E. Taylor, *op.cit.*, pp. 165-166.

likewise received an important post in the government. In January, at the suggestion of the Eighth Route Army, north-eastern Shansi was joined with parts of Hopei and Chahar to form the Shansi-Hopei-Chahar Border Region (*Chin-Chi-Ch'a pien-ch'ü*).[123] The committee in charge of the new border region met under the chairmanship of Sung Shao-wen and exercised the authority normally wielded by a provincial government. The Japanese, as well as persons loyal to Yen, imply that he approved of this arrangement[124] and, according to a Communist writer, he was instrumental in persuading the central government to sanction it.[125] Thereafter, his followers referred to the government of Shansi as a *yu-chi cheng-chih*, a guerrilla administration.[126]

Yen's intransigence must have angered the Japanese because in February 1938 they halted their operations against the Eighth Route Army in the north and invaded southwestern Shansi.[127] The Chinese armies were as unpopular in the southwest as they had been in the north,[128] and the new Japanese offensive provoked so much fear and confusion in Lin-fen that Yen lost track of his divisions and could not recall which of them were at the front.[129] When asked to describe his strategy, he became hysterical and merely shouted: "China must break the Japanese political plan. We must counter this plan by developing the national revolutionary struggle."[130] Nevertheless, at Ling-shih Pass, north of Lin-fen, provincial troops and Central forces, fighting under the command of General Wei Li-huang, put up such stiff resistance that the Japanese drive bogged down and there almost occurred another bloody and inconclusive battle comparable to the struggle

[123] Michael Lindsay, *Notes on Educational Problems in Communist China* (New York, 1950), p. 9.

[124] *Jōhō*, No. 35 (Feb. 1, 1941), p. 3, and Wang Ch'ien, *op.cit.*, pp. 24a-25a. The Japanese account says that the Communists had to be extremely careful not to provoke Yen because of "his knowledge of power politics" and for this reason agreed to let younger people from his own regime, such as Sung Shao-wen, dominate the Border Region government. It would seem that as a result Yen raised no objection to the creation of the new government.

[125] Israel Epstein, *The People's War* (London, 1939), p. 235.

[126] Wang Ch'ien, *op.cit.*, p. 25b.

[127] *NYT*, Feb. 19, 1938, 3:7.

[128] James Bertram, *op.cit.*, pp. 191-192.

[129] Evans Carlson, *op.cit.*, p. 124.

[130] *Ibid.*

waged at Hsin-k'ou three months earlier.[131] But once again the Chinese were obliged to fall back in order to avoid being outflanked, this time by a Japanese column which attacked Lin-fen from the east.[132] Although Central troops commanded by Wei Li-huang defeated Japanese efforts to seize the strategic Chung-t'iao mountain range in southern Shansi, the loss of Lin-fen and Ling-shih-kuan compelled Yen to flee with what was left of his army across the Yellow River into the neighboring province of Shensi.

[131] *Japanese Monograph No. 178*, pp. 126-128.
[132] *Ibid.*

CHAPTER THIRTEEN

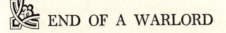 END OF A WARLORD

The Struggle against Japan

In the spring of 1938 the Japanese removed many of their troops from Shansi for use in other parts of China, and Yen succeeded in reestablishing his authority in the southwestern Corner of Shansi.[1] There he set up his headquarters at K'o-nan-po in the remote and mountainous district of Chi-hsien. The Japanese retaliated by mounting another offensive against the Shansi Army. After devastating the cities of southwestern Shansi and killing many of Yen's officials, they withdrew,[2] only to return the following year and again in 1940, when Yen's forces attacked Japanese-occupied areas to the north and east. During each of these offensives, the Japanese were obliged to overcome bitter resistance.[3] Yen's troops avoided clashes with the bulk of the Japanese Army and instead harassed its communications and otherwise waged a guerrilla war like the one being fought elsewhere in Shansi by the Communists and the New Army.[4] In the winter of 1939 a foreign visitor encountered much enthusiasm for Yen's cause in Chi-hsien and came away with the impression that there existed a high degree of cooperation between Yen's forces and the local population.[5] In his speeches, Yen repeatedly exhorted his soldiers to treat civilians with consideration.[6] But his army probably owed most of its new popularity to the efforts of the Sacrifice League, which continued to play an important role in Yen's campaign to mobilize the masses. On several occasions, the Communists and the New Army also came to Yen's aid by assaulting from the rear Japanese forces invading southeastern Shansi.[7]

[1] *NYT*, May 17, 1938, 4:3, June 1, 1938, 10:2, and *CWR*, June 4, 1938, p. 27.

[2] *NCH*, April 5, 1939, 10:1, April 19, 1939, 98:1.

[3] *NCH*, Nov. 15, 1939, 272:4, Nov. 22, 1939, 317:5, and *Japanese Monograph No. 178*, pp. 221-223, 308-312.

[4] *NCH*, April 5, 1939, 10:1-3, April 19, 1939, 98:1, and Paul O. Elmquist, *op.cit.*, p. 29.

[5] *NCH*, April 5, 1939, 10:4.

[6] For example, see *Lectures*, iii-C, pp. 165-168 (Aug., Sept. 1938).

[7] Haldore E. Hanson, *Humane Endeavour*, pp. 289-291, *NYT*, Aug. 12, 1938, 8:1, and *NCH*, Nov. 22, 1939, 317:5.

Although Yen remained in alliance with the Communists, the spectacular growth of their power and influence in Shansi frightened him and caused him to become more and more hostile to them. By 1939 the New Army was inclining toward the Communists and together they controlled most of the territory in Shansi not occupied by the Japanese.[8] At the suggestion of his son-in-law, General Wang Ching-kuo, Yen tried to arrest the progress of communism in his own domain by setting up the National Revolutionary Comrades Association (*kuo-min ke-ming t'ung-chih hui*) to oppose the increasingly pro-Communist Sacrifice League and its Dare-to-Die Corps.[9] Yen's fears must have persisted, however, because in the spring of 1939 his troops stood by without interfering while bands of armed men attacked schools, newspaper offices, and other establishments maintained in Yen's territory by the Sacrifice League.[10] According to the Communists, hundreds of persons seized in these raids were mutilated and buried alive by the marauders.[11] When the Sacrifice League retaliated by issuing a manifesto insinuating that Yen was reactionary and pro-Japanese,[12] he suppressed the League and tried to disarm its Dare-to-Die Corps, which fled north and placed itself under the protection of the New Army. In the winter of 1939, after the central government ordered him to initiate another offensive against the Japanese, Yen attempted to decimate the New Army by making it do most of the fighting,[13] resulting in a war between Yen's forces and the New Army. This conflict lasted more than a month and destroyed the "united front" in Shansi, since Yen received assistance from troops belonging to the central government[14] and the Communists intervened on behalf of the New Army.[15]

[8] Paul O. Elmquist, *op.cit.*, p. 17.

[9] Chao Shu-li, *op.cit.*, pp. 105, 108, 110, and the biography of Wang Ching-kuo in *Kuomintang Biographies*.

[10] George E. Taylor, *op.cit.*, p. 165.

[11] Chao Shu-li, *op.cit.*, pp. 113-115.

[12] George E. Taylor, *op.cit.*, p. 165.

[13] *NCH*, Jan. 24, 1940, 124:4, and *CWR*, Jan. 27, 1940, p. 314.

[14] *Japanese Monograph No. 178*, p. 230, and George E. Taylor, *op.cit.*, p. 166.

[15] *CWR*, May 11, 1940, 366:1, and Tada butai sanbōbu (Tada Corps, Chief of Staff), pub., *Chūgoku kyōsantō undō no kaisetsu* (*Explanation of the Chinese Communist Movement*) (Peiping, Feb. 17, 1941), pp. 27-28.

Although Yen succeeded in expelling the Communists and their sympathizers from the territory he governed in southwestern Shansi, control of the rural areas in northwestern Shansi passed into the hands of the Eighth Route Army. In 1941 they were made a part of the so-called Shansi-Suiyuan Border Region (*Chin-Sui pien ch'ü*).

The Communists say that Yen wanted to stop fighting Japan as early as the spring of 1938 and accuse him of allying with the Japanese before attacking the New Army.[16] Yen's speeches, as well as the testimony of Chinese and foreign observers, indicate that these charges are untrue.[17] It would appear, however, that after the Communists and the New Army joined forces against him, Yen retaliated by entering into negotiations with the Japanese. The Japanese initiated these negotiations in the spring of 1940, following the appointment of Yen's friend, Tanaka Ryūkichi, as chief of staff of the Japanese First Army, stationed in Shansi.[18] Tanaka's aim was to check the growth of communism in China by inducing first Yen and then the central government at Chungking to form an anti-Communist alliance with Japan.[19] Although the Shansi Army continued to resist the Japanese in southwestern Shansi, Yen exchanged letters with General Itagaki, the chief of staff of Japan's North China Expeditionary Force, expressed sympathy for Tanaka's objectives, and agreed to send a high-ranking officer to confer with the Japanese.[20] According to a Jap-

[16] Hsü Fan-t'ing, *Letter*, pp. 3-4, Hsi Jung, *op.cit.*, p. 5, and Anonymous, "Po I-po t'ung-chih hsieh-lu Yen Hsi-shan t'ung-ti p'an-kuo nui-mu," pp. 2-4, Ch'en Po-ta, *Yen Hsi-shan p'i-p'an.*

[17] *Lectures*, III-C, p. 163 (April 1938), *NCH*, April 5, 1939, 10:5, and April 19, 1939, 98:2, C. Y. W. Meng, *op.cit.*, p. 60, and Stanton Lautenschlager, *op.cit.*, pp. 20-22. According to an unimpeachable Japanese source, Yen's troops continued to battle with the Japanese throughout 1940. See Tanaka Ryūkichi, *Hai-in o tsuku: gumbatsu sennō no jissō* (*The Cause of Defeat Revealed: The Truth about Domineering Militarists*) (Tokyo, 1956), p. 16. Among the accusations which the Communists have leveled at Yen in an effort to discredit him is a completely false charge that in 1937 he "handed over the entire province to the Japanese invaders without a struggle." See Wu Hsiang, "Taiyuan Rising Industrial Center," *China Reconstructs*, May 1964, p. 36. Yet at the time of the Japanese invasion several high-ranking Chinese Communist leaders, including Mao Tse-tung, repeatedly lavished praise on Yen for waging an uncompromising struggle against the Japanese. For example, see *HPCY*, pp. 140-141, 145-148, 153, and *TPLC*, p. 154.

[18] Hata Ikuhiku, *op.cit.*, p. 160.

[19] Tanaka Ryūkichi, *op.cit.*, p. 15.   [20] See *ibid.*, p. 16.

anese writer, Yen obtained from Chungking permission to co-operate with the Japanese if they promised to remove all of their troops from Shansi as soon as the Communists were suppressed.[21] He stopped negotiating with them in December, however, when Tanaka's superiors recalled him to Japan, perhaps because they were unwilling to meet Yen's demands.[22] Two months later, the Japanese reiterated their charge that Yen was a "dupe" of the Communists.[23]

In May 1941 Tanaka Ryūkichi returned to Shansi and reopened negotiations with Yen, in spite of considerable opposition on the part of Japanese military authorities in North China.[24] This may be why Yen remained aloof from the fighting and even disarmed Chiang Kai-shek's fleeing soldiers when the Japanese mounted a spring offensive against Central troops defending the Chung-t'iao Mountains in southern Shansi.[25] Tanaka went back to Tokyo in August, but his visit paved the way for talks between Yen and General Iwamatsu, the commander of the Japanese First Army.[26] In the summer of 1942 Yen told the Japanese that he would aid them in their fight against communism in China if they withdrew a large part of their forces from Shansi and helped him strengthen his own army by giving him food, weapons, and CH$15 million worth of specie.[27] Yet when Iwamatsu sent his chief of staff, General Hanatani, to Chi-hsien for the purpose of delivering what Yen demanded, Yen called Japan's concessions inadequate and refused to negotiate with Hanatani.[28] According to Tanaka Ryūkichi, Yen resented the arrogance of the Japanese. Tanaka also says that after learning of Japan's defeat in the battle for Midway, Yen concluded that the Japanese would lose the war in the Pacific and therefore was unwilling to compromise himself by becoming their ally.[29]

[21] Maruyama Shizuo, op.cit., p. 175.

[22] See ibid., p. 176, and Tanaka Ryūkichi, op.cit., pp. 17-18. In 1944 Yen admitted that in 1940 he was approached by the Japanese but implied that he merely rebuked them for their aggression against China. See Harrison Forman, op.cit., p. 32.

[23] Jōhō, No. 35 (Feb. 1, 1941), p. 1.

[24] Tanaka Ryūkichi, op.cit., p. 18.

[25] Japanese Monograph No. 178, p. 240, and NCH, June 11, 1941, 403:3.

[26] Tanaka Ryūkichi, op.cit., p. 18.

[27] Maruyama Shizuo, op.cit., p. 176.

[28] Hirano, Komoto, pp. 195-196.

[29] Tanaka Ryūkichi, op.cit., p. 18.

Another Japanese writer tells a different story. He claims that while Yen was talking to Hanatani a messenger reported the arrival of the paper currency or *fa-pi* which the Japanese intended to give Yen. Since Yen was under the impression that he would receive specie instead of *fa-pi*, when his interpreter mistranslated this term and pronounced it *p'ao-p'in* rather than *fa-pi*, Yen jumped to the conclusion that Japan's *p'ao-ping* or "troops and artillery" were approaching and hastily terminated his conversation with Hanatani for fear of being ambushed. "Consequently, the second phase of 'Operation Yen Hsi-shan' ended on a tragi-comic note," comments this writer.[30] Because they had allowed Yen to deceive them, Iwamatsu lost his command and Hanatani was transferred to the Pacific.[31] Thereafter, in an effort to avoid being further humiliated by Yen, the Japanese Army negotiated with him clandestinely and through civilian intermediaries like his friend Kōmoto Daisaku.[32] In 1943, Kōmoto became head of the *Sansei sangyō kabushiki kaisha*, the Shansi Industrial Company, which operated the industries Yen had built in and around Taiyuan. Yen immediately sent two of his closest supporters to Taiyuan, where they joined Kōmoto's staff and helped him arrange a cease-fire between Yen's forces and the Japanese.[33] Is it possible that in return for Yen's cooperation the Japanese gave him a degree of control over his former industries? "The Japanese seemed not to press Yen too hard and there was more than a suspicion that they regarded Yen as a possible successor to the Generalissimo, should Chiang Kai-shek be defeated," says an American reporter who visited Yen's domain in 1944. "He was thought of not necessarily as a puppet but rather as a compromise between the extremes of treason at Nanking and national resistance Chungking."[34] Communist writers charge that Japan was planning to make Yen "the little emperor" of North China.[35] Thus Yen stopped

[30] Maruyama Shizuo, *op.cit.*, pp. 176-177. Although in 1944 Yen told an American reporter about his negotiations with Iwamatsu, he did not admit that he encouraged the Japanese and inferred that he rejected their overtures without a moment's hesitation. See Harrison Forman, *op.cit.*, p. 32.

[31] Hirano, *Komoto*, p. 197.   [32] *Ibid.*

[33] See *ibid.*, pp. 198-199.

[34] Harrison Forman, *op.cit.*, pp. 31-32.

[35] "Po I-po t'ung-chih hsieh-lu Yen Hsi-shan t'ung-ti p'an-kuo nui-mu," p. 5.

fighting the Japanese only after they gave up their efforts
to reduce him to subservience and began treating him like
an ally.

By 1944 Yen's troops were battling the Communists,[36] and
a Japanese writer maintains that frequently the Japanese
took part in the fighting.[37] In areas which Yen governed,
persons even suspected of sympathizing with the Eighth
Route Army were seized by the police and often executed.
The police took their orders from Yen's once radical but
now fanatically anti-Communist nephew, Liang Hua-chih,[38]
whose career illustrates vividly the kaleidoscopic changes
which frequently took place in the thinking of individual
Chinese between 1937 and 1949. Nonetheless, Yen did not
assail the Communists openly until the summer of 1944, when
he told a group of visiting American newsmen that for several
years the Communists in Shansi had been violating the spirit
of the united front.[39] The enraged Communists lashed back
at Yen by making him the target of a vitriolic propaganda
campaign. They accused him of selling out to the Japanese as
early as 1938, denounced him for virtually enslaving his subjects, and even wrote songs about his crimes.[40] "His regime
is a mixture of fascism and medievalism," charged one of
his attackers.[41]

Yen's wartime relations with Chiang Kai-shek's regime in
Chungking also were stormy. He continued to be a member
of Chiang's Council of State, as well as the Generalissimo's
Military Affairs Commission, and one of his generals was
in charge of the Department of Military Affairs in the central
government;[42] however, Americans who visited Yen's capital
in the summer of 1944 encountered no Kuomintang flags or
portraits of Chiang and came away with the impression that
Chungking exercised hardly any authority in territory controlled by Yen.[43] Instead of praising Chiang, Yen told the

[36] Harrison Forman, op.cit., p. 31, and Guenther Stein, The Challenge of Red China (New York, 1945), p. 52.

[37] Hirano, Komoto, p. 199.   [38] Hirano, Prisoner, p. 68.

[39] NYT, June 5, 1944, 9:1-2.

[40] Ch'en Po-ta, op.cit., pp. 3-4, 17-21, 39, Hsü Fan-t'ing, Letter, pp.
10-11, and Hsi Jung, op.cit., pp. 1-16.

[41] Ch'en Po-ta, op.cit., p. 60.

[42] F. F. Liu, op.cit., p. 124.

[43] Harrison Forman, op.cit., p. 31, and Guenther Stein, op.cit., p.
51.

Americans that unless Chiang's government improved considerably the masses would turn to the Communists.[44] An official
in Yen's government even admitted that often there occurred
clashes between the Shansi Army and Central troops under
the command of General Hu Tsung-nan.[45] According to a
Communist writer, these clashes began in 1940, when troops
belonging to the central government drove Yen's forces out
of several districts in southern Shansi.[46] As one of Yen's American guests put it, "Resisting pressure from three sides—from
Japan, Central Forces, and Communists—fence-sitter Yen
somehow manages to hold his own."[47]

Although the territory Yen governed after 1938 comprised
less than an eighth of Shansi,[48] he came to enjoy within the
confines of his tiny domain the absolute power he had tried
in vain to acquire before Japan invaded Shansi. "Merchants
had to surrender all trade to Yen's monopoly administration,"
observed an American who traveled through Chi-hsien in 1944.
"Thus, they were forced to work [in other words, to take up
another occupation] or leave and Yen became the only merchant in the area."[49] Yen accomplished this by actually putting
into effect his plans for the circulation of product certificates
in lieu of money and the distribution of goods according to
labor.[50] The Communists say that even itinerate peddlers were
forced out of business and their functions taken over by Yen's
monopolies.[51] Yen abolished the private ownership of land,
moreover, and redistributed land in such a way as to give every
able-bodied peasant between the ages of eighteen and forty-
eight a plot of equal size. The peasants worked their new
holdings in groups of three, and each farmer was obliged to
serve for several years in Yen's army while his two partners
supported him by cultivating his land as well as their own.[52]

[44] Guenther Stein, *op.cit.*, p. 53.
[45] Harrison Forman, *op.cit.*, p. 31.
[46] Chao Shu-li, *op.cit.*, p. 119.
[47] Harrison Forman, *op.cit.*, p. 31.
[48] *NYT*, June 5, 1944, 9:2.
[49] Guenther Stein, *op.cit.*, p. 52.
[50] Stanton Lautenschlager, *op.cit.*, p. 23, Harrison Forman, *op.cit.*,
pp. 27-33, *NYT*, June 5, 1944, 9:1, and Anonymous, "Yen Hsi-shan
k'e-cheng hsia te jen-min sheng-huo" ("The Life of the People under
Yen Hsi-shan's Cruel Rule"), p. 3, Ch'en Po-ta, *Yen Hsi-shan p'i-p'an*.
[51] "Po I-po t'ung-chih . . . ," p. 3.
[52] Harrison Forman, *op.cit.*, pp. 34-35, Ch'en Po-ta, *op.cit.*, pp. 16-
22, and *NYT*, June 5, 1944, 9:1.

Yen entitled this program *ping-nung ho-i*, "Every Farmer a Soldier."[53]

The Communists accused him of using it to enslave the rural population. According to them, in areas ruled by Yen peasants could not leave the land allocated to them, were subjected continually to military training and discipline, and dared not disobey the government for fear that it would deprive them of their farms.[54] "Communist armies are strong militarily because they are able to move fast and collect followers," Yen told some visiting Americans in the summer of 1944. "If everyone has land under a farmer-soldier system, nobody will be able to move from the plot he cultivates, so how can they recruit."[55] The Communists charged that Yen also taxed away from the peasants so much of their crop that they rebelled and had to be coerced into accepting his new system of land tenure.[56] On the other hand, he extorted even larger sums from the rich[57] and virtually confiscated a part of their wealth by making landlords surrender land they could not farm with their own labor in return for a mere 5 percent of its annual harvest.[58]

Yen's extraordinary power was the result of conditions created by his defeat at the hands of the Japanese. After 1938 his subjects were so few in number that for the first time he succeeded in bringing all of them completely under the control of his government. Furthermore, his authority within his own regime must have been considerably greater than in the past, since only the most devoted of his followers remained with him during the war. According to American observers, Yen's subordinates treated him with the deference normally shown to a patriarch by other members of his clan.[59]

[53] An elaborate description of Yen's land-reform program after 1938 can be found in the three volume work *Ping-nung ho-i* (*Every Farmer a Soldier*), which he published in Chi-hsien in 1941. For a later and more concise treatment of this subject see his *Chin-pu Shan-hsi* (*Progress in Shansi*) (Chi-hsien, 1945). Ch'en Po-ta's *Yen Hsi-shan p'i-p'an* in the anthology of the same name is a savage but nonetheless informative Communist attack on Yen's social and economic policies during the war against Japan.

[54] Ch'en Po-ta, *op.cit.*, pp. 18-22.   [55] *NYT*, June 5, 1944, 9:2.
[56] "Po I-po t'ung-chih . . . ," pp. 1-4.
[57] *Lectures*, III-C, pp. 167-170 (Aug. 1938), C. Y. W. Meng, *op.cit.*, pp. 59-60, and Stanton Lautenschlager, *op.cit.*, pp. 20, 23.
[58] Guenther Stein, *op.cit.*, p. 51.
[59] *Ibid.*, and *NYT*, June 5, 1944, 9:2.

In their eagerness to demonstrate their loyalty to him, they even swore to commit suicide if they failed in their duty or otherwise betrayed his confidence.[60] All of this caused one American to describe Yen's wartime capital as a "mixture of the Syrian retreat of the old man of the mountain, a medieval baron's eyrie, early American phalanstery, and Upton Sinclair's plan."[61]

The Last Struggle

After Japan surrendered in the summer of 1945, Yen thwarted Communist efforts to seize Taiyuan and other cities in Shansi by enlisting the support of the Japanese, who allowed him to reestablish his authority in the areas they occupied.[62] This provoked a bitter struggle between Yen's forces and the Communists. Instead of repatriating the Japanese troops in Shansi, Yen incorporated them into his own army and used them against the Communists.[63] As late as February 1947 the streets of Taiyuan still were crowded with Japanese soldiers, dressed in Yen's uniforms but fighting under their own commanders.[64] "They are really no problem," Yen replied when an American newsman questioned the wisdom of letting the Japanese retain their weapons. "We shall get rid of them eventually."[65] Thus in Shansi the Japanese were obliged to enter into an alliance dominated by a man who they initially had set out to reduce to the status of a puppet.

Yen's principal aim was to create in the areas he governed an economy viable enough to sustain his forces in their fight against communism. He compelled hundreds of Japanese technicians to remain in Shansi and with their help maintained and even increased the output of the factories he and the Japanese had built in and around Taiyuan.[66] Since much of the

[60] Harrison Forman, *op.cit.*, p. 35.

[61] *NYT*, June 5, 1944, 9:2.

[62] Agnes Smedley, *The Great Road*, pp. 418-426, Graham Peck, *op.cit.*, p. 613, and Theodore White and Anna Lee Jacoby, *Thunder Out of China* (New York, 1946), p. 284.

[63] Hsi Jung, *op.cit.*, pp. 8, 11-13.

[64] Henry Lieberman, "Gen. Yen Governs Again in Shansi with Japanese General as His Aide," *NYT*, Feb. 13, 1946, 10:6-7 and Benjamin Welles, "Japanese Soldiers Are Still in Shansi," *NYT*, Feb. 10, 1947, 18:2-4.

[65] Charles J. V. Murphy, *op.cit.*, p. 114.

[66] Benjamin Welles, *op.cit.*, 18:3, *Japanese Steel Survey*, 407:1, and Henry Lieberman, "State Industries of Shansi Grow but Benefit

rural population lived in territory ruled by the Communists, however, in order to feed his army Yen had to exploit unmercifully the peasants in his own domain.[67] This alienated them completely and caused many to defect to the Communists.[68] As a result, Yen's troops were obliged to withdraw from the countryside into the cities, which the Communists besieged and captured one by one until by the winter of 1947 Yen controlled little more than Taiyuan and its environs.[69]

Yen admitted that the Communists were growing stronger and predicted that within six months they would rule half of China.[70] Nevertheless, he prepared to defend Taiyuan to the death, perhaps in the hope that if he and other anti-Communist leaders held out long enough, the United States would enter the war on their side and save his regime from destruction. Inside Taiyuan were tens of thousands of Yen's troops, equipped with 700 pieces of artillery and protected by at least 5,000 stone pill boxes, some of them bearing colorful nicknames like "Old Tiger" and "Plum Blossom."[71] The Communists were unable to penetrate this maze of fortifications when they attacked Taiyuan in the summer of 1948 and fell back after suffering heavy casualties.[72] In this battle, as well as in the others which Yen fought with the Communists, Japanese soldiers comprised the mainstay of his forces.[73] Early in October Yen attempted a counteroffensive, but the Communists killed or captured most of the troops who attacked them.[74]

---

to People is Delayed," *NYT*, Feb. 14, 1947, 17:2-3. Apparently Yen's dream of an industrialized Taiyuan has been realized completely under the Communists. "Today, Taiyuan ranks among the leading industrial cities of China," states an article in a 1964 issue of a Communist periodical. "In the past 15 years 220 large and medium-sized factories and mines have either been newly built or expanded from old ones." See Wu Hsiang, *op.cit.*, p. 36.

[67] Jack Belden, *op.cit.*, p. 353.

[68] Benjamin Welles, "Shansi's Warlord in Unique Battle," *NYT*, Feb. 9, 1947, 33:3.

[69] *Ibid.* A comprehensive and unusually perceptive description of Yen's regime in 1948 can be found in A. Doak Barnett, *China on the Eve of Communist Takeover*, pp. 157-180.

[70] Benjamin Welles, *op.cit.*, 33:4.

[71] P'eng Fei, ed., *T'ai-yüan chih chan* (*The Battle for Taiyuan*) (Peking, 1957), pp. 2-3.

[72] *NYT*, July 19, 1948, 5:4, July 20, 1948, 11:3, July 28, 1948, 18:5, July 30, 1948, 11:1.

[73] Hirano, *Komoto*, p. 210.

[74] *Ibid.*, and P'eng Fei, *op.cit.*, pp. 4-5.

Thereafter, losses on both sides mounted rapidly as the Communists redoubled their efforts to seize Taiyuan. A Communist writer speaks of entire companies of Communist soldiers being wiped out in the course of a single attack.[75] Each army bombarded the other incessantly and there was much hand-to-hand fighting. By December the Communists had overrun most of the fortifications surrounding Taiyuan; however, Chiang Kai-shek air-lifted food and other supplies to Yen's troops, who continued to resist so tenaciously that the Communists still were outside the city walls when the arrival of winter compelled them to halt their offensive.[76] About this time there appeared in the American magazine *Life* a photograph of Yen seated at his desk contemplating a pile of capsules filled with cyanide, which he swore that he and his followers would swallow before they surrendered Taiyuan to the Communists.[77] The Communists charged that as part of an earlier campaign to impress Americans and persons in other parts of China, Yen invited a group of foreign and Chinese newsmen to visit besieged Taiyuan and induced them to lavish praise on his regime by giving them costly gifts and setting them up in a brothel at the expense of the provincial government.[78]

Events during the winter of 1949 underscored the hopelessness of Yen's situation. After completing their conquest of Manchuria, the Communists destroyed the bulk of Chiang Kai-shek's army at Hsüchow and captured Peiping and Tientsin. Meanwhile, in Shansi they used propaganda to demoralize Yen's army. "Soldiers of Yen's Army: Peiping and Tientsin already have been liberated!" they shouted across the lines. "How can Taiyuan still hold out? Come over! The Liberation Army will treat you well!"[79] As proof of their good intentions, they placed dishes of food on the battlefield and urged Yen's increasingly famished soldiers to help themselves.[80] "Come over! Don't give your lives for Yen Hsi-shan!" they yelled. "Your loved ones are waiting anxiously for your return."[81] Thousands of Yen's troops deserted.[82]

[75] P'eng Fei, *op.cit.*, pp. 9-11.
[76] *NYT*, March 19, 1949, 4:4.
[77] *Life*, Nov. 22, 1948, p. 41.
[78] *San Man Po*, Nov. 14, 1958, p. 2.
[79] P'eng Fei, *op.cit.*, p. 15.
[80] See *ibid.*, p. 16.   [81] *Ibid.*   [82] See *ibid.*, p. 17.

In March the Communists renewed their offensive against Taiyuan, and Yen flew to Nanking for the avowed purpose of asking the central government to reinforce his army and supply it with more food and ammunition. But he did not return and took with him most of the gold in the provincial treasury.[83] Furthermore, he refused to talk to an American reporter who approached him in Nanking and reminded him of his promise to commit suicide before letting the Communists occupy Taiyuan.[84] Under the command of General Imamura Hōsaku, Yen's army continued to fight off the Communists until April 20, when they broke through Imamura's lines after attacking from all directions with at least 1,300 pieces of artillery and a force three times larger than Imamura's.[85] As the city defenders fell back, Nanking's pilots stopped dropping food to them, for fear of being shot down by the advancing Communists. Imamura's starving troops kept on fighting, however, and killed or wounded many of their assailants before finally surrendering on April 24.[86] Among the high-ranking officers taken prisoner by the Communists were Yen's son-in-law, Wang Ching-kuo, who was last seen being led down a street at the end of a rope, and the chief of Yen's gendarmerie, Sun Ch'u.[87] General Imamura swallowed poison and Yen's nephew, Liang Hua-chih, killed himself after burning to the ground a prison filled with Communist soldiers captured during the fighting.[88] Thus the struggle for Taiyuan belies the occasionally expressed belief that the Communists triumphed on the Chinese mainland because their opponents lacked the will to resist.

Upon reaching Nanking, Yen quickly insinuated himself into the quarrel between acting president Li Tsung-jen and Chiang Kai-shek. Although Chiang had relinquished the presidency of the central government in January, there remained

---

[83] Hirano, *Komoto*, p. 217.

[84] *San Man Po*, Nov. 14, 1958, p. 2.

[85] Hirano, *Komoto*, p. 211, and P'eng Fei, *op.cit.*, pp. 19-24.

[86] *NYT*, May 24, 1960, 37:3. An especially vivid and detailed account of the last battle for Taiyuan, which suggests that the Communists suffered enormous losses at the hands of the city's defenders, can be found on pages 11-38 of Ti-liu-shih-pa chün cheng-chih pu (Political Department, Sixty-Eighth Army), ed., *Ao-chan T'ai-yüan ch'eng* (*The Bitter Battle for Taiyuan*) (published in 1948 at an unknown place).

[87] Hirano, *Prisoner*, p. 67.   [88] See *ibid.*, pp. 67-68.

in the government and its armed forces a plethora of officials who were loyal to him rather than Li Tsung-jen, with the result that he retained enough power to obstruct and frustrate Li's policies. He likewise antagonized Li by removing to Taiwan more than US$200 million worth of gold and other assets belonging to the central government, which Li needed in order to meet the government's soaring expenses.[89] Yen tried in vain to persuade Chiang to reconcile his differences with Li for the sake of unity against the Communists.[90] In April Li refused to accompany the central government when it moved from Nanking to Canton, but instead expressed his dissatisfaction with Chiang's actions by retiring to Kwangsi. At Chiang's behest Yen visited Kwangsi for the purpose of urging Li to reconsider his decision to withdraw from public life. He broke into tears while talking about the loss of Shansi and warned that the anti-Communist cause was doomed unless Li went to Canton.[91] Li was so moved by Yen's grief that he agreed to reassume the leadership of the central government if Chiang Kai-shek turned over to it most of the gold and American dollars in his possession and stopped overriding Li's authority. Yen communicated Li's demands to Chiang, who promised to comply with them, and Li departed for Canton.[92]

In Canton, Li proceeded to create a new government, made up of not only Chiang's supporters but also persons opposed to Chiang. He even offered the premiership to an outspoken critic of Chiang's regime, Chü Cheng, a veteran member of the Kuomintang, who had served as president of the Legislative Yüan before virtually being driven into exile because of his opposition to Chiang.[93] When the Legislative Yüan rejected Chü, however, Li was obliged to settle for Yen Hsishan.[94] "He [Yen] was well known for his adaptability, and naturally Chiang welcomed him as the president of the Ex-

[89] Henry Lieberman, "Nanking Rebuffed by Chiang on Gold," *NYT*, April 16, 1949, 1:7 and 3:2-5.

[90] See *ibid.*, 1:7.

[91] Liang Sheng-chün, *Chiang Li tou-cheng nui-mu* (*The Inside Story of the Struggle between Chiang and Li*) (Hong Kong, 1954), pp. 132-133.

[92] See *ibid.*, pp. 134-135, and Yin Shih, *Li Chiang kuan-hsi yü Chung-kuo* (*The Relationship between Li and Chiang and China*) (Hong Kong, 1954), p. 130.

[93] The biography of Chü Cheng in *Kuomintang Biographies.*

[94] Yin Shih, *op.cit.*, pp. 130-131.

ecutive Yüan," recalls Li.[95] Yet, in spite of Yen's pleas, Chiang refused to surrender more than a fraction of the wealth he had taken to Taiwan, so that under Yen the currency issued by the central government continued to decline in value until soon it became utterly worthless.[96] Moreover, Chiang kept on giving orders to the army, much of which obeyed him rather than Li and Yen.[97] All of this caused Li to put into effect a plan that he and other members of the so-called Kwangsi Clique had contemplated as early as the winter of 1948.[98] Instead of attempting to defend all of South China against the Communists, he ordered what was left of the Nationalist armies to withdraw into Kwangsi and Kwangtung, in the hope that by concentrating in this smaller and therefore more easily defended area the anti-Communist forces could maintain a foothold on the Chinese mainland until events compelled the United States to enter the war in China on their side.[99] Chiang Kai-shek was bound to oppose this scheme

[95] P. 2 of ch. 51 of the English-language version of Li Tsung-jen's unpublished autobiography. Li's statement contradicts the assertions of a Communist writer, who maintains that Yen antagonized Chiang by accepting the premiership in Li's government. See *San Man Po*, Nov. 14, 1958, p. 2. Two of Li's followers disagree about the degree of solidarity between Yen and Li. Yin Shih, *op.cit.*, p. 131, says that Yen was "a prisoner of feudal forces" and called his selection a blow to Li Tsung-jen. On the other hand, according to Liang Sheng-chün, *op.cit.*, pp. 158-160, 166-168, Yen thoroughly approved of Li's policies and lent them his utmost support. Perhaps neither writer is either entirely correct or wholly mistaken. In a letter to me, dated April 21, 1964, Dr. T. K. Tong, who translated Li Tsung-jen's autobiography into English, writes as follows: ". . . after Chü Cheng was voted down by the Legislators, Li found no other suitable persons competent in seniority and capability of taking this high position, who could get the necessary votes from the CC Opposition in the Legislative Yüan. Yen was then almost alone in Canton; he was an astute politician, who could win Chiang's approval and get as well the CC votes from the Legislative Yüan. Thus, he was selected. According to Li, Yen's appointment involved nothing on 'policy' matters. He was sure that Yen would not do exactly as Li wanted him to do, but Yen was certainly the only person then able to tide over the emergency." I am very much indebted to Dr. Tong and General Li for taking the time to answer my questions about the circumstances surrounding Yen's appointment as premier.

[96] Liang Sheng-chün, *op.cit.*, pp. 158-160.

[97] See *ibid.*, pp. 160-162.

[98] Ch'en Shao-hsiao ("Major" Ch'en), *Chiu-p'an t'an ping-lü* (*Wine Talk about Military Affairs*) (Hong Kong, 1963), pp. 136-142, 164, 195-199.

[99] Liang Sheng-chün, *op.cit.*, pp. 164-166, and Yin Shih, *op.cit.*, p. 135.

because it would have the effect of bringing most of the troops still loyal to the central government completely under the control of Li Tsung-jen and Chiang's other rivals from Kwangsi and Kwangtung. Consequently, Li began ousting Chiang's adherents from the central government.[100] Yen sympathized with Li's objectives, but dared not lend them much support for fear of antagonizing Chiang.[101] This created among Li's supporters the impression that Yen was a "stooge" for Chiang Kai-shek.[102] Chiang, on the other hand, must have resented bitterly Yen's willingness to cooperate with Li.[103] Thus, Yen alienated both sides by indulging in the kind of fence-sitting that for many decades had been his principal trademark in Chinese politics.

The final years of Yen Hsi-shan's life were filled with disappointments and unhappiness. According to supporters of Li Tsung-jen, Chiang Kai-shek refused to let Nationalist troops in neighboring provinces go to the defense of Kwangsi and Kwangtung, with the result that in October the Communists occupied Canton.[104] After denouncing Chiang, Li fled to the United States, but Yen accompanied the central government to Szechwan and then to Taiwan, where he continued to serve as its premier until March 1950, when Chiang reassumed the presidency. Thereafter, Yen enjoyed the title of *tzu-cheng* senior advisor, to Chiang; in reality, he was utterly powerless and may have been virtually a prisoner in Taiwan, owing to Chiang's antagonism toward him because of his activities on behalf of Li Tsung-jen while at Canton. At least this is the opinion of a Communist writer, who says that on one occasion Yen asked for permission to go to Japan, but was told that he could not leave Taiwan until he turned over to the central government most of the wealth he had taken with him and invested abroad when he fled from Taiyuan in 1949.[105] Deserted by all but a handful of his followers,[106] he remained in Taiwan and spent most of his

[100] Liang Sheng-chün, *op.cit.*, p. 167.   [101] *Ibid.*

[102] *NYT*, Feb. 21, 1950, 16:3.   [103] *Ibid.*

[104] Yin Shih, *op.cit.*, pp. 135-137, and Liang Sheng-chün, *op.cit.*, pp. 169-172.

[105] *San Man Po*, Nov. 14, 1958, p. 2.

[106] Interview with Yen's former English-language secretary, Wang Huai-i, Taipei, Taiwan, Jan. 13, 1957. According to an unusually well-informed person, whose identity I cannot disclose, during the years

time writing books, which he frequently had translated into English. Their titles include *The Error of Communism*, *The Impending World Crisis*, *Peace or World War*, *The Road to Cosmopolitanism*, and *How to Impede War and Establish the Foundation of the World Unit*.[107] He died in Taiwan on May 24, 1960.

---

immediately following Japan's surrender Yen persuaded many of his supporters to invest heavily in a certain American-run concern operating in China. When this concern subsequently defaulted on its obligations to them, they blamed Yen for their losses and stayed away from him in Taiwan.

[107] *NYT*, May 24, 1960, 37:3.

CHAPTER FOURTEEN

 CONCLUSIONS

THE PICTURE that emerges from this study is one of a conservative and, by contemporary standards, backward people struggling to adapt itself to the conditions of the modern world under the leadership of a man whose own limitations were among the most formidable obstacles in his path. Yen Hsi-shan governed a domain with an economy too underdeveloped to provide sufficient food for its inhabitants and a population so unsophisticated and opposed to innovation that its members resisted tenaciously efforts to make them send their children to school and unbind the feet of their women. Such conditions could be overcome only by bringing about far-reaching changes in the structure of society in Shansi, as well as in the outlook and values of its people. Yet, although Yen was aware of the need for radical change and continually spoke about its desirability, until the 1930's he remained too conservative and too attached to the existing order to attempt anything even approaching the kind of reforms necessary in order to modernize Shansi. Many of the reforms he proposed in the 1920's were undertaken sixty years before by Tseng Kuo-fan and other leaders of the T'ung Chih Restoration. Tseng's immediate successors had found them to be an inadequate solution to the problems that confronted the China of their time, and under the sponsorship of the Model Governor they were an equally unsatisfactory answer to the dilemmas of twentieth century China. The fact that Yen placed his faith in them long after more sophisticated Chinese had rejected them as obsolete reveals the degree to which the political leaders of modern China have lagged behind the leaders of the Chinese intellectual community.

After 1930, however, Chiang Kai-shek's growing power, together with the Soviet Union's five year plans and the impact of the world depression on Shansi's economy, caused Yen to undertake an ambitious program of rapid industrialization. This raises the possibility that in at least some instances the division of China into competing warlord regimes created an environment favorable to economic growth, since in order to provide their armies with the latest weapons and other necessities warlords were compelled to build factories and otherwise develop the productive resources of their domains. As a soldier, Yen perceived with unusual keenness the military value of modern technology and therefore of industrialization along Western lines. If he is typical of many warlords, they were intensely pragmatic and preoccupied with the need for action—both outstanding characteristics of what might be called the military outlook. Is it possible, moreover, that owing to their lowly origin and their lack of indoctrination in the traditional Confucian ideology, warlords like Yen were less affected by bureaucratic attitudes which in the past had caused even those in charge of modernization projects to regard them as merely sources of revenue rather than as productive enterprises to be subsidized and promoted for their own sake?[1]

Although Yen remained opposed to class warfare and continued to denounce communism, after 1930 his outlook and behavior became increasingly radical. I have in mind his persistent and single-minded efforts to promote industrialization, especially the development of heavy industry, as well as his growing hatred of imperialism and capitalism, his antagonism toward private enterprise and a money economy, and his eagerness to imitate the Soviet Union, the exceedingly functional orientation of his policies with respect to education, an infatuation with planning that found expression in his attempts to organize and direct every aspect of life in Shansi, and his rejection of traditional Chinese conceptions of morality in favor of values borrowed from the West.

Furthermore, his experiences illustrate how the aims of a warlord intent upon industrializing his domain inevitably ran counter to the interests of the gentry, for in order to raise enough capital to erect modern industries it was necessary to tax away much of the wealth possessed by the rich and effect changes in the existing system of land tenure and money lending that threatened to deprive the gentry of their privileged position in the countryside. Yen had much in common with the gentry and wanted their support; however, he

[1] For examples of the earlier attitude toward industrialization see Albert Feuerwerker, *China's Early Industrialization* (Cambridge, 1958), pp. 96-188, 242-251.

was bent on making them subordinate their interests to his own and at times his determination to build an industrialized power state outweighed his desire for their cooperation. It not only caused him frequently to disregard the economic interests of the rich but likewise explains why he at least tried to educate the masses and urged them to participate more actively in public affairs. Without their enthusiastic support and cooperation he could not realize the objectives of his Ten Year Plan, much less hurl back the invading Japanese. This causes me to wonder if the Revolution of 1911 undermined somewhat the authority of the landed gentry in China by bringing to power military leaders, who in many instances were the sons of merchants and peasants and for this reason less committed to defending the preeminent position of the landholding class than were the mandarins they displaced.[2] Yet throughout his career Yen generally was regarded as a "conservative," which suggests that this term must be used carefully within the context of China's recent history. This in turn raises the question of to what degree militarism is the force underlying the changes that have occurred in China over the last sixty years. And I do not exclude the past fifteen, since Chinese communism is in many respects a military movement and therefore may be an outgrowth of warlordism.

Certainly the schemes that Yen tried to carry out in Shansi, especially after 1930, constitute one of the last systematic attempts made in China to bring about reform along conservative lines. Together with the program adopted by Chiang Kai-shek and the Kuomintang, they form a link between the T'ung Chih Restoration and other moderate reform movements of the nineteenth century and the current efforts of the Chinese Communists to revolutionize Chinese society. Like the statesmen of the Restoration, Yen advocated using Western technology to protect traditional Chinese institutions and values; however, unlike his predecessors he contemplated tampering with the political, social, and economic foundations of the

[2] Writing on p. 164 of *The United States and China* (Cambridge, 1958), John Fairbank says: "Of the ten or a dozen leading warlords of this period [1911-1949], one began life as a peddler, another as a fiddler, two rose from the rank of private, one had been a bandit, and another a coolie."

established order and to the extent that he actually did so unwittingly may have subverted them and cleared the way for the radical changes of the future. His experience also illustrates how in some instances innovations introduced by conservative leaders in the hope of bolstering the existing order contributed to the destruction of the very system their proponents wished to preserve. All of this suggests that the "warlord period" of China's history was not merely an era of fruitless strife but rather a period of transition which witnessed changes so significant that without them the unification and modernization of China currently being undertaken by the Chinese Communists would be impossible. Many of these changes came about only because the leadership of China had passed into the hands of men whose semi-Western military training enabled them to appreciate the value of innovation and whose comparative lack of instruction in the Neo-Confucian orthodoxy, with which the more educated mandarins who preceded them had been indoctrinated, made them more inclined to abandon traditional ideas and institutions in favor of new ones when it suited them.[3]

On the other hand, it is not my purpose to suggest that Yen's policies altered profoundly the social and economic structure of Shansi. Hostility from rivals like Chiang Kai-shek kept him from soliciting or earning outside Shansi the capital to modernize the economy of his mineral-rich but otherwise impoverished domain. Thus the division of China into

[3] In *The Military in the Political Development of New Nations* (Chicago, 1964), the sociologist Morris Janowitz arrives at much the same conclusion after surveying the behavior of the military in a score or more of "new" nations. He points out (p. 42) that the military is a crisis organization which must be prepared to act and respond to the immediate environment. In other words, it must be prepared to mobilize its resources in a crisis and especially to challenge tradition. He goes on to say that engineering and the need to adjust to technological innovations are important day-to-day professional concerns of career army officers and that skills developed, especially of a managerial kind, are easily transferred to middle-level civilian administration, notably of factories and industries. This would seem to be what differentiated warlords like Yen Hsi-shan from the mandarinate which preceded them. Janowitz says, with respect to the role played by army officers in underdeveloped nations, that "the combination of hinterland and middle-class origins plus professional military education does not produce a traditional conservative outlook but, in varying forms, a modernizing and collectivistic orientation (p. 45)." I am indebted to Professor Robert Marsh of Duke University for calling my attention to Janowitz's book.

mutually antagonistic warlord states had the paradoxical effect of encouraging but at the same time limiting economic growth in Shansi. If Yen did not achieve many of his objectives, however, this was chiefly because he failed to mobilize effectively the agricultural resources of Shansi. His Ten Year Plan, along with the social and political changes it provoked in Shansi, are examples of what might be called "fragmentary" or "incomplete" modernization. They affected largely the urban population, especially in Taiyuan, rather than the countryside. Perhaps this was characteristic of modernization under the warlords, who usually made their headquarters in the cities, where they concentrated most of their troops and built the arsenals and other factories they needed. Significantly, when the Communists attacked Yen in 1936 and again in 1948 and 1949, the cities of Shansi remained loyal to him, while the peasantry went over to the Communists. It would seem that in the countryside the privileged classes were more entrenched than in the cities and therefore better able to resist Yen's demands and frustrate his schemes. In spite of his bold words, Yen had neither the power nor, one suspects, the willingness to initiate a movement aimed at really mobilizing the peasants in his domain. Besides alienating many of his followers, such a policy would have given to the Communists and others who opposed his regime an opportunity to organize the rural population against him. Yet, in the absence of a social revolution in the countryside, he could not create the mass political base he needed in order to realize his economic and military ambitions. To paraphrase Morris Janowitz, although Yen recognized the need for mobilizing the masses behind his program, he did not develop a viable political apparatus outside the organizational structure of his own army, which, together with the existing bureaucracy, remained too archaic and unpopular to shape a minimum level of political consensus in support of his objectives.[4] Therefore, his talk of reform and resistance to the Japanese often lacked real force and momentum. This dilemma plagued him until 1937, when his failure to resolve it resulted in the almost complete destruction of his power in Shansi.

Yen resisted tenaciously Japan's attempts to conquer Shansi;

[4] See Morris Janowitz, *op.cit.*, pp. 84-85, 103.

however, his troops suffered one defeat after another, not only because of the superior firepower and better training of the Japanese Army but also on account of his suicidal policy of fighting a positional war against a much stronger enemy. This policy was forced on him by the unpopularity of his troops and his government in the countryside, which prevented him from employing more fluid tactics. Only the Communists had enough support among the peasants to engage in a partisan struggle with the Japanese Army behind its own lines, and by the spring of 1938 any other kind of warfare was out of the question in Shansi. This is why, as one investigator puts it, "Yen Hsi-shan passed into virtual oblivion while the Communists took and held the initiative. . . ."[5]

5 Paul O. Elmquist, op.cit., p. 49.

BIBLIOGRAPHY

Works in Chinese and Japanese

GOVERNMENT DOCUMENTS

Gaimushō (Japanese Foreign Office), *Honpō no chihō-seifu oyobi kojin no taisuru shakkan kankei zakken: Sansei oyobi Kyōsei shō no bu, ji Shōwa gogatsu shidō roku-nen gogatsu* (*Miscellaneous Matters Relating to Our Country's Loans to Local Governments and Individuals: Section on Shansi and Shensi Provinces, May, 1930 to May, 1931*). Tokyo, 1931.

Naikaku sōri daijin kambō chōsashitsu (Cabinet Research Office), comp., *Chūkyō tekkōgyō chōsa hōkokusho* (*Survey Report on the Steel Industry of Communist China*). Tokyo, 1956.

Shan-hsi sheng cheng-fu (Provincial Government of Shansi), pub., *Chin-pu Shan-hsi* (*Progressive Shansi*). No place of publication, 1945.

————, pub., *Shan-hsi liu-cheng san-shih hui-pien* (*A Collection of Documents Pertaining to Government in Shansi*). Taiyuan, 1929.

————, pub., *Shan-hsi sheng-cheng shih-nien chien-she chi-hua an* (*A Draft of the Shansi Provincial Government's Ten Year Plan for Economic Reconstruction*), Volume I. Taiyuan, 1933.

————, pub., *Shan-hsi sheng t'ung-chi nien-chien* (*Shansi Statistical Annual*), Volumes I and II. Taiyuan, 1934.

Tada butai sanbōbu (Tada Corps, Chief of Staff), pub., *Chūgoku kyōsantō undō no kaisetsu* (*Explanation of the Chinese Communist Movement*). Peiping, February 17, 1941.

Tsou Lu, ed., *Chung-kuo Kuo-min-tang shih-kao* (*A Draft of History of China's Kuomintang*), Volume I. Changsha, 1938.

Yen Hsi-shan, pub., *Chin Shan hui-i lu* (*The Records of the Conference for the Promotion of Progress in Shansi*). Taipei, 1957.

Zai Pekin nippon taishikan keimubu (Japanese Embassy in Peking, Police Affairs Division), pub., *Saikin Hokushi ni okeru Chūgoku kyōsan undō no gaikyō* (*A Current*

Survey of the Chinese Communist Movement in North China). Tientsin, 1939.

PUBLICATIONS OF SEMIOFFICIAL AND INDEPENDENT
ORGANIZATIONS

Chin-Sui she-hui ching-chi tiao-ch'a t'ung-chi hui (Association for the Promotion of Statistical Investigation of the Economies and Societies of Shansi and Suiyuan), pub., *Chin-Sui she-hui ching-chi tiao-ch'a t'ung-chi she nien-kan (Annual of the Association for the Promotion of Statistical Investigation of the Economies and Societies of Shansi and Suiyuan).* Taiyuan, 1935.

Chung-hua shih-yeh hsieh-hui (Chinese Industrial Association), pub., *Chung-hua shih-yeh yüeh-k'an (Chinese Industrial Monthly),* September 1, 1935. Taiyuan.

Chung-kuo ti-cheng hsüeh-hui (Chinese Land Policy Study Association), pub., *T'u-ti ts'un-yu wen-t'i (The All Land to the Villages Question).* Nanking, 1935.

Ch'üan-kuo ching-chi wei-yüan-hui (National Economic Committee), pub., *Shan-hsi k'ao-ch'a pao-kao shu (Report on an Investigation of Shansi).* Shanghai, 1936.

Koain seimu pu (Asia Development Board, Political Affairs Bureau), pub., "Sansei shō no shigen to kōgyō" ("The Industries and Material Resources of Shansi"), *Jōhō (Intelligence),* No. 1 (September 1, 1939), pp. 47-52.

————, pub., "Shin-Satsu-Ki henku no jōkyō" ("The General Situation in the Chin-Ch'a-Chi Border Region"), *Jōhō,* No. 35 (February 1, 1941), pp. 1-73.

Nung-ts'un chiao-yü kai-chin she (Society for the Improvement of Village Education), pub., *Hsin nung-ts'un (New Village),* May 15, 1936. Taiyuan.

Chien-cheng chou-k'an min-chung chien-sheng yün-tung hui (Shansi Association for the Promotion of Popular Supervision of the Government), pub., *Chien-cheng chou-k'an (Supervisorial Weekly),* January 1, 1935. Taiyuan.

Shih-yeh pu, Kuo-chi mao-i chü (Industry Section, Board of International Trade), pub., *Chung-kuo shih-yeh chih, Shan-hsi sheng (The Chinese Industrial Gazetteer, Shansi Province).* Shanghai, 1937.

Shiryō-ka, Sōmu bu, Minami Manshū kabushiki kaisha (Research Section, General Affairs Department, South Manchurian Railroad Company), pub., *Hoku Shi jijō sōran* (*General Survey of Conditions in North China*). Hsinking, 1935.

Taiheiyō Sensō gen'in kenkyūbu, Nihon kokusai seiji gakkai (Committee to Study the Origins of the Pacific War, The Japanese Association of International Relations), ed., *Taiheiyō sensō no michi: kaisen gaikō shi* (*The Road to the Pacific War: A Diplomatic History before the War*), Volume II, *Manshū jihen* (*The Manchurian Incident*). Tokyo, 1962-1963.

COMPILATIONS

Hatano Ken'ichi, *Gendai Shina no kiroku* (*Modern China Archives*). Tokyo, 1924-1932.

ALMANACS AND ENCYCLOPEDIAS

Chung-kuo fen-sheng t'u (*A Provincial Atlas of China*). Hong Kong, 1954.

Gaimusho, Ajia kyoku (Japanese Foreign Office, Asia Bureau), comp., *Gendai Chūgoku jimmei jiten* (*A Biographical Dictionary of Modern China*). Tokyo, 1962.

Gaimushō jōhō bu (Information Section, Japanese Ministry of Foreign Affairs), comp., *Gendai Chūka minkoku manshu teikoku jimmei kan* (*Current Survey of Important Men in the Chinese Republic and the Manchu Empire*). Tokyo, 1937.

Tō yō rekishi daijiten (*An Historical Dictionary of the Far East*) Volume III. Tokyo, 1937.

NEWSPAPERS AND PERIODICALS

Ch'en Pao (*The Morning Paper*), 1924-1932. Peking.

Chiao-t'ung jih pao (*Communications Daily*), 1920-1932. Peking.

Ching-chi (*Economics*), 1924. Peking.

Chieh-fang (*Liberation*), 1938-1940. Yenan.

Ching Pao (*The Peking Times*), 1924-1932. Peking.

Chung-wai ching-chi chou-k'an (*Sino-Foreign Economic Weekly*), 1924-1932. Peking.

Hsien-tai p'ing-lün (*The Contemporary Review*), 1925-1926. Peking.

Hsin Chung-kuo (New China), 1919. Peking.

Hsin Min-kuo (New Republic), 1924. Peking.

Hsin-wen Pao (The News), 1924-1932. Peking.

Hsin Wen-hua (New Culture), 1936. No place of publication.

Hua-pei jih-pao (North China Daily News), 1924-1932. Peking.

Huang Pao (The "Yellow" News), 1924-1932. Peking.

I Shih-pao (Wide World Daily), 1924-1934. Tientsin.

————, 1934. Peking.

Kuang-chou min-kuo jih-pao (Kwangchow Republican Daily), 1935. Kwangchow.

Kuo-wen chou-pao (The Weekly Gazette), 1927-1938. Tientsin.

San Man Po (The New Evening News), 1958. Hong Kong.

Shanghai Chung-hua jih-pao (The Shanghai Chinese Daily), 1935. Shanghai.

Shanghai yin-hang chou-pao (The Shanghai Bankers Weekly), 1936. Shanghai.

Shih-chieh jih-pao (The Daily World), 1924-1932. Peking.

Ta Kung Pao (Impartiality), 1936-1938. Tientsin and Shanghai.

Ti-hsüeh tsa-chih (The Geography Magazine), 1916. Peking.

Tu-li p'ing-lün (Independent Commentary), 1935. Peiping.

Tung-fang tsa-chih (Far Eastern Miscellany), 1936. Peking.

REMINISCENCES AND AUTOBIOGRAPHIES

Li Tsung-jen, unpublished autobiography.

Yen Hsi-shan, *Shan-hsi kuang-fu chih ching-kuo (An Account of the Revolution of 1911 in Shansi)*. Taiyuan, 1945.

ARTICLES

Anonymous, "Shan-hsi yü-ts'ai lien-kang chi-ch'i ch'ang" ("The Northwestern Yü-ts'ai Steel and Machine Plant"), *Chung-hua shih-yeh yueh-k'an*, September 1, 1935, pp. 119-123.

Anonymous, "Po I-po t'ung-chih hsieh-lu Yen Hsi-shan t'ung-ti p'an-kuo nui-mu" ("Comrade Po I-po reveals the inside story of Yen Hsi-shan's treason"), pp. 1-10 in Ch'en Po-ta, *Yen Hsi-shan p'i-p'an* (*A Criticism of Yen Hsi-shan*). Kalgan, 1945.

Anonymous, "Yen Hsi-shan k'e-cheng hsia te jen-min sheng-huo" ("The Life of the People under Yen Hsi-shan's Cruel Rule") pp. 1-4 in Ch'en Po-ta, *Yen Hsi-shan p'i-p'an.*

Chang Chih-chieh, "Yang-ch'üan mei-yeh pu chen chih wang-yin yü ch'ao-su ho-tso chih pi-yao" ("The Principal Causes of the Depression Afflicting the Coal Industry in Yang-ch'üan and the Necessity of Speedy Cooperation"), *Chung-hua shih-yeh yueh-k'an*, September 1, 1935, pp. 1-4.

Chang Tso-hua, "Nui-Meng wen-t'i yü kuo-fang" ("The Inner Mongolian Question and National Defense"), *Kuo-wen chou-pao*, September 7, 1936, pp. 1-6.

Chang Wei-lu, "Shan-hsi chih-yeh chiao-yü chih chien-t'ao chi ch'i chiang-lai ying ch'ü chih t'u-ching" ("An Examination of Vocational Education in Shansi and the Road It Ought to Take in the Future") *Hsin nung-ts'un*, May 15, 1936, pp. 62-68.

"Chao," "Shan-hsi wen-t'i" ("The Shansi Question"), *Hsien-tai p'ing-lün*, September 19, 1925, pp. 3-4.

Chao Lien-Ch'eng, "Tsai Hu-yen nung-ts'un chiao-yü shih-yen hsüeh-hsiao i-nien-lai sheng-huo chung te chi-ko p'ien-tuan" ("Some Snatches of Life during the Past Year at the Hu-yen Experimental School for Village Education"), *Hsin nung-ts'un*, May 15, 1936, pp. 178-198.

Chen Ming-t'ing, "Lün wu-ch'an cheng-chüan" ("A Discussion of Product Certificates"), *Chien-cheng chou-k'an*, January 1, 1935, pp. 1-4.

Ch'en Fang-t'ung, "T'ai-yüan lüeh-ying" ("Fleeting Impressions of Taiyuan"), *Kuo-wen chou-pao*, December 7, 1936, pp. 27-31.

Chi Sheng, "T'u-ti wen-t'i chih shih te yen-chiu" ("An Historical Investigation of the Land Question"), *Chin-Sui she-hui ching-chi tiao-ch'a t'ung-chi she nien-kan*, December 1, 1935, pp. 21-64.

Ch'i Chih-chin, " 'T'u-ti ts'un-yu' hsia chih Chin-pei nung-ts'un" ("Peasant Villages of Northern Shansi under [Yen's] 'All Land to the Village' Scheme"), *Kuo-wen chou-pao*, March 23, 1936, pp. 21-26.

Ch'i Chih-chin, "T'u-ti ts'un-yu chih chih chien-t'ao" ("An Investigation of [Yen's] All Land to the Village Scheme"), *Kuo-wen chou-pao*, December 23, 1935, pp. 1-6.

Ch-i T'ien-shou, "Lün nung-ts'un hsin-yung ho-tso chüan" ("A Discussion of Village Credit Cooperative Certificates"), *Chien-cheng chou-k'an*, January 1, 1935, pp. 1-9.

Ch-i T'ien-yü, "I-nien-lai Shan-hsi chih ts'ai-cheng" ("Fiscal Administration in Shansi During the Past Year"), *Chien-cheng chou-k'an*, January 1, 1935, pp. 1-23.

Chu Chang-pao, "P'ing Yen Hsi-shan chih t'u-ti ts'un-yu pan-fa" ("A Criticism of Yen Hsi-shan's All Land to the Village Scheme"), *Tung-fang tsa-chih*, November 1, 1936, pp. 11-15.

Chu Ch'eng, "Sui chü chieh-k'ai" ("What's Happening in Suiyuan"), *Kuo-wen chou-pao*, November 30, 1936, pp. 1-8.

Ch'u Chih-sheng, "Shan-hsi te ching-chi hsien-chuang yü ching-chi t'ung-chih" ("Economic Controls and Present Economic Conditions in Shansi"), *Kuo-wen chou-pao*, March 12, 1934, pp. 1-5.

Fan Ch'ang-chiang, "Shan-hsi chi-hsing" ("Recollections of a Trip through Shansi"), *Kuo-wen chou-pao*, March 29, 1937, pp. 21-26.

————, "Sui chan te chien-t'ao" ("An Investigation of the Fighting in Suiyuan"), *Kuo-wen chou-pao*, January 1, 1937, pp. 1-3.

Han Lu, "Ai Shan-hsi" ("Alas for Shansi"), *Hsien-tai p'ing-lün*, July 3, 1926, pp. 6-7.

Han Mei, "Ts'ung fu-nü wen-t'i shuo tao Shan-hsi fu-nü te yün-tung" ("The Question of Women and the Women's Movement in Shansi"), *Chien-cheng chou-k'an*, January 1, 1935, pp. 1-5.

Heng San, " 'K'ai-fa Hsi-pei wen-t'i' chih shang-chiao" ("What About the So-called 'Problem of Developing the Northwest' "), *Chien-cheng chou-k'an*, January 1, 1935, pp. 1-9.

Ho Lien, "Hua-pei Chi Lü Chin Ch'a Sui wu-sheng ching-chi tsai cheng-ko Chung-kuo ching-chi chih ti-wei" ("The Position Occupied by the Economies of the Five Provinces of North China, Honan, Shantung, Shansi, Chahar, and

Suiyuan, in the Economy of China as a Whole"), *Tung-fang tsa-chih*, April 1, 1936, pp. 5-12.

Ho Tung, "Sui-yüan tsai kuo-fang shang te ti-wei" ("Suiyuan's Position with Respect to National Defense"), *Kuo-wen chou-pao*, November 2, 1936, pp. 5-10.

Hsia Ching-feng, "Shan-hsi lü-hsing chi" ("Diary of a Trip through Shansi"), Part I, *Ti-hsüeh tsa-chih*, January 1, 1916, pp. 1a-6a.

————, "Shan-hsi lü-hsing chi," Part II, *Ti-hsüeh tsa-chih*, February 2, 1916, pp. 5a-7b.

Hsiao Lin, "Tsai T'ai-yuan te i t'ien" ("A Day in Taiyuan"), *Kuo-wen chou-pao*, December 27, 1936, pp. 56-58.

Hsin San, "Chen-hsing Shan-hsi shang-yeh ch'u-i" ("My Humble Opinion About How to Promote Commercial and Industrial Prosperity in Shansi"), *Chung-hua shih-yeh yüeh-k'an*, September 1, 1935, pp. 9-12.

Hsu Fan-t'ing, "Chi Shan-hsi t'u huang-ti Yen Hsi-shan te i-feng wu-ch'ien yen-shu" ("A Five Thousand Word Letter to the Local Emperor of Shansi, Yen Hsi-shan"), Ch'en Po-ta, *Yen Hsi-shan p'i-p'an*, pp. 1-18.

————, "San nien bu yen chih yen" ("Words Unsaid for Three Years"), Ch'en Po-ta, *Yen Hsi-shan p'i p'an*, pp. 1-7.

Hsu Hsin, "Mei-kuo pai-yin cheng-ts'e chih yen-chiu" ("A Study of American Silver Policy"), *Chin-Sui she-hui ching-chi tiao-ch'a t'ung-chi she nien-kan*, December 1, 1935, pp. 1-6.

Hsu Tso-hsin, "Shan-hsi nung-ts'un hsien-chuang chi ch'i kai-chin fang-fa" ("Present Conditions in the Villages of Shansi and Methods of Improving Them"), *Chien-cheng chou-k'an*, January 1, 1935, pp. 1-6.

Hsu Ying, "Chui-hua Shan-hsi" ("Shansi in Retrospect"), *Kuo-wen chou-pao*, November 22, 1937, pp. 50-51.

Hsueh Ch'in "Tang-shih hui-i" ("Party Matters in Retrospect"), *Chien-cheng chou-k'an*, January 1, 1935, pp. 1-6.

Huang Li-ch'uan, "Hsü" ("Introduction"), *Hsin nung-ts'un*, May 1936, pp. 1-3.

Jen Pi-shih, "Shan-hsi k'ang-chan te hui-i" ("Recollections About the Fighting in Shansi"), *Chieh Fang*, January 28, 1938, pp. 15-19.

Jen Ying-lun and Kuo Chien-fu, "Chin shih nien-lai chih
    Shan-hsi min-chung yün-tung" ("The Mass Movement
    in Shansi during the Past Ten Years"), *Chien-cheng
    chou-k'an*, January 1, 1935, pp. 1-6.

Kan Hsiu-ch'i, "K'ang-jih t'ung-i chan-hsien tsai Shan-hsi"
    ("The Anti-Japanese United Front in Shansi"), *Chieh
    Fang*, October 31, 1938, pp. 13-16.

Kuang Ch'ing-i, "Jih-pen hua-hsüeh kung-yeh chih chin-
    k'uang" ("Recent Conditions in the Japanese Chemical
    Industry"), *Chung-hua shih-yeh yüeh-k'an*, September 1,
    1935, pp. 35-49.

Kuo Hung-shih, "Mu hsiao (Hu-yen nung-ts'un chiao-yü shih-
    yen hsueh-hsiao) ch'eng-li i-nien-i-lai" ("The First Year
    of Our School [the Hu-yen Experimental School for
    Village Education]"), *Hsin nung-ts'un*, May 15, 1936,
    pp. 151-177.

———, "Nung-chia fu-yeh chih yen-chiu" ("A Study of Peas-
    ant Handicraft Industry"), *Hsin nung-ts'un*, May 15,
    1936, pp. 319-334.

Li Ch'ang-sheng, "Pen hui kung-tso chih hui-ku yü ch'an-
    wang" ("The Work of Our Association in Retrospect
    and Its Possibilities for the Future"), *Chien-cheng chou-
    k'an*, January 1, 1935, pp. 1-21.

———, "P'o-ch'an te Chung-kuo ching-chi chih ch'u-lu" ("The
    Way Out for the Bankrupt Chinese Economy"), *Chien-
    cheng chou-k'an*, January 1, 1935, pp. 1-7.

———, "Shan-hsi te ch'ien-t'u" ("The Road Ahead for
    Shansi"), *Chien-cheng chou-k'an*, January 1, 1935,
    pp. 1-10.

Li Fei, "So-wei 't'u-ti ts'un-yu' " ("The So-called 'All Land to
    the Village Scheme' "), *Hsin wen-hua*, February 1, 1936,
    pp. 13-15.

Li Hsi-chen, "Wo hsien chiao-yü ying yu te hsin tao-hsiang"
    ("The New Direction which Our District Education
    Ought To Take"), *Hsin nung-ts'un*, May 15, 1936, pp.
    82-85.

Li Shu-hua, "Shan-hsi ts'un-cheng te kuo-ch'ü yü hsien-tsai"
    ("Past and Present Village Administration in Shansi"),
    Chien-cheng chou-k'an, January 1, 1935, pp. 1-6.

Li Teh-hsien, "Kai-chin Shan-hsi nung-yeh chih wo chien"
    ("My Views On How To Improve Agriculture in

Shansi"), *Chung-hua shih-yeh yüeh-k'an*, September 1, 1935, pp. 13-15.

Liu Kuan-san, "Pen she ch'eng-li chih ching-kuo" ("The Experiences of Our Association since Its Creation"), *Chin-Sui she-hui ching-chi tiao-ch'a t'ung-chi she nien-kan*, December 1, 1935, pp. 1-2.

Liu Po-ying, "Hu-yen nung-ts'un chiao-yü shih-yen hsüeh-hsiao san-nien-lai chih ching-kuo lüeh-shu" ("A Résumé of Events during the Past Three Years at the Hu-yen Experimental School for Village Education"), *Hsin nung-tsun*, May 15, 1936, pp. 1-66.

"Lü," "Shan-hsi shu-cheng t'an," ("On the Government of Shansi"), Part I, *Hsien-tai p'ing-lün*, August 14, 1926, pp. 5-7.

———, "Shan-hsi shu-cheng t'an," Part II, *Hsien-tai p'ing-lün*, August 21, 1926, pp. 7-9.

———, "Shan-hsi shu-cheng t'an," Part III, *Hsien-tai p'ing-lün*, August 28, 1926, pp. 6-11.

———, "Shan-hsi shu-cheng t'an," Part IV, *Hsien-tai p'ing-lün*, September 11, 1926, pp. 8-10.

———, "Shan-hsi shu-cheng t'an," Parts V and VI, *Hsien-tai p'ing-lün*, September 25, 1926, pp. 9-13.

———, "Shan-hsi shu-cheng t'an," Part VII, *Hsien-tai p'ing-lün*, October 9, 1926, pp. 10-13.

Ma Shao-po and Ts'ao Tzu-chung, "I-nien-lai Shan-hsi chih chiao-yü" ("Education in Shansi during the Past Year"), *Chien-cheng chou-k'an*, January 1, 1935, pp. 1-12.

Mi Pao-min, "I-nien-lai Chung-kuo te tsai-ch'ing" ("Calamities in China during the Past Year"), *Hsin nung-ts'un*, May 15, 1936, pp. 371-389.

P'eng Shih-hung, "Chia-t'ing kung-yeh" ("Cottage Industry"), *Chung-hua shih-yeh yüeh-k'an*, September 1, 1935, pp. 5-6.

P'ing Fan, "Min-chung yün-tung chih tso-jih chin-jih yü ming-jih" ("The Mass Movement in Shansi: Yesterday, Today, and Tomorrow"), *Chien-cheng chou-k'an*, January 1, 1935, pp. 1-9.

Shih I-hsiang, "Chung-kuo nung-ts'un te chia-shih chiao-yü" ("Home Handicraft Training in the Villages of China"), *Hsin nung-ts'un*, May 15, 1936, pp. 415-420.

Shun Wu, "I-nien-lai Shan-hsi chih chien-she" ("Economic Reconstruction in Shansi during the Past Year"), *Chien-cheng chou-k'an*, January 1, 1935, pp. 1-25.

Ta Pei, "I-nien-lai Shan-hsi chih ch'u-pan chieh" ("Publishing in Shansi during the Past Year"), *Chien-cheng chou-k'an*, January 1, 1935, pp. 1-12.

T'ang Ch'i-yü, "P'ing Yen Hsi-shan shih chih 't'u-ti ts'un-yü' " ("A Criticism of Mr. Yen Hsi-shan's 'All Land to the Village' Scheme"), *Tung-fang tsa-chih*, November 1, 1936, pp. 5-10.

Teng-Li-hao, "Shan-hsi cheng-chih te chien-t'ao" ("An Examination of Government in Shansi"), *Chien-cheng chou-k'an*, January 1, 1935, pp. 1-5.

Tuan Liang-ch'en, "I-nien-lai chih Shan-hsi ching-chi" ("The Economy of Shansi during the Past Year"), *Chien-cheng chou-k'an*, January 1, 1935, pp. 1-25.

Wang Chen-i, "Mo-fan tu-chün chih-hsia Shan-hsi chih kai-kuan" ("A Picture of Shansi under the Rule of the Model Governor"), *Hsin min-kuo*, June 1924, pp. 1-10.

Wang Meng-chou and Chang Lan-t'ing, "I-nien-lai Shan-hsi chih chin-tu" ("The Fight against Narcotics in Shansi during the Past Year"), *Chien-cheng chou-k'an*, January 1, 1935, pp. 1-10.

Wang Ta-san, "Lün Chung-kuo hsü-yao ho-chung chih-yeh chiao-yü" ("A Discussion of What Kinds of Vocational Training Are Needed in China"), *Hsin nung-ts'un*, May 15, 1936, pp. 1-25.

Wen Ch'i-an and Ku P'ei-ying, "Shan-hsi ching-cheng chih t'an-t'ao" ("An Investigation of Police Administration in Shansi"), *Chien-cheng chou-k'an*, January 1, 1935, pp. 1-7.

Wu Pao-san, "Ch'a Sui Chin lü-hsing kuan-kan" ("Impressions from a Trip through Chahar, Suiyuan, and Shansi"), Part I, *Tu-li p'ing-lün*, November 10, 1935, pp. 14-18.

———, "Ch'a Sui Chin lü-hsing kuan-kan," Part II, *Tu-li p'ing-lün*, November 17, 1935, pp. 14-20.

Wu P'i-mu and Li Shu-chi, "I-nien-lai Shan-hsi chih tsai-huo" ("Disasters in Shansi during the Past Year"), *Chien-cheng chou-k'an*, January 1, 1935, pp. 1-6.

Ying Ch-iu, "I-nien-lai chih ta-shih shu-p'ing" ("A Résumé of Important Events in Shansi during the Past Year"), *Chien-cheng chou-k'an*, pp. 1-31.

GENERAL WORKS

Anonymous, *Shan-hsi ch'ing-tang ch'ien-hou chi-lüeh* (*A Brief Description of Events Leading Up To and Following the Party Purification Movement in Shansi*). Date and place of publication unknown.

Chao Shu-li, *Li-chia-chuang te pien-ch'ien* (*Li Village Turns Over*). Shanghai, 1947.

Chao Tai-wen, *Shan-hsi hsien-cheng* (*Archival Compilations of Shansi*), 5 volumes. Taiyuan, 1936.

Ch'en Ch'i-t'ien, *Shan-hsi p'iao-chuang k'ao-lüeh* (*A Survey of Shansi Banks*). Shanghai, 1936.

Ch'en Po-ta, *Yen Hsi-shan p'i-p'an* (*A Criticism of Yen Hsi-shan*). Kalgan, 1945.

Ch'en Shao-hsiao, *Chiu-p'an t'an ping lü* (*Wine Talk about Military Affairs*). Hong Kong, 1963.

Fan Ch'ang-chiang, *Sai shang hsing* (*A Journey in the North*). Shanghai, 1937.

Fan Ch'ang-chiang, *et al.*, *Hsi-hsien feng-yün* (*Wind and Clouds on the Western Front*). Shanghai, 1937.

———, *Hsi-hsien hsieh-chan chi* (*An Account of the Bloody Fighting on the Western Front*). No date or place of publication.

———, *Hsi-pei chan-yün* (*War Clouds over the Northwest*). Shanghai, 1938.

———, *Hsi-pei hsien* (*Northwestern Front*). Hankow, 1938.

Fang Yen-kuang, *Yen Po-ch'uan hsien-sheng yü cheng-chih te k'e-kuan chi-shu* (*Objective Accounts of Mr. Yen Hsi-shan and the Government of Shansi*). Nanking, 1948.

Fukada Yūzō, *Shina kyōsangun no gensei* (*The Current Condition of the Chinese Communist Army*). Tokyo, 1939.

Hata Ikuhiku, *Nitchū sensō shi* (*A History of the Sino-Japanese War*). Tokyo, 1961.

Hatano Ken'ichi, *Chūgoku kyōsantō shi, ichi ku san roku nen* (*The History of the Chinese Communist Party, 1936*). Tokyo, 1961.

Hatano Ken'ichi, *Chūgoku kyōsantō shi, ichi ku san shichi nen* (*The History of the Chinese Communist Party, 1937*). Tokyo, 1961.

———, *Gendai Shina no seiji to jimbutsu* (*Politics and Outstanding Men in Contemporary China*). Tokyo, 1937.

Hattori Takushirō, *Dai-Tōa sensō Zenshi* (*The Complete History of the War for Greater East Asia*), Volume I. Tokyo, 1953.

Higuchi Hiromu, *Nippon no tai Shina tōshi kenkyū* (*A Study of Japanese Investments in China*). Tokyo, 1939.

Himeno Tokuichi, *Hoku-Shi no seijō* (*Political Conditions in North China*). Tokyo, 1936.

Hirano Reiji, *Chūkyō ryoshū ki* (*I Was a Prisoner of the Chinese Communists*). Tokyo, 1957.

———, *Manshu no imbōsha: Kōmoto Daisaku no ummei teki na ashioto* (*The Manchurian Intriguer: The Fateful Trail of Kōmoto Daisaku*). Tokyo, 1959.

Horiba Kazuo, *Shina jihen sensō shidō shi* (*An Historical Guide to the China Incident*). Tokyo, 1962.

Hsi Jung, *Yen Hsi-shan te tsui-chuang* (*The Crimes of Yen Hsi-shan*). Yenan, 1945.

Hsüeh Hui-tzu, *Chin-jih chih hua-pei* (*North China Today*). Nanking, 1939.

Hsüeh Mu-ch'iao, *Chung-kuo nung-ts'un wen-t'i* (*The Question of China's Peasant Villages*). Place of publication unknown, 1936.

Kao K'e-fu, ed., *Ti-pa-lu chün tsai Shan-hsi* (*The Eighth Route Army in Shansi*). Shanghai, 1938.

Kojima Seiichi, *Hoku-Shi keizai tokuhon* (*An Economic Primer for North China*), Volumes I and II. Tokyo, 1937.

Lai Yen-yü, ed., *Kuang-hsi i-lan* (*Glimpses of Kwangsi*). Nanning, 1935.

Liang Sheng-chün, *Chiang Li tou-cheng nui-mu* (*The Inside Story of the Struggle between Chiang and Li*). Hong Kong, 1954.

Maruyama Shizuo, *Ushinawaretaru kiroku* (*The Story of Defeat*). Tokyo, 1950.

P'eng Fei, ed., *T'ai-yüan chih chan* (*The Battle for Taiyuan*). Peking, 1957.

Po Li, *Chin Ch'a Chi p'ien-ch'ü yin hsiang chi* (*Impressions of the Shansi-Chahar-Hupei Border Region*). Hankow, 1938.

Takagi Rikurō, *Hoku-Shi keizai annai* (*An Economic Guide to North China*). Tokyo, 1937.

Tanaka Ryūkichi, *Hai-in o tsuku: gumbatsu sennō no jissō* (*The Cause of Defeat Revealed: The Truth about Domineering Militarists*). Tokyo, 1956.

Ti-liu-shih-pa chün cheng-chih pu (Political Department, Sixty-Eighth Army), ed., *Ao-chan T'ai-yüan ch'eng* (*The Bitter Battle for Taiyuan*). Place of publication unknown, 1949.

Ts'ai Tung-fan, *Min-kuo t'ung-su yen-i* (*A Popular Account of the Chinese Republic*). Shanghai, 1926.

Sun Yat-sen, *Tsung-li ch'üan-shu yen-chiang* (*The Complete Lectures of the Premier*), Volume I. Taipei, 1951.

Wan Ya-kang, *Chung-kuo kung-ch'an-tang chien-shih* (*A Short History of the Chinese Communist Party*). Hong Kong, 1951.

Wang Ch'ien, *Erh-shih-ch'i nien Shan-hsi cheng-chih kai-k'uang* (*Twenty Seven Years of Government in Shansi*). Unpublished manuscript, written in 1938.

Wang Chu-hsien, *Shan-hsi ta-hsueh chiao-chih* (*A Sketch of Shansi University*). Unpublished manuscript, written in 1954.

Wen Kung-chih, *Tsui-chin san-shih nien Chung-kuo chün-shih shih* (*A Military History of China during the Last Thirty Years*), Volume I. Shanghai, 1930.

Yen Hsi-shan, *Ping nung ho-i* (*Every Farmer a Soldier*), Volumes I-III. Place and time of publication unknown.

——, ed., *Sung-k'an hsien-sheng ch'üan-chi* (*The Collected Works of Mr. Hsü Chi-yu*), Volume I. Wu-t'ai, Shansi, 1915.

——, *Ts'un-cheng fa-kuei ling-wen chi-yao* (*A Compilation of Rules Governing Village Administration*). Taiyuan, 1925.

——, *Wu-ch'an cheng-ch'üan yü an-lao fen-p'ei* (*Product Certificate and Distribution According to Labor*). Taiyuan, 1939.

Yen Hsi-shan, *Yen Po-ch'uan hsien-sheng yen lün lei-pien* (*The Collected Addresses of Mr. Yen Hsi-shan*). Volumes I-IX. Shanghai, 1939.

———, *Yen tu-chün cheng-shu* (*The Political Handbook of Military Governor Yen*). Shanghai, 1930.

———, *Yen yüan-chang cheng-lun chi-yao* (*The Collected Speeches of Premier Yen*), Volume I. Taipei, 1950.

Yin Shih, *Li Chiang kuan-hsi yü Chung-kuo* (*The Relationship between Li and Chiang and China*). Hong Kong, 1954.

Yoshimo Sakuzō and Katō Shigeru, *Shina kakumei shi* (*A History of the Chinese Revolution*). Tokyo, 1922.

Works in Western Languages

GOVERNMENT DOCUMENTS

Bureau of Industrial and Commercial Information, Ministry of Industry, Commerce and Labor, National Government of the Republic of China, *The Chinese Economic Bulletin*, Nanking, 1929-1937.

Chinese Ministry of Information, comp., *China Handbook*, New York, 1937-1945.

International Military Tribunal for the Far East, *Proceedings*, Tokyo, 1946.

The Chinese Government, Bureau of Economic Information, comp., *The Chinese Economic Bulletin*, Peking, 1920-1926.

The Chinese Government, Bureau of Economic Information, comp., *The Chinese Economic Monthly*, Peking, 1925-1926.

United States Army, Forces in the Far East, *North China Area Operations Record, July 1937–May 1941*, Japanese Monograph Number 178, Washington, 1955.

United States Department of State, pub., *Papers Relating to the Foreign Relations of the United States, 1930*, Vol. II. Washington, 1945.

———, *Foreign Relations Papers, 1936*, Washington, 1954.

———, *Foreign Relations Papers, 1943*, Washington, 1954.

Uyehara, Cecil H., comp., *Checklist of Archives in the Japanese Ministry of Foreign Affairs, Tokyo, Japan, 1868-1945*. Washington, 1954.

PUBLICATIONS OF SEMIOFFICIAL AND INDEPENDENT
  ORGANIZATIONS

American Red Cross, pub., *Report of the American Red Cross,
  1929*. Washington, 1929.
China International Famine Relief Commission, pub., *Famine
  China's Northwest*, Series B, No. 41. Peiping, 1930.
————, pub., *Annual Report*, Peiping, 1930-1934.

ALMANACS, HANDBOOKS, AND ENCYCLOPEDIAS

Millard's Review, pub., *Who's Who in China, 1920*. Shanghai,
  1920.
Rawlinson, Frank, ed., *The China Christian Year Book, 1924*.
  Shanghai, 1924.
The China Weekly Review, pub., *Who's Who in China, 1926*.
  Shanghai, 1926.
————, pub., *Who's Who in China, 1936*. Shanghai, 1936.
Bell, H. T. M., and H. G. W. Woodhead, eds., *The China
  Year Book, 1916*. London, 1917.
————, eds., *The China Year Book, 1919-1920*. London, 1920.
Woodhead, H. G. W., ed., *The China Year Book, 1921-1922*.
  London, 1923.
————, *The China Year Book, 1923*. Tientsin, 1924.
————, *The China Year Book, 1925-1926*. Tientsin, 1927.
————, *The China Year Book, 1928*. Tientsin, 1929.
————, *The China Year Book, 1929-1930*. Tientsin, 1931.
————, *The China Year Book, 1931*. Tientsin, 1932.
————, *The China Year Book, 1933*. Shanghai, 1934.
————, *The China Year Book, 1934*. Shanghai, 1935.
————, *The China Year Book, 1935*. Shanghai, 1936.
————, *The China Year Book, 1936*. Shanghai, 1937.
————, *The China Year Book, 1938*. Shanghai, 1939.
————, *The China Year Book, 1939*. Shanghai, 1940.

NEWSPAPERS AND PERIODICALS

Asia, 1924. New York.
China Reconstructs, 1964. Peking.
China Today, 1934-1941. New York.
International Press Correspondence, 1935-1936. Moscow.
Japan Weekly Chronicle, 1937. Kobe.
Life Magazine, 1945-1950. New York.

Monthly Review of Economic Statistics, 1934-1938. Shanghai.
Pacific Affairs, 1936. New York.
The China Weekly Review, 1920-1950. Shanghai.
The Chinese Economic Journal, 1926-1937. Shanghai.
The Chinese Recorder, 1919-1920. Shanghai.
The New York Times, 1931-1950. New York.
The North China Herald, 1910-1941. Shanghai.
The People's Tribune, 1931-1937. Shanghai.
The Trans-Pacific, 1924. Tokyo.

COMPILATIONS

Chinese Communist Party, comp., *Biographies of Kuomintang Leaders*. Yenan, 1945. English translation published by Harvard University Committee on International and Regional Studies. Cambridge, 1948.

ARTICLES

Anonymous, "Agricultural Practices in Shansi," *The Chinese Economic Monthly*, August, 1925, pp. 1-8.
———, "China's Great North West," *The People's Tribune*, March 1, 1934, pp. 274-283.
———, "Coal Mining in Shansi," *The Chinese Economic Monthly*, November 1925, pp. 26-31.
———, "Economic Conditions in Suiyuan Province," *The Chinese Economic Journal*, October 1933, pp. 385-400.
———, "Labor Conditions in Shansi," *The Chinese Economic Monthly*, June 1925, pp. 20-24.
———, "Model Governor's Example for China," *The Trans-Pacific*, March 29, 1924, p. 5.
———, "Plight of the Shansi Peasantry," *The People's Tribune*, January 16, 1932, pp. 132-136.
———, "Prison Life in Shansi," *China Today*, April 1935, p. 134.
———, "Sericulture in Shansi," *The Chinese Economic Monthly*, December 1925, pp. 8-16.
———, "Survey of Forest Conditions and Lumber Production in Shansi," *The Chinese Economic Journal*, February 1926, pp. 155-160.
Chan, Hansu, "Chinese Red Army in New Offensive," *China Today*, April 1936, pp. 128-130.

Chang Chiao-fu, "Living Conditions of Peasants in Middle Shansi," in *Agrarian China* (Shanghai, 1938), pp. 199-203.

Chen Han-seng, "The Good Earth of China's Model Province," *Pacific Affairs*, September 1936, pp. 370-380.

Chie Hua, "A Further Step Towards the Annexation of North China," *International Press Correspondence*, June 13, 1936, pp. 745-746.

———, "The Chinese Red Army and Its Struggle for an Anti-Japanese United Front," *International Press Correspondence*, July 25, 1936, pp. 916-917.

Corbin, Paul L., "General Yen and his Work in Shansi," *The China Mission Year Book*, 1924, pp. 486-489.

Dreyer, F. C. H., "Yen Shi-shan: A Progressive Governor," *The Chinese Recorder*, July 1920, pp. 476-484.

Durdin, Tillman, "Chinese Nationalists Move Their Capital to Formosa; Now Plan a Guerrilla War," *The New York Times*, December 9, 1949, pp. 1:8 and 3:4.

Elmquist, Paul O., *The Nature of the Chinese Foothold in Shansi, 1937-1938*. Unpublished manuscript, 55 pages.

Emerson, John P., *Yen Hsi-shan, A Warlord and His Province, 1911-1948*. Unpublished manuscript, 55 pages.

Fairfield, Wynn C., *China's Model Province and Its Governor*. Unpublished manuscript, 3 pages.

Fisher, Sterling, "Shansi Tries Out Radical Reforms," *The New York Times*, February 2, 1936, p. 7:6.

Freeman, Mansfield, "Has China Found a New Moses?" *Asia*, April 1924, pp. 295-298 and 323-324.

Hanson, Haldore E., "Chinese War Lord Dreams of Russia," *The China Weekly Review*, February 8, 1936, p. 356.

———, "Leaks in the Opium Barrel," *The China Weekly Review*, March 7, 1936, p. 20.

———, "Toy Railroad Thrives in Shansi," *The China Weekly Review*, February 22, 1936, pp. 421 and 432.

Hearn, Lawrence, "Suiyuan—Heart of Eastern Asia," *China Today*, December 1936, p. 21.

Hosie, Lady, "Shansi After Twenty-Five Years," *The North China Herald*, December 16, 1936, p. 470.

Hsieh, C. Y., "Is Japan Planning to Assist Shansi against the Chinese Reds?" *The China Weekly Review*, March 28, 1936, p. 114.

Kann, E., "Copper Banknotes in China," *The Chinese Economic Journal*, July 1929, pp. 549-577.

Ku Chi-kang, "Farm Settlements in the Rear Loop," in *Agrarian China*, pp. 46-50.

Levenson, Joseph R., "Ill Wind in the Well Field: The Erosion of the Confucian Ground of Controversy," in Arthur F. Wright, ed., *The Confucian Persuasion* (Stanford, 1960), pp. 268-287.

Lieberman, Henry, "Gen. Yen Governs Again in Shansi with Japanese General as His Aide," *The New York Times*, February 13, 1946, p. 10:6-7.

————, "Nanking Rebuffed by Chiang on Gold," *The New York Times*, April 16, 1949, pp. 1:7 and 3:2-5.

————, "Peiping Convicts 17 Tokyo P.O.W.'s," *The New York Times*, June 22, 1956, pp. 1:8 and 5:4.

————, "State Industries of Shansi Grow But Benefit to People Is Delayed," *The New York Times*, February 14, 1947, p. 17:2-3.

Ma, C. F., "Notes on Chinese Labor Population," *The Chinese Economic Journal*, November 1930, pp. 1257-1266.

Meng, C. Y. W., "Japan's Plans to Attack China's 'First Line of Defense,'" *The China Weekly Review*, June 19, 1937, pp. 90-91.

————, "'Model Governor' Yen Hsi-shan Advocates Abolition of Private Ownership of Land," *The China Weekly Review*, September 21, 1935, pp. 88-89.

————, "Nippon Conquest of Shansi Still a Distant Dream," *The China Weekly Review*, December 9, 1939, pp. 59-60.

Murphy, Charles J. V., "China Reborn," *Life Magazine*, November 12, 1945, pp. 113-114.

Otsuka, Reizo, "Recent Developments in the Chinese Communist Movement," in *Problems of the Pacific* (Chicago, 1936), pp. 343-375.

————, "The Red Influence in China," in *Data Papers, Institute of Pacific Relations, 6th Congress*, Volume 7:2 (Tokyo, 1936), p. 49.

Phillips, J. W., "The Rising Tide in North China," *China Today*, July 1936, p. 195.

Smedley, Agnes, "China's Silent Heroes—Wounded Soldiers of Shansi," *The China Weekly Review*, November 6, 1937, pp. 214-215.

Strong, Anna Louise, "An Interview with General Yen Hsi-shan," *China Today*, April 1938, p. 8.

Swallow, R. W., "Taiyuanfu Revisited," *The North China Herald*, November 2, 1932, p. 196:1-5.

Tan Shin She, "The Policy of the C. P. of China and the Chinese Red Army," *International Press Correspondence*, May 16, 1936, pp. 630-631.

Thomson, James C., "Communist Policy and the United Front in China, 1935-1936," Harvard University, Committee on International and Regional Studies Seminar, *Papers on China*, Volume 11.

Wan Min, "For a Change in All Spheres of Our Work," *International Press Correspondence*, February 8, 1936, pp. 223-224.

———. "Replies to Chief Arguments against the Anti-Imperialist Front in China," *International Press Correspondence*, January 11, 1936, pp. 39-40.

———, "The New Situation and the New Tactics in Soviet China," *International Press Correspondence*, December 8, 1935, pp. 1658-1659.

Wales, Nym, "Is the Sleeping Giant Awakening?" *The China Weekly Review*, October 8, 1938, pp. 180-181 and 190.

Wang Ching-wei, "Suiyuan as a Symbol of National Unity," *The People's Tribune*, April 1, 1937, pp. 1-3.

Welles, Benjamin, "Japanese Soldiers Are Still in Shansi," *The New York Times*, February 10, 1947, p. 18:2-4.

———, "Shansi's Warlord in Unique Battle," *The New York Times*, February 9, 1947, p. 33:3-4.

Wright, Harrison K., "What the People Ought to Know," *The Chinese Recorder*, November 1919, pp. 743-748.

Wu Hsiang, "Taiyuan Rising Industrial Center," *China Reconstructs*, May 1964, pp. 36-37.

Wu, H. P. Tasmania, "Chinese Red Army in Shansi," *China Today*, January 1937, pp. 38-39.

Yen Ching-yüeh, "Militarizing the Model Province," *The China Weekly Review*, May 31, 1930, pp. 538-539.

GENERAL WORKS

Abend, Hallet, *My Life in China: 1926-1941*. New York, 1943.

Barclay, George, *Colonial Development and Population in Taiwan*. Princeton, 1954.

Barnett, A. Doak, *China on the Eve of Communist Takeover*. New York, 1963.

_____, *Communist China in Perspective*. New York, 1962.

Beckmann, George, *The Modernization of China and Japan*. New York, 1962.

Belden, Jack, *China Shakes the World*. New York, 1949.

Bertram, James M., *First Act in China*. New York, 1938.

_____, *Unconquered*. New York, 1939.

Bisson, T. A., *Japan in China*. New York, 1938.

Booker, Edna Lee, *News Is My Job*. New York, 1940.

Carlson, Evans F., *Twin Stars of China*. New York, 1940.

Chang, Carsun, *The Third Force in China*. New York, 1952.

Ch'ien Tuan-sheng, *The Government and Politics of China*. Cambridge, 1950.

Clark, Grover, *In Perspective (China 1927)*. Peking, 1927.

Elkins, H. P., and Theon Wright, *China Fights for Her Life*. New York, 1938.

Epstein, Israel, *The People's War*. London, 1939.

_____, *The Unfinished Revolution in China*. Boston, 1947.

Fairbank, John K., *The United States and China*. Cambridge, 1958.

Feuerwerker, Albert, *China's Early Industrialization*. Cambridge, 1958.

Forman, Harrison, *Report from Red China*. New York, 1945.

Gamble, Sidney D., *North China Villages*. Berkeley, 1963.

Gannes, Harry, *When China Unites*. New York, 1937.

Gould, Randall, *China in the Sun*. New York, 1946.

Gunther, John, *Inside Asia*. London, 1939.

Hahn, Emily, *The Soong Sisters*. New York, 1943.

Hanson, Haldore, *Humane Endeavour*. New York, 1939.

Hogg, George A., *I See a New China*. Boston, 1945.

Holcombe, Arthur, *The Chinese Revolution*. Cambridge, 1930.

Institute of Pacific Relations, pub., *Agrarian China*. Shanghai, 1938.

Janowitz, Morris, *The Military in the Political Development of New Nations*. Chicago, 1964.

Kent, Percy H., *The Twentieth Century in the Far East*. London, 1937.

Kiang Kang Hu, *China and the Social Revolution*. San Francisco, 1914.

Kotenev, Anatol, *New Lamps for Old*. Shanghai, 1931.

Latourette, Kenneth, *A History of Christian Missions in China*. New York, 1939.

――――, *The Chinese, Their History and Culture*. New York, 1934.

Lautenschlager, Stanton, *With Chinese Communists*. London, 1941.

Levenson, Joseph, *Liang Ch'i-ch'ao and the Mind of Modern China*. Cambridge, 1953.

Li Chien-nung, *The Political History of China 1840-1928*. English translation by Teng and Ingalls. Princeton, 1956.

Lindsay, Michael, *Notes on Education's Problems in Communist China*. New York, 1950.

Liu, F. F., *A Military History of Modern China 1924-1949*. Princeton, 1956.

Lynn, Jermyn Chi-hung, *Political Parties in China*. Tientsin, 1930.

MacNair, Harley F., *China in Revolution*. Chicago, 1931.

MacNair, Harley F., and Donald F. Lach, *Modern Far Eastern International Relations*. New York, 1950.

Mallory, W. H., *China, Land of Famine*. New York, 1927.

Mao Tse-tung, *The Situation and Tasks in the Anti-Japanese War after the Fall of Shanghai and Taiyuan*. Peking, 1956.

Maurer, Herrymon, *The End Is Not Yet*. New York, 1941.

Misselwitz, Henry F., *The Dragon Stirs*. New York, 1941.

Morse, Hosea B., and MacNair, Harley F., *Far Eastern International Relations*. Cambridge, 1931.

Payne, Robert, *Mao Tse-tung*. New York, 1950.

Peck, Graham, *Two Kinds of Time*. Boston, 1950.

Peffer, Nathaniel, *The Far East*. Ann Arbor, 1958.

Reinsch, Paul, *An American Diplomat in China*. London, 1922.

Rosinger, Lawrence K., *China's Crisis*. New York, 1945.

Scalapino, Robert, and George Yü, *The Chinese Anarchist Movement*. Berkeley, 1961.

Schwartz, Benjamin, *Chinese Communism and the Rise of Mao*. Cambridge, 1951.

Selle, Earl, *Donald of China*. New York, 1948.

Shepherd, Charles R., *A Nation Betrayed*. New York, 1954.

Smedley, Agnes, *Battle Hymn of China*. New York, 1943.

————, *China Fights Back*. New York, 1938.

————, *The Great Road*. New York, 1958.

Snow, Edgar, *Random Notes on Red China (1936-1945)*. Cambridge, 1957.

————, *Red Star over China*. New York, 1944.

————, *The Battle for Asia*. New York, 1941.

Stein, Guenther, *The Challenge of Red China*. New York, 1945.

T'ang Leang-Li, *The Inner History of the Chinese Revolution*. London, 1930.

Taylor, George E., *The Struggle for North China*. New York, 1940.

Todd, Oliver J., *Two Decades in China*. Peiping, 1938.

Van Dorn, Harold, *Twenty Years of the Chinese Republic*. New York, 1932.

Wales, Nym, *Red Dust*. Stanford, 1952.

White, Theodore, ed., *The Stilwell Papers*. New York, 1948.

White, Theodore, and Anna Lee Jacoby, *Thunder Out of China*. New York, 1946.

Wieger, Leon, *Chine Moderne*, Vol. iv. Hien-hien, 1924.

————, *Chine Moderne*, Vol. viii. Hien-hien, 1927.

————, *Chine Moderne*, Vol. ix. Hien-hien, 1931.

Wilbur, C. Martin and Julie Lien-ying How, *Documents on Communism, Nationalism, and Soviet Advisers in China 1918-1927*. New York, 1956.

Wright, Arthur F., ed., *The Confucian Persuasion*. Stanford, 1960.

Yanaga, Chitoshi, *Japan since Perry*. New York, 1949.

CORRESPONDENCE

Anonymous, Report, April 27, 1915, in a letter to author from Wynn C. Fairfield, dated September 25, 1958.

Fairfield, Wynn C., Letter to author, dated July 18, 1958.

———, Letter to author, dated September 12, 1958.

———, Letter to author, dated September 23, 1958.

———, Letter to author, dated September 25, 1958.

Hutchins, F. S., Letter to author, dated September 5, 1957.

K'ung, H. H., Letter to author, dated December 5, 1957.

Lao Kan, Letter to author, dated May 1, 1958.

Leonard, Margaret H., Letter to author, dated July 24, 1957.

Moyer, Raymond T., Letter to author, dated October 8, 1962.

Tong, T. K., Letter to author, dated January 15, 1964.

Watson, Percy T., Letter to author, dated October 5, 1957.

Williamson, H. R., Letter to author, dated December 11, 1957.

Yang Ai-yüan, Letter to author (in Chinese), dated April 12, 1958.

INTERVIEWS

Buck, John L., Interview with author, Stanford University, January 30, 1963.

Buss, Claude C., Interview with author, Stanford University, April 10, 1963.

Chai Chien-pang, Interview with author, Taiwan, February 22, 1957.

Ch'uan Han-sheng, Interview with author, Taiwan, October 3, 1956.

Keng Shih, Interview with author, Taiwan, January 19, 1957.

Liu, James T. C., Interview with author, Stanford University, November 1, 1962.

Lo Chia-lun, Interview with author, Taiwan, May 17, 1957.

Uno Shigeaki, Interview with author, Stanford University, November 27, 1962.

Vetch, Henri, Interview with author, Hong Kong, March 31, 1958.

Wang Huai-i, Interview with author, Taiwan, January 13, 1957.

Yen Hsi-shan, Interview with John Philip Emerson, Taiwan, September 22, 1956.

———, Interview with author, Taiwan, December 27, 1956.

———, Interview with author, Taiwan, January 13, 1957.

———, Interview with author, Taiwan, June 11, 1957.

INDEX

agriculture, 92-99, 101-02, 194-207; land reform, 57, 201-07; status of the peasantry, 57-58, 94-96, 125-27, 198-99; reforestation, 92-93, 97; animal husbandry, 93-94, 97; cotton growing, 93, 99, 194-95; agricultural extension program, 94, 99, 196-98; failure of Yen's efforts to step up agricultural output, in the 1920s, 94-99, 101-02, in the 1930s, 198-99; sericulture, 94, 97; water control, 96, 195-96; agriculture under Yen's Ten Year Plan, 194-207. *See also* land reform; Ten Year Plan

airpower, 29; role in Yen's defeat by Chiang Kai-shek, 118; Yen's respect for, 248-49; devastating impact of Japanese air superiority, 258. *See also* armed forces; Chiang Kai-shek; Feng Yü-hsiang; Japan

American Red Cross, 37, 91. *See also* famines

anarchism, 207

Anfu Clique, 22-23. *See also* warlords

Annam, 165

armed forces, in Shansi: recruiting and training, 13, 24-31, 128; role of militia, 25, 30-31; Japanese impact on training, 26-27; vocational training for soldiers, 27; Taiyuan Arsenal, 27-29, 186, 191, 211; airpower, 29; suppression of banditry, 30-31; defeat by Chiang Kai-shek in 1930, 113-14; unrest in, 128, 222; neglect in 1930s, 139, 182; defeat by Communists in 1935, 220-27, 285-88, 297; reorganization for resistance to Japan, 243-46; tactics and orientation, 243-48, 258-59; defeat by Japanese, 257-63, 271-77, 297; poor quality, 258-60; unpopularity with civilian population, 260-61; organization of New Shansi Army, 262, 274, 275-78; Yen adopts Communist methods of fighting, 273-77; Yen attacks New Army, 279; defeat by Communists in 1945-1949, 285-288.

See also airpower; Communists; education; industry; Japan; law enforcement; militia; Shansi Army; Ten Year Plan

Association for the Promotion of Statistical Investigation of the Economies and Societies of Shansi and Suiyuan, 130

Association in Charge of the Movement for Putting into Effect Mass Education in Shansi, 144-45

Australia, 93

banditry in Shansi, 30-31. *See also* armed forces; law enforcement

Bank of China, 156

Bertram, James, 265

Blood and Iron Society, 13

Blood and Iron National Salvation Corps, 211. *See also* Japan

Boxer Uprising 12, 79. *See also* Manchus

British-American Tobacco Company, 166. *See also* Great Britain; foreign influence

Buck, Pearl, 206. *See also* Chiang K'ang-hu

Buddhism, 6; influence on Yen's ideology, 62-63, 167; pro-Japanese inclinations of Buddhists in Shansi, 254, 261. *See also* ideology; Japan

bureaucracy in Shansi, 47-51, 97-98. *See also* government; law enforcement; Ten Year Plan

Burma, 165

Buss, Claude, 234

Canton, 104, 236, 289-91. *See also* National Government

CC Clique, 290

Chahar, 3, 236, 241, 243; importance to Shansi, 128; Japanese threat to, 212-14, 216, 229-30, 240, 247

Chang Hsüeh-liang, 118-19, 120; Yen's relations with, 108-09, 114-15, 233; role in Sian Incident, 239-41. *See also* Feng Yü-hsiang; Manchuria; National Government; Sian Incident

to mobilize peasants against Japan, 260-61; Communists use social reforms to rally peasants against Japanese, 264-71, 297. *See also* agriculture; Communists; economy; gentry; Japan; land reform; Ten Year Plan

Peffer, Nathaniel, 75, 236
Peiping, 112-13, 162, 179, 231, 236, 242, 287
Peking, 3, 86, 108-09, 118
Peking, University of, 206
Peking and Tientsin Times, the, 193
Peking (Peiping)–Suiyuan Railroad, 80, 89, 180
Peking Union Medical College, 36
Pen-chi-hu Steel Mill, 187
P'eng Chen, 105. *See also* Communists
P'eng Teh-huai, 265, 272. *See also* Communists
People's Normal School, Shansi, 70, 73-74. *See also* education
People's Political Supervisorial Association, 147. *See also* gentry; government
People's Revolutionary University, 274
People's Self-Defense Corps, 251
People's Tribune, the, 238
P'ing-hsing-kuan, battle for, 263-64, 271-72. *See also* Communists; Japan
P'ing-ting, 4, 87. *See also* Shansi
P'ing-yao, 4. *See also* Shansi
Po I-po, 105, 209, 231-33, 274. *See also* Communists
product certificates, 161-63, 283
Provincial Bank of Shansi, 99-100, 116, 134-35, 156, 178
Provincial College of Agriculture, 94. *See also* agriculture; education; Ten Year Plan
public health, 116-17, 137-38, 199, 210, 242; role of missionaries, 36-38

Red Army, Chinese, 218-29, 246, 266. *See also* Communists
Red Guards, 249. *See also* Communists
Revolution of 1911, 12-20, 295. *See also* Manchus; Sun Yat-sen
Roosevelt, Franklin, 166-67

Russo-Japanese War, 10-11, 247. *See also* Japan; Yen Hsi-shan

Sang Kan River, 195, 213
science in Shansi, 189
Shang Chen, 26, 119-22, 241
Shanghai, 162, 179, 209, 236
Shansi: geography of, 3, 4, 5, 7; population of, 4, 6, 8; history of before 1900, 6; Yen's attitude toward population control in, 170-71
Shansi Academy for Research into the Natural Sciences, 189
Shansi Army, 24-31, 139, 182, 220-27, 242-48, 257-63, 271-77, 285-88, 297. *See also* armed forces; Communists; Japan; law enforcement
Shansi Cadre Training Force, 235
Shansi Dare-to-Die Corps, 249, 262, 278. *See also* Communists; Japan
Shansi-Hopei-Chahar Border Region, 275
Shansi Industrial Company (*Sansei sangyō kabushiki kaisha*), 281
Shansi Industrial Technical College, 199
Shansi Marketing Cooperative for Locally Made Goods, 132
Shansi-Suiyuan Border Region, 279
Shansi-Suiyuan Railroad Bank, 134
Shansi University, 75-77. *See also* education
Shansi Water Conservancy Commission, 195
Shansi Women's Vocational Training Factory, 34, 170
Shantung, 108, 110-11, 113, 192, 215, 241
Shensi, 3, 184, 192, 219, 222, 225, 227, 238, 247, 276
Shih Yü-san, 121. *See also* warlords
Shihchiachuang, 181, 215
Shimbu Gakkō, 9. *See also* Japan; Yen Hsi-shan
Sian Incident, 232-33; Yen's role in, 239-41. *See also* Chiang Kai-shek; Communists; National Government
Siemens Company, 168
Sinkiang, 218
Snow, Edgar, 222, 227, 238, 241